W9-CCX-530

LOEB CLASSICAL LIBRARY

FOUNDED BY JAMES LOEB 1911

EDITED BY

JEFFREY HENDERSON

[QUINTILIAN]

THE MAJOR DECLAMATIONS

I

LCL 547

[QUINTILIAN]

THE MAJOR DECLAMATIONS

VOLUME I

EDITED BY

ANTONIO STRAMAGLIA

TRANSLATED BY

MICHAEL WINTERBOTTOM

WITH NOTES BY
BIAGIO SANTORELLI AND
MICHAEL WINTERBOTTOM

HARVARD UNIVERSITY PRESS
CAMBRIDGE, MASSACHUSETTS
LONDON, ENGLAND
2021

Copyright © 2021 by the President and Fellows
of Harvard College
All rights reserved

First published 2021

LOEB CLASSICAL LIBRARY® is a registered trademark
of the President and Fellows of Harvard College

Library of Congress Control Number 2021932924
CIP data available from the Library of Congress

ISBN 978-0-674-99740-0

*Composed in ZephGreek and ZephText by
Technologies 'N Typography, Merrimac, Massachusetts.
Printed on acid-free paper and bound by
Maple Press, York, Pennsylvania*

CONTENTS

PREFACE   vii

GENERAL INTRODUCTION   ix

ABBREVIATIONS   lxxv

GENERAL BIBLIOGRAPHY   xcv

SIGLA   cxxi

DECLAMATIONS

1 The handprints on the wall   1

2 The blind man on the threshold   51

3 Marius' soldier   111

4 The astrologer   159

5 Sick son ransomed   221

PREFACE

"No Latin text is more continuously testing, not to say tormenting, to the reader than the *Major Declamations.*" These words—all too true—by the late Donald Russell (1985, 43) perfectly explain why, in 1999, an international series of volumes devoted to each of these nineteen rhetorical pieces was started in Cassino. The collection was completed in 2020; the present Loeb largely builds on these forerunners, while not hesitating to differ from their conclusions. It should be pointed out that the footnotes to the translation seek mainly to complement the extensive commentary in the Cassino volumes, to which the reader should always be prepared to turn.

The title page names those who take ultimate responsibility: AS for the Latin text, MW for the translation, BS and MW for the prefaces and notes to the individual pieces. But that bald statement needs to be glossed. The general introduction is the work of BS and AS (and the latter gave minute attention to every aspect of the book). The notes had as their basis a skeleton assembled at an early stage by MW—with the constant help of Donald Russell—but in their final form they are largely the work of BS, as are the introductions to the individual declamations; some contributions made by AS and Russell (DAR) are signaled as such in the notes. As to the translation, MW's first faltering draft was greatly improved by DAR.

PREFACE

It was then worked on jointly by AS and MW over a long period, as the text and the interpretation of the difficult Latin evolved. The translation, it should be stressed, is keyed to AS's text, and does not necessarily reflect in every detail MW's personal judgments. That said, the mistakes that remain are his own. He also acted, not without trepidation, as guardian of the English language for the whole work.

The authors wish to record, first of all, their profound gratitude to the colleagues connected with the Cassino project: Bé Breij, Graziana Brescia, Nicola Hömke, Gernot Krapinger, Giovanna Longo, Lucia Pasetti, Oronzo Pecere, Catherine Schneider, Danielle van Mal-Maeder, Thomas Zinsmaier; their kindness and friendship over the last twenty years have been an invaluable enrichment. Warmest thanks are further due to Philip Barras, Federico Capizzi, Armando Carosi, Francesco Citti, Leonardo Costantini, Riccardo Macchioro, Giuseppe Russo, Stéphane Ratti, Iolanda Ventura.

It had been hoped that these volumes would be dedicated to Donald Russell on his hundredth birthday, October 13, 2020. In the event, they are fondly dedicated to his memory. His work has been seminal to the advance in the understanding of ancient declamation, and his unstinting help and encouragement constantly inspired the present project. Many examples of his acumen in interpreting a difficult text and of his felicity in emending the idiosyncratic Latin will be found in the following pages.

ANTONIO STRAMAGLIA
MICHAEL WINTERBOTTOM
BIAGIO SANTORELLI
April 2021

GENERAL INTRODUCTION

1. DECLAMATION AND GRECO-ROMAN EDUCATION[1]

A *controversia* is a speech purporting to be delivered on behalf of either the prosecution or the defense in an imaginary trial. Slightly simpler is the *suasoria*, a speech of advice addressed to a mythological or a historical character on the verge of making an important decision. Learning how to compose and deliver such speeches, known collectively as declamations (Lat. *declamationes*, Gk. *meletai*),[2] was the final stage in the traditional Greco-Roman rhetorical training, which was considered the necessary preparation for public activity throughout the Roman imperial age. Although criticized for the often far-fetched nature of its subjects, declamation remained for more than six centuries the keystone of education for any young citizen who could afford a "high-school" training. At the same time, this school practice quickly earned the favor of a large audience of professional rhetoricians, enthusiasts, and people of average education: by the first century AD, public performances of fictive speeches were among the

[1] §§1–4 are by Biagio Santorelli, 5–8 by Antonio Stramaglia.

[2] But there were alternative words in both languages: see for the terminology Russell (1983, 9–12); Civiletti (2002); Stroh (2003); Spangenberg Yanes (2012); Feddern (2013, 13–35).

most popular events in the cultural life of the Roman empire. With its fictional universe of characters, laws, and recurring situations, declamation shaped a cultural background common to the writers and readers of the Greco-Roman world, who all shared the same—more or less standardized—rhetorical education.[3]

Despite its pervasive presence in Greco-Roman culture, declamation has left behind only limited remains. Very little is known about its origin and earliest stages: according to Quintilian,[4] the composition of speeches on fictional subjects in imitation of the law courts was already practiced in schools at the time of Demetrius of Phalerum (ca. 345–283 BC); Philostratus[5] states that declamation stemmed from the rhetorical school of the Athenian orator Aeschines (389–314 BC), but the practice is clearly foreshadowed as early as the fifth century BC by Gorgias (*Encomium of Helen*; *Palamedes*) and "Antiphon" (*Tetralogies*).[6] The earliest extant fragments of speeches that can properly be classified as declamations date back to the Hellenistic period: the scanty evidence preserved by a number of papyri[7] testifies that the composition

---

[3] For a recent survey of the history of declamation, its role in Greco-Roman education, and the surviving sources, see Lentano (2017, 13–32); Corbeill (2007) and Bloomer (2007) are also helpful.

[4] Quint. 2.4.41.

[5] Philostr. *VS* 1.pr.4.2 Stefec.

[6] See especially Fairweather (1981, 114–15); Winterbottom (1983–2019, 112ff.), (1988–2019, 141–46); Dmitriev (2020).

[7] Now listed in Stramaglia (2015b, 167–71); add Hatzilambrou (2015).

of fictional speeches was by now an established part of the rhetorical curriculum in the Greek world; such authors as Polybius give clear, if indirect, confirmation of this.[8]

By the first century BC the precepts of Greek rhetoric had been taken over by the Romans, and declamation, with its own set of rules and peculiar features, had become part of their educational practices. Subjects of declamations are mentioned in Cicero's *On Invention* and in the anonymous *Rhetoric for Herennius*;[9] some traces of the earliest age of Roman declamation are preserved also in Suetonius' *On Rhetoricians*.[10] But it is in the very last years of the Republic that the popularity of the practice soars, so much so that the Elder Seneca (ca. 54 BC–AD 39) can state that declamation "was born" *after* him.[11]

It is to the Elder Seneca, indeed, that we owe our earliest direct evidence on Latin declamation. With the declared aim of fostering the education of his three sons, Seneca collected the most brilliant passages from the speeches of the rhetoricians he had heard during his long life, most of whom would otherwise be unknown to us. The result is an anthology of highlights from the declamations of about 120 rhetoricians who flourished between the late first century BC and the Tiberian age, which Seneca arranged in ten books of *controversiae* and at least two

[8] Russell (1983, 19–20); most recently, Candau (2017, 64–65, 69–75).

[9] Winterbottom (1974, 1:vii–viii); Calboli (2020[3], 1.59–62).

[10] Suet. *Rhet.* 25.5. See now Costa (2017, 202–9).

[11] Sen. *Controv.* 1.pr.12.

of *suasoriae*;[12] half of the work has come down to us in full, the rest only in excerpts. The passages selected by Seneca record the words of experienced rhetoricians, whose speeches may have been delivered in a variety of venues (including public recitations and lectures in declamation schools)[13] and perhaps in some cases circulated in more or less refined written form;[14] Seneca himself takes the floor in the preface to each book and in numerous comments appended to the quotations, highlighting the qualities and shortcomings of the rhetoricians he reviews.

Overall, Seneca's work portrays the circulation of declamatory speeches within an elite of professional rhetoricians and amateurs, all skilled enough to appreciate the literary value of the rhetorical production that Seneca aims to preserve. Our knowledge of how Roman students

[12] Only one book of *suasoriae* survives, at the end of which the manuscripts preserve the incipit of a now lost second book. Seneca's work bears the title: *Oratorum et rhetorum sententiae, divisiones, colores*, which reflects the internal arrangement of the material: after giving the theme of a declamation, Seneca quotes *sententiae* (the "epigrams" devised by a number of rhetoricians on each side of the dispute); then he moves on to their *divisiones* (the "plans of the speeches," i.e., how a speaker organized the material of his oration); and, finally, he reports *colores* they suggested (the "colors," i.e., how they would lay out the facts to their own advantage). Cf. Winterbottom (1974, 1:xvi–xx); Berti (2007, 25–28); Huelsenbeck (2018, 9–11).

[13] Cf. Huelsenbeck (2015, 57n44).

[14] Cf. [Santorelli-]Stramaglia (2015, 272–76) on the written circulation of declamations in general; Huelsenbeck (2018, 12–13 and n. 16) in particular on Seneca's sources.

were *trained* to compose a declamation, however, rests largely on a different Latin source: the so-called *Declamationes minores* (*Minor Declamations*) ascribed to Quintilian. The manuscript tradition has preserved 145 *controversiae*, out of the 388 of the original collection. For each piece a theme is given. Then, typically, the unknown author ("the Master") discusses the peculiarities and the major difficulties of the case; he subsequently exemplifies his remarks by outlines of and/or extracts from speeches of his own composition, varying in length and elaboration. We seem to have here the notes that a teacher of rhetoric prepared for his own lectures. This Master was hardly Quintilian himself, but he was certainly very close to the latter's theoretical approach. The *Minores* are most likely to be dated to the late first century AD.[15]

A further collection of excerpts has reached us under the name of Calpurnius Flaccus: fifty-three themes of *controversiae*, accompanied by short extracts from the speeches on behalf of one or both the parties involved. We lack information on the author of these declamations, as well as on the compiler of the surviving extracts.[16] Rhythm

[15] For a full introduction to the *Declamationes minores*, see now Pasetti (2019).

[16] On the basis of some surviving paratextual data, it has long been believed that the excerpts of Calpurnius Flaccus were originally included in an otherwise lost *Corpus decem rhetorum minorum*, which also contained the surviving portion of the pseudo-Quintilianic *Declamationes minores* and the abridged version of the Elder Seneca's anthology (see Stramaglia [2006, 572n71] for details). This hypothesis, however, has been recently challenged by Huelsenbeck (2016, 366n41).

and style suggest that the pieces should be dated to the late second century AD.[17]

From the second century onward, direct Greek sources at last add to the available evidence: we have three declamations by Lesbonax of Mytilene; two by Polemon of Laodicea; a few disputed fragments from Hadrian of Tyre; some pieces by Lucian of Samosata; and, most important, several speeches by Aelius Aristides.[18] Later on, we owe the bulk of the surviving body of Greek declamations to Libanius of Antioch (fourth century) and, especially, to Choricius and the other rhetors of the "school of Gaza" (sixth century).[19]

[17] Håkanson (2014d, 130); Santorelli (2017b, 131–39).

[18] Cf. Russell (1983, 4–5); most recently, see Iglesias-Zoido (2010) on Lesbonax; de Martini (2019) on Polemon's declamations; Amato-Ventrella (2009, 156–58) on the fragments of Hadrian of Tyre; Guast (2018) on Lucian; Oudot (2017) for a detailed introduction to Aelius Aristides. Janiszewski-Stebnicka-Szabat (2015) provides a prosopography—with individual bibliographies—of the Greek sophists of the Roman imperial age.

[19] On Libanius' declamations, see the overview by Penella (2014); on Choricius and the "school of Gaza," see the studies collected in Amato-Thévenet-Ventrella (2014) and Amato-Corcella-Lauritzen (2017). Our knowledge of declamation, and especially of its most technical features, is further enhanced by a number of theoretical works from the imperial age, both in Greek and in Latin. The Greek treatises handed down under the names of Hermogenes of Tarsus (2nd century) and Sopatros (?4th century) are paramount; several Latin tracts, mostly translating and commenting on the works of Greek predecessors, are gathered in *Rhetores Latini Minores* (Halm [1863]). See the overviews by Webb (2017, esp. 146–50), and Kraus (2017); also Pepe (2013, 378–84, 488n80), and—on papyri—Longo (2020).

Among all the extant sources, the nineteen *Major Declamations* wrongly ascribed to Quintilian (see §4) stand out for their contribution to our understanding of ancient declamation. They are virtually the only fully-developed *controversiae* surviving from pre-medieval Latinity, invaluable because they show how a student was expected to handle the themes, the recurring situations and arguments, the technical rules. And what is more, they lay bare the mistakes that were often made in the process.

2. THEMES, CHARACTERS AND LAWS IN THE *MAJOR DECLAMATIONS*

If a student refuses to pay the tuition fee for his rhetorical training, says Juvenal, his teacher is forced to leave the school and argue his own case before a real court; meanwhile, in the deserted classroom, *The Rapist* and *The Administering of Poison* go silent, and so do *The Wicked, Ungrateful Husband* and *The Cures for Chronic Blindness*.[20] In that same classroom, Juvenal's teacher was accustomed to listening to his students while they killed cruel tyrants day in, day out:[21] in the second century AD, it seems, not much had changed since the days of Petronius, when students spoke of nothing but "pirates standing on the beach, dangling manacles, tyrants writing orders for sons to cut off their fathers' heads, oracles advising the sacrifice of three or more virgins during a plague";[22] and,

[20] Juv. 7.166–70; for the declamation themes alluded to in these lines (trans. Braund), see Santorelli (2016, 298–99).

[21] Juv. 7.151.

[22] Petron. 1.3 (trans. Sullivan). On the declamatory background of this tirade see Stramaglia (2015b, 148–50).

if we compare these indirect witnesses with the themes of the *controversiae* surviving from later times, we can see that this novel-like universe was to remain the normal background for rhetorical exercises throughout antiquity.

From this perspective, the *Major Declamations* are generally consistent with the expectations and the literary taste of the imperial age. The themes preserved in the collection show in varying proportions realistic elements, recurring situations dictated by the genre, and pure fantasy. Only one of the preserved speeches, *Marius' Soldier* (*DM* 3), has a historical Roman setting (the camp of Gaius Marius, during the Cimbrian war) and is based on an allegedly real event (the killing of a tribune by a soldier whom the former had attempted to rape);[23] at the opposite end, one speech, *The Friends Who Stood Surety* (*DM* 16), is clearly inspired by a well-known traditional anecdote (the story of Damon and Phintias).[24] Some speeches are set in fairly realistic scenarios: we encounter cases arising from charges of murder (*DM* 7, *Torture for a Poor Man*), treason in time of war (*DM* 11, *The Rich Man Accused of Treason*), unlawful damage to a neighbor's property (*DM* 13, *The Poor Man's Bees*). Most of the cases are set in motion by events that in themselves were not necessarily unlikely in the ancient world, yet could give rise to complex plots close to novel or tragedy. Such events include parricide, or attempted parricide, in connection with inheritance (*DM* 1, *The Handprints on the Wall*; 2, *The Blind Man on the Threshold*; 17, *The Spilled Poison*); kidnappings by pirates, resulting in death or misfortune for their

23 Cf. Introduction to *DM* 3.
24 Cf. Introduction to *DM* 16.

victims (*DM* 5, *Sick Son Ransomed*; 6, *The Body Cast Up by the Sea*; *DM* 9, *The Gladiator*); an illness curable only by an unconventional therapy (*DM* 8, *The Sick Twins*); administering of poison and other illegal substances (*DM* 17, again; 14–15, *The Hate Potion*); alleged incest (*DM* 18–19, *The Son Suspected of Incest with His Mother*). Even the dire case of *The People Who Fed on Corpses* during a famine (*DM* 12) is not without historical precedents.[25] The widespread belief in magic and the supernatural is evident in *The Astrologer* (*DM* 4), which is based on the prediction of glory and parricide for a child who is about to be born, and in *The Spell on the Tomb* (*DM* 10), where a sorcerer casts a spell on a tomb to prevent the shade of a dead youth leaving it.

Most declamations envisage family conflicts: besides the two speeches on behalf of a son against his stepmother, with the parties accusing each other of the father's murder (*DM* 1–2), four times in our collection a son opposes his father. The causes and circumstances of these conflicts vary from case to case: a son seeks permission to take his own life, against his father's will, because an astrologer predicted at his birth that he would commit parricide (*DM* 4); a father in need requests to be fed by the son he had not rescued from the pirates, ransoming his other sick son instead (*DM* 5); a son, who has been secretly feeding his father's enemy out of gratitude, challenges in court his father's decision to disown him (*DM* 9); and a son whom his father has unsuccessfully tried to disown three times is eventually charged with attempted parricide, when he is caught preparing poison (*DM* 17). In addition, in one

25 Cf. Introduction to *DM* 12.

case a son challenges his blind mother's prohibition to leave her side (*DM* 16). Fathers and mothers, too, are often at odds in our speeches: a father speaks against a blind mother who denies burial to their son, guilty of leaving her to save his father (*DM* 6); however, a mother may accuse a father of ill-treatment when he has authorized a doctor to cure one of their twin sons at the cost of the other's life (*DM* 8), when he has enchanted the tomb of their son—preventing his soul from visiting the mother at night (*DM* 10), and also when he has tortured their son to death due to a rumor of incest, without revealing what he has discovered (*DM* 18–19).

Outside the family sphere, a motif largely exploited in declamations is the enmity between a rich man and a poor man.[26] The *Major Declamations* preserve three themes in which these characters confront each other directly. In one case, a poor man claims to be the sole witness of the murder of his own son at the hands of a rich man, and he demands to be tortured to corroborate his accusation (*DM* 7); in another speech, a poor man asks for compensation for the loss of a swarm of bees that his rich neighbor has killed by poisoning the flowers growing in his own field (*DM* 13); we also hear a rich man as a plaintiff, when a poor man causes the death of his three sons by accusing him of treason: the rich man, after leading the city army to victory, demands that the poor man's sons be killed now in their turn (*DM* 11). Also, the enmity between these two characters is part of a case in which a rich man's son argues against his father to challenge his own disownment (*DM* 9).

[26] Cf. Breij (2020, 13–32).

In addition to the stock characters and situations of the declamatory universe, our collection features some less conventional ones, including a doctor who performs vivisection on a boy in order to cure his twin brother (*DM* 8), or a prostitute who gives her lover a potion that makes him stop loving her (*DM* 14–15). In the background, too, we see at work some of the characters most censored by the critics of declamation,[27] such as pirates (*DM* 5, 6, and 9) and a tyrant (*DM* 16); we learn of the prediction of an astrologer (*DM* 4) and of the spells of a sorcerer (*DM* 10), and encounter "stepmothers more cruel than any in tragedy" (*DM* 1–2): all unrealistic elements that Quintilian advised against in declamation.[28] Yet, at least in our speeches, the unreal features blamed by the critics generally have a precise narrative function: they put obstacles in the way of the protagonists of the story, so as to prepare for the conflicts that will be eventually brought to court. We may assume that the authors of such themes exploited sensational elements so as to capture the students' interest and maintain their engagement in an educational process that might well be prolonged and repetitive.[29] Our collection, however, shows that such fictional cases raised ethical, social, and legal questions not so remote from the issues that the young would face outside the declamation hall: although they sprang from unrealistic situations, the conflicts of our *controversiae* exposed students to a variety of reflections often deeply rooted in Roman cul-

[27] See, e.g., §1, above.

[28] Quint. 2.10.4; cf. also 4.2.94 and 10.5.14. See Reinhardt-Winterbottom (2006, 161–67).

[29] See again the testimony of Juv. 7.150–54.

ture and able to contribute to their preparation for adulthood.[30]

An important clue to the educational value seen in the practice of declamation is the frequent occurrence of family conflicts in the cases preserved in our collection (cf. above). An exercise based on a character arguing against a family member demands reflection on the traditional roles and relationships within a household. On several occasions, the Master in the *Minor Declamations* instructs students to make their points without showing disrespect for a family member, as that would have been an unacceptable violation of *pietas*.[31] The *Major Declamations* document how this would work out in practice: a son, or a mother, will never challenge Father's authority, however dire the circumstances;[32] on the other hand, a good father should not abuse his ultimate power to impose his will on the family, but rather resort to moderation and mercy.[33] Our extant speeches show that the very concept of the traditional *patria potestas* is constantly in question when fathers and sons argue against each other,[34] while the cases

[30] Cf., e.g., Kaster (2001), with an analysis of the intended purposes of declamations centered on cases of rape; see below for further references.

[31] Cf., e.g., *Decl. min.* 259.1, 280.1; see also Quintilian's recommendations on this matter (7.4.27–28), with Regali (1986, 162–63).

[32] An extreme example of this is *DM* 18, where Mother does not deny Father's right to torture Son in his investigation on the alleged incest (see the Introduction to *DM* 18).

[33] Cf., e.g., 6.14.6–7, where Father claims that he *could have* resorted to his supreme power, but in fact did not do so.

[34] Further references in Santorelli (2019, 73–76).

for ill-treatment of a wife prove to be an appropriate venue for reflection on the role of the mother and the authority of the wife in her household.[35] Consideration of moral issues is also required of the speaker when characters involved in the dispute are disabled, or poor, or otherwise in need: two declamations (*DM* 6 and 16) confront the speaker with a son's obligation to provide assistance to a blind mother, while two others (*DM* 1 and 2) raise the question of the attitude of a good father toward a blind son. The duty to support a person in need is imposed on sons toward their parents by law (*DM* 5), but it resurfaces also outside the household, as a moral obligation for a good friend (*DM* 9). In such cases, developing a *controversia* was not just a purely rhetorical exercise for a Roman schoolboy: although set in a fictional world, the disputes between fathers, mothers, and sons required students to reflect on issues that they would encounter soon in their real life, and on the implications of their future role as head of their own household.

If we return to the speeches that revolve round the enmity between Rich Man and Poor Man, we see that each of these cases compels the speaker to address a legal issue: Is evidence extracted under torture reliable (*DM* 7)?[36] Can bees be considered the property of the beekeeper (*DM* 13)?[37] Is retaliation an appropriate punishment for false accusations (*DM* 11)?[38] In addition to all this, such themes required students—normally from fam-

---

[35] See, e.g., 8.6.7–8.1.
[36] Cf. Introduction to *DM* 7.
[37] Cf. Introduction to *DM* 13.
[38] Cf. Introduction to *DM* 11.

ilies wealthy enough to pay for a higher education—to speak from the point of view of a person of lower status, confronting the implications of inequalities and facing the challenge of opposing social superiors.[39]

In some cases, the questions raised by our themes preserve a noticeable echo of debates in Roman society: the case of *The Sick Twins* (*DM* 8), for instance, concerns the timeless issue of the ethical limits of medicine and is inspired by a debate on vivisection that had gone on in Rome since the early imperial age;[40] in *The Hate Potion* (*DM* 14–15), the accusation and the defense exploit the two different answers given by Roman jurists as to whether the administration of a nonlethal potion amounts to poisoning—a sign of some awareness in the declaimers of contemporary jurisprudence.[41]

In short, the misdeeds of pirates, poisoners, and sorcerers were meant to generate conflicts that, although clearly fictional, would give students an opportunity to develop the critical skills considered crucial for any activity in the public sphere—while acquiring the rhetorical technique necessary to speak persuasively in public.

In order to create a suitable occasion for reflection and debate, the themes of our declamations usually feature one or more laws, intended to channel their far-fetched

[39] See Bernstein (2013, 6–7).

[40] Cf. Introduction to *DM* 8.

[41] Cf. Introductions to *DM* 14 and 15. The same applies, to some extent, to *DM* 11 (which probably reflects the contemporary approach to the crime of *calumnia*) and 13 (which voices two opposing interpretations on the right of ownership over bees).

starting situation into a judicial hearing: here, before an imaginary court, the speaker will be required to exercise the analytical and rhetorical skills developed in his curriculum.

With few exceptions, the laws and the legal procedures featured in the themes of our collection derive from the Greek rhetorical (and sometimes legal) tradition and, in themselves, have little or no correspondence with actual Roman laws. A clear example of this is given by *The Astrologer* (*DM* 4): the case envisages one law granting a war hero a reward of his choice, and another prescribing that anyone committing suicide without prior authorization should be left unburied. Both provisions are well attested in Greek and Roman declamation: while the former is entirely fictional, the latter seems to be inspired by a custom occasionally attested in the Greek world, but neither is known to Roman jurisprudence.[42] The same applies to the action for damage to the state, brought against an envoy in *The People Who Fed on Corpses* (*DM* 12): this is probably inspired by Greek trials—both real and rhetorical—for misconduct of an embassy; the Roman rhetorical tradition envisages this action as applying to physical damage to public buildings, but we do not know for sure if any of this had a counterpart in Roman legal practice.[43]

Even in this respect, however, the fictions of the school could offer students a valuable preparation for the challenges of a real courtroom. For instance, the charge of ill-treatment, leveled by a wife against her husband in four

[42] Cf. Introduction to *DM* 4.
[43] Cf. Introduction to *DM* 12, n. 1.

of our speeches (*DM* 8, 10, 18, 19), is an invention of the schools of rhetoric; still, Quintilian points out that this fictive law was inspired to some extent by a real procedure, which allowed a wife to recover her dowry in case of divorce.[44] Since our declamations take for granted that a wife would *not* divorce the husband to whom she had borne children, the action for ill-treatment is the only proceeding available to mothers who need to prosecute their husbands for more serious reasons than mere marital bickering.[45]

Three speeches presuppose the obligation on a son to assist his parents in distress: either by feeding them, if they are in need (*DM* 5), or by staying at their side, if they are disabled (*DM* 6 and 16). Provisions of this kind, already mentioned by the Elder Seneca and Quintilian, probably had some counterparts in the Greek world, whereas Roman law would enforce such a duty only after the second century AD: in this case, declamation seems to have anticipated jurisprudence, by making a law out of what was already perceived to be a moral obligation.[46]

Two of our pieces (*DM* 9 and 17) imply a law granting to fathers the right to disown their children, and to disowned children the possibility of challenging such decisions in formal trials. Such proceedings were not allowed by Roman law: a father could indeed impose punishments on his children by his own authority or by the judgment of a domestic court, but a son could be disinherited only by will, and therefore his punishment would be effective only

---

44 Quint. 7.4.11; see also Introduction to *DM* 8.
45 Cf. 8.6.1–4; see also Introduction to *DM* 8.
46 Cf. Introduction to *DM* 5.

after the father's death. However, Roman law granted a disinherited son the right to challenge the father's will: as Quintilian did not fail to point out,[47] rhetorical trials about disownment resembled real-life actions challenging disinheritance, and the former may be seen as preparatory exercises for the latter.[48]

A closer agreement with actual Roman law can be detected in the provisions forbidding the use of torture on freeborn citizens (*DM* 7),[49] prescribing death for treason (*DM* 11), and subjecting slanderers to the same penalty they sought to inflict on their victims (*DM* 11, again).[50] One speech, finally, hinges on a real Roman law: this is *The Poor Man's Bees* (*DM* 13), in which Poor Man charges Rich Man with malicious damage under the *Lex Aquilia de damno*.[51]

Overall, a lack of verisimilitude, and a certain distance from the real proceedings of Roman courts, is undeniable in most of the themes preserved in our collection. However, a variety of ethical, social, and legal questions appears beneath the surface of the fictional world conjured up by the rhetoricians: the unrealistic, and even absurd, features of the themes of declamation seem to provide a "safe space" in which a student could confront a wide range of complex issues, so as to attain both the technical knowledge necessary to speak persuasively and the "soft skills" needed to manage the challenges of adult life.

[47] See again Quint. 7.4.11.
[48] Cf. Pasetti (2011, 90–91n2).
[49] Cf. Introduction to *DM* 7, nn. 4–5.
[50] Cf. Introduction to *DM* 11.
[51] Cf. Introduction to *DM* 13.

3. COMPOSING A *CONTROVERSIA*

A *controversia* is based on a fiction tacitly accepted both by the speaker and by its audience: whether he is a student presenting his work to his teacher, or a teacher addressing his students, or a professional performing in public, the speaker assumes the role of plaintiff or defendant in a trial. In its structure, therefore, a *controversia* has ideally to be as close as possible to a real judicial oration, and the speaker follows the traditional precepts of rhetoric in order to compose a speech capable of persuading his audience.[52]

In our collection each piece is identified by a short title, indicating in a couple of words the essence of the case, sometimes in an allusive or even enigmatic fashion. It is impossible to tell with certainty whether these titles are the work of the authors of the speeches or an addition by a late antique editor; the former hypothesis seems however more likely, since all the other fully developed "Quintilianic" declamations known to us that are now lost bore equally short and tantalizing titles, though they were *not* included in the "edited" collection that has survived.[53]

The declamation proper is preceded by an *argumentum* or *thema* ("subject," or "theme"), a short account of the background of the case. The theme was not necessarily invented by the author of a given declamation: indeed, some themes enjoyed a lasting success and were devel-

[52] On the standard structure of a *controversia*, see in further detail Berti (2007, 43–78).

[53] On this thorny issue, see now Stramaglia (2017, 198–99; 2018a).

oped by a variety of rhetoricians over time.[54] The *Major Declamations* preserve seventeen themes, two of which are developed on both sides (*DM* 14–15 and 18–19), probably by different rhetoricians;[55] in at least one case, it is arguable that the author of a theme (*DM* 2) intended to improve on that of another case included in our collection (*DM* 1).[56] The theme specifies briefly and in simple language the facts, the characters, and the law(s) involved in the case. In composing his speech, the declaimer was meant to conform to the theme; however, not infrequently the pieces in our collection introduce points not stated in the theme or inconsistent with it.[57]

The first task of a declaimer was to identify the fundamental issue raised by the theme.[58] In our collection, three cases arise from a dispute over facts: two feature characters accusing each other of a homicide, the responsibility for which has to be determined (*DM* 1–2),[59] while

[54] See Stramaglia (2015b) on the circulation (and the fading) of themes of declamations.

[55] See Introductions to these four pieces.

[56] See Introduction to *DM* 2.

[57] Cf. Håkanson (2014a, 6–12).

[58] The basic issue of a case was called its *status*, or *constitutio causae* (*stasis* in Greek). The Greek rhetorical tradition devised a detailed classification of all cases according to their *status*; the canonical form of this classification, referred to as *status*-theory, or *stasis*-theory, was ascribed to the Greek rhetorician Hermagoras of Temnos (second century BC). See now Berti (2014, 100n1) for further references.

[59] In the *status*-theory, such cases were defined as "double conjecture" (*duplex coniectura*): cf. [Santorelli-]Stramaglia (2017, 26n56).

in a third it has to be decided whether a son was making an attempt on his father's life (*DM* 17).[60] Several cases are triggered by dispute over the interpretation of the law: four raise the problem of the conflict between the literal application of the wording of the law and a deeper interpretation of its intended meaning (*DM* 5, 7, 11, 12),[61] while one dispute arises from a conflict of laws (*DM* 4).[62] In most of the *Maiores*, though, there is no doubt that the defendant has done what he is charged with, but it has to be determined whether he is in fact guilty:[63] in one case, the defendant does not deny having committed a homicide but maintains that he acted in self-defense (*DM* 3);[64] in other cases it has to be decided whether a father's actions amount to ill-treatment of his wife (*DM* 8, 10, 18–19);[65] whether a son deserves to be disowned (*DM* 9);[66] whether a rich man intended to damage a poor man's property by poisoning his flowers (*DM* 13);[67] whether a prostitute was justified in administering a hate potion to her lover (*DM* 14–15);[68] whether a son's decision to leave

---

[60] This is an instance of "simple conjecture" (*simplex coniectura*): cf. Pasetti (2011, 41).

[61] This *status* is known in Latin as *scriptum et voluntas* (wording and intention). Cf. van Mal-Maeder (2018, 17) on *DM* 5; Breij (2020, 60–64) on *DM* 7; Santorelli (2014b, 33) on *DM* 11; Stramaglia (2002, 131n117) on *DM* 12.

[62] *Leges contrariae* (conflict of laws). Cf. Stramaglia (2013b, 83–84n1).

[63] I.e., the "quality" (*qualitas*) of the action must be determined.

[64] Cf. Schneider (2004, 29).   [65] Cf. Breij (2015, 64).

[66] Cf. Krapinger (2007b, 19).

[67] Cf. Krapinger (2005, 109–10n217).

[68] Cf. Longo (2008, 38).

his blind mother is justified by the need to rescue his father (*DM* 6)[69] or a friend (*DM* 16).[70]

Once the basic issue of the case has been identified and the most suitable strategy has been devised, the speaker has to construct his speech. In accordance with rhetorical theory, this consists of four main parts:

EXORDIUM (proem): the opening section of the speech, meant to present in brief the terms of the question in the most favorable perspective; its purpose is to inform the judge(s)—and the wider audience—of the facts and, at the same time, to make them well disposed toward the speaker.

NARRATIO (narration): a (more or less) concise account of the facts of the case; in a number of pieces,[71] the main narration is followed at some distance by an "additional narration," mainly designed to arouse the emotions of the audience.

ARGUMENTATIO (argumentation): the core of the speech, offering a detailed defense of the speaker's case; this section is normally further divided into:

CONFIRMATIO (confirmation), presenting the arguments in favor of the speaker;

REFUTATIO (refutation), rebutting the arguments of the opposing party.

The order of these two subsections may vary, and they sometimes merge rather indistinctly.[72] The ar-

[69] Cf. Zinsmaier (2009, 15, 66–67).
[70] Cf. Santorelli (2014b, 197–98).
[71] Cf. Introduction to *DM* 5, n. 4.
[72] Cf. Introductions to *DM* 10 and 13.

gumentation may be introduced by a *PROPOSITIO CAUSAE* (statement of the case), announcing the intended goal of the speech;[73] and/or by a *PARTITIO* (division), listing the main arguments to be used in the argumentation.[74]

EPILOGUS (epilogue): the conclusion of the speech, meant to wrap up the case (sometimes with a summary of the most salient facts) and ensure the judge's sympathy.

The aims and the technical features of each of these parts of a speech were discussed and variously defined by Greek and Roman specialists; however, the *Major Declamations* do not adhere systematically to a single theoretical approach. Some speeches follow the precepts and the recommendations set out by Quintilian in the *Institutio oratoria*,[75] while others make choices that he would have certainly disapproved of; in some cases, it can be argued that the authors deliberately disregard the guidelines set by the great master, perhaps with the aim of competing with him.[76]

For instance,[77] Quintilian recommends that the **proem**

[73] Thus in *DM* 1–2, 5, 11–15, 17–19.

[74] Thus in *DM* 1, 13.

[75] Thus, e.g., *DM* 4 (see Introduction to that piece).

[76] Thus *DM* 19: Quintilian blames the practice, apparently widespread in the schools of rhetoric, of developing the theme of *The Son Suspected of Incest with His Mother*, from the father's perspective, as a figured speech; yet our declamation follows precisely this strategy. See Introduction to *DM* 19.

[77] See in detail Longo (2021), on which the following outline is based; also Corcella (2021, 91ff.).

of a declamation should explain the case and that the speaker should not assume that the judge already knows all the facts; any excess in rhetorical ornament, as well as any display of animosity against the opposing party, should also be avoided in this section of the speech.[78] But in our collection we find some speeches introduced by elaborate proems,[79] delaying or omitting any account of the dispute,[80] and even lashing out at the opponent.[81] The **narration**, according to Quintilian, should account for the facts of the case in a complete yet concise way, with consistency and plausibility, while bringing forward only the "seeds" of the arguments to be exploited in the subsequent argumentation.[82] But the *Maiores* repeatedly disregard these precepts: some of them offer either incomplete or over-long narrations,[83] others discuss arguments extensively in this section[84] or resort to blatantly implausible accounts of the facts.[85] As for the **argumentation**, Quintilian recommends smooth and coherent transitions between one topic and another, and the arrangement of the

---

[78] Quint. 4.1.14, 34, 60.

[79] Cf., e.g., 5.1.1–2.4.

[80] Cf., e.g., 17.2.4 for a delayed mention of the facts of the case, and 19.1.1–2.4 for a complete omission of them.

[81] Cf., e.g., 12.1.3, 12.2.5.

[82] Quint. 4.2.45–47, 54.

[83] Two extremes are 7.3.1–3 (exceedingly short) and 10.3.1–9.1 (very long in itself, and followed by an additional narration in 10.13.4–16.7).

[84] See, e.g., *DM* 1; it appears that this weakness was intentionally corrected in *DM* 2: see Introductions to *DM* 1 and 2.

[85] Again, this is the case with *DM* 19: see Introduction to that piece.

various points in order of increasing strength.[86] In the argumentations of the *Maiores*, however, consistency and consequentiality are not always achieved, and in at least one case the speaker indulges in a digression entirely irrelevant to the case, thus falling into one of the mistakes most criticized by the theorists.[87] The **epilogue**, finally, should according to Quintilian consolidate the points made throughout the speech and win over the judges. But some of our pieces fail to find a good balance between these two needs, either delaying to the epilogue some details better placed in the narration,[88] or relying exclusively on pathos in this section of the speech,[89] or even risking hostility toward the speaker himself.[90] Taken together, these factors make a strong case against the attribution of the *Major Declamations* to a single author, let alone Quintilian.

4. AUTHORSHIP AND DATING[91]

With a few notable exceptions (Francesco Filelfo, Erasmus of Rotterdam, and Juan Luis Vives among them),[92] what we call the *Major Declamations* were until the nineteenth century generally considered the work of a single

[86] Quint. 7.1.10.

[87] Cf. 12.16.6.

[88] Cf., e.g., 8.22.5.

[89] Cf. 3.19.1–6.

[90] Cf. 19.16.2–6.

[91] For a fuller treatment, see Santorelli (2021b).

[92] See Pagliaroli (2006, 45–46) on Filelfo (whose standard edition is now De Keyser [2015, 1:229]); van der Poel (2010, 281 with n. 8) on Erasmus; Krapinger (2003, 298–99) and Bernstein (2013, 154) on Vives.

author, the celebrated Roman rhetorician Quintilian (first century AD).[93] In 1881, a ground-breaking study by Constantin Ritter proved that the nineteen speeches *cannot* be ascribed to one and the same hand: arguing from the language, style, and rhetorical technique of the individual pieces, Ritter singled out a group of five declamations (*DM* 3, 6, 9, 12–13) closer to the standpoints of the real Quintilian, which might have been the work of a pupil of his; then, he ascribed a larger group of twelve speeches (*DM* 2, 4, 5, 7–8, 11, 14–19) to an unknown author dating to a time between the early second and the late third century AD; finally, he suggested that *DM* 1 was composed by a third author, somewhat earlier than the group of later speeches, while *DM* 10 would have been the most recent piece in the whole collection.[94] About a century later, and after further inquiries by Georg Golz and Nikolaj Deratani,[95] Lennart Håkanson carried out a seminal study of the rhythmical clausulae of our collection, which enabled him to allocate the composition of the individual speeches in a timespan between the late first and the mid-third century AD. Håkanson's study was published posthumously in 2014;[96] since 1999, however, an international

---

[93] It should be pointed out that no ancient source or medieval manuscript gives *Declamationes maiores* as a title: this seems to be a *modern* convention, only introduced to distinguish these pieces from the much shorter *Declamationes minores*, equally wrongly attributed to Quintilian. The earliest traces of these titles may date from as late as the seventeenth century: see Stramaglia (2006, 556n5).

[94] Ritter (1881, in particular 181–84, 267–68).

[95] Golz (1913); Deratani (1927).

[96] Håkanson (2014d, with a synopsis at 95).

research group had been publishing a series of individual volumes devoted to the nineteen *Maiores*,[97] with further analysis of the language, style, and legal background of the individual speeches. On the basis of such a wealth of scholarship, it is now possible to suggest more specific datings.

DM 3, 6, 9, 12, and 13, besides being the closest to Quintilian's views and language, are the only pieces showing a truly Roman color: *DM* 3, set in Marius' camp, mentions a specifically Roman form of debt-slavery[98] and makes use of a number of traditional Roman *exempla*;[99] in *DM* 6 the speaker claims the rights granted by his Roman citizenship,[100] alludes to his status as *pater familias*,[101] and mentions Verres with a quotation from Cicero;[102] *DM* 9 adduces examples of impressive magnanimity or gratitude drawn from Roman history;[103] *DM* 12 alludes to the voting procedures of the Roman senate;[104] *DM* 13 is grounded on an actual Roman law and exploits the theoretical positions of Roman jurists.[105] Arguing from prose rhythm, Håkanson concluded that *DM* 3 was the earliest piece, *DM* 6, 9, 13 were composed around the same time or slightly later, and *DM* 12 came shortly after. *DM* 6, 9, 13 were arguably composed under Hadrian's reign (AD 117–138): *DM* 6 seems to share the view of *patria potestas* that

[97] See in detail below, §7 and n. 220.
[98] The *addictio*: see 3.17.2–3.
[99] 3.11.1–3, 3.17.5.
[100] 6.17.6.
[101] 6.14.6.
[102] 6.9.2–4.
[103] 9.17.7, 9.20.6.
[104] 12.6.1.   [105] See Introduction to *DM* 13.

became prevalent in the Hadrianic age,[106] and *DM* 9 is very close to this speech in language and style; *DM* 13 shows a considerable affinity to the positions of the jurist Celsus, active under Hadrian.[107] *DM* 3 must have been composed before Hadrian determined that homicide in self-defense against a sexual assault should not be prosecuted, for that principle is never mentioned in the speech (even though it would have excused the defendant).[108] *DM* 12, finally, has striking similarities with Juvenal's satire 15 (datable shortly after AD 127),[109] and arguably inspired it.[110] Therefore, it is plausible that *DM* 3 was written at the outset of the second century,[111] *DM* 12 around AD 127, and *DM* 6, 9, 13 some time between them.

[106] Cf. Santorelli (2019, 76–82).

[107] Cf. Mantovani (2006–7, 331).

[108] Cf. Pietrini (2012, 105–6).

[109] This *terminus post quem* is drawn from Juv. 15.27, mentioning one of the consuls of that year.

[110] See in detail Santorelli (2021b, 372–75).

[111] Catherine Schneider (2004, 34–37; cf. 2003, 69, 76; 2005, 118–22) tentatively dated this speech to the mid-fourth century, and Stéphane Ratti (2007–10, 241–48; 2010a; 2014–16, 48–49) went so far as to ascribe it to the hand of Nicomachus Flavianus Senior (†394). Such datings are hardly tenable for both cultural-historical (Cameron [2011, 842–45]; Brendel [2013, 1046–50]; Cameron [2016]) and prose-rhythmical (Cameron [2016]) reasons. The same applies to the ascription of *DM* 10 to Marius Victorinus (†364), suggested by Schneider (2013, 49–51) and endorsed by Ratti (2014–16, 49–52); to the dating of *DM* 18–19 in the late fourth century (Calboli [2008]; see *contra* Santorelli [2021b, 395]); and to the broader idea that the *Maiores* may have been "either composed or reworked . . . between 382 and 394" (Calboli [2010, 141], translated).

The language and the prose rhythm of *DM* 1 and 10 are consistent with a dating to the mid-second century:[112] these speeches were probably composed slightly later than the previous five, by two different authors. *DM* 16 and 7 must have been written around the same time;[113] the two speeches share several linguistic similarities, and *DM* 16 might have been influenced by *DM* 6 and 9 in its description of the imprisonment of a youth kidnapped by pirates.[114]

DM 2 and 17 share some similarities in language and contents, as they both feature a son caught by his father while allegedly preparing poison. *DM* 2 was certainly written after *DM* 1;[115] its language points to the late second century, while *DM* 17 appears to be slightly later and may be dated in the first half of the third century AD.[116]

The early third century is the most likely date for the composition of a further cluster of declamations united by a number of linguistic similarities, namely *DM* 4, 5, 11, 18, 19. Among these, *DM* 4 seems quite close to *DM* 17, and the author of the latter may well have known the former;[117] the dating of this group of speeches to the third century seems to be confirmed by the interpretation of the

[112] Cf. Santorelli[-Stramaglia] (2017, 31–36). On *DM* 10 see previous note.

[113] Cf. Breij (2020, 18–21 and 75 on *DM* 7); Santorelli (2014b, 202–4 on *DM* 16).

[114] Compare, e.g., 16.8.6–7 with 6.4.1 and 9.4.3; 16.3.6–7 and 16.9.7–8 with 6.5.6–7.

[115] See above, §3 and n. 56; [Krapinger-]Stramaglia (2015, 61–62).

[116] Cf. Pasetti (2011, 42–45); Stramaglia (2013b, 36–37).

[117] Pasetti (2011, 49–51); Stramaglia (2013b, 29).

crime of slander exploited in *DM* 11, which appears to be consistent with the Roman legislation of the Severan epoch.[118] *DM* 18 and 19 share the same theme but are written for the two opposing sides by two different authors, who display very different levels of technical skill and do not seem to take each other's work into account.[119] *DM* 5, finally, appears closely tied to the other speeches of this group by a network of linguistic and thematic similarities.[120]

The latest pieces of our collection are *DM* 14–15 and 8. *DM* 14–15 develop the speech for the prosecution and the defense on a theme centered on the administering of a nonlethal potion: whether this could be considered poisoning was a question debated in the jurisprudence of the mid-third century AD, which is the most likely epoch for the dating of this pair of speeches. It is not possible to determine whether either of the two was written earlier than the other: neither speech takes into account the arguments of the other, and the opposing pieces might have been penned independently by two different authors in the same milieu.[121] Finally, *DM* 8 (a case of ill-treatment featuring twin brothers, one of whom is vivisected with his father's permission) has a number of striking similarities with *DM* 4[122] and, most notably, with *DM* 10 (a case of

[118] See Introduction to *DM* 11, n. 3.

[119] See Santorelli (2020b); Longo (2021, 230).

[120] See the references collected in Stramaglia (2013b, 29n68); Santorelli (2014b, 42–43); Breij (2015, 110–11).

[121] Cf. Longo (2008, 39–45).

[122] See Stramaglia (2013b, 29 and 91–92n17 with further references).

ill-treatment)[123] and 5 (one of two kidnapped brothers is ransomed and dies, while the other is left by his father in the hands of the pirates); indeed, the author of *DM* 8 seems to have drawn from *DM* 5 a number of expressions that are sometimes quite out of place in the context of his speech.[124] If, as argued above, *DM* 10 dates to the mid-second century and *DM* 5 to the early third, it is possible that the author of *DM* 8 knew both the other speeches and devised his declamation by the mid-third century AD or slightly later.[125]

To summarize, the chronological pattern of the individual *Maiores* could be arranged as follows:

3	ca. 100
6, 9, 13	(Early) age of Hadrian
12	No(t much) later than 127
1	
10	Mid-2nd century
16	(ca. 140–170)
7	
2	Late 2nd century
4, 5	
11	Early 3rd century
18, 19	

[123] Cf. Deratani (1927, 308–9).

[124] L. Greco in Stramaglia (1999b, 17–21), in the wake of Reitzenstein (1909, 67–68) and Deratani (1927, 297–303).

[125] See in detail Santorelli (2021a).

17   Early/Mid-3rd century

14, 15   Mid-3rd century

8   Mid-/Late 3rd century

5. THE FORMATION OF
THE COLLECTION

What we have is thus a set of speeches by several authors of different dates, reflecting various theoretical positions and technical levels. How such heterogeneous material came to be assembled into a collection, and for what purposes, are questions that can be at least partly answered thanks to some scanty evidence preserved by our manuscript tradition.

After the end of the text of *DM* 10, some of our manuscripts record the following subscription: "I, Dracontius, felicitously read and emended this with my brother Hierius, peerless orator of the city of Rome, in the school of Trajan's forum;" then, after *DM* 18: "I, Domitius Dracontius, felicitously copied and emended this from the manuscript of my brother Hierius, for me, for my uses, and for all pupils."[126] These subscriptions, along with other textual clues, testify that our entire tradition of the *Major Decla-*

---

[126] After *DM* 10: *Legi et emendavi ego Dracontius cum fratre Hierio incomparabili oratore* (Lommatsch: *arrico* codd.) *urbis Romae in schola fori Traiani feliciter*; after *DM* 18: *Descripsi et emendavi Domitius Dracontius de codice fratris Hieri feliciter mihi et usibus meis et d(iscipul)is* (Haase) *omnibus*. The text of these subscriptions, and the discussion that here follows, are based on the radically new assessment by Pecere (2021).

mations ultimately descends from a single manuscript produced by a certain Domitius Dracontius in Rome, somewhere in the area of Trajan's forum.[127] We have no further information on the identity of this Dracontius; the reference to his pupils, and the mention of his "brother"[128] Hierius, point to his being a teacher of rhetoric. Hierius, in fact, is probably to be identified with a rhetorician of Syrian origins, salaried by the city of Rome, to whom Augustine dedicated his work *De pulchro et apto* about the year AD 380 and whom he also praised in the *Confessions*.[129] In all likelihood, Dracontius was a colleague of Hierius in Rome, and the uses he envisaged for his collection of speeches were connected with his rhetorical teaching.

The first subscription suggests that, at first, Dracontius had a manuscript containing only *DM* 1–10; we do not know if he assembled the individual pieces himself, or if he drew the collection from elsewhere: all we know is that, at some point in the late fourth century, he checked with the help of Hierius the correctness of the copy he owned in the area of Trajan's forum. Some time later, according to the second subscription, Dracontius transcribed from a manuscript belonging to Hierius the text of *DM* 11–18, which he emended, this time, without the help of his colleague. The original collection of ten speeches was thus supplemented by the addition of eight more pieces; the second subscription, with the solemn mention of Dra-

---

[127] On the topographical issues, see Stramaglia (2017, 195n3).

[128] This definition implies that Dracontius and Hierius shared an equal rank, i.e., were colleagues (cf. Pecere [1986, 49–50]); see below.

[129] August. *Conf.* 4.13.20–14.21. See now Stramaglia (2017, 200–201).

contius' full name, seems to suggest that at that point he thought his work was completed. *DM* 19 must have been appended to the collection at a later stage, either by Dracontius himself or by someone else, in order to supplement *DM* 18 with a speech for the opposing side.

The pieces that Dracontius included in his collection must already have been circulating under the name of Quintilian: a passage from *DM* 1 is ascribed by Servius to Quintilian,[130] and the same applies to a quotation from *DM* 4 in a late antique commentary on Lucan.[131] Jerome knows *DM* 13 as Quintilianic;[132] later, the sixth-century bishop of Pavia, Ennodius, stated that he was replying to Quintilian when he wrote a declamation on the same theme as *DM* 5;[133] and an anonymous reply to *DM* 3 seems to date from around AD 600.[134] Besides these explicit testimonies, a number of allusions to our *Major Declamations* may be found in Jerome, who must have read and studied the "Quintilianic" *controversiae* quite thoroughly;[135] echoes or (at times extensive) "borrowings" from passages of our speeches, additionally, have been detected in Firmicus Maternus,[136] the *Panegyrici Latini*,[137] and the *Historia Augusta*.[138]

Throughout antiquity, many more declamations must

[130] Cf. 1.3.1 and Introduction to *DM* 1.
[131] Cf. 4.10.6 and Introduction to *DM* 4.
[132] Cf. 13.2.3 and Introduction to *DM* 13.
[133] See Introduction to *DM* 5.
[134] See Introduction to *DM* 3.
[135] Cf. 1.11.4 and Introduction to *DM* 1; 3.16.2–3 and Introduction to *DM* 3; 10.2.8 and Introduction to *DM* 10; and, in general, Introduction to Fragments, n. 1.   [136] Cf. Introduction to *DM* 4.   [137] Cf. 3.16.2–3 and Introduction to *DM* 3.
[138] Cf. 3.3.2 and Introduction to *DM* 3.

have been ascribed to Quintilian that are now lost.[139] What has come down to us is just a limited sample of a production that probably began while the great master was still alive[140] and went on growing for centuries. A late antique testimony affords a unique glimpse into this process of gradual agglutination of pieces of diverse origin and epoch.[141] Among the "Thirty Tyrants" who tried to overturn emperor Gallienus (253–268) there was, according to the *Historia Augusta*, one Postumus Junior; he must have been hardly more than a boy when he died, but he had at least one memorable feature:

> He was . . . so skilled in declaiming that his *controversiae* are said to have been inserted among those of Quintilian, who, as the reading of even a single chapter shows at the very first glance, was the sharpest declaimer of the Roman race.[142]

[139] As shown by the allusions to, and quotations from, "Quintilianic" speeches not included in our collection: see Fragments. The attribution of rhetorical pieces to Quintilian, the most popular master of rhetoric in the Roman tradition, was clearly meant to vouch for their value, according to a practice widespread since antiquity (and not only in the field of rhetoric): see Stramaglia (2016, 44).

[140] See Stramaglia (2006, 555).

[141] See Stramaglia (2016, 47). Variety of subjects and characters may have been consciously pursued in the gradual development of the corpus: cf. Lentano (2021).

[142] SHA *Tyr. Trig.* 4.2: *Fuit . . . ita in declamationibus disertus, ut eius controversiae Quintiliano dicantur insertae, quem declamatorem Romani generis acutissimum vel unius capitis lectio prima statim fronte demonstrat.* The relevance of this passage to the *Maiores* was definitively demonstrated by Deratani (1925, 101n1); see now Stramaglia (2017, 206–7).

After shaping the Roman education and culture for centuries, these texts disappeared almost entirely. Only an anthology prepared by a fourth-century teacher escaped the shipwreck fairly unscathed; and so, what was designed as no more than a didactic tool ended up playing a key role for future knowledge of Roman declamation.

6. THE MANUSCRIPT TRADITION

No solid evidence for the *Major Declamations* seems to survive from ca. AD 600 (above, §5) until the late tenth century, when Gerbert of Aurillac (later, Pope Silvester II; 940/50–1003) commissioned our earliest extant manuscript, B (see below), and annotated it.[143] How the *Maiores* managed to survive the Dark Ages, and then gradually spread again in the West, can nevertheless be gathered to a large extent from the surviving medieval and Renaissance manuscripts. They number over eighty,[144] though only a few of them are relevant for the establishment of

---

[143] Gerbert's hand was recognized by Hoffmann (1995, 26–28); see most recently Stoppacci (2016, 24, 30–31).

[144] Thus (in passing) Håkanson (1973, 318), confirmed by some sampling kindly made by Riccardo Macchioro. Dessauer (1898), whose catalog is still the most complete, recorded only fifty-eight items; a full survey including unexplored witnesses would certainly be rewarding in terms of *Überlieferungsgeschichte* and cultural history (see Marshall [1978, 182]; Cortesi [1984, 243–53]; Winterbottom [2014–19] for some case studies), but, given that all the manuscripts seem to descend from a single exemplar, it is not likely to affect the text of the *Maiores* appreciably (as the case studies cited above ultimately confirm). I thus resolved—just as Håkanson did—to forgo a systematic search for new witnesses, in view of the scope of this Loeb edition.

the text: after a first attempt by Caspar Hammer,[145] they were identified in 1898 in an outstanding dissertation by Hugo Dessauer.[146] He arranged the manuscripts in four classes—subsequently[147] named α β γ δ—and confirmed Hammer's conclusion that they all descend from a single archetype.[148] Class α included the already mentioned B, then V, π, M (all sigla resolved below, cxxi–cxxiii). Dessauer rightly recognized B and V as the best individual witnesses in our whole surviving tradition;[149] for the rest, the value and the stemmatic position of manuscripts π M and of classes β γ δ have been assessed quite differently by Dessauer (followed *in toto* by Lehnert [1905]), Reitzenstein (1909), Helm (1911), and Håkanson (1982b). This lively debate has been conveniently summarized elsewhere:[150] here I shall refer to the latest appraisal of the whole subject.

In a recent paper,[151] Michael Winterbottom has convincingly argued that:

1. π and M in fact descend from B, through a lost intermediary (ϵ);
2. γ β δ (better arranged in this order, according to the age of the oldest witness to each group) all go back to a common subarchetype (Φ);
3. "contamination from Φ—bearing both good and bad

145 Hammer (1893).

146 Dessauer (1898).

147 Since Lehnert (1905). Dessauer spoke of A B C D.

148 Hammer (1893, 27–28); Dessauer (1898, 80ff.).

149 Dessauer (1898, 19–20 and *passim*, in the wake, again, of Hammer [1893, 28]).

150 Håkanson (1986^2, 335–36); Stramaglia (2006, 564–68).

151 Winterbottom (2019b).

readings—affected (at least) the ancestor common to M and π [= ϵ] . . . , as well as M itself via its corrector [= M^2]",[152]

4. π and M, *not* being primary manuscripts, "can and should be used as carriers of scribal conjecture. But otherwise their evidence can be disregarded, and on two counts: they descend from a surviving manuscript, and they are subject to contamination from a source that can more readily be reconstructed without their help."[153]

For the sake of clarity, I reproduce the *stemma codicum* drawn by Winterbottom:[154]

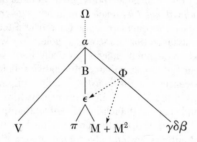

The basic fact is that α now indicates no longer a class of manuscripts, but the archetype: that is, in "Maasian" terms, the oldest forebear that the surviving manuscript evidence allows us to reconstruct—in this case, through the agreement of B V Φ. I will revert in a while to the "top

[152] Winterbottom (2019b, 297).
[153] Winterbottom (2019b, 298).
[154] Winterbottom (2019b, 310 fig. 2).

down" consequences of this, that is, to its ecdotic implications; first, some further "bottom up" reflections are in order.

Winterbottom has made it clear that the archetype of our tradition is medieval (more on this below). Its ultimate source was Dracontius' exemplar (Ω in the stemma), as proved by the subscriptions that still survive in a number of our codices (above, §5; and see below). But how did the *Maiores* get from Ω to α? It is unthinkable that Dracontius' actual manuscript survived that far: as one of his subscriptions states, it was a working copy for his own teaching purposes; it probably was not even a bound codex, but rather an "open book" made of detachable fascicles (*codex disligatus*), each containing a given text or set of texts—a frequent practice for didactic tools.[155] It is fair to assume that Dracontius' collection was transcribed at some point (maybe precisely because it was felt to bear the imprint of an authoritative scholar),[156] in the sixth century at the latest, in some well-crafted library copy intended for long term preservation.[157] It is such a single copy[158] (which I shall call ω) that must have ensured the survival of the nineteen declamations until ancient authors started to be copied again in the Carolingian revival. That exemplar itself was arguably tran-

[155] See in detail Pecere (2021, 310–11).

[156] Pecere in Stramaglia (2017, 208).

[157] For the manuscript evidence pointing to this, see Pecere (2021, 311–12).

[158] To my knowledge, only Reitzenstein (1908, 104) had hitherto envisaged an "einzige ins Mittelalter herübergerettete Handschrift."

scribed into α and then soon discarded, as was the fate of such antique manuscripts once they had "done their duty." This is a speculative reconstruction, but one that reflects a widely attested pattern in the history of Latin texts. It may therefore be not too bold to date the archetype α some time in the ninth century, and to term ω a prearchetype, deserving a place in the final stemma (below).

All this can draw some external support from the single trace of extra-stemmatic tradition so far identified. Ms. Paris, Bibliothèque nationale de France, lat. 7900A, a Carolingian school book manufactured in Northern Italy in the ninth to tenth century,[159] is in fact a palimpsest; below the "final" text there are faint, tantalizing remains of a collection of declamatory extracts, where the name "Quintilian" seems to appear twice. The only fully identifiable item is the theme (no traces of the rest) of *DM* 2, with just a few adjustments evidently made to enhance clarity for didactic purposes. These excerpts are written in an early Carolingian script, roughly datable within the first half of the ninth century:[160] but palaeographic and codicological arguments make it virtually certain that a late antique exemplar was being transcribed.[161]

[159] See most recently Longobardi (2017, 9–15).

[160] Ronconi in Stramaglia (2006, 585–86).

[161] See for all details Stramaglia (2006, 568–73, with Ronconi's appendix, 585–88; 2010, 139–43); [Krapinger-]Stramaglia (2015, 20–22). Regrettably, the *scriptio inferior* is now almost illegible, due to the chemical agents used in the nineteenth century; the transcription given by Dessauer (1901) is therefore indispensable. See also Santorelli (2014a).

We may now go back to the "main stream" of our tradition, and first of all envisage a slightly revised stemma:[162]

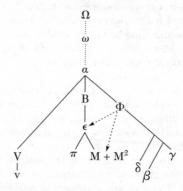

Something needs to be said on the salient features of *a*. It bore a good number of more or less typical errors;[163] those arising from incorrect word division[164] stand out: they reflect the *scriptio continua* used in late antique manuscripts, and so either came about because ω was misread, or were inherited *via* ω. *a* was also marred by various glosses or annotations, as well as by a number of interpolations:[165] all of them must have been originally either mar-

[162] For v see below, n. 177. The individual witnesses of γ δ β are detailed in the Sigla; their mutual relationships are—somewhat tentatively—drawn in Håkanson's stemma (1982b, xiii).

[163] Håkanson (1982b, xix–xxv).

[164] Dessauer (1898, 93–94); Håkanson (1982b, xxiii–xxiv).

[165] Håkanson (1982b, xix–xx). Previous treatments are often biased, but still useful: see Dessauer (1898, 83ff.); Reitzenstein (1909, 73–84); Helm (1911, 384–88).

ginal or interlinear but were then transcribed into the text; it is hard to tell, though, whether the copyist of α was responsible for that or simply reproduced what he found in his model. In any case, these "concretions" were the result of a *gradual* process, as is vividly shown by, for example, 6.9.3[166] (a remark embedded within an interpolation, to which it refers).

Also notable is α's treatment of the rubricated elements (titles; initial letters/words of speeches)[167] and the paratext (*subscriptiones*, etc.)[168] that it found in ω: they were copied along with the main text—though space was left for some initials that were not in the event added by the rubricator, thus causing, for example, the small lacuna at the beginning of *DM* 17 in *all* our manuscripts. This same process went much further in α's progeny, where forgotten initials became more and more common (with such consequences as, for instance, the muddled beginning of *DM* 16), and the paratext was more often left out than not—which explains why Dracontius' subscriptions survive only in very few witnesses.

Oddly enough, a hallmark of α has been mainly neglected hitherto: the highly uneven textual correctness of the individual speeches. Some of them are overall quite well transmitted (e.g., *DM* 4 and 9), various others are more or less problematic (e.g., *DM* 6), still others are a real disaster—like *DM* 16, which in all extant manuscripts is disfigured by lacunae, glosses, and much more, and is abruptly truncated at the end. Such a "schizophrenic" un-

---

166 See apparatus *ad loc.*
167 On which see now Winterbottom (2019b, 296, 305–6).
168 On which see now Pecere (2021) and above, §5.

evenness surely cannot be attributed to α itself: it must have to do with its ancestry.

It is fair to argue that Dracontius—or any predecessor of his—when first assembling "Quintilianic" *controversiae* into a codex, had to resort to different exemplars (papyrus rolls, pretty certainly) for different speeches or groups of speeches; and some of those exemplars were clearly more correct than others, hence, an oscillating textual standard in the final result of the process—our collection.[169] A professional like Dracontius (or Hierius before him) could not but be aware of this, and one of the goals of the revision that his subscriptions record must have been to remedy such defects; but he also certainly knew that declamations of even the greatest rhetoricians would soon be hard to come by,[170] so he seems to have aimed at collecting as many "Quintilianic" pieces as he was able to find.[171] This explains two important things:

1. why his corpus was seemingly made up in three stages (*DM* 1–10 + 11–18 + 19: see §5)—he increased his collection as he managed to get hold of further pieces;

---

[169] For parallels to this well-known type of process in the history of Latin texts, see Stramaglia (2017, 207n72).

[170] Already in the early first century AD, the Elder Seneca complained: "In general . . . there are no extant drafts from the pens of the greatest declaimers, or, what is worse, there are forged ones" (*Controv.* 1.pr.11: *Fere . . . aut nulli commentarii maximorum declamatorum extant aut, quod peius est, falsi*). See on the general issue [Santorelli-]Stramaglia (2015, 272–76).

[171] See Stramaglia (2017, 207–8).

l

2. why other analogous pieces never entered his collection—hardly by choice, but rather because they were unavailable to him.[172]

However, such professionals as Hierius and Dracontius would never have included in their collections a piece like *DM* 16 in the mutilated and extremely corrupt form in which we have it.[173] In a case like this, some "disaster" must have taken place later on: whether because the (unbound? see above) fascicle containing that piece suffered especially serious damage in Ω, before being (precariously) copied into ω; or because ω deteriorated over time at least in part, before becoming the model of α.

This second option brings us to one last issue that requires special consideration. What modern editions reckon as declamation 1—the individual pieces bearing no (authoritative) number in our codices,[174] it should be noticed—is never located at the beginning of the collection in the manuscripts; and the heading and the original theme of this piece are missing in all witnesses. Three orderings are attested:

2, 3, . . . , 19, 1: B A δ
2, 1, 3, . . . , 19: V πM CDE
2, 1, 13, 8, 5, 16, 17, 10, 3, 11, 12, 9, 4, 6, 7, 18, 19, 14, 15: β

Håkanson brilliantly explained the puzzling order in the β manuscripts as the result of the dismemberment of their

---

[172] See Introduction to Fragments.
[173] Pecere *per verba*.
[174] See Håkanson (2014c, 40 and n. 4).

model.[175] For the rest, I surmise that (?a general title of the collection, then) the individual title and theme—plus the pertinent paratext—of *Paries palmatus* are missing because the first folium in ω was lost at some point during its centuries-long life. Since the first declamation in the series was now acephalous, the scribe of α, when copying from ω, appended that piece to the end, thus starting his job with *DM* 2. The resulting sequence was kept in B (painstakingly true in every respect to its model) and, probably, Φ (as reflected by A, one of its most faithful and least contaminated descendants).[176] The ever "interventionist" scribe of V, however, on realizing that (our) *DM* 1 concerned more or less the same topic as (our) *DM* 2, placed 1 after 2, so as to form another pair like 14–15 and 18–19.[177] Contamination and scribes' whim must have

[175] Håkanson (2014c).

[176] Marco Antonio Siciliani (*per litteras*) has kindly dated this manuscript to the early/mid-fifteenth century and located its production in the area between northwestern Germany and the current Netherlands.

[177] Interestingly, V in its turn lost its first folium (Hammer [1893, 16]), so it was *DM* 2 that now came to be mutilated—losing not only the theme, but also the initial part of the speech. The readings of this missing portion can fortunately be recovered through what I shall call v, a faithful copy of V produced before the loss occurred (see Dessauer [1898, 20]; Winterbottom [2014–19, 254]; and the Sigla, below). V—and in turn v—also lacks the final part of *DM* 19, but for a different reason. The text in V stops abruptly at 19.11.6 in the middle of a sentence at fol. 136v, l. 9, then the rest of that folium and the subsequent one are left blank; the same happens in v, true to its model. This means that either α

meanwhile started to play their part, producing the oscillations in the rest of our tradition.

We can deal more quickly with the main features of the individual components of a's offspring. A detailed description of each manuscript would exceed the scope of the present edition; for this, the reader is referred to the excellent treatments by Dessauer, Håkanson, and (for the datings) Munk Olsen.[178] In what follows, I shall succinctly concentrate only on the ecdotic value of the main witnesses viz. classes.

B ($s.$ X^2, as already mentioned) and V ($s.$ XII^2) stand out for complementary reasons, partly hinted at above: "in terms of the degree of general correctness, V stays ahead, in terms of the degree of approximation to the spelling and the textual corruptions of the archetype, it lags behind B."[179] What is more, both witnesses are practically exempt from contamination and interpolation. On π and M, both descendants of B, the essential points have been made above; I add only that π displays many striking conjectures among a mass of interpolations, thus commanding attention in spite of its low stemmatic value.

As for Φ, it is in essence a (conjecturally) emended

---

had lost—by my reckoning—its final bifolium (still present when B and Φ were produced) by the time it was used as V's model, or that such a loss occurred in some unknown intermediate copy that was V's antigraph. The former hypothesis seems more economical, but certainty is not attainable.

[178] Dessauer (1898, 5ff.); Håkanson (1982b, iv–xi); Munk Olsen (1985, 292–305). Add, for B, Hoffmann (1995, 134 and *passim*).

[179] Translated from Dessauer (1898, 20). See also below, §8.

version of α; but "[i]t should be emphasized that Φ was an excellent text even before it was corrected, for it avoids the multitudinous individual errors of B and V."[180] (Unanimous) readings of Φ are therefore of primary importance in the reconstruction of α and must be given all due consideration (see below, §8). When Φ's witnesses split, they may carry conjectures as well as corruptions, and their respective value will be a matter for debate. Only a fresh investigation of Φ's progeny[181] could shed full light on this, but at least the following seems reasonably warranted:

1. in class γ, A stands out for its relative purity (see above); C^2 (C's contemporary corrector) for a number of brilliant readings—whether due to himself or drawn from some other manuscript (many of those readings are shared with E);[182] E for being the only carrier of various correct readings—among much dross;[183]

2) class β is sometimes certainly correct (as a result of clever conjecturing) against the rest of the tradition; its readings should therefore be assessed without bias, though they come from late manuscripts.[184]

For the consequences of all this on the text and apparatus of the present edition, see §8.

[180] Winterbottom (2019b, 303).

[181] A major desideratum, impracticable for the present edition—though its result would affect the history of the text, rather than its constitution (cf. n. 144).

[182] See Håkanson (1982b, ix and n. 9).

[183] See Håkanson (1982b, x).

[184] See in detail (though with some exaggerations in favor of β) Helm (1911, 354–67, 380).

7. BEYOND THE MIDDLE AGES: THE *MAJOR DECLAMATIONS* IN THE AGE OF THE PRINTED BOOK

In terms of cultural history, the manuscripts reviewed so far are only a part of the lively reception that the *Major Declamations* enjoyed after their "recovery."[185] In the Middle Ages they were a source of *bons mots* for at least four different *Florilegia*, the quarry for two systematic sets of excerpts,[186] the object of vernacular translations,[187] and the inspiration for no less than four poetical reworkings of three pieces from the collection.[188] None of these can be used to correct the text of the *Maiores*, since all this "literature in the second degree" ultimately goes back to the same archetype as the main stream of our tradition;[189] but such enthusiasm explains why, for example, a Gerbert of Aurillac (in whose school at Reims "the *Declamationes maiores* were used for training in public oratory")[190] or a

[185] An excellent overview on this long neglected field is now provided by Macchioro (2021).

[186] Conventionally called *Excerpta Monacensia* and *Excerpta Parisina*. The former are halfway between an epitome and a summary of the *DM*; the latter rework the *DM* as dialogues. The standard edition is still Lehnert (1905, 355–431), but a new one is being prepared by Riccardo Macchioro.

[187] Since at least the mid-thirteenth century, when a "translation" into Florentine was made: on this work, and its disputed authorship, see now Lorenzi Biondi (2013; 2016, 61 and 63).

[188] See Introductions to *DM* 4, 8, and 13.

[189] As recognized long ago, and now confirmed by Macchioro (2021, 240ff.).

[190] See above, §6. Quote from Kauntze (2014, 46 [with references]).

William of Malmesbury[191] commissioned their own copies of the *Major Declamations* and worked quite intensively on them.

It was only with Humanism and the Renaissance, however, that "Quintilian's" *causae*—as they were now called—acquired paramount importance in the new approach to antiquity. Petrarch, Boccaccio, and many others owned, read, annotated, and praised or criticized these texts, which became an integral part of the Latin that any learned man was supposed to be familiar with.[192] A leading role in this multifaceted process was played by Lorenzo Valla: he drew extensively on the *Maiores* for his monumental *Elegantiae linguae Latinae* and contributed a number of valuable conjectures and technical annotations—as well as concocting what was to become the standard formulation of the theme of *DM* 1, deprived of its original *argumentum* in all manuscripts. Valla's personal copy still survives and bears vivid witness to his intensive engagement, which was to make his text influential in the future.[193]

The real turning point, however, was the age of print. To be sure, the *editio princeps* of (only) *DM* 8, 9, 10 published

191 See Winterbottom (2014–19).

192 For details and further bibliography, see Stramaglia (2006, 565–67); Fernández López (2011, 239–41); Bernstein (2013, 149ff.).

193 Valla's manuscript is Oxford, Bodleian Library, Selden Supra 22; in one of its annotations, the great scholar's hand was recognized by Cortesi (1984, 251–52; 1986, 373–74 and pl. XIII); cf. Sanzotta (2013, 416 [nr. 6]). On Valla's *argumentum* to *DM* 1, see now Santorelli-Stramaglia (2017, 44, 85n1); his contributions to the text of the *Maiores* have been helpfully singled out and tabulated by Charlet (2015). Dessauer (1898, 55–56) went so far as to postulate a *recensio Valliana* within the later manuscript

in Rome in 1475 by Domizio Calderini was no more than a perfunctory textbook for his courses, practically useless for modern editors.[194] But the first *complete* printed edition, which came out in Venice in 1481,[195] was prepared with great care by Jacopo Grasolari, who also benefited from the revision of his renowned teacher, Giorgio Merlani (Georgius Merula). The merits of this editorial enterprise[196] have not been duly acknowledged by modern scholarship:[197] we owe to it many fine corrections, and a punctuation often preferable to that of the main editions that came later; what is more, it gives the declamations in the "modern" order (1, 2, . . . 19; see above, §6) that was to become standard.

The editions that followed, for far more than a century, were not of quite the same distinction.[198] They were mostly based on mediocre manuscripts, or simply on previously printed books, and this gave gradual rise to a

---

tradition of the *Maiores*, but see the wise qualifications of Pagliaroli (2006, 49–50).

[194] Calderini (1475; *IGI* 8253). On this extremely rare book, never consulted—as far as I can tell—for subsequent editions of the *Maiores* before the present one, see Campanelli (2001, 73).

[195] Grasolarius-Merula (1481; *IGI* 8254). It was lavishly reprinted as early as 1482 (*IGI* 8255; see degli Agostini [1754, 592–93]; Lemaire [1825, 281]), as well as being copied into a luxurious contemporary manuscript (Paris, Bibliothèque nationale de France, lat. 14115; see Dessauer [1898, 3, 58]).

[196] On whose genesis see degli Agostini (1754, 589, 592–93).

[197] What is more, since Burman (1720b) its readings have been ascribed in apparatuses to "Lucas": but "Lucas Venetus" was the printer, not the editor of the Latin text.

[198] See Lemaire (1825, 280–300) for a full survey of the editions up to the early nineteenth century; and now van der Poel (forthcoming).

faulty vulgate text. At least one achievement, though, deserves mention: the *Commentarii familiares*, with which the Flemish humanist and printer Jodocus Badius Ascensius[199] equipped the first (1519) and—in enlarged form, and in a separate volume (1528)—the second of his four editions of the *Maiores* (along with Quintilian's *Institutio*).[200] The text volume is hardly remarkable; but the *Commentarii* are a kind of running commentary, the first attempt at a systematic elucidation of these contorted and obscure texts. Even today, no commentator can do without this pioneering work: it often grasps the truth where later attempts have failed, especially when legal matters are involved, and contributes in the process a number of fine conjectures (oddly absent from the corresponding text volume).

Further progress in editions came only as late as the second half of the seventeenth century, when the modern textual history of the *Maiores* (by now usually printed together with the *Minores*) really began. In 1665, the Dutch printer Hack brought out a complete edition of the *corpus Quintilianeum*; its second volume, containing the declamations, was ornamented by Johann Friedrich Gronov with "a galaxy of fine emendations"[201] (in the footnotes),

[199] The vernacular form of his name is uncertain: see Renouard (1908, 1:4–7); White (2013, 4–6).

[200] Badius Ascensius (1528). The tangled history of Badius' four editions of the Latin text (1519, 1528, 1531, 1533), and of the two editions of his *Commentarii* to the *Maiores*, is elucidated by Renouard (1908, 1:153–54; 3:197–207, 471). See now also White (2013, 95).

[201] Thus Winterbottom (1984, xxiv): he was referring to the *Minores*, but the same applies to the *Maiores*.

which have often won general acceptance thereafter.[202] Emendation was pursued even more determinedly by Ulrich Obrecht, in his 1698 edition of the Quintilianic corpus:[203] even when they do not persuade, his proposals often play an important diagnostic role. What is more, Obrecht's punctuation marks an enormous advance: subsequent editors have too often overlooked this, to their loss. Death prevented Obrecht from completing his edition with a commentary volume;[204] a similar fate had a few years earlier befallen Johannes Schultingh, who planned an edition with commentary of the "Quintilianic" declamations but could leave behind only a highly promising torso.[205] The challenge was successfully taken up by Pieter Burman (the Elder: 1668–1741), who in 1720—in the second volume of his complete Quintilian—equipped the text of the *Maiores* with a wide, still indispensable commentary.[206] This included the complete notes of Gronov (1665), some extracts from Badius Ascensius (1528), many helpful references to published books that would have

[202] Gronov (1665). On his editorship of volume two (only) of the *Hackiana*, and on its hurried production, see Burman (1720a, **** 2v–3r).

[203] Again, the declamations are in volume two: Obrecht (1698).

[204] Cf. Burman (1720a, **** 3v).

[205] Cf. Burman (1720a, **** 3r).

[206] Burman (1720b), on which see now Robles Sánchez (2020, 11–22). The *praefatio* to the first volume (Burman [1720a], containing the *Institutio oratoria*) helpfully surveys earlier scholarship on the *Maiores* (see the previous and following footnotes); it is reprinted in Lemaire (1825, 68–92) and—with ample explanatory notes—in Robles Sánchez (2020, 164–207).

otherwise fallen into oblivion, and a good number of contributions by Burman himself. What makes this commentary invaluable, however, is the unpublished material it brought to light: namely, the marginal annotations of Pieter de Fransz (Francius) and Theodor Jansson van Almeloveen (Almelovenius) to their copies of the *Institutio oratoria* and *Declamationes*;[207] and, most remarkably, Schultingh's extensive notes recovered from his papers on his death—a lasting landmark in the correction and elucidation of the *Major Declamations*.[208]

Burman took little account of the edition of the *Maiores* published (along with Tacitus' *Dialogus*) in Oxford in 1675 (1692²) by an unknown scholar; but its explanatory footnotes are often as succinct as they are acute.[209] Even worse, scholarship has until recently all but ignored the massive work of the Venetian Lorenzo Patarol, posthumously published in 1743. In his early years he composed full replies (antilogies) to all the *Maiores*—except for the existing pairs 14–15 and 18–19—and provided annota-

---

[207] Cf. Burman (1720a, **** 2r–v); and, on the little known de Fransz (1645–1704), Winterbottom (2017–19, 272).

[208] Cf. Burman (1720a, **** 3r).

[209] Ed. Oxon. (1692²). The anonymous editor was *perhaps* the same shadowy John Warr (most recently hinted at in Smith [2017, 613n35]), who based on the Oxford edition (1675¹) his fine translation of the *Maiores* published in 1686 (see below in the main text). In his preliminary address "to the Reader," Warr (1686) writes rather ambiguously: "I have spent some time in translating XIX of the Declamations of Quintilian, printed apart in Latin at the Theater in Oxford, for the use of schools." Certainly, both edition and translation are the work of a clever man.

tions to the fifteen "Quintilianic" declamations he was replying to.[210] Patarol was largely unaware of previous scholarly debate,[211] but his notes are sometimes the only ones that explain a baffling passage.

After the first half of the eighteenth century, scholarly interest in the *Major Declamations* waned dramatically. Burman's text and commentary were simply reprinted, more than once;[212] and no systematic exploration and assessment of the manuscript tradition was attempted until Hammer (1893) and, most notably, Dessauer (1898) (see §6). The latter sadly died very young, in 1900; he was thus unable to undertake the edition he had planned, for which he had already collated all the relevant manuscripts. These invaluable materials (as well as a number of unpublished conjectures of his own) passed to Georg Lehnert, who based on them his own Teubner edition (1905). Unfortunately, Lehnert inspected no manuscripts himself and—what is worse—had a far too optimistic opinion of the state of the transmitted text;[213] additionally, he made only minimal use of previous scholars' conjectures and contributed very few of his own (a pity, for they are usually of value). As a result, his text is all too often incom-

---

[210] Patarol (1743). On this learned and versatile man (1674–1727), and his remarkable work on the *Maiores*, see now Bernstein (2013, 149–50, 158–64); Martella (2015, 435–37 and notes).

[211] See, however, Bernstein (2013, 158–59).

[212] Most accessibly in Dussault (1823), which however reprints Burman's commentary only in part.

[213] Cf., e.g., Lehnert (1905, xxvii): "Ipse pauca novavi neque id sine consilio. Melius enim quam primo aspectu credideris, declamationum verba tradita sunt."

prehensible, and his apparatus both inadequate and unreliable.[214]

The great advance came in 1982, with Lennart Håkanson's new Teubner.[215] No praise is too great for this piece of scholarship, as admirable in assessing and reporting on the manuscript tradition as in establishing the text and, wherever necessary, emending it with the highest acumen. The edition was preceded by a number of textual studies of the same standard[216] and accompanied by some other papers, equally important though not strictly text-critical, which were only published long after Håkanson's untimely death in 1987.[217] Detailed appraisals of his contribution to the *Major Declamations*—and to Latin philology overall—have been given elsewhere.[218] Suffice it here to say that we owe to Håkanson the first readable text of the *Maiores* and that, in addition, his apparatus often helps the reader to comprehend problematic passages.[219]

The need for the elucidation of these tremendously difficult texts, however, could not be fully met by a text edition alone, however outstanding. For this reason an in-

214 On Lehnert's (1871–1944) rather shadowy figure and scholarship, see now Winterbottom (2017–19, 273–75).

215 Håkanson (1982b).

216 Håkanson (1973, 317–22; 1974; 1976; 1978; 1982a, 242).

217 See the essays collected in Håkanson (2014e).

218 Most notably, by Winterbottom (2016). But see already, e.g., Shackleton Bailey (1976a, 73): Håkanson's critical powers "would have been remarkable at any period in the history of philology."

219 A long-standing desideratum: see Kroll (1905); Winterbottom (1976–2019, 314); and the acknowledgments by Fairweather (1985, 183); Russell (1985, 43).

ternational project was launched in 1999 in Cassino, with the aim of producing full individual commentaries on all the nineteen declamations, to be published in a special series. The project was completed in 2020. Without the enormous amount of spadework undertaken in these volumes, the present edition would have been unthinkable. The reader is always tacitly referred to the Cassino commentaries for in-depth clarification and further bibliography.[220]

One last resource for the exegesis of the *Maiores* and, occasionally, the establishment of their text should be mentioned here: the translations, at least five of which are relevant for scholarly purposes. Du Teil (1659^2, in French) often gives no more than a paraphrase, but he is sometimes the only one to make sense of a vexed passage; Warr (1686, in English) is a major achievement in terms of both elegance and acuity, still indispensable for editors; Steffens (1766, in German; *DM* 1, 2, 5, 6, 7, 8 only) is neat and accurate—though rarely helpful when uncertainties arise—and the facing Latin text occasionally improves on Burman; Sussman (1987, in English) constantly aims at rendering the original in the clearest possible way—which somewhat detracts from faithfulness to the Latin, but greatly helps in the struggle to interpret; Pagliaro (2008^3,

[220] The individual *Maiores* have been covered as follows: 1: Santorelli-Stramaglia (2017); 2: Krapinger-Stramaglia (2015); 3: Schneider (2004) (add Brescia [2004]); 4: Stramaglia (2013b); 5: Van Mal-Maeder (2018) (add Stramaglia [2018b]); 6: Zinsmaier (2009); 7: Breij (2020); 8: Stramaglia (1999b); 9: Krapinger (2007b); 10: Schneider (2013); 11: Santorelli (2014b); 12: Stramaglia (2002); 13: Krapinger (2005); 14–15: Longo (2008); 16: Santorelli (2014b); 17: Pasetti (2011); 18–19: Breij (2015).

in Italian), finally, deserves special praise for many valuable insights in both the translation and the accompanying notes.

All further secondary literature on textual and exegetical matters (including key contributions by—among others—Hammer, Becker, Reitzenstein, Helm, Englund, Shackleton Bailey, Watt, Russell, and Pasetti, as well as a number of items hitherto overlooked)[221] can be found in the Abbreviations below.

8. THE PRESENT EDITION

As explained above (§6), the text of the present edition is based in principle on the agreement of B V Φ. When they split, according to Maasian rules two witnesses should outvote one; but things are not so simple. In fact:

---

[221] Burman (±1700) stands out among these. This handwritten set of anonymus notes can be confidently recognized (Winterbottom) as "a little sketch of what might be done to the *Major Declamations*," drafted by Burman some years before his edition and perhaps submitted as a specimen to Jakob Voorbroek (= Perizonius, Burman's predecessor in Leiden University), in whose library it remained. The notes are to be dated between 1698 (reference is made to Obrecht's edition, as well as to the writer's own edition of Phaedrus, both published in that year) and 1715 (the year of Perizonius' death). Burman took over some of the ideas in his later edition, but surprisingly discarded (or forgot about?) at least three striking emendations, which anticipate modern scholars (Hammer at 4.17.3: *eminui*; Russell [*per litteras*] at 8.22.4: *nemore*; Håkanson at 16.10.2: *tenent*); see also below, Introduction to *DM* 4, n. 11. The present apparatus records only the most significant proposals; for a full *editio princeps* see Capizzi (2020–21).

When V Φ agree, most of the times they are right against B; but this normally applies only to trivialities, which B (all too) painstakingly[222] reproduced from *a*, and which V Φ easily corrected.[223] In a number of cases, however, B proves superior to V Φ; this typically happens when this faithful copy has preserved readings of the archetype *a prima facie* suspicious, but actually correct (linguistic peculiarities being often involved): in other terms, *lectiones difficiliores* that V and Φ misread or—more likely—tampered with.[224]

When (less frequently) B Φ agree, in the majority of cases they are obviously right against V;[225] but not only trivialities are here involved. On many occasions V has clearly endeavored to improve on *a*: often wrongly, but also not seldom with success.[226]

222 See above, §6.

223 As such, these cases are rarely included in the present apparatus. There are, e.g., about twenty-five of them in *DM* 1, according to Håkanson's apparatus.

224 Cf., e.g., 1.14.4, 4.8.7, 5.9.4, 6.9.6, 8.13.4, 8.19.1, 10.17.3, 12.19.3, 13.15.4, 15.6.5.

225 This happens, e.g., in seventeen out of nineteen cases in *DM* 1, according to my reckoning based on Håkanson's apparatus. Most of these minor details are not recorded in the present apparatus.

226 See especially 1.7.5 (same conjecture in π); 1.14.4, 2.24.7 (same conjecture in π); 3.4.4, 3.10.3, 3.18.2, 4.1.1, 5.13.5 (same conjecture in M); 5.15.5 (same conjecture in C²); 6.15.5, 6.23.2, 7.8.9 (same conjecture in π E); 7.11.1, 8.4.4, 8.10.1, 8.13.6, 8.14.4 (same conjecture in A); 8.18.3 (Φ splits); 8.22.4, 9.12.1, 9.15.3, 10.9.4, 10.12.3 (same conjecture in π); 10.17.6, 12.12.3, 12.21.1 (Φ splits); 13.9.6 (Φ splits); 13.11.1 (same omission in S); 13.18.1,

V alone can thus be superior to B Φ, usually[227] by conjecture.

When (very often) B V agree against Φ, they are often right, but in *very* many other cases[228] it is Φ alone that gives the correct reading.

The ultimate reason for all this is quite clear: B strove to reproduce *a*, whether its text made sense or not; whereas V and—yet more—Φ were inclined to intervene when either (or both) of them distrusted *a*'s text: sometimes wrongly, sometimes rightly. The resulting muddle was further complicated by contamination, which especially operated from Φ (or portions of it) to B's descendants π M.[229] Maasian rules thus prove to be of little or no help to an editor of the *Maiores*. Vis-à-vis the manuscript readings, he basically has to decide *case by case* whether to follow:[230]

1. B or B V, which are most likely to *represent* the archetype—be it correct or faulty;
2. V or Φ individually (or V Φ together, where applicable), which may have *preserved* a given reading

---

15.3.3 (same conjecture in π δ); 15.9.2, 16.3.4, 16.3.6 (same conjecture in E); 16.10.2, 17.16.3 (Φ splits); 18.12.8, 19.5.5.

[227] But V alone seems to have *preserved* a *lectio difficilior* (or a clue to it) in such cases as 5.23.1, 13.5.3; cf. also 2.9.3, 15.2.2.

[228] Winterbottom (2019b, 307–9) lists nearly 250 instances.

[229] See Winterbottom (2019b, 304).

[230] I single out only the *basic* options; of course, a number of "minor" combinations (e.g., B or V agreeing with a given manuscript or branch of the Φ class) may also occur.

of the archetype, but are rather more likely to have conjecturally *emended* α—whether for good or ill;

3. π and/or M and/or branches or even single witnesses of Φ (plus, occasionally, N or W),[231] in the awareness that all these readings—whether individual or more or less widely shared (because of contamination, usually)—are certainly *conjectural emendations*.

In a very large number of cases, however, none of these options is practicable: for when serious textual uncertainties present themselves, *all* manuscripts tend to be (whether unanimously or variously) faulty. This is altogether obvious, since the manuscript tradition of the *Major Declamations* offers a perfect example of "closed recension": all surviving witnesses ultimately descend from one and the same late antique ancestor (§5). Therefore, if something is more or less badly wrong in this single line of transmission, there is no hope for remedy except from conjectural emendation. This is provided to a certain extent by our medieval manuscripts; but a lot more is needed.

Under these circumstances, when B V Φ did not agree, in the present edition I have followed options 1, 2, and 3 (above) in decreasing order of preference, whenever a satisfactory solution was offered by any one of them. In all the other *very* numerous cases, I have resorted to the conjectures provided by "modern" scholars (for the lead-

---

[231] These sigla are resolved below, cxxiii. On W see there; on N, akin to M and cited only (after Håkanson or Hammer) at 2.16.7, 3.9.6, 13.12.2, see Dessauer (1898, 17); de Meyier (1946, 19–20); Håkanson (1982b, xi).

ing ones see §7) and attempted a number of my own. In terms of method, the basic criterion for textual criticism in the *Maiores* remains the one that was lucidly—if somewhat harshly as regards the texts themselves—stated by Dessauer:

> The faults that mar the tradition are admittedly great and multifarious, but their healing is eased by the marked individuality of the diction, the schoolmasterish narrowness of the ideas, the limited vocabulary, the ever-recurring phrases, in short by the whole coloring that characterizes the declamations.[232]

The many ways in which these key aspects of *usus scribendi* can be exploited are superbly illustrated by Håkanson's work, which also pays all due attention to another prime factor in textual decisions: rhythm. It would be beyond the scope of this book to rehearse all such technical aspects;[233] suffice it here to broadly state that departing from Håkanson's choices is often necessary, but always done at one's own risk. However, in the thorny process of constituting the text for the present edition, I have had the privilege to constantly exchange opinions with Michael Winterbottom: and when we disagreed, our arbiter was none other than Donald Russell. Whatever its intrinsic merits, the Latin text here offered has benefited enormously from both these scholars.

[232] Translated from Dessauer (1898, 101–2).

[233] Many of them were lucidly singled out by Håkanson's reviewers: cf. Rahn (1976, 410); Winterbottom (1976–2019); Fairweather (1985, 183); Russell (1985, 44).

Regarding orthography, like Håkanson I generally abide by B, our oldest witness, when manuscripts oscillate—whether on morphological issues (gen. pl. *-um/-ium*; abl. sing. *-e/-i* . . .), or on assimilations/dissimilations of prefixes and the like.[234] But B also contains a lot of blatantly unacceptable forms, as was already pointed out by Friedrich Enderlein and as Håkanson himself acknowledged;[235] among these I include the unassimilated forms *-nb-*, *-nm-*, *-np-*, whose legitimacy in our text does not seem to be sufficiently backed up by general evidence:[236] I have thus systematically restored the standard *-mb-*, *-mm-*, *-mp-*, though it should be emphasized that full certainty in such matters is hardly attainable.[237] For more details on all these minutiae, the reader is referred to Håkanson's preface and apparatus.

As to punctuation, I have used special care in making it as clear and "explanatory" as possible, bearing constantly in mind that "punctuation shows the understanding and the degree of independence of an editor in the most unmistakable way."[238] The manuscript evidence in this area cannot be used, because—as is well known—it follows very different principles from the modern ones;[239] but older editions and more recent scholarship yield many decisive contributions, recorded in the present apparatus

234 Cf. Håkanson (1982b, xxv–xxvi).

235 See Enderlein (1870, 5); Håkanson (1982b, v).

236 On which see Prinz (1953, 36–37, 40–41, 45–46, 48).

237 For instance *-nb-*, *-nm-*, *-np-* are sometimes to be admitted in the text of Quintilian's *Institutio* according to Winterbottom (1970, 44, 45–46).

238 Translated from Reitzenstein (1909, 85).

239 Cf. Golz (1913, 14ff.).

with more care than has hitherto been customary, given the importance of this feature.[240]

The layout of the text has also been the object of attention. Håkanson sometimes diverges from his predecessors in the positioning of the chapter numbers[241] introduced by Burman and consistently kept until Lehnert; yet such discrepancies are patently not of intentional choices but of misprints (misalignments). I have therefore tacitly restored the chapter numbers to their original positions—even where logic might have recommended different choices—to avoid unwelcome complications in citations.[242] To this same end, I have divided all chapters into subsections (ideally corresponding to units of thoughts, mostly of a couple of sentences). This subdivision is entirely new, though for some of the speeches it was *partly* anticipated in the corresponding volumes of the Cassino collection. I hope that citing the *Major Declamations* in the future will be made easier by this innovation.

Finally, the critical apparatus. The *Maiores* are extraordinarily difficult pieces, whose readers need to know at each stage not only *what* they are reading—whether trans-

---

[240] On the other hand, I have refrained from Håkanson's "rather Germanic procedure of putting commas to mark subordinate clauses," as it "produces consistency, but also a fussy impression" (Russell [1985, 44]).

[241] Namely, at 2.24 (deleted), 3.16, 4.8, 4.14, 5.17, 5.18, 6.3, 6.5, 6.8, 6.10, 6.20, 7.2, 7.12, 10.3, 10.8, 10.16, 11.10, 12.7, 12.13, 12.14, 12.23, 12.27, 13.5, 13.17, 15.6, 15.11, 16.5, 17.18, 18.17.

[242] The few other misprints in Håkanson (1982b) (mostly listed by Shackleton Bailey [1984–97, 211–12]) I have also corrected tacitly; a note in the apparatus is made only in two doubtful cases (3.7.4, 12.13.4).

mitted text or modern conjecture—but also *why*. Reconciling this need with the customary restrictions of a Loeb apparatus would have been impossible, had not the editors of the collection generously allowed much more space than usual for the apparatus criticus (and also for the footnotes to the translation, its inseparable complement). Still, a fairly "extreme" use of abbreviations in reporting lemmas etc. was unavoidable; and no distinction could be made, in attributing conjectures, as to the degree of confidence with which they had been originally proposed (main text; apparatus . . .). More important, a number of other limitations imposed themselves. As a general rule, an entry in the apparatus has been made only when the text printed:

1. is *not* the more or less unanimous reading of the manuscripts, or else a reading with no feasible variants; when neither of these is the case, the main manuscript variants have been recorded;
2. departs from the paradosis; if so, the apparatus records the accepted emendation—and one or more alternatives, in case of *significant* doubts; it should be pointed out that no *cruces* appear in the text, because of the constant need to provide a(n albeit tentative) translation;
3. is more or less doubtful; one or more possible alternatives are then signaled;
4. accepts/introduces a *semantically relevant* change in the punctuation (see above);
5. does *not* follow Håkanson in substantial matters of orthography (for the rest, the reader is tacitly referred to his apparatus: see above).

Also, with regard to the manuscripts:

1. details of portions lacking are given only for the important V (including its readings that can be recovered through v);[243] for all other incomplete witnesses (in the Φ branch), the reader is referred to Håkanson's preface and apparatus;

2. π M, both *codices descripti*,[244] are reported only when they carry a valuable individual reading (= conjecture), or when they join a *portion* of Φ in a given reading: in the latter case, the most likely reason for the agreement is contamination (which is virtually certain when π and/or M match the *whole* of Φ), but independent conjecture cannot be ruled out *a priori*; as a consequence, in the present apparatus *"codd."* means B V Φ, not necessarily also π M (let alone further secondary witnesses, like N W)—and the same principle applies to *"cett."*;

3. paratext is recorded only when it contributes to the constitution of the main text.

I have systematically collated (on scans) B V, and wherever necessary π M, as well as Valla's codex;[245] Michael Winterbottom has kindly checked the readings of v for the portion where it replaces V. Of the Φ manuscripts, I have checked A[246] on a digital reproduction; for all the others,

---

243 See above, §6.

244 See above, §6.

245 See above, §6 and n. 193.

246 Of special interest, in spite of its relatively late date: see above, §6 and n. 176.

I have relied on Håkanson's apparatus.[247] For the Paris palimpsest I have used Dessauer's transcription;[248] for N W see below, Sigla. The readings of ϛ are taken in general from Burman, occasionally also from other—mostly older—editions.

[247] See above, §6 and n. 181.
[248] See above, §6 and n. 161.

ABBREVIATIONS

The abbreviations of scholars' names below are used in the apparatus criticus; such names have been kept latinized—where applicable—only for publications prior to 1650. When reprints of articles are referred to, pages are cited according to the reprint; and most books and articles prior to the twentieth century have been consulted in freely accessible online reproductions. All "Harvard style" abbreviations (e.g., Burman 1720b) referred to in this section are resolved in the General Bibliography.

AAP	*Atti dell'Accademia Pontaniana*
AAT	*Atti della Accademia delle Scienze di Torino, Classe di Scienze morali, storiche e filologiche*
AJPh	*American Journal of Philology*
Alm.	Almeloveen, Th. J. van. In Burman 1720b.
ALMA	*Archivum Latinitatis Medii Aevi (Bulletin Du Cange)*
ANRW	*Aufstieg und Niedergang der römischen Welt*
Axel.	Axelson, B. In Håkanson 1982b.
Baden	Baden, T. 1822. "Obss. in Quinctiliani Decl. XIX." In *Miscellanea maximam partem critica*, edited by F. T. Friedemann, J. D. G. Seebode, 1:749–50. Hildesheim, 1822.

B. Asc.[1] Badius Ascensius, J. 1528. *Commentarii familiares . . . in M. Fabii Quintiliani declamationes, nuper editi.* Paris.

B. Asc.[2] Badius Ascensius, J., ed. 1533[4]. *M. F. Quintiliani Institutiones Oratoriae, ac Declamationes, cuiuscuius sint.* Paris. (Mostly repr. of 1519[1].)

Bech. Becher, F. 1887. "Bericht über die Litteratur zu Quintilian aus den Jahren 1880–1887." *JAW* 51:1–82.

Beck.[1] Becker, A. 1902. "Julius Firmicus Maternus und Pseudo-Quintilian." *Philologus* 61:476–78.

Beck.[2] ———. 1904. *Pseudo-Quintilianea. Symbolae ad Quintiliani quae feruntur Declamationes XIX maiores.* Progr. Ludwigshafen am Rhein.

Bendz Bendz, G. In Håkanson 1982b.

Best Best, W. 1707. *Ratio emendandi leges.* Utrecht.

BICS *Bulletin of the Institute of Classical Studies of the University of London*

BMCR *Bryn Mawr Classical Review*

BphW *Berliner philologische Wochenschrift*

Breij[1] Breij, B., ed., trans., comm. 2015. [*Quintilian*]. *The Son Suspected of Incest with His Mother* (Major Declamations, 18–19). Cassino.

Breij[2] ———, ed., trans., comm. 2020. [*Quintilian*]. *The Poor Man's Torture* (Major Declamations, 7). Cassino.

Breij[3]   ———. "*Inter ignes et flagella*: Uses of
                Torture in the *Major Declamations*."
                In Lovato-Stramaglia-Traina 2021,
                1–31.

BstudLat   *Bollettino di studi latini*

Bur.[1]   Burman, P. ±1700. See Capizzi 2020–21.

Bur.   ———, ed. and comm. 1720b. *M. Fabii
                Quinctiliani, ut ferunt, Declamationes
                XIX majores, et quae ex CCCLXXXVIII.
                supersunt CXLV minores. et Calpurnii
                Flacci Declamationes. cum notis docto-
                rum virorum.* Leiden.

Cal.   Calderini, D., ed. 1475. *Declamationes
                tres.* Rome.

Cappelli   Cappelli, A. 2011[7] (1899[1]). Lexicon Ab-
                breviaturarum. *Dizionario di Abbrevia-
                ture latine ed italiane.* Rev. and enl.
                by M. Geymonat and F. Troncarelli.
                Milan.

Cast.   Castiglioni, L. 1943/4–54. "Decisa forfici-
                bus. IV." *RIL* s. III 77 (1943/4): 409–30.
                Repr. in Castiglioni, *Decisa forficibus*,
                79–107. Milan, 1954.

CCSL   *Corpus Christianorum. Series Latina*

CEA   *Cahiers des études anciennes*

Char.   Charlet, J.-L. 2015. "Les déclamations du
                Pseudo-Quintilien dans le *Cornu copiae*
                de Niccolò Perotti." In Poignault-
                Schneider 2015, 397–415.

Corb.   Corbeill, A. 2017. Review of Santorelli
                2014b. *Gnomon* 89:331–34.

ABBREVIATIONS

Corbino	Corbino, A. 2009. "*Actio in factum adversus confitentem.* Quint., *Declam. Maior* XIII.*"* In *Studi in onore di Antonino Metro*, edited by C. Russo Ruggeri, 1:511–24. Milan, 2009.
CPh	*Classical Philology*
CR	*Classical Review*
CSEL	*Corpus Scriptorum Ecclesiasticorum Latinorum*
De Fel.	De Felice, P. 2001. "Pseudo-Quintiliano *Declamazioni maggiori* 16, 1." *InvLuc* 23:53–54.
Der.	Deratani, N. 1930. "De poetarum vestigiis in declamationibus Romanorum conspicuis." *Philologus* 85:106–11.
Dess.[1]	Dessauer, H. 1898. *Die handschriftliche Grundlage der neunzehn grösseren pseudo-quintilianischen Declamationen*. Leipzig.
Dess.[2]	———. In Lehnert 1905.
Dim.	Dimatteo, G. 2019a. "Ps. Quint. *decl.* 13, 7 (p. 272, 15–18 Håkanson)." *Latinitas* n.s. 7.1:15–16.
Di St.	Di Stefano, A. 2015. "Alcuni recenti studi sulle declamazioni pseudoquintilianee." *BstudLat* 45:601–10.
Du Teil	Du Teil, [B.], trans. 1659[2]. *Les Grandes et entieres declamations du fameux orateur Quintilien, mises en François . . . .* Paris. (Corr. repr. of *Les Grandes declamations de Quintilien, nouvellement traduites en François . . . .* Paris, 1658[1].)

Ed. Oxon.	Editio Oxoniensis (Anonymous), ed. and ann. 1692[2] (1675[1]). *M. Fab. Quintiliani Declamationum liber. Cum ejusdem (Ut nonnullis visum) Dialogo de causis corruptae eloquentiae.* Oxford.
EEAth	*Epistemonike Epeteris tes Philosophikes Scholes tou Panepistemiou Athenon*
Ellis	Ellis, R. 1909. "Notes on the Nineteen Larger Declamations Ascribed to Quintilian." *Hermathena* 35:328–46.
Eng.	Englund, Y. 1934. *Ad Quintiliani quae feruntur Declamationes maiores adnotationes.* Uppsala.
Fairw.[1]	Fairweather, J. 1981. *Seneca the Elder.* Cambridge.
Fairw.[2]	———. 1985. Review of Håkanson 1982b. *Gnomon* 57:182–84.
Franc.	Francius (de Fransz), P. In Burman 1720b.
G&R	*Greece and Rome*
Gand.	Gandiglio, A. 1913. Review of Tosato 1912. *RFIC* 41:318–22.
GFA	*Göttinger Forum für Altertumswissenschaft*
GGA	*Göttingische Gelehrte Anzeigen*
Golz	Golz, G. 1913. *Der rhythmische Satzschluss in den grösseren pseudoquintilianischen Declamationen,* Breslau.
Gr.-Mer.	Grasolarius (Grasolari), J., and G. Merula (Merlani), eds. 1481. *M. Fabii Quintiliani eloquentissimi Declamationes.* Venice.

Grassi	Grassi, C. 1971. In *Seneca il Vecchio. Quintiliano*, edited, translated, and annotated by M. Bonaria and C. Grassi, 43–255. Brescia, 1971.
Gron.	Gronov, J. F., ed. and ann. 1665. *M. Fab. Quintiliani Declamationes undeviginti. M. Fabii Avi et Calpurnii Flacci Declamationes. Auctoris Incerti Dialogus De causis corruptae Eloquentiae*. Leiden-Rotterdam.
Gron.[1]	———. 1672. In Vv. Aa. 1672.
Gron.[2]	———. 1755[3]. *Observationum libri quatuor*. Edited by F. Platner. Leipzig. (*Observationum libri tres*, Leiden 1639[1], 1662[2].)
Grut.	Gruterus, I. (J. Gruter). 1591. *Suspicionum libri IX*. Wittenberg.
Gryph.	Gryphius (Greyff), S., ed. 1531 (1591[12]). *Mar. Fabii Quintiliani Declamationes*. Lyon.
Håk.[1]	Håkanson, L. 1973. "Textkritisches zu den unter dem Namen Quintilians überlieferten sog. kleineren und grösseren Deklamationen." In *Classica et Mediaevalia Francisco Blatt septuagenario dedicata*, 310–22. Copenhagen, 1973.
Håk.[2]	———. 1974. *Textkritische Studien zu den grösseren pseudoquintilianischen Deklamationen*. Lund.

Håk.[3] ———. 1976. "35 Emendationsvorschläge zu den grösseren pseudoquintilianischen Deklamationen." *Eranos* 74:122–38.

Håk.[4] ———. 1978. "Einige textkritische Bemerkungen zu den größeren pseudoquintilianischen Deklamationen." *WS* 91:151–58.

Håk.[5] ———. 1982a. "Miscellanea critica." *Phoenix* 36:237–42.

Håk. ———, ed. 1982b. *Declamationes XIX maiores Quintiliano falso ascriptae.* Stuttgart.

Håk.[6] ———. 2014b. "Zu den literarischen Vorbildern der *Declamationes maiores*: Cicero, Seneca, *Declamationes minores.*" In Håkanson 2014e, 15–38.

Håk.[7] ———. 2016. *Unveröffentlichte Schriften,* II (*Kommentar zu Seneca Maior,* Controversiae, *Buch I*). Edited by F. Citti, B. Santorelli and A. Stramaglia. Berlin-Boston. (B. Santorelli, "Aktualisierung," 143–48.)

Håk.-Wint. Håkanson, L., and M. Winterbottom. 2015. "*Tribunus Marianus.*" In Del Corso-De Vivo-Stramaglia 2015, 61–90.

Hamm.[1] Hammer, C. 1893. *Beiträge zu den 19 grösseren quintilianischen Deklamationen.* Progr. Munich.

Hamm.[2] ———. 1899. Review of Dessauer 1898. *BphW* 19:521–24.

Helm[1] Helm, R. 1911. Review of Reitzenstein 1909. *GGA* 173:337–89.

Helm[2]   ———. 1955. "Observatiunculae ad Ps.
              Quintiliani declamationes pertinentes."
              In *Ut Pictura Poesis. Studia Latina Petro
              Iohanni Enk septuagenario oblata*, 87–
              98. Leiden, 1955.
Hine   Hine, H. M. In Winterbottom 2019a.
Hömke   Hömke, N. 2002. *Gesetzt den Fall, ein Geist
              erscheint. Komposition und Motivik der
              ps-quintilianischen* Declamationes maio-
              res *X, XIV und XV*. Heidelberg.
HSPh   *Harvard Studies in Classical Philology*
H.-Sz.   Hofmann, J. B., and A. Szantyr. 1972[2].
              Lateinische Syntax und Stilistik. Munich.
              (Corr. repr. of 1965[1].)
Hüb.   Hübner, W. In Stramaglia 1999b.
Hüb.-Hei.   Hübner, W., and S. Heilen. In Stramaglia
              2013b.
IFC   *Incontri di filologia classica*
IGI   *Indice generale degli incunaboli delle biblio-
              teche d'Italia*, I–VI. Rome, 1943–1981.
InvLuc   *Invigilata lucernis*
JAW   *Jahresbericht über die Fortschritte der
              classischen Altertumswissenschaft*
JHM   *Journal of the History of Medicine and Al-
              lied Sciences*
JRA   *Journal of Roman Archaeology*
Klotz[1]   Klotz, A. In Lehnert 1905.
Klotz[2]   ———. 1906. "Über die *Expositio totius
              mundi et gentium*." *Philologus* 65:97–
              127.
Kr.[1]   Krapinger, G., ed., trans., comm. 2005.
              [*Quintilian*]. *Die Bienen des armen*

*Mannes (*Größere Deklamationen, *13).* Cassino.

Kr.[2] ———, ed., trans., comm. 2007b. [*Quintilian*]. *Der Gladiator (*Größere Deklamationen, *9).* Cassino.

Kr.-Str. Krapinger, G., trans., comm., and A. Stramaglia, ed., comm. 2015. [*Quintilian*]. *Der Blinde auf der Türschwelle (*Größere Deklamationen, *2).* Cassino.

Kroll K(roll), W. 1905. Review of Lehnert 1905. *Literarisches Zentralblatt* 56:1296.

K.-S. Kühner, R., and C. Stegmann. 1976[5]. *Ausführliche Grammatik der lateinischen Sprache*, 2:1–2 (*Satzlehre*). Rev. by A. Thierfelder. Hanover.

Kuy. Kuyper (Cuperus), F. In Burman ±1700.

Leh.[1] Lehnert, G. 1903. "Zum Texte der Pseudo-Quintilianischen *declamationes maiores*." *Philologus* 62:419–44.

Leh. ———, ed. 1905. *Quintiliani quae feruntur Declamationes XIX maiores*. Leipzig.

Leu. Leumann, M. 1977. *Lateinische Laut- und Formenlehre*. Munich.

Lips Lips (Lipsius), J. In Burman ±1700.

Longo Longo, G., ed., trans., comm. 2008. [*Quintiliano*]. *La pozione dell'odio (*Declamationes maiores, *14–15).* Cassino.

Longo[1] ———. 2016. "La medicina nelle *Declamazioni maggiori* pseudo-quintilianee." In Dinter-Guérin-Martinho 2016, 167–87.

ABBREVIATIONS

Luc.   Lucarini, C. M. 2020. "Zu den lateinisch-griechischen Musterbriefen (*P. Bonon.* 5)." *ZPE* 216:73–77.

Lund.[1]   Lundström, S. 1973–74. "Textkritische Bemerkungen zu den grösseren pseudoquintilianischen Deklamationen." *Kungliga Humanistiska Vetenskapssamfundet i Uppsala Årsbok*, 63–86.

Lund.[2]   ———. In Håkanson 1982b.

Mant.[1]   Mantovani, D. 2006–7. "I giuristi, il retore e le api. *Ius controversum* e *natura* nella *Declamatio maior* XIII." *Seminarios Complutenses de Derecho Romano* 19 (2006): 205–83. Repr. in *Testi e problemi del giusnaturalismo romano*, edited by D. Mantovani and A. Schiavone, 323–85. Pavia, 2007.

Mant.[2]   ———. *per litteras*.

Marsh.   Marshall, P. 1978. Review of Håkanson 1974. *CPh* 73:180–82.

MD   *Materiali e discussioni per l'analisi dei testi classici*

Meurs.[1]   Meursius, I. (J. van Meurs). 1597. *Ad Theocriti Syracusani Poetae Idyllia Spicilegium*. Leiden.

Meurs.[2]   ———, ed. and comm. 1599[2] (1597[1]). *Lycophronis Chalcidensis Alexandra*. Leiden.

Meurs.[3]   ———. 1599. *Exercitationes criticae*, I–II. Leiden.

Ne.-W.   Neue, F., and C. Wagener. 1902–1905[3]. *Formenlehre der lateinischen Sprache*, I–IV. Berlin. (= Hildesheim, 1985.)

Obr.   Obrecht, U., ed. 1698. *M. Fabii Quincti-
              liani Declamationes innumeris locis
              emendatae*. Strasbourg.

Pagl.   Pagliaro, R. L., ed., trans., ann. 2008[3].
              [*Quintiliano*]. Declamationes XIX maio-
              res. *Proposta di traduzione* [*in CD-
              Rom*]. Caserta, 2011[2] (*Introduzione*) +
              CD-Rom 2008[3]. (Naples, 2004[1].)

Pas.[1]   Pasetti, L. 2004. Review of Stramaglia
              2002. *Eikasmos* 15:568–75.

Pas.[2]   ———. 2008a. "[Quint.] *Decl.* 3,19
              (59,14s. H.)." *Eikasmos* 19:237–40.

Pas.[3]   ———. 2008b. Review of Brescia 2004 and
              Schneider 2004. *Eikasmos* 19:533–39.

Pas.[4]   ———. 2008c. Review of Krapinger 2005.
              Lexis 26:443–46.

Pas.[5]   ———. 2009b. Review of Krapinger
              2007b. *Gnomon* 81:604–8.

Pas.   ———, ed., trans., comm. 2011. [*Quinti-
              liano*]. *Il veleno versato* (Declamazioni
              maggiori, *17*). Cassino.

Pass.   Passerat, J. In Gronov 1665.

Pat.   Patarol, L., ed. and ann. 1743. *M. Fabii
              Quintiliani Declamationes, Cum earum-
              dem Analysi, & Adnotatiunculis Diffi-
              ciliores, & conditiores sensus explicanti-
              bus. In singulas praeterea declamationes
              Antilogiae. Auctore Laurentio Patarol*. In
              Patarol, *Opera Omnia quorum pleraque
              Nunc primum in lucem prodeunt*, 2:93–
              402. Venice, 1743.

PhilolAnt   *Philologia Antiqua*

Pi.[1]   Pieri, B. 2001."I medici e la *humanitas* (Ps.
             Quint. *decl.* 8,3)." *Eikasmos* 12:477–80.
Pi.[2]   ———. 2002. Review of Stramaglia 1999b.
             Paideia 57:369–78.
Pir.   Pirovano, L. 2012. Review of Krapinger
             2007b. *Eikasmos* 23:545–48.
PL   *Patrologia Latina*
Plas.   Plasberg, O. In Reitzenstein 1909 (whose
             pages are straightforwardly cited).
QUCC   *Quaderni urbinati di cultura classica*
Reitz.[1]   Reitzenstein, R. 1908. "Zu Quintilians
             grossen Declamationen." *Hermes*
             43:104–19.
Reitz.[2]   ———. 1909. *Studien zu Quintilians
             grösseren Deklamationen*. Strasbourg.
REL   *Revue des études latines*
RFIC   *Rivista di filologia e di istruzione classica*
RG   Walz, Ch., ed. 1832–1836. *Rhetores Graeci*,
             I–IX. Stuttgart. (= Osnabrück 1968.)
RhM   *Rheinisches Museum*
RIL   *Rendiconti dell'Istituto Lombardo, Classe
             di Lettere, Scienze morali e storiche*
Ritt.   Ritter, C. 1881. *Die quintilianischen Decla-
             mationen. Untersuchung über Art und
             Herkunft derselben*. Freiburg-Tübingen.
             (= Hildesheim, 1967.)
Rizz.   Rizzelli, G. 2021. "Il fr. 3 Stramaglia delle
             Declamazioni maggiori e la circolazione
             di temi fra retori e giuristi." In Lovato-
             Stramaglia-Traina 2021, 343–60.
RPh   *Revue de philologie, de littérature et
             d'histoire anciennes*

RPL	*Res Publica Litterarum: Studies in the Classical Tradition*
Ruardi	Ruardi, J. 1769. *Specimen criticum inaugurale ad nonnulla juris et aliorum auctorum loca*. Franeker.
Russ.[1]	Russell, D. A. 1985. Review of Håkanson 1982b. *CR* n.s. 35:43–45.
Russ.[2]	———. In Winterbottom 2019a (whose pages are straightforwardly cited).
Russ.[3]	———. *per litteras*.
Salm.	Salmasius (Saumaise), C. 1638. *De usuris liber*. Leiden.
S&T	*Segno e Testo: International Journal of Manuscripts and Text Transmission*
Sant.[1]	Santorelli, B. 2013. "Note critiche a Ps.-Quint., *Decl. mai.* 16." *Prometheus* 23:227–36.
Sant.	———, ed., trans., comm. 2014b. [*Quintiliano*]. *Il ricco accusato di tradimento* (Declamazioni maggiori, *11*)—*Gli amici garanti* (Declamazioni maggiori, *16*). Cassino.
Sant.[2]	———. 2018b. "Il *debitor delicatus* tra due scogli (Ps.-Quint. *decl. mai.* 9, 19)." *Maia* 70:544–50.
Sant.[3]	———. In this Loeb edition.
Sant.-Str.	Santorelli, B., comm., and A. Stramaglia, ed., trans., comm. 2017. [*Quintiliano*]. *Il muro con le impronte di una mano* (Declamazioni maggiori, *1*). Cassino.
SC	*Sources Chrétiennes*
Sch.	Schultingh, J. In Burman 1720b.

Scheff.   Scheffer, J. 1737. "Adversariorum liber
               ἀνέκδοτος. XV, XVII." *Miscellaneae
               observationes criticae in auctores veteres
               et recentiores* 8:438–44, 449–56.

Schn.[1]   Schneider, C., ed., trans., comm. 2004.
               [*Quintilien*]. *Le soldat de Marius*
               (Grandes déclamations, *3*). Cassino.

Schn.[2]   ———, ed., trans., comm. 2013. [*Quin-
               tilien*]. *Le tombeau ensorcelé* (Grandes
               déclamations, *10*). Cassino.

SCO   *Studi classici e orientali*

Set.   Setaioli, A. 2000. Facundus Seneca. *Aspetti
               della lingua e dell'ideologia senecana*.
               Bologna.

Sh. B.[1]   Shackleton Bailey, D. R. 1976a. Review of
               Håkanson 1974. *AJPh* 97:73–79.

Sh. B.[2]   ———. 1976b. "Emendations of Pseudo-
               Quintilian's Longer Declamations."
               HSPh 80:187–217.

Sh. B.[3]   ———. 1982. In Håkanson 1982b.

Sh. B.[4]   ———. 1984–97. "More on Pseudo-
               Quintilian's Longer Declamations." *HSPh*
               88 (1984): 113–37. Repr. with *addenda*
               in Shackleton Bailey, *Selected Classical
               Papers*, 188–212. Ann Arbor, 1997.

SIFC   *Studi italiani di filologia classica*

Steff.   Steffens, J. H., trans. 1766. *Versuch einer
               Uebersezzung einiger Declamationen des
               Quinctilianus*. Zelle.

Str.[1]   Stramaglia, A. 1996–97. "Note critiche ed
               esegetiche alla X *Declamazione maggiore*

pseudo-quintilianea (*Sepulcrum incantatum*)." *InvLuc* 18–19:275–84.

Str.[2] ———. 1999a. Res inauditae, incredulae. *Storie di fantasmi nel mondo greco-latino*. Bari.

Str.[3] ———, ed., trans., comm. 1999b. [*Quintiliano*]. *I gemelli malati: un caso di vivisezione* (Declamazioni maggiori, 8). Cassino.

Str.[4] ———, ed., trans., comm. 2002. [*Quintiliano*]. *La città che si cibò dei suoi cadaveri* (Declamazioni maggiori, 12). Cassino.

Str.[5] ———. 2006. "Le *Declamationes maiores* pseudo-quintilianee: genesi di una raccolta declamatoria e fisionomia della sua trasmissione testuale." In *Approches de la Troisième Sophistique. Hommages à Jacques Schamp*, edited by E. Amato, 555–84. Brussels, 2006. (Appendix: F. Ronconi, "Il codice palinsesto *Paris. Lat.* 7900A: una nuova ispezione della *scriptio inferior*," 585–88.)

Str.[6] ———. 2008. "Pseudo-Quintilianus, *Declamationes maiores*, 1: *Paries palmatus*." *InvLuc* 30:195–233.

Str.[7] ———. 2009a. "Note critiche ed esegetiche alle *Declamationes maiores* pseudo-quintilianee." *Graeco-Latina Brunensia* 14:297–313.

Str.[8] ————. 2009b. "Pseudo-Quintilianus, *De-clamationes maiores*, 2: *Caecus in limine*." *InvLuc* 31:193–240.

Str.[9] ————. 2013a. "Ps.-Quint., *Decl. mai.* 2, 22 (p. 40, 3 Håkanson)." In *Per Gabriella. Studi in ricordo di Gabriella Braga*, edited by M. Palma and C. Vismara, 4:1723–28. Cassino, 2013.

Str.[10] ————, ed., trans., comm. 2013b. [*Quintiliano*]. *L'astrologo* (Declamazioni maggiori, 4). Cassino.

Str.[11] ————. 2015a. "Note critiche ed esegetiche alla V *Declamazione maggiore* pseudo-quintilianea (*Aeger redemptus*)." *InvLuc* 37:105–12.

Str.[12] ————. 2016. "The Hidden Teacher. 'Metarhetoric' in Ps.-Quintilian's *Major Declamations*." In Dinter-Guérin-Martinho 2016, 25–48.

Str.[13] ————. 2017. "I frammenti delle *Declamazioni maggiori* pseudo-quintilianee." *SIFC* s. IV 15:195–214.

Str.[14] ————. 2018a. "Il titolo della VI *Declamazione maggiore* pseudo-quintilianea." *Maia* 70:160–62.

Str.[15] ————. 2018b. "Pseudo-Quintilianus, *De-clamationes maiores*, 5: *Aeger redemptus*." *PhilolAnt* 11:25–76.

Str.[16] ————. 2018c. "Si può mentire sotto tortura? Nota a Ps. Quint. *decl.* 7,6." *Paideia* 73:1455–58.

Str.[17] ————. 2020. "Note critiche ed esegetiche alla XIII *Declamazione maggiore* pseudo-quintilianea (*Apes pauperis*)." In Polara 2020, 2:993–98.

Suss. Sussman, L. A., trans. and ann. 1987. *The Major Declamations Ascribed to Quintilian. A Translation*. Frankfurt.

Tab.[1] Tabacco, R. 1979a. "*Apes pauperis* [ps.-Quint. XIII]. Articolazione tematica ed equilibrio strutturali." *AAP* 28:81–104.

Tab.[2] ————. 1979b. "Ps.-Quint. XIII 15. Un problema di interpretazione." *BstudLat* 9:279–80.

Tab.[3] ————. 1980. "Le declamazioni maggiori pseudoquintilianee (Rassegna critica degli studi dal 1915 al 1979)." *BstudLat* 10:82–112.

Tab.[4] ————. 1985. "[Quintilianus], *Declamationes maiores*, XIII." In I. Lana, *Letteratura e civiltà in Roma tra il II ed il III secolo d. C. Lezioni e Seminari*, i–xxx. Turin, 1985.

Tos. Tosato, C. 1912. *Studio sulla grammatica e lingua delle XIX Declamazioni Maggiori Pseudoquintilianee*. Intra.

Tr.-B. Traina, A., and T. Bertotti. 2003[3] (= 2015). *Sintassi normativa della lingua latina. Teoria*. Bologna.

Valla Valla, L. Text of the *Major Declamations* and unpublished—marginal or interlinear—notes to them in his exemplar of

	the work (Oxford, Bodleian Library, Selden Supra 22).
Vass.	Vassis, S. 1906–7. "De locis quibusdam Quintiliani declamationum quae feruntur." *EEAth* 3:113–16.
vDorp	van Dorp, A. 1760. *Dissertatio iuridica inauguralis. Ad loca quaedam iuris et alia observationes*. Franeker.
vM.-M.[1]	Van Mal-Maeder, D. 2013. "Fiction et paredoxe dans les *Grandes déclamations* du Pseudo-Quintilien." In *Théories et pratiques de la fiction à l'époque impériale*, edited by C. Bréchet, A. Videau, and R. Webb, 123–35. Paris, 2013.
vM.-M.	———, ed., trans., comm. 2018. [*Quintilien*]. *Le malade racheté* (Grandes déclamations, 5). Cassino.
vMor.	von Morawski, K. 1895. "De sermone scriptorum latinorum aetatis quae dicitur argentea observationes selectae." *Eos* 2:1–12.
Wag.	Wagenvoort, H. 1927. "Sepulcrum incantatum." *Mnemosyne* s. II 55:425–48.
Wal.[1]	Walter, F. 1925. "Zu lateinischen Schriftstellern." *Philologus* 80:437–53.
Wal.[2]	———. 1942. "Zu Cicero und zu Quintilian mit den Deklamationen." *RhM* 91:1–7.
Warr	Warr, J., trans. 1686. *The Declamations of Quintilian, Being an Exercitation or Praxis upon His XII. Books, Concerning the Institution of an Orator*. London.
Watt[1]	Watt, W. S. In Håkanson 1982b.

Watt[2]   ———. 1982. "Notes on Pseudo-Quintilian, *Declamationes XIX maiores*." *BICS* 29:19–34.

Watt[3]   ———. 1991. "Notes on Pseudo-Quintilian, *Declamationes XIX maiores*." *Eranos* 89:43–59.

Wiles   Wiles, J. J. 1922. "Emendations of Quintilian and the Elder Seneca." *CR* 36:68–69.

Wint.[1]   Winterbottom, M. 1976–2019. Review of Håkanson 1974. *CR* n.s. 26 (1976): 276. Repr. in Winterbottom 2019c, 313–14.

Wint.[2]   ———, ed. and comm. 1980 (= 1990). *Roman Declamation. Extracts Edited with Commentary*. Bristol.

Wint.[3]   ———. In Håkanson 1982b.

Wint.[4]   ———, ed. and comm. 1984. *The Minor Declamations Ascribed to Quintilian*. Berlin-New York.

Wint.[5]   ———. 2000–19. Review of Stramaglia 1999b. *CR* n.s. 50 (2000): 305–6. Repr. in Winterbottom 2019c, 345–46.

Wint.[6]   ———. 2014–19. "William of Malmesbury's Work on the *Declamationes maiores*." *S&T* 12 (2014): 261–76. Repr. in Winterbottom 2019c, 252–63.

Wint.[7]   ———. 2019a. "Notes on the text of Pseudo-Quintilian, *Major Declamations*." *MD* 82:133–69.

Wint.[8]   ———. 2019b. "The Manuscript Tradition of [Quintilian]'s *Major Declamations*: A New Approach." In Winterbottom 2019c, 295–310.

Wint.[9]   ———. In this Loeb edition.
WS   *Wiener Studien*
Zins.   Zinsmaier, Th., ed., trans., comm. 2009.
          [*Quintilian*]. *Die Hände der blinden*
          Mutter (Größere Deklamationen, 6).
          Cassino.
ZPE   *Zeitschrift für Papyrologie und Epigraphik*

GENERAL BIBLIOGRAPHY

Amato, E., F. Citti, and B. Huelsenbeck, eds. 2015. *Law and Ethics in Greek and Roman Declamation*. Berlin.

Amato, E., A. Corcella, and D. Lauritzen, eds. 2017. *L'École de Gaza. Espace littéraire et identité culturelle dans l'Antiquité tardive*. Leuven.

Amato, E., L. Thévenet, and G. Ventrella, eds. 2014. *Discorso pubblico e declamazione scolastica a Gaza nella tarda antichità: Coricio di Gaza e la sua opera*. Bari.

Amato, E., and G. Ventrella, eds., trans., comm. 2009. *I Progimnasmi di Severo di Alessandria (Severo di Antiochia?)*. Berlin-New York.

Badius Ascensius, J. 1528. *Commentarii familiares . . . in M. Fabii Quintiliani declamationes, nuper editi*. Paris.

Becker, A. 1904. *Pseudo-Quintilianea. Symbolae ad Quintiliani quae feruntur Declamationes XIX maiores*. Progr. Ludwigshafen am Rhein.

Bernstein, N. W. 2012. "'Torture Her Until She Lies': Torture, Testimony, and Social Status in Roman Rhetorical Education." *G&R* n.s. 59:165–77.

———. 2013. *Ethics, Identity, and Community in Later Roman Declamation*. Oxford.

Berrens, D. 2018. *Soziale Insekten in der Antike. Ein Beitrag zu Naturkonzepten in der griechisch-römischen Kultur*. Göttingen.

Berti, E. 2007. Scholasticorum studia. *Seneca il Vecchio e la cultura retorica e letteraria della prima età imperiale.* Pisa.

———. 2014. "Le *controversiae* della raccolta di Seneca il Vecchio e la dottrina degli *status*." *Rhetorica* 32:99–147.

———. 2015. "Declamazione e poesia." In Lentano 2015b, 19–57.

Bloomer, W. M. 2007. "Roman Declamation: The Elder Seneca and Quintilian." In Dominik-Hall 2007, 297–306.

Boutemy, A. 1949. "Recherches sur le *Floridus Aspectus.* III." *Latomus* 8:283–301.

Braccini, T. 2011. *Prima di Dracula. Archeologia del vampiro.* Bologna.

Breij, B. 2012. "*Oratio figurata.*" *Historisches Wörterbuch der Rhetorik* 10:781–87.

———, ed., trans., comm. 2015. [*Quintilian*]. *The Son Suspected of Incest with His Mother (*Major Declamations, *18–19).* Cassino.

———. 2016. "Rich and Poor, Father and Son in *Major Declamation 7.*" In Poignault-Schneider 2016, 275–90.

———, ed., trans., comm. 2020. [*Quintilian*]. *The Poor Man's Torture (*Major Declamations, *7).* Cassino.

Brendel, R. 2013. Review of Ratti 2010b. *GFA* 16:1041–52.

Brescia, G. 2004. *Il miles alla sbarra.* [*Quintiliano*], Declamazioni maggiori, *III.* Bari.

———. 2009. "Gladiatori per 'caso': modelli antropologici in [*Quintiliano*], *Declamazioni maggiori*, IX." *Rhetorica* 27:294–311.

———. 2021. "L'oracolo e il parricidio. Mito 'in filigrana'

nella *Declamazione maggiore* 4." In Lovato-Stramaglia-Traina 2021, 33–51.

Bureau, B. 2007. "Ennode de Pavie adversaire de 'Quintilien'. Éthique et éloquence autour de la controverse *liberi parentes alant aut vinciantur* (Ennod. *Dict.* 21, Ps. Quint. *Decl. Maior.* 5)." In *Parole, Media, Pouvoir dans l'Occident Romain. Hommages offerts au Professeur Guy Achard*, edited by M. Ledentu, 147–72. Lyon, 2007.

Burman, P. ±1700. See Capizzi 2020–21.

——, ed. and comm. 1720a. *M. Fabii Quinctiliani De institutione oratoria libri duodecim, cum notis et animadversionibus virorum doctorum.* Leiden.

——, ed. and comm. 1720b. *M. Fabii Quinctiliani, ut ferunt, Declamationes XIX majores, et quae ex CCCLXXXVIII. supersunt CXLV minores. et Calpurnii Flacci Declamationes. cum notis doctorum virorum.* Leiden.

Calboli, G. 2008. "Il conflitto tra paganesimo e cristianesimo nel IV sec. d. C.: declamazioni e storiografia." In *Studi offerti ad Alessandro Perutelli*, I, edited by P. Arduini, S. Audano, A. Borghini, A. Cavarzere, G. Mazzoli, G. Paduano, and A. Russo, 159–80. Rome, 2008.

——. 2010. "L'eros nelle declamazioni latine (una pozione di contro-amore)." *Rhetorica* 28:138–59.

——, ed., trans., comm. 2020[3]. *Rhetorica ad C. Herennium*, I–III. Berlin-Boston. (Bologna, 1969[1].)

Calboli Montefusco, L., ed., trans., comm. 1979. *Consulti Fortunatiani Ars rhetorica*. Bologna.

——. 1984. *La dottrina degli* status *nella retorica greca e romana*. Bologna. (= Hildesheim, 1986.)

——. 1988. Exordium, narratio, epilogus. *Studi sulla*

teoria retorica greca e romana delle parti del discorso. Bologna.

Calderini, D., ed. 1475. *Declamationes tres.* Rome.

Cameron, A. 2011. "*Antiquus error/novus error*: The *HA*, Nicomachus Flavianus, and the 'Pagan Resistance.'" *JRA* 24:835–46.

———. 2016. Review of Ratti 2016. *BMCR* 2016.09.10.

Campanelli, M. 2001. *Polemiche e filologia ai primordi della stampa. Le* Observationes *di Domizio Calderini.* Rome.

Candau, J. M. 2017. "Speeches of Historians and Historiographical Criticism: Timaeus' Speeches in Polybius' Book XII." In *Anthologies of Historiographical Speeches from Antiquity to Early Modern Times. Rearranging the Tesserae,* edited by J. C. Iglesias-Zoido and V. Pineda, 63–78. Leiden-Boston, 2017.

Capizzi, F. 2020–21. "Note critiche inedite di Pieter Burman il Vecchio alle *Declamationes maiores* e ad altre opere latine." *IFC* 20 (forthcoming).

Cappello, O. 2016. "*Civitas beluarum*: The Politics of Eating Your Neighbor. A Semiological Study of Ps.-Quintilian's Twelfth *Major Declamation*." In Dinter-Guérin-Martinho 2016, 209–36.

Carter, M. J. 2015. "Bloodbath: Artemidorus, ἀπότομος Combat, and Ps.-Quintilian's *The Gladiator*." *ZPE* 193:39–52.

Charlet, J.-L. 2015. "Les déclamations du Pseudo-Quintilien dans le *Cornu copiae* de Niccolò Perotti." In Poignault-Schneider 2015, 397–415.

Citti, F. 2014. "Andrea Navagero, *lusus* 39 W." In *Nel cantiere degli umanisti. Per Mariangela Regoliosi,* edited by

L. Bertolini, D. Coppini, and C. Marsico, 415–25. Florence, 2014.

Civiletti, M. 2002. "*Meléte*: analisi semantica e definizione di un genere." In *Papers on Rhetoric*, IV, edited by L. Calboli Montefusco, 61–87. Rome, 2002.

Corbeill, A. 2007. "Rhetorical Education and Social Reproduction in the Republic and Early Empire." In Dominik-Hall 2007, 69–82.

Corbino, A. 2009. "*Actio in factum adversus confitentem.* Quint., *Declam. Maior* XIII." In *Studi in onore di Antonino Metro*, edited by C. Russo Ruggeri, 1:511–24. Milan, 2009.

Corcella, A. 2021. "Le *Declamazioni maggiori* e la prassi declamatoria greca." In Lovato-Stramaglia-Traina 2021, 77–105.

Cortesi, M. 1984. "Una pagina di umanesimo in Eichstätt." *Quellen und Forschungen aus italienischen Archiven und Bibliotheken* 64:227–60.

———. 1986. "Scritti di Lorenzo Valla tra Veneto e Germania." In *Lorenzo Valla e l'umanesimo italiano. Atti del convegno internazionale di studi umanistici (Parma, 18–19 ottobre 1984)*, edited by O. Besomi and M. Regoliosi, 365–98. Padua, 1986.

Costa, S., ed., trans., comm. 2017. *Gaio Svetonio Tranquillo. I grammatici e i retori*. Milan.

Dadson, T. J., ed. 2000. *Gabriel Bocángel y Unzueta. Obras completas*, I–II. Madrid-Frankfurt.

degli Agostini, G. 1754. *Notizie istorico-critiche intorno la Vita, e le Opere degli Scrittori Viniziani*, II. Venice.

De Keyser, J., ed. 2015. *Francesco Filelfo. Collected Letters*. Epistolarum Libri XLVIII, I–IV. Turin.

Del Corso, L., F. De Vivo, and A. Stramaglia, eds. 2015. *Nel segno del testo. Edizioni, materiali e studi per Oronzo Pecere*. Florence.

de Martini, A., ed. and comm. 2019. *Polemone di Laodicea. Le declamazioni per Cinegiro e per Callimaco*. Alessandria.

de Meyier, K. A. 1946. *Bibliotheca Universitatis Leidensis. Codices manuscripti*, IV (*Codices Perizoniani*). Leiden.

Deratani, N. 1925. "De rhetorum Romanorum declamationibus. I: De minorum declamationum auctore." *RPh* s. II 49:101–17.

———. 1927. "De rhetorum Romanorum declamationibus. II: Quaestiones ad originem maiorum, quae sub nomine Quintiliani feruntur, declamationum pertinentes." *RPh* s. III 1:289–310.

Desanti, L. 2015. *La legge Aquilia. Tra* verba legis *e interpretazione giurisprudenziale*. Turin.

Dessauer, H. 1898. *Die handschriftliche Grundlage der neunzehn grösseren pseudo-quintilianischen Declamationen*. Leipzig.

———. 1901. "De codice rescripto Parisino 7900 A." *RhM* 56:416–22.

Dimatteo, G. 2019b. *Audiatur et altera pars. I discorsi doppi nelle* Declamationes minores *e in Calpurnio Flacco*. Bologna.

Dinter, M., Ch. Guérin, and M. Martinho, eds. 2016. *Reading Roman Declamation. The Declamations Ascribed to Quintilian*. Berlin-Boston.

———, eds. 2017. *Reading Roman Declamation. Calpurnius Flaccus*. Berlin-Boston.

Dmitriev, S. 2020. "Rhetoric, Philosophy, and Poetry in Gorgias' *Encomium of Helen*." *RFIC* 148:327–69.

Dominik, W., and J. Hall, eds. 2007. *A Companion to Roman Rhetoric*. Malden, MA-Oxford.

Dussault, J. J., ed. and comm. 1823. *Marci Fabii Quintiliani Declamationes majores et minores item Calpurnii Flacci ex recensione Burmanniana*. Paris. (= *Quintilianus*, collig. N. E. Lemaire, V.)

Du Teil, [B.], trans. 1659[2]. *Les Grandes et entieres declamations du fameux orateur Quintilien, mises en François . . . .* Paris. (Corr. repr. of *Les Grandes declamations de Quintilien, nouvellement traduites en François . . . .* Paris, 1658[1].)

Ed. Oxon. (Anonymous), ed. and trans. 1692[2] (1675[1]). *M. Fab. Quintiliani Declamationum liber. Cum ejusdem (Ut nonnullis visum) Dialogo de causis corruptae eloquentiae*. Oxford.

Enderlein, F. L. 1870. *Codex Bambergensis XIX majores declamationes in libris mss. Quinctiliano adscriptis continens cum textu ed. Burmanni comparatus*. Schweinfurt.

Faber, E. 2020. "Antiker Kannibalismus zwischen Mythos und Historie." In *Zwischen Hunger und Überfluss. Antike Diskurse über die Ernährung*, edited by E. Faber and T. Klär, 217–44. Stuttgart, 2020.

Fairweather, J. 1981. *Seneca the Elder*. Cambridge.

———. 1985. Review of Håkanson 1982b. *Gnomon* 57:182–84.

Feddern, S., ed. and comm. 2013. *Die Suasorien des älteren Seneca*. Berlin-Boston.

Fermi, D. 2014. "Questione di sguardi. Il caso di 'impressione materna' in Heliod. 4, 8, 5 e 10, 4, 7." *QUCC* n.s. 106:165–79.

Fernández López, J. 2011. "Notas para una historia de la

recepción de las *Declamationes maiores* atribuidas a Quintiliano." In *Perfiles de Grecia y Roma. Actas del XII Congreso Español de Estudios Clásicos (Valencia, 22 al 26 de octubre de 2007)*, III, edited by J. de la Villa Polo, J. F. González Castro, and G. Hinojo de Andrés, 237–43. Madrid, 2011.

———. 2018. "Declamación, medicina y mecenazgo en el *Quintiliano respondido* de Gabriel Bocángel." *Minerva* 31:221–48.

Gibson, C. A. 2013. "Doctors in Ancient Greek and Roman Rhetorical Education." *JHM* 68:529–50.

Giomaro, A. M. 2003. *Per lo studio della calumnia. Aspetti di "deontologia" processuale in Roma antica.* Turin.

Golz, G. 1913. *Der rhythmische Satzschluss in den grösseren pseudoquintilianischen Declamationen.* Breslau.

Grasolarius (Grasolari), J., and G. Merula (Merlani), eds. 1481. *M. Fabii Quintiliani eloquentissimi Declamationes.* Venice.

Gronov, J. F., ed. and ann. 1665. *M. Fab. Quintiliani Declamationes undeviginti. M. Fabii Avi et Calpurnii Flacci Declamationes. Auctoris Incerti Dialogus De causis corruptae Eloquentiae.* Leiden-Rotterdam.

Guast, W. 2018. "Lucian and Declamation." *CPh* 113:189–205.

Guerrini, A. 2003. *Experimenting with Humans and Animals. From Galen to Animal Rights.* Baltimore-London.

Håkanson, L. 1973. "Textkritisches zu den unter dem Namen Quintilians überlieferten sog. kleineren und grösseren Deklamationen." In *Classica et Mediaevalia Francisco Blatt septuagenario dedicata*, 310–22. Copenhagen, 1973.

———. 1974. *Textkritische Studien zu den grösseren pseudoquintilianischen Deklamationen.* Lund.

————. 1976. "35 Emendationsvorschläge zu den grösseren pseudoquintilianischen Deklamationen." *Eranos* 74:122–38.

————. 1978. "Einige textkritische Bemerkungen zu den größeren pseudoquintilianischen Deklamationen," *WS* 91:151–58.

————. 1982a. "Miscellanea critica." *Phoenix* 36:237–42.

————, ed. 1982b. *Declamationes XIX maiores Quintiliano falso ascriptae.* Stuttgart.

————. 1986². "[Quintilian]. *Declamationes maiores.*" In *Texts and Transmission. A Survey of the Latin Classics,* edited by L. D. Reynolds, 334–36. Oxford, 1986². (Corr. repr. of 1983¹.)

————. 1986. "Die quintilianischen Deklamationen in der neueren Forschung." *ANRW* II.32.4:2272–306.

————. 2014a. "Zu den Themata der *Größeren Deklamationen.*" In Håkanson 2014e, 5–14.

————. 2014b. "Zu den literarischen Vorbildern der *Declamationes maiores*: Cicero, Seneca, *Declamationes minores.*" In Håkanson 2014e, 15–38.

————. 2014c. "The Murder of a Manuscript." In Håkanson 2014e, 39–46.

————. 2014d. "Der Satzrhythmus der 19 *Größeren Deklamationen* und des Calpurnius Flaccus." In Håkanson 2014e, 75–130.

————. 2014e. *Unveröffentlichte Schriften,* I (*Studien zu den pseudoquintilianischen* Declamationes maiores). Edited by B. Santorelli. Berlin-Boston. (B. Santorelli, "Aktualisierung," 131–35.)

————. 2016. *Unveröffentlichte Schriften,* II (*Kommentar zu Seneca Maior,* Controversiae, *Buch I*). Edited by F. Citti, B. Santorelli, and A. Stramaglia. Berlin-Boston. (B. Santorelli, "Aktualisierung," 143–48.)

Håkanson, L., and M. Winterbottom. 2015. *"Tribunus Marianus."* In Del Corso-De Vivo-Stramaglia 2015, 61–90.

Halm, C. 1863. *Rhetores Latini Minores*. Leipzig.

Hammer, C. 1893. *Beiträge zu den 19 grösseren quintilianischen Deklamationen*. Progr. Munich.

Hand, F. 1832. *Tursellinus seu de particulis Latinis commentarii*, II. Leipzig.

Hatzilambrou, R. 2015. "The Death of Antisthenes, or *P. Oxy.* XI 1366 Revisited." *ZPE* 194:80–90.

Helm, R. 1911. Review of Reitzenstein 1909. *GGA* 173:337–89.

Hoffmann, H. 1995. *Bamberger Handschriften des 10. und des 11. Jahrhunderts*. Hanover.

Hofmann, J. B., and A. Szantyr. 1972². *Lateinische Syntax und Stilistik*. Munich. (Corr. repr. of 1965¹.)

Hömke, N. 2002. *Gesetzt den Fall, ein Geist erscheint. Komposition und Motivik der ps-quintilianischen Declamationes maiores X, XIV und XV*. Heidelberg.

Huelsenbeck, B. 2015. "Shared Speech in the Collection of the Elder Seneca (*Contr.* 10.4): Toward a Study of Common Literary Passages as Community Interaction." In Amato-Citti-Huelsenbeck 2015, 35–62.

———. 2016. "Annotations to a Corpus of Latin Declamations: History, Function, and the Technique of Rhetorical Summary." *Lexis* 34:357–82.

———. 2018. *Figures in the Shadows. The Speech of Two Augustan-Age Declaimers, Arellius Fuscus and Papirius Fabianus*. Berlin-Boston.

Iglesias-Zoido, J. C. 2010. "Una figura olvidada: el rétor Lesbonacte." In *Perfiles de Grecia y Roma. Actas del XII Congreso Español de Estudios Clásicos (Valencia, 22 al 26 de octubre de 2007*), II, edited by J. F. González Castro and J. de la Villa Polo, 497–504. Madrid, 2010.

Janiszewski, P., K. Stebnicka, and E. Szabat. 2015. *Prosopography of Greek Rhetors and Sophists of the Roman Empire.* Oxford-New York.

Kaster, R. A. 2001. "Controlling Reason: Declamation in Rhetorical Education at Rome." In *Education in Greek and Roman Antiquity*, edited by Y. L. Too, 317–37. Leiden, 2001.

Kauntze, M. 2014. *Authority and Imitation. A Study of the* Cosmographia *of Bernard Silvestris.* Leiden-Boston.

Knoch, S. 2018. *Sklaven und Freigelassene in der lateinischen Deklamation.* Hildesheim.

Krapinger, G. 2003. "Vives' Antwort auf Ps. Quintilians *Paries palmatus*: Die Deklamation *Pro Noverca*." In Schröder-Schröder 2003, 289–333.

———, ed., trans., comm. 2005. [*Quintilian*]. *Die Bienendes armen Mannes* (Größere Deklamationen, *13*). Cassino.

———. 2007a. "Die Bienen des armen Mannes in Antike und Mittelalter." In Theatron. *Rhetorische Kultur in Spätantike und Mittelalter – Rhetorical Culture in Late Antiquity and the Middle Ages*, edited by M. Grünbart, 189–201. Berlin-New York, 2007.

———, ed., trans., comm. 2007b. [*Quintilian*]. *Der Gladiator* (Größere Deklamationen, *9*). Cassino.

Krapinger, G., trans., comm., and A. Stramaglia, ed., comm. 2015. [*Quintilian*]. *Der Blinde auf der Türschwelle* (Größere Deklamationen, *2*). Cassino.

Krapinger, G., and Th. Zinsmaier. 2021. "Philosophische Theoreme in den *Declamationes maiores*." In Lovato-Stramaglia-Traina 2021, 141–61.

Kraus, M. 2017. "Das *Corpus Hermogenianum*. Fälschung, Irrtum oder Missverständnis?" In *Verleugnete Rezeption. Fälschungen antiker Texte*, edited by W. Kofler and A. Novokhatko, 153–66. Freiburg-Vienna, 2017.

K(roll), W. 1905. Review of Lehnert 1905. *Literarisches Zentralblatt* 56:1296.

Kühner, R., and C. Stegmann. 1976⁵. *Ausführliche Grammatik der lateinischen Sprache*, 2:1–2 (*Satzlehre*). Rev. by A. Thierfelder. Hanover.

Langlands, R. 2006. *Sexual Morality in Ancient Rome*. Cambridge.

Lehnert, G., ed. 1905. *Quintiliani quae feruntur Declamationes XIX maiores*. Leipzig.

Lemaire, N. E., ed. 1825. *M. F. Quintilianus et Calpurnius Flaccus: de quorum operibus judicia testimoniaque omnia, item annales Quintilianeos, editiones recensuit, et tres indices absolutissimos emendavit, auxit, N. E. L.* Paris. (= *Quintilianus*, collig. N. E. Lemaire, VII.)

Lentano, M. 1998. *L'eroe va a scuola. La figura del* vir fortis *nella declamazione latina*. Naples.

———. 2014. "Musica per orecchie romane. Nota a ps.-Quint. *decl. mai.* 4, 7." *BstudLat* 44:166–77.

———. 2015a. "*Parricidii sit actio*: Killing the Father in Roman Declamation." In Amato-Citti-Huelsenbeck 2015, 133–53.

———, ed. 2015b. *La declamazione latina. Prospettive a confronto sulla retorica di scuola a Roma antica*. Naples.

———. 2017. *La declamazione a Roma. Breve profilo di un genere minore*. Palermo.

———. 2020. "Il colore che non ti aspetti. Per un com-

mento alla seconda declamazione di Calpurnio Flacco."
BstudLat 50:87–104.

———. 2021. "Veder raccolto in breve spazio il mondo. Le
Declamazioni maggiori dello Pseudo-Quintiliano come
collezione." In Lovato-Stramaglia-Traina 2021, 185–203.

Longo, G., ed., trans., comm. 2008. [*Quintiliano*]. *La pozione dell'odio* (Declamationes maiores, *14–15*). Cassino.

———. 2020. "An Approach to Greek and Latin Handbooks on Declamation." *S&T* 18:57–87.

———. 2021. "Le *Maiores* e la precettistica antica sugli er-
rori nella declamazione." In Lovato-Stramaglia-Traina
2021, 205–33.

Longobardi, C. 2017. *Leggere Orazio nella scuola tardo-
antica. Gli* Scholia vetustiora *al quarto libro delle* Odi.
Pisa.

Lorenzi Biondi, C. 2013. "Tra Loschi e Lancia. Nota
sull'attribuzione delle *Declamationes maiores* volgari."
Studi di filologia italiana 71:323–39.

———. 2016. "Filologia del volgare intorno al Salutati.
Una prima giunta." *Filologia italiana* 13:47–108.

Lovato, A., A. Stramaglia, and G. Traina, eds. 2021. *Le*
Declamazioni maggiori *pseudo-quintilianee nella Roma
imperiale*. Berlin-Boston.

Macchioro, R. 2021. "La ricezione medievale delle *Declamationes maiores* tra *florilegia* e riscritture." In Lovato-
Stramaglia-Traina 2021, 235–65.

Mantovani, D. 2006–7. "I giuristi, il retore e le api. *Ius
controversum* e *natura* nella *Declamatio maior* XIII."
Seminarios Complutenses de Derecho Romano 19
(2006): 205–83. Repr. in *Testi e problemi del giusnaturalismo romano*, edited by D. Mantovani and A. Schiavone, 323–85. Pavia, 2007.

Manzione, C. 2014. "Per un'introduzione al *Rhetor* di Coricio (*op.* XLII [*decl.* 12] F./R.)." In Amato-Thévenet-Ventrella 2014, 170–203.

Martella, L. 2015. "Scene di un processo. L'*Antilogia* di Lorenzo Patarol alla VIII *Declamazione maggiore* pseudo-quintilianea." In Poignault-Schneider 2015, 435–49.

Morin, G. 1913. "Pour l'authenticité de la lettre de S. Jérôme à Présidius." *Bulletin d'ancienne littérature et d'archéologie chrétiennes* 3:52–60.

Munk Olsen, B. 1985. *L'étude des auteurs classiques latins aux XIe et XIIe siècles*, II. Paris.

Obrecht, U., ed. 1698. *M. Fabii Quinctiliani Declamationes innumeris locis emendatae*. Strasbourg.

Oudot, E. 2017. "Aelius Aristides." In Richter-Johnson 2017, 255–69 (text) and 702–5 (notes).

Pagliaro, R. L., ed., trans., ann. 2008³. [*Quintiliano*]. Declamationes XIX maiores. *Proposta di traduzione* [*in CD-Rom*]. Caserta, 2011² (*Introduzione*) + CD-Rom, 2008³. (Naples, 2004¹.)

Pagliaroli, S. 2006. "Una proposta per il giovane Valla: *Quintiliani Tulliique examen*." *Studi medievali e umanistici* 4:9–67.

Pasetti, L. 2008c. Review of Krapinger 2005. *Lexis* 26:443–46.

———. 2009a. "*Mori me non vult*. Seneca and Pseudo-Quintilian's IVth *Major Declamation*." *Rhetorica* 27:274–93.

———. 2009b. Review of Krapinger 2007b. *Gnomon* 81:604–8.

———, ed., trans., comm. 2011. [*Quintiliano*]. *Il veleno versato* (Declamazioni maggiori, *17*). Cassino.

———. 2014. "L'eroe in coma. [Quint.] *decl.* 246, 4." *Latinitas* n.s. 2.2, 2014:19–23.

———. 2015. "Cases of Poisoning in Greek and Roman Declamation." In Amato-Citti-Huelsenbeck 2015, 155–99.

———. 2016. "Lingua e stile dell''io' nella declamazione latina." In Poignault-Schneider 2016, 135–159.

———. 2019. "Le *Declamationes minores*: funzione e tradizione di un libro di scuola." In *Le* Declamazioni minori *attribuite a Quintiliano*, I, edited, translated, and commented by L. Pasetti, A. Casamento, G. Dimatteo, G. Krapinger, B. Santorelli, and Ch. Valenzano, xi–xxxviii. Bologna, 2019.

Patarol, L., ed. and ann. 1743. *M. Fabii Quintiliani Declamationes, Cum earumdem Analysi, & Adnotatiunculis Difficiliores, & conditiores sensus explicantibus. In singulas praeterea declamationes Antilogiae. Auctore Laurentio Patarol*. In Patarol, *Opera Omnia quorum pleraque Nunc primum in lucem prodeunt*, 2:93–402. Venice, 1743.

Pecere, O. 1986. "La tradizione dei testi latini tra IV e V secolo attraverso i libri sottoscritti." In *Società romana e impero tardoantico*, IV (*Tradizione dei classici, trasformazioni della cultura*), edited by A. Giardina, 19–81 (text) and 210–46 (notes). Rome-Bari, 1986.

———. 2021. "Le sottoscrizioni di Domizio Draconzio rivisitate." In Lovato-Stramaglia-Traina 2021, 307–18.

Penella, R. J. 2014. "Libanius' *Declamations*." In *Libanius: A Critical Introduction*, edited by L. Van Hoof, 107–27. Cambridge, 2014.

———, trans. and ann. 2020. *Libanius: Ten Mythological and Historical Declamations*. Cambridge.

Pepe, C. 2013. *The Genres of Rhetorical Speeches in Greek and Roman Antiquity*. Leiden-Boston.

Petrucci, A. 2017. "*Mors est aeternum nihil sentiendi receptaculum.* Noterelle sul diritto di scelta di morire nell'esperienza giuridica romana." In *Pluralismo delle fonti e metamorfosi del diritto soggettivo nella storia della cultura giuridica*, I (*La prospettiva storica*), edited by A. Landi and A. Petrucci, 105–22. Turin, 2017.

Pietrini, S. 2012. *L'insegnamento del diritto penale nei libri Institutionum*. Naples-Rome.

Pingoud, J., and A. Rolle. 2020. *Déclamations et intertextualité. Discours d'école en dialogue*. Bern.

Pirovano, L. 2012. Review of Krapinger 2007b. *Eikasmos* 23:545–48.

Poignault, R., and C. Schneider, eds. 2015. *Présence de la déclamation antique (controverses et suasoires)*. Clermont-Ferrand.

———, eds. 2016. *Fabrique de la déclamation antique (controverses et suasoires)*. Lyon.

Polara, G., ed. 2020. Omne tulit punctum qui miscuit utile dulci. *Studi in onore di Arturo De Vivo*, I–II. Naples.

Prinz, O. 1953. "Zur Präfixassimilation im antiken und im frühmittelalterlichen Latein (Fortsetzung und Schluss)." *ALMA* 23:35–60.

Querzoli, S. 2013. *Scienza giuridica e cultura retorica in Ulpio Marcello*. Naples.

Rahn, H. 1976. Review of Håkanson 1974. *Gnomon* 48:409–11.

Ratti, S. 2007–10. "Nicomaque Flavien senior et l'*Histoire Auguste*: la découverte de nouveaux liens." *REL* 85 (2007): 204–19. Repr. in Ratti 2010b, 239–48.

———. 2010a. "L'auteur et la date du *Miles Marianus* (Ps. Quint., *decl.* 3)." In Ratti 2010b, 253–60.

————. 2010b. Antiquus error. *Les ultimes feux de la résistance païenne*. Turnhout.

————. 2014–16. "Les ancêtres d'Émile Ajar." *Médium* 40 (2014): 109–24. Repr. in Ratti, *L'Histoire Auguste. Les païens et les chrétiens dans l'Antiquité tardive*, 41–52. Paris, 2016.

Ravallese, M. 2021. "La città che divora. Aspetti paideutici e giuridici nella XII *Declamazione maggiore* dello Pseudo-Quintiliano." In Lovato-Stramaglia-Traina 2021, 319–41.

Regali, M. 1986. "Osservazioni su alcuni aspetti retorici della *declamatio maior* IX dello Pseudo-Quintiliano." *SCO* 35:161–69.

Reinhardt, T., and M. Winterbottom, eds. and comm. 2006. *Quintilian*. Institutio oratoria. *Book 2*. Oxford.

Reitzenstein, R. 1908. "Zu Quintilians grossen Declamationen." *Hermes* 43:104–19.

————. 1909. *Studien zu Quintilians grösseren Deklamationen*. Strasbourg.

Renouard, Ph. 1908. *Bibliographie des impressions et des oeuvres de Josse Badius Ascensius, imprimeur et humaniste (1462–1535)*, I–III. Paris.

Richter, D., and W. A. Johnson, eds. 2017. *The Oxford Handbook of the Second Sophistic*. Oxford-New York.

Ritter, C. 1881. *Die quintilianischen Declamationen. Untersuchung über Art und Herkunft derselben*, Freiburg-Tübingen. (= Hildesheim, 1967.)

Rizzelli, G. 2021. "Il fr. 3 Stramaglia delle *Declamazioni maggiori* e la circolazione di temi fra retori e giuristi." In Lovato-Stramaglia-Traina 2021, 343–60.

Robles Sánchez, M. Á. 2020. *Pieter Burmann (1668–1741) y la edición de* La Declamatio Maior I: *traducción y comentario*. Beau Bassin, Mauritius.

Russell, D. A. 1983. *Greek Declamation*. Cambridge.

———. 1985. Review of Håkanson 1982b. *CR* n.s. 35:43–45.

Russo, G. 2019. "Ovide dans les *Déclamations majeures* du Pseudo-Quintilien." *Pan* n.s. 8:229–40.

Santorelli, B. 2014a. "*Pauper et dives inimici*. Un perduto tema declamatorio in un palinsesto latino." *RhM* 157:320–26.

———, ed., trans., comm. 2014b. [*Quintiliano*]. *Il ricco accusato di tradimento* (Declamazioni maggiori, *11*)— *Gli amici garanti* (Declamazioni maggiori, *16*). Cassino.

———. 2016. "Juvenal and Declamatory *inventio*." In Stramaglia-Grazzini-Dimatteo 2016, 293–321.

———. 2017a. "Graziano e le mura insanguinate di Lione (Ps.-Quint. *Decl. mai.* 1.11—Hier. *Ep.* 60.15.3)." *Philologus* 161:319–28.

———. 2017b. "Metrical and Accentual *clausulae* as Evidence for the Date and Origin of Calpurnius Flaccus." In Dinter-Guérin-Martinho 2017, 129–40.

———. 2018a. "*Quaeritur an servus sit*. Casi di schiavitù per debiti nella declamazione latina." *Maia* 70:28–41.

———. 2018b. "Il *debitor delicatus* tra due scogli (Ps.-Quint. *decl. mai.* 9, 19)." *Maia* 70:544–50.

———. 2019. "*Poteram quidem fortiter dicere: 'Pater iussi.'* L'autorità paterna a scuola, tra retorica e diritto." In L. Capogrossi Colognesi, F. Cenerini, F. Lamberti, M. Lentano, G. Rizzelli, and B. Santorelli, *Anatomie della paternità. Padri e famiglia nella cultura romana*, 73–88. Lecce, 2019.

———. 2020a. "*Leno etiam servis excipitur*. Vendita e tutela degli schiavi in due *Declamazioni maggiori* pseudoquintilianee (Ps.-Quint. *decl. mai.* 3, 16; 9, 12)." In Polara 2020, 2:11–24.

————. 2020b. "*Sic irasceris parricidae?* Paternità e cronologia relativa delle *Declamazioni maggiori* 18 e 19." *Pan* n.s. 9:131–42.

————. 2021a. "Contro i padri troppo pronti a credere. Per la datazione di [Quint.] *Decl. mai.* 8 (*Gemini languentes*) e 10 (*Sepulcrum incantatum*)." *RFIC* 149:97–113.

————. 2021b. "Datazione e paternità delle *Declamazioni maggiori* pseudo-quintilianee." In Lovato-Stramaglia-Traina 2021, 361–429.

Santorelli, B., and A. Stramaglia. 2015. "La declamazione perduta." In Lentano 2015b, 271–304.

————, comm., and ————, ed., trans., comm. 2017. [*Quintiliano*]. *Il muro con le impronte di una mano* (Declamazioni maggiori, *1*). Cassino.

Sanzotta, V. 2013. "Lorenzo Valla (Roma 1407–1457)." In *Autografi dei letterati italiani. Il Quattrocento*, I, edited by F. Bausi, M. Campanelli, S. Gentile, and J. Hankins, 411–28. Rome, 2013.

Schneider, C. 2001. "La 'réception' de Valère Maxime dans le recueil des *Grandes déclamations* pseudo-quintiliennes." *InvLuc* 23:223–37.

————. 2003. "Lactance, Jérôme et les recueils de déclamations pseudo-quintiliens." In *Autour de Lactance. Hommages à Pierre Monat*, edited by J.-Y. Guillemin and S. Ratti, 63–76. Besançon, 2003.

————, ed., trans., comm. 2004. [*Quintilien*]. *Le soldat de Marius* (Grandes déclamations, *3*). Cassino.

————. 2005. "L'histoire dans la rhétorique: les enjeux politiques du *Miles Marianus* (pseudo-Quintilien, *Grandes déclamations* 3)." *CEA* 42:99–122.

————, ed., trans., comm. 2013. [*Quintilien*]. *Le tombeau ensorcelé* (Grandes déclamations, *10*). Cassino.

————. 2016. "Le *Tribunus Marianus* par Lorenzo Patarol (1674–1727). Un essai de traduction." In Studium in libris et sedula cura docendi. *Melanges en l'honneur de Jean-Louis Charlet*, edited by G. Herbert de la Portbarré-Viard and A. Stoehr-Monjou, 371–87. Paris, 2016.

Schröder, B.-J., and J.-P. Schröder, eds. 2003. Studium declamatorium. *Untersuchungen zu Schulübungen und Prunkreden von der Antike bis zur Neuzeit.* Munich-Leipzig.

Schwennicke, A. 2018. "The *carcer* in Roman Declamation: Formation and Function of a Topos." *AJPh* 139:483–510.

Selinger, R. 1999. "Experimente mit dem Skalpell am menschlichen Körper in der griechisch-römischen Antike." *Saeculum* 50:29–47.

Shackleton Bailey, D. R. 1956. *Propertiana*. Cambridge. (= Amsterdam, 1967.)

————. 1976a. Review of Håkanson 1974. *AJPh* 97:73–79.

————. 1976b. "Emendations of Pseudo-Quintilian's Longer Declamations." *HSPh* 80:187–217.

————. 1984–97. "More on Pseudo-Quintilian's Longer Declamations." *HSPh* 88 (1984): 113–37. Repr. with *addenda* in Shackleton Bailey, *Selected Classical Papers*, 188–212. Ann Arbor, 1997.

Smith, N. 2017. "Legal Agency as Literature in the English Revolution: The Case of the Levellers." In *The Oxford Handbook of English Law and Literature, 1500–1700*, edited by L. Hutson, 604–23. Oxford, 2017.

Spangenberg Yanes, E. 2012. "Discorsi già scritti e discorsi mai scritti: due distinte sfere di applicazione dei verbi *recito* e *declamo*." *RPL* n.s. 15:50–79.

Steffens, J. H., trans. 1766. *Versuch einer Uebersezzung einiger Declamationen des Quinctilianus*. Zelle.

Stoppacci, P. 2016. *Clavis Gerbertiana. Gerbertus Aureliacensis*. Florence.

Stramaglia, A.. 1999a. Res inauditae, incredulae. *Storie di fantasmi nel mondo greco-latino*. Bari.

———, ed., trans., comm. 1999b. [*Quintiliano*]. *I gemelli malati: un caso di vivisezione* (Declamazioni maggiori, 8). Cassino.

———, ed., trans., comm. 2002. [*Quintiliano*]. *La città che si cibò dei suoi cadaveri* (Declamazioni maggiori, 12). Cassino.

———. 2006. "Le *Declamationes maiores* pseudoquintilianee: genesi di una raccolta declamatoria e fisionomia della sua trasmissione testuale." In *Approches de la Troisième Sophistique. Hommages à Jacques Schamp*, edited by E. Amato, 555–84. Brussels, 2006. (Appendix: F. Ronconi, "Il codice palinsesto *Paris. Lat.* 7900A: una nuova ispezione della *scriptio inferior*," 585–88.)

———. 2010. "Come si insegnava a declamare? Riflessioni sulle *routines* scolastiche nell'insegnamento retorico antico." In *Libri di scuola e pratiche didattiche. Dall'Antichità al Rinascimento. Atti del Convegno Internazionale di Studi (Cassino, 7–10 maggio 2008)*, I, edited by L. Del Corso and O. Pecere, 111–51 (pl. 1–2). Cassino, 2010.

———, ed., trans., comm. 2013b. [*Quintiliano*]. *L'astrologo* (Declamazioni maggiori, 4). Cassino.

———. 2015b. "Temi 'sommersi' e trasmissione dei testi nella declamazione antica (con un regesto di papiri declamatori)." In Del Corso-De Vivo-Stramaglia 2015, 147–78.

————. 2016. "The Hidden Teacher. 'Metarhetoric' in Ps.-Quintilian's *Major Declamations*." In Dinter-Guérin-Martinho 2016, 25–48.

————, ed., trans., comm. 2017². *Giovenale, Satire 1, 7, 12, 16. Storia di un poeta*. Bologna. (Corr. repr. of 2008¹.)

————. 2017. "I frammenti delle *Declamazioni maggiori* pseudo-quintilianee." *SIFC* s. IV 15:195–214.

————. 2018a. "Il titolo della VI *Declamazione maggiore* pseudo-quintilianea." *Maia* 70:160–62.

————. 2018b. "Pseudo-Quintilianus, *Declamationes maiores*, 5: *Aeger redemptus*." *PhilolAnt* 11:25–76.

————. 2019. "Come è fatta una declamazione? Una lettura dei *Cadaveribus pasti* (Ps.-Quint. *Decl. mai.* 12)." *Camenae* 23:*1–*12.

Stramaglia, A., S. Grazzini, and G. Dimatteo, eds. 2016. *Giovenale tra storia, poesia e ideologia*. Berlin-Boston.

Stroh, W. 2003. "*Declamatio*." In Schröder-Schröder 2003, 5–34.

Strong, A. K. 2016. *Prostitutes and Matrons in the Roman World*. Cambridge.

Tabacco, R. 1977–78. "L'utilizzazione dei *topoi* nella declamazione XIII dello Pseudo-Quintiliano." *AAT* 112:197–224.

Traina, A. 1966–86². "*Primus dies natalis*." *Maia* 19 (1966): 279–80. Repr. with *addenda* in Id., *Poeti latini (e neolatini)*, I, 281–83. Bologna, 1986² (1975¹).

Traina, G. 2021. "Le *Declamazioni maggiori*: istruzioni agli storici." In Lovato-Stramaglia-Traina 2021, 431–48.

Valla, L. Text of the *Major Declamations* and unpublished—marginal or interlinear—notes to them in his exemplar of the work (Oxford, Bodleian Library, Selden Supra 22).

Van den Berg, Ch. 2016. "Program and Composition

in Pseudo-Quintilian's 13th *Major Declamation*." In Poignault-Schneider 2016, 161–75.

Van der Poel, M. 2010. "Observations sur la déclamation chez Quintilien et chez Érasme." In *Quintilien ancien et moderne*, edited by P. Galland, F. Hallyn, C. Lévy, and W. Verbaal, 279–89. Turnhout, 2010.

———. forthcoming. "Interpretative Survey of Quintilian Editions and Translations from 1470 until the Present." In *The Oxford Handbook of Quintilian*, edited by J. Murphy and M. van der Poel. Oxford (forthcoming).

Van Mal-Maeder, D. 2007. *La fiction des déclamations*. Leiden-Boston.

———, ed., trans., comm. 2018. [*Quintilien*]. *Le malade racheté* (Grandes déclamations, 5). Cassino.

Vottero, D., ed., trans., comm. 2004. *Anonimo Segueriano. Arte del discorso politico*. Alessandria.

Vv. Aa. 1672. *M. Annaei Senecae Rhetoris Opera, quae extant, integris N. Fabri, A. Schotti, J.F. Gronovi & selectis Variorum Commentariis illustrata, & præterea Indice accuratissimo aucta. Accedunt J. Schultingii in eundem notæ & emendationes, hactenus ineditæ*. Amsterdam.

Wallner, Ch. 2008. Review of Krapinger 2007b. *Nikephoros* 21:309–12.

Walz, Ch., ed. 1832–1836. *Rhetores Graeci*, I–IX. Stuttgart. (= Osnabrück 1968.)

Warr, J., trans. 1686. *The Declamations of Quintilian, Being an Exercitation or Praxis upon His XII. Books, Concerning the Institution of an Orator*. London.

Watt, W. S. 1982. "Notes on Pseudo-Quintilian, *Declamationes XIX maiores*." *BICS* 29:19–34.

———. 1991. "Notes on Pseudo-Quintilian, *Declamationes XIX maiores*." *Eranos* 89:43–59.

Webb, R. 2017. "Schools and *paideia*." In Richter-Johnson 2017, 139–53 (text) and 695–96 (notes).

Wetherbee, W., ed., trans., ann. 2015. *Bernardus Silvestris. Poetic Works*. Cambridge, MA-London.

White, P. 2013. *Jodocus Badius Ascensius. Commentary, Commerce and Print in the Renaissance*. Oxford.

Winterbottom, M. 1970. *Problems in Quintilian*. London.

———, ed., trans., ann. 1974. *The Elder Seneca*, I–II. London-Cambridge, MA.

———. 1976–2019. Review of Håkanson 1974. *CR* n.s. 26 (1976): 276. Repr. in Winterbottom 2019c, 313–14.

———. 1983–2019. "Declamation, Greek and Latin." In Ars rhetorica *antica e nuova*, edited by A. Ceresa-Gastaldo, 57–76. Genoa, 1983. Repr. in Winterbottom 2019c, 103–18.

———, ed. and comm. 1984. *The Minor Declamations Ascribed to Quintilian*. Berlin-New York.

———. 1988–2019. "Introduction." In D. Innes and M. Winterbottom, *Sopatros the Rhetor. Studies in the Text of the Διαίρεσις ζητημάτων*, 1–20. London, 1988. Repr. as *Sopatros' Διαίρεσις ζητημάτων*, in Winterbottom 2019c, 135–60.

———. 2003–19. "Ennodius, *Dictio* 21." In Schröder-Schröder 2003, 275–87. Repr. in Winterbottom 2019c, 205–17.

———. 2014–19. "William of Malmesbury's Work on the *Declamationes maiores*." *S&T* 12 (2014): 261–76. Repr. in Winterbottom 2019c, 252–63.

———. 2016. "Lennart Håkanson: der Mensch, der Gelehrte." In Håkanson 2016, ix–xiii.

———. 2017. "The *Tribunus Marianus* and the Development of the *cursus*." In Ingenio facilis. Per Gio-

vanni Orlandi (1938–2007), edited by P. Chiesa, A. M. Fagnoni, and R. E. Guglielmetti, 231–47. Florence, 2017.

———. 2017–19. "The Editors of Calpurnius Flaccus." In Dinter-Guérin-Martinho 2017, 141–60. Repr. in Winterbottom 2019c, 264–82.

———. 2019a. "Notes on the text of Pseudo-Quintilian, *Major Declamations*." *MD* 82:133–69.

———. 2019b. "The Manuscript Tradition of [Quintilian]'s *Major Declamations*: A New Approach." In Winterbottom 2019c, 295–310.

———. 2019c. *Papers on Quintilian and Ancient Declamation*. Oxford-New York.

Zinsmaier, Th., ed., trans., comm. 2009. [*Quintilian*]. *Die Hände der blinden Mutter* (Größere Deklamationen, 6). Cassino.

———. 2015. "Truth By Force? Torture as Evidence in Ancient Rhetoric and Roman Law." In Amato-Citti-Huelsenbeck 2015, 201–18.

Zullo, F. 2016. "Proprietà terriere e metodi 'mafiosi': Iuv. 14, 138–151." In Stramaglia-Grazzini-Dimatteo 2016, 323–30.

SIGLA

Relationships between manuscripts are represented in the stemma above, p. xlviii. Notation of the dates and places where the various manuscripts up to the twelfth century seem to have been written is that of Munk Olsen (1985, 292–305). On that chronological basis the manuscript families and their internal components are listed in descending order:

α consensus of mss. B (and frequently of fam. ϵ, derived from it) V with group Φ

ϵ consensus of mss. πM

γ consensus of mss. ACDE or, where C is lacking, of mss. ADE

ψ consensus of mss. CDE or, where C is lacking, of mss. DE

δ consensus of mss. HO and usually J

β consensus of mss. PS

Φ consensus of fam. $\gamma\delta\beta$

B   Bamberg, Staatsbibliothek, Class. 44 (M.IV.13) (Northern Italy; *s.* X^2)

π Paris, Bibliothèque nationale de France, lat. 1618 (France; *s.* XII^1)

SIGLA

M   Montpellier, Bibliothèque interuniversitaire.
        Section Médecine, H 226 (France?; s. XII^2)

V   Leiden, Universiteitsbibliotheek, Voss. lat. Q.
        111 (NW France; s. XII^2)
v   Oxford, Bodleian Library, Arch. Selden. B.36-I
        (England; s. XII/XIII) [cf. General Introduc-
        tion, §6, n. 177]

A   Saint-Omer, Bibliothèque d'agglomération, 663
        (NW Germany, or Netherlands; s. XV^1)
C   Paris, Bibliothèque nationale de France, lat.
        7800 (olim Colbertinus) (France; s. XII^1)
D   Paris, Bibliothèque nationale de France, lat.
        7802 (France; s. XII$^{med.}$)
E   Paris, Bibliothèque nationale de France, lat.
        15103-II (France; s. XII/XIII)

H   Leiden, Universiteitsbibliotheek, Perizon. O. 4A
        (France; s. XII$^{med.}$)
J   Leiden, Universiteitsbibliotheek, Voss. lat. Q.
        77-II (France?; s. XII/XIII)
O   Città del Vaticano, Biblioteca Apostolica
        Vaticana, Ottobon. lat. 1207 (Italy; s. XIII)

P   Paris, Bibliothèque nationale de France, lat.
        16230 (France; s. XIV)
S   Paris, Bibliothèque interuniversitaire de la
        Sorbonne, 629 (France; s. XV)

Also note:

N   Leiden, Universiteitsbibliotheek, Perizon. F. 14
        (Italy; *s.* XV^1) [cf. General Introduction, §8,
        n. 231]

W   readings from a codex shared by Johan de Witt
        with Alm. and reported in Burman's edition
        (see Burman 1720a, ***3*v*)

ϛ   readings of inferior mss. (mostly drawn from
        Burman) or early editions

*   an asterisk indicates the presence of trivial
        discrepancies within a group (as Φ*) or family
        (as γ*) which are not mentioned

ac   *ante correctionem*
pc   *post correctionem*
sl   *supra lineam*

See also the Abbreviations and General Bibliography,
above.

DECLAMATION 1

INTRODUCTION

Both here and in *DM* 2 a blind son and his stepmother accuse each other of killing his father. Both are "conjectural" cases, arising, that is, from conflicting assertions about facts: "You did it" and "I didn't do it"; the question at issue therefore is whether X did it (Quint. 3.6.5). The heads of "conjecture" are laid down in the handbooks; place, time, opportunity, motive are here especially relevant (cf. *Rhet. Her.* 2.3; Quint. 5.10.23). The speaker in *DM* 1 is Son's advocate. He voices scorn for the "hackneyed topic of the comparison of persons" (13.2), but his whole speech depends on showing that points that seem to go against Son in fact suggest Stepmother's guilt; that is natural in a case of mutual accusation (*antikategoria*)[1] like the present one.

The exciting and unparalleled circumstances of this piece naturally dominate the argumentation. The main

---

[1] A case (which would not arise in a real lawcourt) where it is agreed that a crime has been committed, and each party must both defend itself and accuse the other of committing the crime (Quint. 7.2.8–9). In our piece the two sides are argued separately, with a clear transition from defense to accusation at 13.1. In *DM* 2, on the other hand, the individual points are argued pro and con. For these two methods, see Quint. 7.2.22 and the other sources in [Krapinger-]Stramaglia (2015, 51n114).

points are foreshadowed early on (2.1–2) and recur throughout: the marks of blood on the wall (5.1–2, 11.4–12.5, 15.1–2), the choice of night for the crime (13.7), the use of Son's sword (3.1–3, 8.1–6, 14.1–2, 15.3), the fact that only one blow was struck (4.1–3, 14.4). These last motifs are brought together in the last words of the declamation, where Son's suicide is predicted (17.6–8). Other important points for discussion are the provision of a secluded room for the blind man (2.5, 15.5–16.5), Stepmother's sleeping through the fracas (4.3, 9.4–6), and her not becoming a second victim of Son (10.1–4).

Along with argument from the circumstances, arguments from character and motive are important (both stressed at 5.4). At 1.2 the advocate draws attention to the sterling character of the blind man. His record hitherto is unblemished, he had got on well with his father (6.3), and one does not start a career of crime by committing parricide (6.1–2); anyway, someone who is blind lacks enterprise (6.4–5) and is incapable of vice (6.7–8; this ploy had been rejected at 1.1) or strong feelings (6.7–8). What is more, he has no reason to kill a father who loves him (2.5, 13.3, 15.5–16.5; cf. 1.2) and whose help is all-important to him (6.9, 17.2, 17.5); he, not Stepmother, will miss the dead man (16.8–17.6). On the other hand, Stepmother—wicked and spiteful as always in declamation—has the inheritance to motivate her (2.4, 16.6), whereas Son is represented as not even knowing he is the heir (2.7; though see 16.6–7); and she dislikes and resents him (2.5, 13.3, 16.4).

The advocate starts by asserting that he wishes to prove Son to be innocent without taking his handicap into account (1.1), but, as he says later, "I am forced to argue from his blindness quite frequently" (10.5). He has no difficulty in showing how incredible is the story that a blind man could plan and carry out this crime (3.4, 7.1–6, 9.1–3, 10.5–6), whereas a sighted person could easily enough give the impression that someone sightless had (1.3–4, 5.1–3). But blindness is little exploited to arouse pathos for the defendant; we are asked to feel hatred for scheming Stepmother rather than pity for Son.

The structure may be analyzed thus:[2]

> PROEM 1.1–4
> NARRATION 2.1–5.3
> ARGUMENTATION
> > *Propositio causae* and *Partitio* 5.4
> > *Refutatio* 6.1–12.6
> > *Confirmatio* 13.1–17.6
> EPILOGUE 17.7–8

These sections, however, are not quite kept within their usual confines. The "narration" is less concerned to tell the story than to show how its various elements militate against Stepmother. The last chapter starts with argumentation (a contrast of the feelings of Son and Stepmother in the face of the Father's death), but passes seamlessly into the brief epilogue, which consists of a pathetic evocation of the plight of the blind man. In general, there is some failure of coherence. In fact, the declaimer blatantly disregards Quintilian's precept to develop arguments only in the *argumentatio*, confining oneself before that to mere "seeds of proofs" (*semina probationum*: 4.2.54; cf. 4.2.108):

---

[2] [Santorelli-]Stramaglia (2017, 26–28).

in *DM* 1 arguments are deployed throughout, from the exordium to the very brink of the epilogue!

DM 1 was arguably written before *DM* 2,[3] and its composition may be dated to the middle of the second century AD.[4] A sentence of the *Paries palmatus* (3.1) is quoted—with textual variants—by Servius;[5] also, in referring to the image of a bloodstained wall in one of his letters, Jerome seems to have our speech in mind.[6] A reply to the speech was composed in the Renaissance by the Spanish humanist Juan Luis Vives,[7] and another later by the Venetian Lorenzo Patarol.[8]

[3] See Introduction to *DM* 2.

[4] See General Introduction, §4.

[5] Serv. *in Aen.* 3.661 (p. 226 Harv.), *Hinc Quintilianus dixit: "Magnum caecitatis solatium est habere rem videntis."*

[6] Cf. *Ep.* 60.15.3 (*CSEL* 54, p. 569), *Gratianus ab exercitu suo proditus et ab obviis urbibus non receptus ludibrio hosti fuit, cruentaeque manus vestigia parietes tui, Lugdune, testantur,* with a possible allusion to 11.4: see Santorelli (2017a).

[7] Edited, with translation and notes, by Krapinger (2003). See also Bernstein (2013, 151–57).

[8] Patarol (1743, 95–113); the Latin text is reproduced and equipped with an English translation in Bernstein (2013, 171–94), with a French translation and some notes in Pingoud-Rolle (2020, 240–77).

1

Paries palmatus

‹Quidam, cui erat filius caecus et quem heredem institue-
rat, induxit illi novercam. Iuvenem in secreta domus parte
seposuit. Noctu, dum in cubiculo cum uxore iaceret, occisus est inventusque postero die habens gladium filii
defixum in vulnere, pariete ab ipsius ad filii cubiculum
vestigiis palmae cruentato. Accusant se invicem caecus et
noverca.›[1]

1. Si iuvenis innocentissimus, iudices, uti vellet ambitu
tristissimae calamitatis, poterat allegare vobis amissam
cum oculis cogitationum omnium temeritatem; sed, cum
ostendere innocentiam suam moribus malit quam adversis, neque pietatis neque conscientiae suae gravem ferre
contumeliam potest, ut parricidium non fecisse videatur
2   beneficio caecitatis. Quare igitur non petit ut illum miserum putetis, nisi et innocens fuerit; non petit ut adflictum

---

[1] *argumentum deperditum sic reformavit Valla (vd. Sant.-Str.
43–45, 85.1)*

---

[1] Supplied by Valla: see General Introduction, §7.

1

The handprints on the wall

‹A man had a blind son, whom he had appointed his heir. He gave him a stepmother, and kept the young man out of the way in a secluded part of the house. One night, when he was lying in his bedroom with his wife, he was killed. Next day he was found with his son's sword buried in the wound. The wall from his room to his son's had been covered with bloody handprints. The blind man and the stepmother accuse each other. ›[1]

(Speech of the son's advocate)

1. If this totally innocent young man, judges, wanted to win favor by parading his tragic calamity,[2] he might try to persuade you that together with his eyes he has lost any reckless thoughts.[3] But as he wishes to demonstrate his innocence from his behavior rather than from his adversities, he cannot tolerate incurring the grave reproach to his filial affection and to his conscience involved in being thought not guilty of parricide only because he is blind. (2) That is why he does not ask you to think him pitiful unless he is also innocent; he does not ask you to alleviate

---

[2] I.e., the loss of sight. Cf. 7.12.5, 16.5.2.
[3] Cf. 1.6.4–8.

allevetis, nisi et probaverit esse se[2] infeliciorem quod patrem amisit, quam quod oculos. Aestimate iuvenem his
moribus, quibus videntem aestimaretis: vita, pudore, pietate. Quae si omnia sibi, ut erant[3] promissa, constiterint,
3 nullo terrebitur crimine. Nec quod sceleratissima feminarum calamitatem nostram cruentato pariete imitata est
expavescimus: quo[4] diligentia sollicitior fuit ne deprehen-
4 deretur, hoc magis indicavit sibi oculos non defuisse. Gratias agimus quod nimium avide suspiciones[5] in nostram
transtulit partem: non esse caeci scelus difficilius probare-
tur, nisi omnia sic acta essent, ut fecisse caecus videretur.

2. Quare igitur, iudices, non improbe speraverim futurum ut suspecta sint vobis quae tam inconsiderate ficta
sunt contra miseram caecitatem. Primum quod spatium
illud ingens domus, quod in medio fuit, ita digesto cruore
satiatum est usque ad cubiculum miserrimi iuvenis, tamquam plane timuerit parricida ne non deprehenderetur.
2 Deinde sceleri nox potissimum electa, quo tempore inveniri maritus sine uxore non posset. Tum ‹in›[6] caede, in

---

2 -rit esse se *Reitz.*[2] *63.10*: -ritis (-rit Φ) sese *codd.*
3 era- M E: eru- *cett.*
4 quo C[2]: quae (quae dil- quo E) *codd.*
5 -nes ⤻ (*vd. Dess.*[1] *100*): -nis *codd.*   6 *add.* S[2]C[2]

---

4 I.e., are proved by me.
5 I.e., if we prove he has always been and still is such an excellent character, as he had "announced" with his behavior since his
early youth. For this use of *promittere*, cf. 1.6.1 and 5.5.6.
6 I.e., made the killing look like the work of a blind man (cf.
1.15.1). With "our calamity" the advocate associates himself with
the blindness of his client, so as to show emotional closeness: cf.
also 1.7.4, 1.14.3.

his afflictions unless he also proves that the loss of his father made him more unfortunate than the loss of his eyes. Judge the young man by the same criteria of character as you would judge him if he were sighted: his manner of life, his sense of shame, his filial affection. If all these traits turn out[4] to be present in him in fulfillment of his earlier promise,[5] he will not be frightened by any charge. (3) Nor are we scared because the most wicked of women mimicked our calamity[6] by marking the wall with blood: the more careful she was not to be caught, the clearer she made it that *she* had the use of her eyes. (4) We are grateful to her for being so very eager to cast suspicion on our side: it would have been harder to prove that the crime was not that of a blind man, if everything had not been done to make it look as if a blind man was responsible.

2. Therefore, judges, I have good reason to hope that you will feel suspicious of the reckless fictions invented to blacken a poor blind man. First of all (it is alleged), the great extent of the house in between[7] was filled with bloodstains, in a series going right up to the wretched youth's bedroom, as if the murderer was positively afraid of *not* being detected. (2) Next, night was specially chosen for the crime, a time when the husband could not be found apart from his wife.[8] Further, <in> a murder case, where

---

[7] All the wall between the two rooms. We are not given a detailed description of the house, but the existence of a remote and almost separate wing of the building is presupposed here (cf. 1.2.5) as in the other speeches envisaging domestic crimes (cf. *DM* 17, 18–19).

[8] Cf. 1.13.7.

qua nemo utitur suo ferro, omnis[7] alieno, gladius adulescentis, ne argumentum deesset novercae, relictus. Postremo peractum vulnere uno scelus, quod obiceretur mani-
3 bus errantis. Et tamen contra tam multa incredibilia solum
advocat noverca testamentum, vultque illud esse pretium
parricidii, ut rerum intellectu in diversum coacto occisum
4 eo probet patrem, quod non meruit[8] occidi. Nos vero istud, si crimen putatis, agnoscimus: iuvenis hic patris sui
heres solus est. Hoc testamentum si vivente adhuc miser-
rimo sene notum esse in domo potuit, scitis quis illi debuerit irasci.
5   Nam quod invisum fuisse filium patri iactat, crimen
novercae erat, si confiteremur; idque probari ex hoc putat,
quod secretum non filius accepit[9] a patre, sed caecitas.
Quo loco dissimulare satis callide conatur invidiam suam:
pater, qui filium caecum in semota penatium parte sepo-
6 suit, eripuit novercae oculis voluptatem. Namque ista cum
invasisse vacuos penates videretur, cum patri filium caecum hoc esse crederet quod orbitatem, excogitavit indul-
gentissimus senex quemadmodum hic miser patri suo in
eadem domo esset, novercae in alia: accepit secretum

---

[7] omnis (*sing., cf. ThlL IX.2.618.67ss.*) *Marsh. 181 coll. 2.8.6*:
nisi *codd.* (*frustra def. Eng. 50–51*)
[8] -uerit V Φ   [9] -cep- A: -cip- *cett.*

---

[9] Cf. 1.3.3, 1.8.1–2, 1.8.6.
[10] Son would have allegedly killed Father to obtain his inheritance—but the latter did not deserve such a fate, as he had
bequeathed Son the whole estate. Cf. 1.16.6–7.
[11] I.e., the man's wife, who had been excluded from the will.

no one uses his own weapon, everyone someone else's, the boy's sword was left to make sure the stepmother did not lack a proof.[9] Finally, the deed was done with a single blow, even though it was to be attributed to the hand of someone who could take no proper aim. (3) Yet to offset so many impossibilities the stepmother can only adduce the will, representing it as the prize to be won from the parricide; hence, by means of a forced misinterpretation of the facts, she proves that the father was killed because he did not deserve to be killed.[10] (4) But this we do acknowledge, if you think it a crime: this young man is his father's sole heir. If this will could have been known of around the house while the pitiable old man was still alive, you know *who* had reason to be angry with him.[11]

(5) For as to her claim that the son was hated by his father, this would be the stepmother's fault if we confessed it to be true.[12] Indeed, she thinks that this hatred can be proved in the following way: his father gave him a secluded room not because he was his son but because he was blind. By this insinuation she is trying, quite cleverly, to cover up her own dislike of the boy: in shutting away his blind son in a remote part of the house, the father robbed the stepmother of a source of pleasure to her eyes. (6) In fact, whereas she imagined she had come into an empty house[13] and thought that for a father a blind son was the same as having no son at all, that most indulgent old man devised a means by which the poor boy should be in the same establishment for his father but a different one for his stepmother: he was given the sort of seclusion he would

---

[12] If Father had come to hate Son, that would be Stepmother's doing.   [13] Cf. 1.13.3.

qui[10] erat petiturus. Quo sit animo senis factum, potestis
7 interrogare testamentum. Neque ego gravissimum patrem
suprema sua iuveni iactasse crediderim: ut heredem filium
scriberet,[11] non est res quae imputetur. Istam magis oportet vel aliquo indicio vel suspicione muliebri arcana mariti
deprehendisse et statim omnibus nuptiarum renuntiasse
pignoribus. Nam cum propter pecuniam ames, idem amo-
ris et spei finis est.

3. Habuerat adulescens gladium in cubiculo suo semper, sive antequam in hanc fortunam incideret paratum,
sive quia caecitatis miserae solacium est habere rem videntium. Certe numquam illum pater timuerat, numquam noverca obiecerat; palam positum est, sub oculis
2 omnium tota domo notissimum ferrum. Scitis quanto ne-
glegentius custodiat ferrum bona conscientia, quam etiam
extra suspicionem sit res sine usu. Innocentia facit ut fer-
3 rum subtrahi possit etiam videnti. Sive igitur aliquis ex
servulis corruptus est, praesertim [e] tam[12] facili occa-
sione, sive ipsi novercae non defuit audacia ad ferendum,[13]
quod facere poterat etiam praesente privigno, utique—
quod dubitari non potest, quod facit certum sceleris auc-

---

10 qui *Str.*[7] *298*: quod *codd.*
11 *hic* (non ante ut) *gravius dist. Bech. 66, sed vd. Sant.-Str.*
12 [e] tam *Håk.*[3] *123*: etiam *codd.*: in tam ⊊
13 ad auf- ⊊ *et Gron., sed vd. ThlL VI.1.556.23ss.*

---

14 And so decided on murder. *Pignora* here refers to the emotional bonds established by marriage (cf. 1.6.3, on parents-
children bonds). *Renuntiare* is the technical word for "terminat-
ing" a contract: see Ulp. *Dig.* 42.5.17.1.

himself have asked for. If you want to know what the old man's intentions were, you can ask the will! (7) I am not inclined to believe that this upright father made a boast of his last dispositions to the youth; to name your son as your heir is not something to claim credit for. This woman must, rather, have detected her husband's secret plan, by picking up some hint or because women are suspicious creatures, and immediately renounced all the ties of marriage.[14] When you love for money's sake, the end of hope is the end of love.

3. The youth had always kept a sword in his bedroom, either because he procured it before he suffered this misfortune,[15] or because the wretchedness of the blind is comforted by the possession of something that sighted people[16] make use of. At any rate, his father had never felt afraid of it, his stepmother had never raised objections. The thing was on full display, well known to the whole household, there for all to see. (2) You know how much more casually someone with a good conscience looks after a sword, you know too how a thing that is of no use to us doesn't make us worry about it. If you are *innocent*, you may have your sword stolen even if you are sighted! (3) So either one of the slaves was bribed, especially when it was so easy to find an opportunity, or the stepmother herself was bold enough to carry it off, something she could readily do even in the presence of her stepson. At all events— there is no doubt about this, and it makes quite clear who was responsible for the crime—, anyone who is going to

---

[15] I.e., became blind.

[16] This sentence is cited, with textual variations, by Servius: see Introduction to the present declamation.

13

torem—mavult in caede alieno uti quam suo gladio quisquis illum relicturus est.

4   Reliqua, iudices, si fieri possunt, facta aestimate: dicitur caecus sine rectore, sine duce, ex illa penatium parte
secreta et paene ex alia domo per inane longum, per tot
offensa limina, per excubantes servulos errasse cum ferro;
cubiculum deinde patris ingressum[14] in neutram deflexisse
partem, sed recto gradu, sicut ducere oculi solent, ad lectulum accessisse leviter, non in torum incidisse, non ante
pervenisse quam crederet. 4. Vos, iudices, criminum tu-
multum ex rerum fide ducite. Dormiens senex, quem caecus percussor quaereret, excitatus ante esset quam inveniretur. Iungunt his multo incredibiliora: ut occiderit
patrem, pepercerit novercae, parricidium autem uno ictu
explicuerit—quod fere vix etiam his contingere solet, qui

2   oculos manu sequuntur. Nulla ergo luminum virtus, sed
homo ferrum missurus in casum, satis felix si percussisset
quamcumque corporis partem, in ipsam protinus animam
incidit et, an morti satisfecisset, intellexit? Officium, iudices, oculorum est renuntiare manibus quid actum sit.

3   Caeci percussoris una securitas fuerat saepius ferire. Negat praeterea quicquam se ex his noverca sensisse, cum
iuxta iaceret, nec explicat unde illud acciderit maximae

---

[14] -um B V δ (*def. Dess.*[1] *76, Eng. 61*): -us *cett.*

---

[17] You can determine what a confused mass of accusations (cf.
17.9.1) Stepmother is throwing at us by considering the (scant)
credibility the facts have in her reconstruction.

[18] The other side: cf. 1.11.7.   [19] Cf. 1.7.2–3.

[20] *Anima* is here a physical part of the body in which the "vital
breath" itself resides: cf. 1.10.6, 1.14.4.   [21] Cf. 1.6.8.

leave a sword behind will prefer to kill with someone else's rather than his own.

(4) Weigh up the rest of what happened, judges, if it falls within the realms of possibility. A blind man, with no one to guide him, no one to lead him, is said to have wandered, carrying a sword, from that secluded wing—almost, indeed, from a separate house—through a long empty area, through so many doorways to trip over, through slaves sleeping on guard. Then, it is alleged, he went into his father's bedroom, and, straying neither to left nor to right, but marching straight ahead, the way people do when their eyes are guiding them, came gently to the bed, without bumping into it, without arriving at it before he expected. 4. It is for you, judges, to reckon how confused the charges are from what is plausible.[17] A sleeping old man sought out by a blind murderer would have woken up before he was found. They[18] add to all this details far more incredible: how he killed his father, spared his stepmother, and completed the murder with a single blow—something that rarely befalls even those who have eyes to guide their hands.[19] (2) Was there then no need of eyes, but someone who had to direct his sword at random, who would have been happy enough if he struck any part of the body at all, hit straight off upon the vital spot,[20] and knew whether he had done all that was needed to kill? The role of the eyes, judges, is to report[21] to the hands what they have done. The only safe course for a blind murderer would have been to strike more than once. (3) Further, the stepmother says she heard nothing of all this, though she was lying by his side; and she has no explanation for one

signum trepidationis, si et pater uno ictu periit[15] neque ista vigilabat: numquam gladium reliquit percussor securus.

5. Reliqua, iudices, nimium suspecta, improbe adsimulata: spatiosissimus paries et longissimum domus latus habuit notas sanguinis, quas reliquisse videretur manus revertentis. O quam bene, quicquid volunt, imitantur

2 oculi! Stupeo, si qua est fides. Omnia privignus[16] illa nocte fecisse dicitur ad votum novercae: gladium in vulnere reliquisse, quem suum negare non posset, deinde per totum parietem quid aliud inscripsisse quam se parricidam?[17] Sanguinem[18] patris usque ad cubiculum suum perduxisse

3 et viam sequentibus reliquisse. Haec fecit aliquis negaturus? Gratulor tibi, adulescens: si non potuisti parricidium illud admittere, nisi ut relinqueres argumentum caecitatis, habuisti innocentiae necessitatem.

4 Causam igitur miserrimi adulescentis sic apud vos agere proposui, ut primum ipsum defendam, quasi reus tantum sit; deinde, cum esse securus de huius innocentia coepero, tunc ingrediar novercae accusationem. Spectabitis utrumque suis moribus, suis causis; erit facilior via ves-

[15] -iit *Reitz.*[2] *61*: -ierit *codd.*

[16] -us *Sh. B.*[2] *188* (*post* fides *et* novercae *distinguens*): -um *codd.*

[17] *dist. Hamm.*[1] *48*

[18] -nem AD (*def. Helm*[2] *87–88*): -ne *cett.*

[22] Unless one planning to blame someone else for the murder: cf. 1.2.2.

[23] Casually repeated from 1.3.4.

[24] = a sighted person.

thing: if the father died at a single stroke *and* she was asleep, why that telltale sign of extreme agitation?—a killer with no worry in the world never left his sword behind![22]

5. The rest, judges,[23] is all too suspect, a wicked series of fictions. The extensive wall forming the longest side of the house carried marks of blood which looked as though they had been left by the hand of someone coming back. How well can eyes[24] make things appear the way they want! (2) Believe me, I am astonished. That night the stepson is alleged to have done all the stepmother could have prayed for: left a sword in the wound that he could not deny was his; then written all along the wall the clear message "I killed my father." He is said to have brought his father's blood right to his own bedroom, leaving a trail for others to follow. (3) Did someone do these things if he was proposing to deny responsibility? I congratulate you, young man: if you were unable to carry out the murder without leaving behind proof of your blindness, you had a compelling reason to preserve your innocence.[25]

(4) Accordingly, I have decided to plead before you the case of a most pitiful young man in the following manner: first I shall defend him, as if he were the accused and no more;[26] then, when I start feeling confident that I have proved his innocence, I shall go on to accuse the stepmother. You will be looking at the two of them together, in the light of their characters, their motives. In that way, you will find it easier, in the discharge of your sacred

[25] Cf. also 1.6.5.
[26] And not an accuser as well.

trae religionis: quamquam duos indicia complexa sint, vos tamen tamquam de singulis cognoveritis.

6. Et primum sic agam tamquam iuvenis habeat oculos, tamquam impetus eius nulla corporis debilitate frangantur. Interrogabo quid ante perdite, quid flagitiose, quid impie fecerit, per quae se parricidam scelera promiserit.

2 Innocentia per gradus certos ab homine discedit, et, ne in maximis trepidet audacia, diu vires in minoribus colligit.

3 Nemo inde coepit, quo incredibile est pervenisse. Dicas necesse est quae huic cum patre odia fuerint, quam violenta dissensio inter sacrorum infinita nominum pignora, crede, mulier, etiam tua causa: nam si facile est patrem filio occidere, facilius est uxori maritum.

4 Loquar nunc de infirmitate miserae caecitatis. Temeritas omnis animorum calamitate corporum frangitur, et frigescunt impetus mentium quos[19] non explicant ministeria membrorum; ad solum se alligat destituta maerorem.

5 Vultus ille perpetua nocte coopertus ac timidus non concipit nefas, ad quod ducibus oculis pervenitur. Cogitat semper errare et offendere, cogitat eundi redeundique difficultatem. Magna innocentiae necessitas est neminem

6 facilius posse deprehendi. Semper sibi custodiunt miseri

---

[19] quod B

---

[27] I.e., the duty to scrupulously seek truth, in keeping with the oath that the judges had to swear prior to the trial (*Cod. Iust.* 3.1.14). Cf. 6.12.6.   [28] Parricide is the most terrible of crimes, the *ultimum nefas* (*Decl. min.* 377.1; cf. 2.1.3); as such, it is traditionally believed to be heralded by a crescendo of minor delicts. Cf. 17.9.3; Sen. *Controv.* 7.5.6 (Triarius).

[29] "Father" and "son." Cf. 5.7.4, 5.14.10; see also 18.3.4.

duty,[27] to follow my argument: though the pieces of evidence involve two people, you will judge them (as it were) separately.

6. And first I shall plead as though the young man had his sight, as though his impulses were shattered by no physical disability. I shall ask what he has done in the past that is the act of a depraved, a villainous or an undutiful man, by what crimes he has given promise of a future parricide.[28] (2) Innocence takes its leave of a man by marked stages, and audacity gathers strength over time in minor enterprises for fear it may falter when the big moment comes. Nobody starts at a point, arrival at which is beyond belief. (3) You must tell us what grudges this man had against his father, what violent disagreement sundered the countless ties that bind those sacred names[29] together; yes, you must—believe me, woman—for your own sake as well: if it is easy for a son to kill his father, it is easier for a wife to kill her husband.

(4) I come on to speak of the handicaps of those unhappy enough to be blind. All the daring of the mind is shattered by the disaster that has afflicted the body: its impulses grow cold, when the limbs refuse their services in carrying them through. Blindness is forlorn, and can cling only to melancholy. (5) Such a man, shrouded in perpetual night and full of fear, has no conception of a crime at which one arrives when there are eyes to lead. He always has in mind getting lost and bumping into things, always has in mind the difficulty of getting there and getting back. The knowledge that no one can be more easily detected makes innocence imperative. (6) The poor things

ne esse miserabiles desinant, et quisquis amisit oculos laborat ne merito perdiderit. Quid aliud caecitas discit
7 quam rogare, blandiri? Odium omne adiuvant oculi, et hunc in pectoribus humanis furorem lumina accendunt, nec levis animis accedit insania, quotiens quem execreris aspicias. Caecus miserior est quam ut invisus sit, timidior
8 est quam ut oderit. Praeterea nocentibus liberis frequentissimas ad parricidium causas suggessit illud, quod videbant. Vitiis enim nostris in animum per oculos via est. Aliis tradidit in parentum sanguinem luxuria ferrum: luxuria, videntium crimen; aliis meretriculae amor immodica poscentis: amor, cui renuntiant oculi. Caecus infelix patrem
9 occidit: deinde cui manum porriget securior? Cuius humeris levior incumbet? Quis contumelias servorum castigabit severius? Quis calamitatem tam obnoxiam maiore
10 reverentia proteget? Inter felices alius est ordo votorum; caecus filius optat superstitem patrem.

7. Volo nunc scire quemadmodum dicat explicitum tam difficile facinus. Caecus parricidium cogitavit: cum quo? Cuius se commisit oculis? Iturus per domum totam quem
2 ducem elegit? Ille, qui erat in cubiculo suo solus, secum— opinor—, secum deliberat, sufficit sibi: cum homine expeditissimo loquitur. Cur enim socium conscientiae quaerat?

---

30 The eyes are traditionally considered the gates for vices and passions (cf., e.g., 2.10.7, 15.12.7).   31 Sc., love for etc. that hands the blade.   32 Cf. 1.4.2.   33 I.e., look for help in walking.   34 Cf. 5.22.4 and 16.6.2; this imagery probably goes back to Verg. *Aen.* 5.325, *incumbens umero* (Becker [1904, 24]).   35 Blindness exposes the young man to the insults of the servants: cf. 1.17.2.   36 That a father may outlive his son is considered against the laws of nature by fortunate people; how-

are always on guard for fear they cease to merit pity, and anyone who has lost his eyes is concerned that the loss does not seem deserved. What do the blind learn except to beg, to wheedle? (7) It is the eyes that aid and abet every feud, it is the eyes that make this madness blaze up in the human heart:[30] no trivial matter is the insanity that comes over the mind when you see a man you loathe. A blind man is too unhappy to be hated, too timid to hate. (8) What is more, guilty children are frequently motivated to kill parents by the very fact that they can see. For our vices enter the mind by way of the eyes. To some men it is debauchery that hands the blade to shed parents' blood: debauchery, a crime of the sighted; to others it is love[31] for some demanding prostitute: and to love the eyes report back.[32] (9) An unfortunate blind man has killed his father. To whom then will he hold out his hand with more confidence?[33] To whose shoulders will he be less of a burden?[34] Who will punish the insults of slaves more severely?[35] Who will have greater respect for a handicap so open to abuse? (10) The prayers of the fortunate have a different order of priority: the blind man asks that his father may survive.[36]

7. Now I want to know how she says so difficult a crime was carried through. A blind man had planned to kill his father. With whom? Whose eyes did he trust himself to? Whom did he choose to guide him as he set out through the whole house? (2) Alone in his bedroom, he plots—with himself, I suppose, with himself; he is sufficient unto himself: he is talking to a person capable of instant action. Why should he look for an accomplice? *He* can do everything.

ever, a blind son who depends entirely on his father wishes not to outlive his parent, as he will lose his main support.

Omnia potest:[20] scire primum, nox quando sit; deinde, prospicere sollicite an omnis familia dormiat, gradu suspenso ponere certa vestigia, et in omnem timoris sui par-

3 tem sollicitum circumagere vultum. O quam parum est in metu ipsos etiam oculos habere! Ita non iste sibi dixit: "Occidere quidem patrem volo, sed quem sequentur hae manus? Nocte solus egrediar, sed quando perveniam?"

4 Putes[21] nos iunctis habitare liminibus? Domus inter patrem filiumque media: quantum erroris, quantum morae!

5 Spatium ingens et vix metiendum. Caecitas inconsulta, quid agis? Nox ante deficiet. Quid, si deinde uterque vigi-

6 laverit?[22] Quid, si noverca? "Age limen inveniam, cardinem sine strepitu movebo, dormientis cubiculum intrabo, quiescentem feriam patrem, semel satis erit, nec noverca vigilabit; securus egrediar, sciente nullo revertar." Vota sunt ista, sed oculorum; caecus desperaret, etiamsi tam multa nox[23] polliceretur.

8. Hoc loco quaeram necesse est, quae ratio fuerit ut iuvenis ad parricidium suo potissimum gladio uteretur.

2 Nimirum illud in mentem venit, quia erat relicturus! Nam si alienum et ignotum in vulnere patris gladium reliquisset, potuerat de percussore dubitari. Hic attulit suum ut,

[20] dist. Obr. (firm. Sant.-Str.)
[21] -tas γ β, sed vd. Hamm.[1] 49, Sant.-Str.
[22] -rit V π (def. Wint. ap. Sant.-Str.): -rint cett.
[23] non Sh. B.[2] 188

---

[37] Cf. 1.4.1.   [38] I.e., before you can reach your father's room, kill him, and return to your room.

[39] Only at night would such things be possible, but exclusively to a sighted person.

First, he can know when it is nighttime. Next, he can anxiously make sure if the whole household is asleep; he can go on tiptoe without faltering, and cast an anxious look around wherever there is something to fear. (3) How little it helps even to have eyes, when you are afraid! Didn't he in fact say to himself: "I want to kill my father, but who will go ahead of my hands?[37] I shall set out at night, alone; but when shall I arrive?" (4) Perhaps you imagine we lodge next door to each other? The whole house lies between father and son: what scope for getting lost, for delay! The distance is vast, scarcely to be covered. (5) Heedless blindness, what are you about? The night will be over too soon.[38] What if after all that they both turn out to have stayed awake? What if the stepmother does? (6) "Fine, I shall find the threshold, I shall open the door without making a noise, I shall enter the bedroom where he is sleeping, I shall strike my father as he slumbers; once will be enough, and the stepmother will not be awake. I shall leave without any problem, I shall return with no one the wiser." That is the wish list—for someone with eyes. A blind man would be in despair, even though night promised so many advantages.[39]

8. At this point I have to ask what made the young man use his own sword in particular for the murder.[40] Obviously, it occurred to him to do that because he was going to leave it behind! (2) If he had left someone else's, an unknown sword, in his father's body, there could have been doubt as to the murderer.[41] He took along his own

<hr />

[40] Cf. 1.2.2, 1.5.2.

[41] The son's sword, on the contrary, was well known to the whole household: cf. 1.3.1, 1.8.5.

3 etiamsi evasisset, tamen ferro suo teneretur. "Cur ergo"
   inquis "gladium in cubiculo tuo habebas?" "Quia habue-
4 ram semper, quia usurus illo non eram. Ferrum ego parricidio meo tot ante annos praeparavi, et secundum illum,
   quem minabar patri, ⟨gladium⟩[24] tamdiu innocens fui?
   Ego eram ferro ac mente paratus, et tot abiere noctes?
5 Ante gladium illum familiarem oculis tuis feci, ante omnibus servulis notum. Pependit in cubiculo tamquam testis
   conscientiae meae, palam, in medio, neglegenter, sic ut
   subtrahi posset. Non illum conscientia trepida velavit; tam
6 notus in cubiculo fuit quam caecitas domini." Quisquis
   ferrum praeparat sceleri, sic illud habet, ut possit suum
   negare.

   9. Ponite nunc ante oculos actum parricidii: deprehen-
   detis difficultatem. Dono illud: dum a suo limine egredi-
   tur, dum illos, quos accepit a patre, servulos fallit, ecce
   cubiculum senis invenit aliquando, ecce paries ille defecit
   et percussoris manus subito destituit, cessere fores sine
2 strepitu. Quid postea agit? Utrum ipsum cubiculi parietem circumit, an se committit in medium et per spatia
3 tenebrarum armatam manum iactat? Ecce patris lectulum

---

[24] *add. Hamm.[1] 50 sive ante sive post* illum, *huc transp. Dess.[1]*
87

---

[42] Stepmother.

[43] Ethopoeia: the speaker pretends that his client answers
directly to Stepmother's objection.

[44] Cf. 1.3.2.

[45] Stepmother's.

[46] = keeps it hidden.

so that even if he got clean away he would be betrayed by his weapon. (3) "Why then," you[42] ask, "did you keep a sword in your bedroom?" "Because I[43] had always kept it there,[44] because I was not going to use it. (4) Did I get the weapon ready for my parricide years before, and, while living next to ⟨the sword⟩ I was thinking of using on my father, did I remain innocent for so long? Was I ready, steel and mind, and yet so many nights went by? (5) No, I ensured in advance that the sword was a familiar sight to your[45] eyes, was well known to all the slaves. It hung in my room like a witness to my clear conscience, quite openly, for all to see, casually, in such a way that it could be filched. It was not kept under wraps by a fearful conscience. It was as well known a sight in the bedroom as its blind owner." (6) Anyone who is intending to use a sword for a crime keeps it at hand in such a way that he can deny it belongs to him.[46]

9. Now picture the execution of the murder:[47] you will not fail to see the difficulty involved. This I grant: he set off from his door, he evaded the slaves posted for him by his father[48] and, look! he eventually found the old man's room, look! the wall gave out and suddenly failed the killer's hands, the door opened quietly.[49] (2) What does he do next? Does he go round the wall of the room, or launch out into the middle, and swing his armed right hand through the dark space? (3) Look, he has hold of his

[47] The speaker invites the audience to form a visual reconstruction (*diatyposis*): a common declamatory device.

[48] Cf. 1.15.7.

[49] These difficulties have been repeatedly surveyed since 1.3.4.

tenet et iam dormientium anhelitus imminens audit; unde sciet quo dirigat ferrum, quem potius feriat ex duobus? Temptabit ergo vultus et pectus obiectum, brevissimam perituræ animæ viam quaeret?[25] Et quantus erit sopor,

4 qui ista non sentiat? Dices: "Neque ego sensi." Ideo intellegis quam malam causam habeas, cuius et una et incredi-

5 bilis defensio est. Ita feritur in sinu tuo maritus, et tu nihil sentis? Ad latus tuum fata hominis peraguntur; tu iaces,[26] tamquam te privignus occiderit priorem? Ita non ille[27]

6 percussus est, homo quem caecus occidit? Te vero, si nihil aliud, calens ille denique cruor suscitasset. Sed quam manifesta est conscientia quae te ad hanc compellit necessitatem, ut, cum occisum a privigno tuo patrem videri

7 velis, cogaris dicere nihil sensisse! Sufficit: vicimus, innocentes sumus! Cum in eodem lectulo fueris, cum amplexa sis forsitan illum, qui occisus est, tam incredibilem profiteris soporem? Cur ergo tu incolumis es? Quae tam iratis

8 manibus sanguinem tuum fortuna subtraxit? Certe dormiebas, certe nihil senseras: ita privignus te reliquit, qui deprehendi non timebat. 10. Occidit ergo aliquis patrem et novercae pepercit? Maximum omnium nefas fortiter

---

25 temptabit *et* quaeret *Håk.²* 20–21: -avit *et* -rit *codd.*
26 ia- A (*def. Håk.²* 21): ta- *cett.*
27 ille <saepius> *Wint.⁷ 134*

---

50 Plural for singular, as at, e.g., 2.3.1. Contrast the parallel scene in 2.17.1.
51 I.e., look for the quickest way to kill. The vital breath, according to ancient lore, would abandon the body at the moment of death through a natural orifice (nose, mouth . . .) or a wound.
52 The sword stroke, as well as the groans of the victim (cf.

father's bed, and hanging over it can hear the deep breathing of people already asleep. How will he know where to aim the blade, which of the two he should choose to strike? Will he then feel the face[50] and the chest presented to him, and look for the shortest route for the doomed breath to depart?[51] And how deep will be a sleep be that does not notice all that? (4) You will say: "I didn't notice it either." You can see how bad your case is if you have only one defense, and that beyond belief. (5) So your husband is struck down in your arms, and you feel nothing? A man meets his fate at your side, and you lie there as if the stepson had killed you first? Now really, was a man, whom a blind man killed, not struck?[52] (6) As for you, you would have been woken by that warm gush of blood, if nothing else. How plain is the guilty conscience which brings you to such a pass: since you want it to look as if your stepson killed his father, you are forced to say you felt nothing! (7) That is enough, we've won, we are innocent! When you were in the same bed, when, maybe, you had your arms round the victim, do you lay claim to a slumber so incredible? How then do *you* come to be safe and sound? What good fortune put *your* blood out of the reach of those angry hands? (8) Of course you were asleep, of course you had felt nothing. That is why your stepson left you:[53] he was not afraid of being detected! 10. Did someone then kill his father and spare his stepmother?[54] Did he have the

2.18.1ff.), should have awakened the woman who was lying in the same bed; since this did not happen, the speaker asks ironically if the man was killed without being struck.

53 Sc., still alive.

54 Cf. 1.4.1.

fecit, minori sceleri statim par non fuit? Omnia humana
sacra confudit, violare non ausus est pectus odiosum?[28]
Incredibile est, sine fide est non occidere novercam cui
2 imputes quod patrem occidat. Quid ais, adulescens? Tune
circa illum sanguinem defecisti? Illa te blandius rogavit
anima? Perdidisti ergo illud, quod nihil senserat, quod
nox, quod silentium, quod tempus supererat sceleris alte-
3 rius? Tu si facere parricidium posses, ideo patrem tantum
occidisses, ut tibi et novercam liceret occidere.

4   Non video qui[29] videri velint relictam mulierem ideo
tantum, ut videretur illud nefas illa[30] fecisse. Callide satis,
sed hoc alio protinus argumento subvertetur:[31] non est
eiusdem consilii novercae parcere, ut substituat ream, et
gladium relinquere, quo ipse deprehendatur.

5   Saepius uti necesse habeo argumento caecitatis, et hoc
etiam loco, quo de illo vulnere disputandum est. ⟨Si⟩[32]
mehercule percussor intrasset, qui videret, qui[33] lumen
prae se tulisset, non tamen tam feliciter librasset ictum
quem, etiamsi nullae fallerent tenebrae, metus et consci-
6 entia incertum magni sceleris tremore[34] fecissent. Raro

28 -osum *Franc.*: -orum *codd.*   29 qui (= quomodo, *velut*
1.12.5) [*Sant.*-]*Str.*: cur M S: cur nisi E: cui *cett.*: (nam video) qui
Sh. B.[2] *188–89*   30 ipsa *Håk., fort. recte*

31 -tetur π (*vind. Sh. B.*[2] *189*): -teretur *cett.*

32 *add. Reitz.*[2] *76*   33 si *Håk.*

34 tremore (*def. Håk.*[2] *21–22) vel* tristi timore C[2]: tristem
morae *vel* -re B V Φ*: timore *Wint.*[1] *314*

55 Cf. n. 28.
56 Cf. Cic. *Rosc. Am.* 65, *omnia divina atque humana iura*
scelere nefario polluisset (in another case of alleged patricide).

fortitude to carry out the most appalling crime of all,[55] yet straight after was not equal to a lesser crime? Did he turn upside down all that men hold sacred,[56] but shrank from violating a breast he hated? It is incredible, past belief that a man whom you charge with killing his father did not kill his stepmother. (2) What do you say, young man? Did you falter when it came to shedding *that* blood? Did *that* life beg you more winningly?[57] Did you then waste such an opportunity?—her being unconscious, the night, the silence, the time available for a second crime. (3) If you were capable of killing your father, you would have done it only in order to be able to kill your stepmother too.

(4) I don't see how they[58] can want it to be thought that the woman was passed over only so that it might look as if *she* did the deed. A cunning enough idea, but one that will immediately be overthrown by another argument: it is not a coherent plan to spare the stepmother in order to accuse her, and to leave a sword behind to bring about one's own detection.

(5) I am forced to argue from his blindness quite frequently:[59] and here too, where the wound has to be discussed. <If>—for heaven's sake—a murderer had entered who had eyes, who had shone a light in front of him, he would not have been as lucky as this in aiming a blow which, even without darkness to mislead him, fear and a guilty conscience would have made problematic, as the hand trembled at the enormity of the crime. (6) It rarely

---

[57] I.e., was the prospect of killing the stepmother more intolerable than the thought of murdering your own father?

[58] Cf. n. 18.

[59] Despite the claim made in 1.1.1–2.

contingit[35] semel ferire carnifici, quamvis componat ipse
cervicem et spectata[36] manus homicidium novissime velut
quoddam genus artis exerceat. Sic ergo libravit manum
7 caecus, ut ipsam protinus feriret animam? Ego mehercules etiam illud admiror, quod, cum patrem vellet, non
novercam percussit. Praeter animum nil virium habet parricidae primus ictus; ille trepidat, ille cogitat, ille erubes-
cit, ille est ab innocentia proximus, ille praestat hoc solum,
ut sequens fortius feriat.

11. Interrogare nunc volo, quae iuveni causa fuerit ut
reliquerit gladium. Scilicet noluit novercam suam infa-
mari, abstulit sibi omnem defensionem et se parricidam
2 confessus est. Ferrum in vulnere reliquit: si nondum occiderat, iterum feriret, si iam perfectum nefas intellegebat,
3 auferret indicium. Sed quid ego rem manifestissimam
colligo? Si vultis, iudices, scire a quo sit relictus gladius,
cogitate cui expedierit ut inveniretur.
4   "Sed paries usque ad cubiculum privigni vestigio manus cruentatus est." Cogitate, iudices, ante omnia non esse
incallidum hominem neque consilii iacentis, qui caecus
explicare conetur facinus etiam oculis difficile. Ille ergo
non aestimat, cum manum cruentam parieti adplicat, ves-

---

35 -ting- A (*def. Håk. coll. 1.4.1*): -tig- *cett.*
36 et sp- *Leh.* (*firm. Sant.-Str.*): exp- B V: et (ut A) exp- Φ (*def.*
Wint.[7] 134–35)

---

60 Cf. *Decl. min.* 315.25 (a father addressing the executioner
of his son), *Hoc saltem fortunae meae praesta: semel ferias.*
61 Cf. Luc. 8.673, *nondum artis erat caput ense rotare* ("it was
not yet a knack to send a head spinning with a sword-cut") (trans.
Duff).

happens that an executioner needs to strike only once,[60] even though he arranges the neck himself, and though the admired hand in the end performs the killing like a kind of art.[61] Did then a blind man direct his hand in such a way as to strike a fatal blow straight off? (7) Indeed I am also surprised that, though he wanted to strike his father, he did not in fact strike his stepmother. The first blow aimed by a parricide is feeble—it merely shows the intention; that blow falters, it deliberates, it blushes, it is just a step away from being innocent: its only contribution is to make the next one stronger.

11. I want now to ask what motivated the youth to leave the sword behind. Of course he did not want his beloved[62] stepmother's name to be blackened: he deprived himself of any defense, and confessed himself to be the murderer. (2) He left the sword in the wound. Yet if he had not yet succeeded in killing, he should have struck a second time; if he realized the crime was complete, he should have taken the evidence away with him. (3) But why do I go on deducing something so patently obvious? If, judges, you are interested in knowing who left the sword behind, think who benefited from it being found.

(4) "But the wall was stained by the traces of a hand right up to the stepson's bedroom."[63] Bear in mind, judges, above all else, that if a man, despite being blind, tries to carry through a crime that even the sighted would find difficult, he is not stupid or dimwitted. Does he not then take into account, as he presses his bloodstained hand to

[62] For this ironic nuance of the possessive, cf. 12.18.3 and 10.

[63] This passage is probably alluded to in Jer. *Ep.* 60.15.3: cf. Introduction to the present declamation.

5 tigium a se parricidii sui relinqui? Cum dexteram, qua
duce utebatur, veste tegere atque ita abire sine vestigio
posset, totum parietem cruentabat et ubique aliquid de
patre misero relinquebat. Quid futurum esset postero die,
quantam exspectaret invidiam luce,[37] non cogitabat, sed
disponebat indicium certum, indubitatum, sine errore,
quod noverca sequeretur usque ad cubiculum suum, usque ad limen ipsum. O admirabilem casum! Nec cruor
6 ante defecit? Utar hoc loco natura ipsius rei. Palmatus
sanguine paries inventus sic est: totam manum explicuit,
omnes digitos diligenter expressit. Totum ergo sanguinem
7 consumet[38] intra prima vestigia. Pone enim manum
cruentatam atque adeo, ut istis etiam blandiar, madentem,
pone mensuram itineris, spatium parietis—diu enim in
secretam domus partem revertendum est—: debet proxima
pars a cubiculo patris habere plurimum sanguinis, sequens minimum, ultima nihil. 12. Nam cruor, quotiens
admotus est, transit, aut in manu tarde reptantis arescit.
2 Hoc quid esse dicamus, quod circa cubiculum utrumque
sanguinis istius vestigium quasi incipit, hinc est paries palmatus et illinc? Quomodo pertulit manus quod relin-
3 quebat? Noverca istud, noverca oculis, illa miserum dextra
sanguinem tulit et manum subinde renovavit. Palmatus

---

[37] -e M (*et vd. Helm*[2] *88–89*): -em *cett.*
[38] -eret S[2] E, *sed cf. H.-Sz. 311 (γ), Sant.-Str.*

---

[64] Cf. n. 18.　　　[65] I.e., it is as fresh at the end of the trail
as at the beginning.　　　[66] The blood.
[67] I.e., she kept putting more blood on her own hand.

the wall, that he is leaving behind the traces of his guilt?
(5) Although he might have used a piece of clothing to
cover the right hand he was using to find his way, and so
made his escape without leaving any trace, he stained the
wall all the way along and left something of his unhappy
father everywhere. He did not think of what would happen next day, how much odium he could expect when it
grew light. In fact, he was laying a trail of evidence that
was certain, beyond doubt, with no chance of error, for the
stepmother to follow all the way to his bedroom, right to
the very threshold. What a wonderful stroke of luck: the
gore didn't run out before he arrived! (6) I shall at this
point appeal to the way things are. This is how the wall was
found marked by palm prints: he spread his whole hand
out, being careful to leave an impression of all his fingers.
So he will use up all the blood on the first prints. (7) Suppose the hand bloodstained and even, to indulge my op-
ponents,[64] dripping, take into account the length of the
journey, the extent of the wall (for it takes some time to
return to his secluded wing of the house): the part nearest
the father's bedroom must have most blood, the next part
already very little, the last part nothing. 12. For every time
blood is applied to a surface, it is either transferred to it
or it dries on the hand of someone creeping slowly along.
(2) What are we then to make of the fact that this trail of
blood as it were starts near *both* bedrooms?[65]—the wall is
marked with the palm of the hand both from this point and
from that. How did the hand carry through to the end
what[66] it kept on leaving behind? (3) It was the stepmother, yes the stepmother, who produced this effect,
with her unimpaired sight. She smeared the unlucky blood
on her right hand, and kept renewing her hand.[67] The wall

est paries, habet distantiam, vacat aliquid loci, integrum
4 ubique vestigium est; caecus manus traxisset. Quaero
nunc: unde tantum sanguinis in manu? Tunc enim ex omni
vulnere cruor profluit et effunditur, cum ferri recentem
viam sequitur; at quotiens eodem, quo factum est, cluditur
5 ‹iter›[39] telo, latet tota mortis invidia. Praeterea cum manus ex parte, qua palmare vestigium potest, plicetur in
capulo et se, dum telum occupat,[40] claudat, necesse est
exteriore ut parte respersa sit. Tuus autem qui palmatus
est paries? Vestigium eius partis ostendit, ad quam cruor
6 pervenire non potuit! Vestrum est nunc omnia ista com-
parare, perpendere. Cur prudentior sit iudex in de-
prehendendo scelere quam reus in admittendo, hoc esse
in causa puto, quod alter tantum pro se cogitat, alter pro
parte utraque.

13. Tuitus sum adulescentis miserrimi causam. Nunc
inspicere volo quanto certioribus argumentis noverca te-
2 neatur. Transeo illum vulgarem et omnibus notum de

---

[39] *add. Håk. post* quotiens, *huc transp. [Sant.-]Str.*

[40] telum occu- π E S²: telocu- B: occu- M: telo occu- *cett.*: telo
del. Dess.¹ 83 (post M) *utpote gloss. ad* capulo

---

[68] The wall is described as showing a series of perfect prints
separated by gaps, not a long smear.

[69] I.e., the gore, which makes the sight of the body more appalling when it is pouring out of the wound.

[70] I.e., the wall that you (Stepmother) bring as evidence
against Son. Cf. 15.6.3, *venefica tua.*   [71] Judges.

[72] This phrase seems to imply an inquisitorial system, whereby
the judge is in charge of detecting a crime and gathering evidence
against the defendant, not of judging the case as an impartial third
party.   [73] In his attempt to pin the crime on someone else,

has been marked with prints; it[68] bears them at intervals, with an empty space in-between, and each trace is perfect; a blind man would have dragged his hands along. (4) I now ask: where did so much blood on the hand come from? For from any wound the gore flows and floods out when it is following the fresh path of a sword. But whenever ⟨the route⟩ is closed by the same weapon that made it, the whole horrid sight of death is hidden.[69] (5) Further, since the palm of the hand, which is capable of making a print, is clasped around the hilt and clenches in gripping the sword, it must get spattered on the outside. How then did your[70] wall get prints of a *palm*? It shows marks of the part of the hand which the blood could not have reached. (6) It is up to you[71] now to compare and think through all these points. Why should a judge be wiser in detecting a crime[72] than a defendant in committing it? I think the reason is that the one is thinking only from his own point of view, the other from that of both sides.[73]

13. I have made the case for this most unhappy young man. Now I want to examine how much more forceful are the proofs that implicate the stepmother. (2) I shall pass over the threadbare and hackneyed topic of the comparison of persons.[74] Someone else might say that a husband

---

the criminal thinks only of what he deems best for himself, and this can lead him to miscalculations, whereas the judge considers the standpoints of *both* parties on trial, and this enables him to unmask the mistakes made by the guilty one.

[74] *Synkrisis*: cf. Quint. 9.2.100. Such an omission would be unconceivable in a real trial; Quintilian himself (10.5.21) criticizes teachers who allowed students to omit the less appealing sections of a speech.

comparatione personarum locum. Alius diceret maritum
et uxorem, nisi liberis initiarentur, non fortissimis corporum vinculis inhaerere; ego illud potius dicam: decepta
3 est, mulier, exspectatio tua. Veneras quasi in vacuam domum et sine herede: exspectaveras ut infelix iste iuvenis
ab ipsis protinus nuptiarum tuarum expelleretur auspiciis,
extorrem et inopem summoveret pater blando corruptus
amplexu, et ominosum[41] calamitate corporis occurrere
delicatis uxoris oculis vetaret; invenisti pium et devotum
unico senem, et de omnibus coniugis tui desperasti obiter
4 affectibus. Miserrimus est maritus, quisquis inducit filio
novercam, quod uxori non videtur posse utrumque amare.
5   Quaero igitur ante omnia: ubi occisus est maritus? In
cubiculo suo. Hoc paulo ante privigno defendendum non
6 fuit. Occisus est in cubiculo senex: ita ille percussor non
timuit uxorem? Audeo[42] secretum nuptiarum et matrimo-
nialis lectuli solitudinem occisurus[43] intrare; quin[44] quae-
7 ram ubi relinquitur maritus ab uxore innocenti?[45] Noctem
autem ad scelus quis elegit? Nox tuum tempus est. Quid,
si accedit huc[46] etiam sceleris occasio? Non venire debes

[41] ominosum *Dess.*[2] *post* -sam (calamitatem) *Gron.*: omnino
summa B V Φ*

[42] -deo M S[2] (*def. Bur.*): -dio *cett.*

[43] -us M[2]: -um *codd.*

[44] quin *Sh. B.*[4] *188*: quem *codd.*

[45] -nti *Lund.*[2] *post Obr.* (-nte), *meliore sensu et clausula*: -ns
codd.: del. *Wint.*[7] *135 utpote ex inseq.* noctem *ortum*

[46] huc ς: hunc B: hinc V: huic Φ

[75] Cf. 1.2.6.   [76] Cf. Sen. *Controv.* 10.4.8 (Gallio), *Oc-
currunt* (sc., crippled beggars) *nuptiis dira omina.*

and wife, in the absence of the blessing of children, are not joined by very close physical bonds. I prefer to say: Woman, your expectations were disappointed. (3) You had come into a household you thought empty[75] and lacking an heir, you assumed that this unlucky youth would be driven out right at the start of your marriage, that the father, seduced by your winning embrace, would send him packing to exile and poverty, and forbid the ill-omened[76] sight of his afflicted body to encounter his wife's fastidious eyes. What you found instead was a principled old man, devoted to his only son, and you thereupon gave up all hope of winning the affections of your partner. (4) Unhappy indeed is the husband who installs a stepmother for his son: his wife does not think he can love both of them.

(5) So first of all I inquire: where was the husband killed? In his bedroom. That was not a point on which the stepson had to defend himself just now.[77] (6) The old man was killed in his bedroom. Did the killer then not fear the wife? Ready to kill, I dare[78] to enter the privacy of the marriage chamber and the isolation of the matrimonial bed; why don't I look instead for a place where the husband is left alone by his innocent wife?[79] (7) Further, who chose night for the wicked deed? Night is *your* time.[80] What if there is also the opportunity to commit the crime?

[77] This point weighs against Stepmother; therefore, the speaker did not have to examine it while defending Son, but he will exploit this argument in the present counteraccusation against Stepmother.

[78] = Suppose that I, ready to kill, dare . . .

[79] = by his wife, who is on this hypothesis innocent.

[80] Cf. 1.2.2: the time when you were sure to be alone with him.

37

a secreta domus parte,[47] nec tota tibi penatium spatia[48]
peragenda[49] sunt; tu non cogitas quemadmodum suspensa
manu sonantem blande cardinem flectas. Iaces secundum
8 occasionem, et expeditum tibi in proximo facinus est. Non
times ne quis deprehendat. Ipsi quoque servuli longius
quiescunt: [et][50] praestatur grande secretum genio loci,
9 tibique ferire cum velis, scire an dormiat, licet. Nox et
ferrum et securus maritus: quid isto delicatius scelere?
Occisum esse miserum senem cum tu volueris scimus.

14. "Quomodo tamen" inquit "gladius pervenit in
meam potestatem, qui privigni fuit?" Haeremus: hic diffi-
cilis expugnandus est locus. Quis credet mihi, si dixero:
"Gladium perdidit caecus, illae perpetua nocte clausae
2 genae non custodierunt"? Fingere nimirum ad tempus
videbor et rem nimium manifestam impudenter colorare.
Scilicet semper isti adposita capulo manus, hae[51] diebus
3 ac noctibus curae. Nolo tamquam callido glorieris ingenio:
non decepisti trucem horridumque latronem; nostri tibi
4 occasionem praebuere mores. Nam quod uno ictu occisus

---

47 a (ab *Wint.*[1] *314*) -ta d. -te *Valla* (*ut vid.*), *corrob. Hâk.*[2]
23–24: ad -tam d. -tem *codd.*
48 spatia *Sch.* (*cf. Hâk.*[2] *24 et 19.3.6*): sacra *codd.*
49 -granda *Warr, sed vd. ThlL X.1.1181.35ss. et denuo 19.3.6*
50 *del.* [*Sant.-*]*Str.*   51 hae *Sch.*: ac B V Φ*

---

81 On the Latin idiom (*suspensa manu*) see Citti (2014, 419–
20).   82 Literally, "cushier." Cf. 17.15.3.
83 Achronic present tense (as in all this section). No one in the
house can be aware of the murder before the woman announces
it: this gives her all the time she needs to arrange the crime scene
so as to frame the stepson.   84 Irony; cf. Juv. 6.280–81.

You don't need to come from a distant part of the house, you don't have to traverse the whole extent of the mansion. You don't wonder how to open the door gingerly,[81] so that the hinge does not creak. You are lying alongside your opportunity, and the dreadful deed is next to you, ready at hand. (8) You are not afraid of someone surprising you. Even the slaves are resting some way off: absolute privacy is guaranteed to the spirit of the hallowed place. You can strike when you want, you can know when he is asleep. (9) Night, a sword, an unsuspecting husband: what crime could be less demanding?[82] We can know[83] that the poor old man was killed only when *you* wanted us to know.

14. "But how," she says, "did the sword, which belonged to my stepson, get into *my* hands?" We are at a loss.[84] Here is a really difficult point to be overcome. Who will believe me if I say: "He was blind, and he mislaid his sword. Those eyes, imprisoned in continual night, couldn't keep watch over it"? (2) People will no doubt think I am making a story up for the occasion, and giving a shameless spin[85] to something quite obvious. Of course his hand is always on the hilt, this is his care day and night.[86] (3) Please don't boast of being unduly clever: you didn't have to deceive some fierce and frightful brigand; it was our[87] habits that gave you the opportunity. (4) As for the fact

---

[85] *Colorare* is metarhetorical: as the blind man insists that his sword was stolen from him, Stepmother objects (using a technical term from rhetoric: see General Introduction, n. 12) that such a claim is unlikely and can be maintained only with a blatant twist of the facts.

[86] Again ironic. In fact the sword was just hanging on the wall (1.8.5).   [87] Cf. n. 6.

est senex, ad quem suspicio magis respicit? Tu praeparare corpus illuc[52] ad ictum[53] potes, dum videris amplecti; tu blanda manu praetemptare pectus, ubi adsiduo visceris pulsu non quiescat anima, ubi statim mors sit; tibi[54] de spiritu sanguinis locum[55] explorare ante et cognoscere licet. Potes[56] et uno ictu ⟨tu⟩,[57] mulier, occidere.

15. Venio nunc ad vestigia parietis cruentati, quibus te satis abundeque pressimus, dum adulescentem defendimus. Haec sunt tamen, quae contra te reservata sunt: cum maritus tuus in cubiculo occideretur, sciebas nullum tibi relictum patrocinium, nisi aliquid caecitatis simile fecisses, ideoque sanguinem in illam partem induxisti, in quam quaeri volebas, ut postero die omnis invidia sanguinis notas et vestigia praeparata sequeretur. Infamans[58] caecum consilium ex calamitate sumpsisti; sciebas illum non aliter, si dux defecisset, ingredi posse quam ⟨ut⟩[59] vestigia parietis perpetuitate dirigeret. Simulasti itaque caecitatem, et, ne quid sceleri impio deesset, mariti tui cruore lusisti. Omnia tibi composita atque simulata sunt per otium et securitatem, tamquam scelus transferretur

---

[52] -uc B (*cf. Ne.-W. II.428, Leu. 469*): -ud V Φ

[53] ad ictum *Franc.* (*firm. Sant.-Str.*): addictus B V: ad ictus Φ

[54] tibi ς: ubi *codd.*   [55] locum π (*vind. Hamm.[1] 54*): hoc cum B V: exitum A: ictum *cett.*

[56] -es V^{ac} (*def. Håk.*): -est B V^{pc} Φ

[57] *add. [Sant.-]Str.*   [58] -mans B. Asc.[1] *vii v.*: -masset π: -mas *cett.* (*unde* ⟨dum⟩ -mas *Wint.[7] 135*)

[59] *add. Håk.*: ⟨si⟩ ς

---

[88] Cf. n. 20.   [89] Contrast 1.9.3 (Son).   [90] I.e., as the chest goes up and down, in inspiration and expiration.

that the old man was killed at a single blow, on whom does more suspicion fall? *You* can get that body ready to be struck, when he thinks you are hugging him; *your* caressing hand can feel his chest beforehand to find where the steady beat of the organ inside keeps life pulsing,[88] where death is immediate;[89] *you* may ascertain his vital spot in advance from his breathing[90] and familiarize yourself with it. It is ⟨*you*⟩, woman, who can kill even with a single blow.[91]

15. I come now to the traces on the bloodstained wall: we pressed you quite enough about that while we were defending the young man, but here are some points I have reserved to use when accusing you. As your husband was being killed[92] in the bedroom, you knew you would have no possible defense unless you did something that looked like the work of a blind man. Accordingly, you made the blood go in the direction toward which you wanted attention to be drawn, so that next day all the indignant household would follow the prearranged traces. (2) In scheming to blacken the blind man, you drew inspiration from his calamity: you knew that, in the absence of a guide, he could not get along unless he guided his steps by feeling the wall all the way. So you counterfeited blindness, and, to make sure that your wicked crime should lack for nothing, you played a game with your husband's blood. (3) You arranged and simulated everything at leisure and with perfect security, the crime being, as it were, transferred by your cleverness to another: *now* you are innocent,

[91] This corresponds to 1.14.4, *quod uno ictu occisus est senex, ad quem suspicio magis respicit?*

[92] Sc., in your plan.

41

ingenio: nunc enim tu innocens quia privigni gladius in
4 vulnere, quia paries cruentatus. Hoc sufficere utrumque
iudicio putabas? Quam facili momento causae fata vertun-
tur, quod fecisse etiam is scelus frequenter inventus est,
qui obiciebat!

5 "Sed causas" inquit "parricidii iste habuit, quem iratus
pater in secretam domus partem relegaverat." Mulier,
erras.[60] Illa forsitan ignominia felicioris videretur esse pri-
6 vigni; caecitatis beneficium est, cum illi secretum datur. O
praeclaram senis optimi singularemque pietatem! Quam
blande[61] ille seposuit miserum suum, quam diligenter
uxoris gaudentis exclusit oculos, quam multo caecum pu-
7 dore donavit! "Si felicior" inquit "essem pater, ego tibi
potius cederem domo tota! Nunc miser illam occupa partem, in qua nemo te videat, in quam solus ego veniam. Sint
circa te servuli fideles. Non gemitus tuos audiat quisquam,
non flebili maerore pascatur. Nihil est quod te sollicitet
8 conversatio[62] nostri." Secretum quod caecitati praestatur,
ideo praestatur ut minus oculi desiderentur.

16. Aliquis odit filium caecum et hac tantum ultione
contentus est, ut illi adsignet quietam et sepositam et[63]
meliorem domus partem? Ista ergo sic intellegenda,[64]
quasi abdicaret, quasi expelleret?[65] Iratus igitur senex

[60] mulier, erras *Sh. B.*[4] *188–89*: mulierum B V: -eri π: -er *cett.*

[61] -de M E: -do (*hapax*) *cett., sed cf. 1.13.7 et Sant.-Str.*

[62] -io *Gron.*: -ione *codd.*

[63] et <ei> *Sh. B.*[4] *189, sed vd. Sant.-Str.*

[64] ista ergo sic -legenda *Håk.*[2] *25–26*: ita ego sic -legebam
codd.: id ego sic -legam *Wint. ap. Sant.-Str.* (*at* id *in hac decl. non
legitur, neque h.l. placet coniunct. praes.*)

[65] abdicaret . . . expelleret ς (*vind. Russ.*[3]): -res . . . -res *codd.*

because the stepson's sword was there in the wound, because the wall was marked with blood. (4) Did you think these two facts enough to persuade a jury? How easily the issue of a case can turn around! Often even a man who was accusing another of a foul deed turns out to have perpetrated it himself!

(5) "But," she says, "he had reasons for killing a father who out of anger had banished him to a remote part of the house." Woman, you are mistaken. That might perhaps seem an insult to a more fortunate stepson; to a blind man it is a boon to be given a private retreat. (6) What a fine and remarkable mark of affection on the part of an excellent old man! How kind he was to set his unhappy son apart, how carefully he kept him from the gaze of his gloating wife, how much shame he spared the blind man! (7) "If I were better off," said the father, "I should prefer to give up the whole house to you. As it is, poor boy, move into that wing, where no one will see you, where only I shall come to visit you. Let loyal slaves surround you, let no one hear your groans or feed off your tearful grief.[93] There is no reason why you should be disturbed by *our* company."[94] (8) A blind man is given privacy so that he can regret the loss of his sight less keenly.

16. Does someone hate his blind son—and is content to punish him by assigning him a part of the house that is tranquil, secluded, *better*? Should all this be taken to mean that he was driving him out, that he was expelling him? So an angry old man keeps his youthful son in (as it

[93] This would be part of the gloating of Stepmother (cf. 1.15.6, *gaudentis*).

[94] I.e., mine and your stepmother's.

tenet iuvenem suum velut interiore complexu et a limine
2 obstat? Rogo, quod duos separat media domo, te inte-
gram, sanam, illum infelicem, caecum, contumeliae op-
portunum, iniuriae facilem, utrum filio irascatur an uxori.
3 "Nolo," inquit, "iuvenis, utaris amoena domus parte, ne, si
quae[66] nitidioribus tectis elaborata sunt, pertineant ad
oculos tuos." Quis tam stulte irascitur caeco, ut putet illius
4 interesse ubi habitare iubeatur? Te potius ille summovit,
tuis invidiam fecit odiis, tibi dixit:[67] "Sufficiat, satis est:
habeas maiorem domus partem. Absentem puta miserum,
5 in paternis sedibus aliquem angulum relinque." Pater, qui
filio sub noverca adsignat secretam domus partem, con-
fitetur uxori se abdicare non posse.
6   Transit ad aliud genus defensionis: sibi causam caedis
non fuisse, cum hic heres inventus sit omnium bonorum.
Quis enim alius esse debebat,[68] ut huic properandum fuerit ad hereditatem? Filius scriptus non timet paeniten-
tiam testamenti. Omnium bonorum heres relictus est; non
ergo irascebatur pater, cum daret secretam domus par-
7 tem. Non possunt tibi diversa prodesse: eadem obiceres
reo, si exheredatus esset. Elige utrum voles: si scivit se

---

66 ne, si quae *Sh. B.*[4] *189*: nescisque B V Φ*: ne haec quae ς
67 dixit *Håk.*: dicit *codd.*
68 -bebat *Sh. B.*[2] *189*: -beat (-buerat S[2]) *codd.*

---

95 Sc., far from driving him out.
96 I.e., you, Wife, rather than Son.   97 Sc., of the boy.
98 I.e., cannot bring himself to.   99 Note that the speaker
had initially questioned whether Son could be aware of his father's will before the murder (1.2.4–7).   100 And so would
not need to think of killing his father in a hurry.

44

were) a close embrace, without letting him out over the threshold?[95] (2) When he puts a house between the two of you, you sound of limb, healthy, him unfortunate, blind, easily insulted, prone to injury, is he—I ask—angry with his son or his wife? (3) "Young man," he says, "I don't want you to have the run of the agreeable part of the house, to make sure no rooms embellished with particularly brilliant ceilings belong to *your* eyes." Who is angry with a blind man so stupidly that he thinks it matters to him where he is told to live? (4) The fact is that it was you, rather,[96] whom he removed from the scene: it was your hatred[97] he reproached, it was to you that he said: "Let it suffice, it is enough: take the larger part of the house. Imagine the poor boy is not there; leave him some corner in his father's residence." (5) If a father allots a separate part of the house to a son who has been given a stepmother, he is confessing to his wife that he is unable to[98] drive him out.

(6) She goes on to another type of plea in her defense: that she had no reason to kill him, for he was found to be heir to the whole property.[99] Well, who else could it have been, so that he had to take such hasty steps to secure the inheritance? A son who has been written into a will does not fear a change of mind over its provisions.[100] He was left heir to all the estate: therefore his father was not angry when he gave him a separate part of the house. (7) Contradictory assertions cannot avail you: you would be bringing the same objection against a defendant who had been disinherited.[101] Take your choice: if he knew he was the

[101] Had Son been disowned, Stepmother would have accused him of killing his father out of resentment.

esse heredem, amare patrem debuit; si ignoravit, non habuit quod speraret ex patris morte.

8   Reliquum est ut intueamur, ille qui periit, ab utro magis vestrum desideretur. 17. Te, opinor, hic gravius afficit dolor, impatientius hic luctus exanimat, te, quae absoluta protinus nubes,[69] et tempori accommodata lugubria flam-

2 meo revertente mutabis. At[70] hic vero iuvenis, qui, si fortunae suae mala cum praeteritis comparet, caecus coepit esse nunc primum, quid non miser in hoc sene perdidit! Vivebat illi magna pietas, aderant, quodcumque iusserat, de facie patris oculi: non inludere infelicibus tenebris contumaces servuli poterant, nec, quod extremum contu-

3 meliarum genus est, ut dominum ageret rogabant. Nunc quanta, di boni, ludibria sunt ineunda! Iunxere se pariter

4 caecitas et solitudo. Quid tibi nunc, miserrime adulescens, hereditas prodest, quam tantum audis? Quid enim circa te pecunia potest? Quae fruendi voluptates, quid aliud

5 quam spoliorum facilis occasio? Quam bene ista omnia paterni oculi custodiebant! Quam facile decipi, quam facile denudari, quam sine labore falli potes, quam cito

6 inops fieri! Morte patris exheredatus es. Quid nunc tibi nisi perpetuus imminet maeror et execratio vitae? Miser post omnia et lacrimas perdidit, nec dolentem adiuvant oculi.

[69] absoluta . . . nubes *Reitz.*[2] 58: -leta . . . -be B V Φ*
[70] *om.* Φ

---

[102] Cf. Juv. 6.224–25.
[103] The loving father made constantly sure that his blind son's commands were duly obeyed by the servants.

heir, he should have loved his father; if he did not know, he had nothing to hope from his father's death.

(8) It remains to consider which of the two of you more misses the man who died. 17. You, I am quite sure, are more seriously afflicted by this grief, you are more devastated by this sorrow, you who if acquitted will remarry at once, letting your bridal veil make another appearance to replace the widow's weeds you put on just for this occasion.[102] (2) This youth instead, if he compares his present ills with those of the past, he is only now beginning to be blind for the first time. Poor creature, he has lost *everything* in this old man! He enjoyed great affection while his father lived; whatever he ordered, eyes were there for him from his father's face:[103] insolent slaves could not mock his unlucky darkness, or (the worst type of insult) ask him to play the master. (3) Now, ye gods, what mockery must he undergo! Blindness and solitude have joined forces. (4) Most unhappy youth, what does your inheritance profit you now, when you can only hear tell of it? What, after all, can any money you possess do for you? What pleasure can you take in the enjoyment of it? All it does is to make you an easy prey for plunderers. (5) How well your father's eyes used to look after all this! How easily you can be deceived, how easily stripped bare, how effortlessly tricked, how quickly made a pauper! You have been *disinherited* by the death of your father. (6) What hangs over you now but the prospect of mourning and cursing life for ever? After losing everything, the poor man has lost his tears too,[104] so he has no eyes to help him in his sorrow.

---

[104] According to a commonplace popular among declaimers, blind people can no longer shed tears: cf. Sen. *Controv.* 7.4.9.

7   Incipit apud te gladius habere quod agat. Quaerit, ecce quaerit miser ferrum: "Nunc"[71] inquit "huc[72] reddite illud, innocens, donec habuit meas manus tantum. Si mori necesse est, illi potissimum incumbam. Hoc illa iam olim

8 gravis et infelix anima quaerebat.[73] Ubi nunc meae vires, ubi impetus, ubi dextra tam fortis? Uno ictu, puto, ne me quidem ipsum mihi continget occidere."

[71] huc *Bur.*, *sed vd. Sant.-Str.*
[72] nunc *Reitz.*[2] *48, sed vd. item Sant.-Str.*
[73] querebat π: querebatur *vel* quaer- *cett.*

(7) Your sword is beginning to have something to do. He is searching, look, the wretched man is searching for the weapon. "Now," he says, "bring it back here; it was innocent so long as it only had my hands to wield it. If I have to die, I shall fall on it for preference. This is what my soul, burdened and unlucky as it is, has long been seeking. (8) Where now is my strength, where my energy, where my so 'brave'[105] right hand? I shall not, I think, succeed in killing even myself with a single blow."

[105] = my supposedly (according to Stepmother's version) bold hand.

DECLAMATION 2

INTRODUCTION

This second piece shares many features with *DM* 1: murdered father, sleeping stepmother, blind son, bloodied sword, counteraccusations. But the author of *DM* 2 clearly aims at "correcting" the weak points of *DM* 1, a piece which he doubtless had in mind and intended to outshine.[1] So the bloody handprints on the wall now disappear (it would have been all too easy to discover the culprit by simply matching the hands of Son and Stepmother with the prints); it is explained why Son was blind (he lost his eyesight while heroically trying, in a house fire, to rescue his mother as well as his father); and there is a whole new element: Son's advocate needs to show not just that Stepmother killed her husband, but that she had earlier accused Son falsely of attempting to poison his father.

As in *DM* 1 (1.1.1), Son's blindness is disallowed as a clinching argument (1.2, 9.1). Again, Stepmother is charged with producing a series of incredible fabrications (1.5, 11.3–5). Again, and inevitably, comparison has to play a major part. Sons are more likely to love their fathers than second wives their husbands (7.1–8.2). Women indeed are just as capable of murder as men (8.3–6). This particular crime was infinitely easier to carry out for Stepmother

[1] Ritter (1881, 92–95 and 183); [Krapinger-]Stramaglia (2015, 61–62); Santorelli[-Stramaglia] (2017, 36–40).

than for Son (16.1–17.4). And greed is a less likely motive
for him than for her (10.5–9; cf. 3.4).

Son, it is argued, was of consistently good character
(1.1). His father loved him, and may have remarried to
help him (3.2). He did not hate his stepmother (3.4, 12.4),
and his father was—as in *DM* 1—essential to his happiness
(10.1, 10.3, 24.4). Points that seem to weigh against him
merely show that he has been framed (2.2). His silence can
be explained away (5.1–2, 13.5–8). Stepmother's sleep can
and must have been pretended (18.1–19.6).

There are vivid evocations: of the discovery of the murder (6.1–3), the evening before it (15.2–3), and Son's
heroism in the burning house (23.2–24.2). This last forms
the bulk of the epilogue, which ends (as in 1.17.6–8) with
a hint that Son is not long for this life.

The structure can be analyzed as follows:[2]

PROEM 1.1–2.2
NARRATION 2.3–6.3
ARGUMENTATION
    Propositio causae (pathetically expanded) 6.4
    Confirmatio/Refutatio 7.1–22.4[3]
EPILOGUE 23.1–24.7

DM 2 was clearly composed after *DM* 1—as mentioned
above—and its language and style suggest a dating to the
late second century AD; additionally, the *Caecus in limine*
might have been known to the author of *DM* 17.[4] The

---

[2] Cf. Krapinger[-Stramaglia] (2015, 52–55).

[3] For the method adopted here in the argumentation, see
Introduction to *DM* 1, n. 1.

[4] Cf. [Krapinger-]Stramaglia (2015, 65–66); see also General
Introduction, §4.

same theme of *DM* 2 (with minimal adjustments, arguably for didactic purposes) is found in a Latin palimpsest bearing in its *scriptio inferior* a collection of declamatory excerpts: it was transcribed in the early Carolingian age, most likely from a late antique exemplar.[5] Also, a nearly identical subject is treated in [Libanius], *Decl.* 49; but the argumentation and style of the Greek speech are very different.[6] An antilogy to *DM* 2 was composed by Patarol.[7]

---

[5] Text and discussion in [Krapinger-]Stramaglia (2015, 20–22); see in more detail General Introduction, §6.

[6] Revised text, with translation and notes, in Krapinger-Stramaglia (2015, 249–316, and cf. 22–24).

[7] (1743, 114–36).

2

Caecus in limine[1]

Ex incendio domus adulescens patrem extulit. Dum matrem repetit,[2] et ipsam et oculos amisit. Induxit illi pater novercam. Quae accessit quodam tempore ad maritum, dixit parari illi venenum, quod iuvenis in sinu haberet, et sibi promissam dimidiam partem bonorum, si illud marito porrexisset. Intravit ad caecum pater interrogavitque an haec vera essent; ille negavit. Exquisivit et invenit in sinu venenum, interrogavit cui parasset; ille tacuit. Recessit pater et mutato testamento novercam fecit heredem. Eadem nocte strepitus in domo fuit: intravit familia in cubiculum domini, invenit ipsum occisum et[3] novercam iuxta cadaver dormienti similem, caecum in limine cubiculi sui stantem, gladium eius sub pulvino cruentatum. Accusant se invicem caecus et noverca.

---

[1] *periit* V *usque ad 2.3.2 iudices, sed suppletur ex* v (*vd. p. lii.177*)

[2] -tit P *necnon Paris. lat. 7900A* (*vd. Kr.-Str.; 2.3.1*): -tiit *cett.*

[3] *om.* v

2

The blind man on the threshold

A young man rescued his father from their burning house. Going back to look for his mother, he failed to save her, and lost his own sight. His father introduced a stepmother for him. One day she went to her husband. She said that poison which the young man had in his pocket[1] was intended for him, and that she had been offered half the estate if she administered it to her husband. The father went to the blind man and asked if this was true; he said it was not. He made a search, and found poison in his son's pocket. He asked him whom he had intended it for; he gave no answer. The father went away, changed his will, and made the stepmother his heir. The same night there was uproar in the house. The household staff went into their master's bedroom and found him murdered, the stepmother at the corpse's side, apparently asleep, the blind man standing on the threshold of his own bedroom, his sword, stained with blood, under the pillow. The blind man and the stepmother accuse each other.

[1] Literally, a "fold" produced by the looping of the toga, which could be used as a pocket.

1. Sentio, iudices, pudori iuvenis, pro quo minimum est quod parricida non est, gravissimum videri quod absolvendus est contra novercam, et plurimum caeco de reverentia deperire⁴ virtutum, cum in patrocinium⁵ summae pietatis

2 affertur⁶ quicquid defenderet alium innocentem. Hoc primum itaque publicis allegamus affectibus, quod pro se reus indignatur uti corporis probatione: solus omnium non remittit sibi ut incredibilior sit in parricidio caecus, quam

3 fuit cum videret. Homo omnium, quos umquam miseros fecere virtutes, innocentissimus, parricidium negavit ante quam pater occideretur, et—ne quid hodiernae sollicitudini praestari putetis—fecit quod est summum in rebus

4 humanis nefas ne vel in alio crederetur. Ignoscite, per fidem, quod indignatur se iuvenis in honorem tantum calamitatis absolvi: filium, qui patrem ex incendio sua caeci-

---

⁴ repe- B (*corr.* B²): pe- M ACD P
⁵ -ium 5: -io *codd.*: -ia *Hâk.*
⁶ aff- v M² J S²: auf- (auff- M) *cett.*

---

² Cf. Introduction to *DM* 1, n. 1.

³ I.e., far more can be said in his favor beyond the negative point that he did not kill his father. Cf. 16.1.1 and 18.1.1.

⁴ The mere fact that she is accusing a *blind* person means that *she* is the culprit: for "whoever brings a counteraccusation against a blind man is the only guilty party" (2.1.5) (AS).

⁵ I.e., his blindness, referred to below as "his physical condition" and "his misfortune."

⁶ I.e., someone as innocent as him, but not as strikingly virtuous. The two points raised in this sentence are dealt with in reverse order (the woman's position from 2.1.5).

DECLAMATION 2

(Speech of the son's advocate)[2]

1. I am aware, judges, that to an honorable young man, the *least* point in whose favor is that he is not a parricide,[3] it is highly distressing that if he is acquitted it must be at the expense of his stepmother,[4] and that a great deal of respect for his virtues is lost to a blind man, when to defend his supreme filial affection he has to adduce something[5] that might defend another innocent person.[6] (2) We accordingly first bring before public opinion the consideration that the defendant thinks it improper to use in his defense proof based on his physical condition:[7] alone of all men, he does not grant it as a point in his own favor that, in a case of parricide, he is a less plausible suspect now that he is blind than he was when he could see. (3) A man, most innocent of all whom their own virtues have ever made unhappy, showed himself not to be a parricide *before* his father was killed:[8] indeed—in case you think that allowance is being made for his present jeopardy—,[9] he made the worst sin in the world incredible even of another.[10] (4) Forgive the young man, I beg you, for not deigning to be acquitted solely out of consideration for his misfortune; it is an outrage, for a son who saved his father at the cost of

---

[7] Yet cf. 2.9.1–5, 2.13.1–4.

[8] By rescuing his father when their house was burning.

[9] I.e., that the claims for his character are being exaggerated for the occasion.

[10] Son's bravery "made it hard to credit, in the face of so shining an example of filial devotion, that *any* son could be guilty of this most monstrous of all crimes" (Shackleton Bailey [1976a], 74).

tate servavit, facinus est hoc tantum innocentem videri,
quod illum non potuerit occidere.

5   Nam quod ad mulierem, iudices, pertinet, quae defendi non potest, nisi[7] patrem caecus occidit, tam impu-
dentem delationis necessitatem malo, quam si tantum
negaret. Viderit qui fiduciam veritatis putat, quod caeco
facinus obiectum est: deprehensa mulieris audacia est,
quod non potest nisi incredibilium comparatione defendi;
6 et quisquis caecum invicem accusat, solus est reus. Aliae,
iudices, esse debuerunt adversus hanc debilitatem probationes: caecus in parricidio non debet suspectus fieri, sed
deprehendi.

    2. Quaeso itaque, iudices, ut haec prima pro causa[8]
iuvenis putetis, quae contra illum nimia sunt. Nihil magis
debet esse pro caeco, quam quod adversus illum fuerunt
multa fingenda; et constat de pietate, de innocentia homi-
2 nis, qui expugnandus fuit parricidii similitudine. Congesta
sunt adversus miseram debilitatem ferrum, cruor, venenum et quicquid non potest esse negligentiae nisi nesci-
entis. Nemo, iudices, nemo diligentior debet esse ad facinus, quam qui parricidium potuit facere caecus.

---

    [7] nisi ς: si *codd.*
    [8] pro causa *Helm*^{2} *89–90* (propterea pro causa *Sch.*): propter
causam *codd.*

---

    [11] Contrast the *argumentum*, 2.3.1 and 2.23.4, where it is as-
serted that Son lost his sight while attempting to save his mother,
after rescuing his father.
    [12] Because it lays bare the flimsiness of her case.

his own sight,[11] to be thought innocent only on the ground that he was incapable of killing his father.

(5) Now as far, judges, as concerns the woman, who cannot be defended unless a blind son killed his father, in my view her having no alternative but to bring so shameless an accusation is preferable[12] to her merely denying the charge. Good luck to anyone who thinks it brings support to the truth that a blind man has been charged with the crime. No, the woman's own effrontery has been laid bare, for she cannot be defended except by a supply of impossibilities; and whoever brings a counteraccusation against a blind man is the only guilty party. (6) Other proofs, judges, ought to have been brought against one so handicapped; in a case of parricide a blind man should not be a suspect: he should be caught in the act.[13]

2. So I ask you, judges, to regard as prime points in favor of the young man the all too many elements against him. Nothing ought to speak more loudly *for* the blind man than the fact that so much had to be fabricated *against* him—despite there being no doubt of the filial affection, of the innocence of a man who had to be defeated by being cast in the role of parricide. (2) Against this poor disabled man have been amassed sword, blood, poison and everything that cannot be the result of negligence—unless on the part of someone unaware. No one, judges, no one ought to be more careful in planning a crime than a man who was capable of committing parricide despite being blind.

[13] Cf. Cic. *Rosc. Am.* 68, *Haec magnitudo maleficii facit ut, nisi paene manifestum parricidium proferatur, credibile non sit.*

3   Iuvenis iste, de quo summa in rebus humanis monstra
finguntur, eius fuit erga parentes semper affectus, quem
nefas est optare de liberis: cum domus ignium saepta vio-
lentia rapuisset miseris senibus omne praesidium, illa festinatione qua fugimus, erumpimus, in medium cucurrit
4 incendium. In quanto tunc periculo fuit[9] rerum natura,
pietas![10] Dum diu multumque attonitus haeret, dum ad
utrumque respicit, ad utrumque discurrit, paene infelicis-
5 simos parentes perdidit pietatis aequalitas. Ut deinde
miserrimos senes cluserat iam propior ignis (audiat licet
invita pietas), patrem iuvenis elegit, et de pariter ardentibus vices disposuit affectus. Vixdum posito sene, cum
illum quoque miraremur[11] explicitum, iterum flammas
aperuit, et undique coeuntis incendii redditus globis arse-
rat iuvenis, si tardius perdidisset oculos. 3. Facinus est,
iudices, non hoc quoque maximis contigisse conatibus, ut
servaretur et mater; minus tamen in utroque fecerat, nisi
perdidisset oculos. Viderint, qui filium in eo magis parente
mirantur, in cuius salutem faciem vultusque consumpsit:

9 fuisti *Wint. ap. Kr.-Str.*
10 -ra, pi- *Håk.* 27–28: -rae pi- *codd.*   11 -entur *Sch.*

---

14 Because of the tragic consequence that this extraordinary
love had for Son. Alternatively, *nefas est optare* = "it would be too
much to hope for . . ." (the affection of this youth exceeds what a
parent should normally wish for).

15 Generalizing: normal people faced with such a contingency.
Cf. Sen. *Ben.* 4.32.4.

16 The old man (as opposed to both).

17 If he had not been blinded, he would have gone on to certain death. Cf. 2.24.2.

(3) This young man, concerning whom the most monstrous acts in the world are being fabricated, had always had feelings toward his parents which it is wrong to pray for in one's children.[14] When the house, cut off by the violence of the fire, had left the unfortunate old people no chance of saving themselves, he hurried into the midst of the conflagration as hastily as we[15] try to make our escape. (4) In what great danger then was his innate filial affection! While he stood there for a long time frozen, quite dumbfounded, while he looked toward both in turn, ran toward both in turn, his equal love for his most unlucky parents came near to destroying them both. (5) Then, when the fire, ever closer, had cut off the wretched old persons, the young man—let his filial feelings listen to this, however unwillingly!—chose his father: affection established an order between the two of them, equally ablaze as they were. He had scarce set down the old man, and we were still astonished that even he[16] had been saved, when the young man for a second time plunged into the flames—and engulfed again in the converging balls of fire, he would have been burned to death if he had not been blinded first.[17] 3. It is outrageous, judges, that his supreme effort was not rewarded by his mother being saved too. But he would have done less in respect of both if he had not lost his sight.[18] Admire, if you like, the son more in respect of the parent[19] in trying to save whom he ruined face and coun-

[18] He would have done less in respect of Mother if he had failed to rescue her, and thus kept his sight; he would have done less in respect of Father if he had not lost his sight while attempting to rescue Father's wife too.

[19] Mother.

patri praestitit caecitatem, qui amisit oculos dum repetit quam reliquerat matrem.

2   Non expectatis,[12] certum habeo, iudices, ut[13] excusem quod pater induxit caeco novercam; factum est eo tempore, quo constabat patrem filio senem solvendo non esse. Contenderim quin immo iuvenis fuisse consilium ut pater, cui matrimonium filiumque abstulerat incendium, residua senectutis alia consolaretur uxore, et ut domus, quae caecum tantum habebat et senem, acciperet ex coniugio 3 ministeria custodita. Facinus est, iudices, quod bonos privignos novercae facilius decipiunt, nec levius oderunt. Quam multis insidiis, quam multis artibus patet caecitas 4 innocentis! Mulier, cui spem invadendae hereditatis praestabat debilitas privigni, senectus mariti, intellexit hoc solum deesse sceleris occasioni, ut prius infamaretur parricidii caecus. Viso igitur hoc, quod sibi iuvenis non videbatur esse privignus, venenum quod in miseri sinu abdiderat deprehensura, nuntiavit patri tamquam parrici- 5 dium pararetur. Et quia mendacium poterat facile nudari, si quem conscium nominasset, totam delationem sic ordinavit, ut sibi crederetur promissam dimidiam partem bonorum, si venenum seni voluisset ipsa porrigere.

---

[12] -tetis B v^{ac}, sed vd. Kr.-Str.   [13] hinc incipit V

---

[20] Son was trying to save Mother's life, but he was doing so for Father's sake (i.e., so that he would not lose his wife). Therefore, blindness also is a sacrifice he offered to Father.   [21] He was too old to look after him without the help of a new wife.

[22] And not Father's.   [23] Son is not dead; but see 2.9.1.

[24] But as a beloved son who would not suspect her.

[25] The speaker assumes here that Stepmother finds the poison on the youth; in 2.4.4, the youth himself searches his garments—

tenance; but it was to his *father* that he presented the gift of his blindness: he lost his eyes when he went back for the mother he had left behind.[20]

(2) You do not expect me, I am sure, judges, to find excuses for my father bringing home a stepmother for his blind son. It happened at a time when it was obvious that the father, old as he was, could not repay his debt to his son.[21] Indeed I should contend that it was the young man's plan[22] that a father, whom fire had robbed of his spouse and his son,[23] should console his remaining years by taking a second wife, and that the household, which consisted only of a blind man and an old man, should gain from the partnership someone to control the servants. (3) It is disgraceful, judges, that stepmothers deceive good stepsons more easily, without hating them any less virulently. How many plots, how many tricks, is a naive blind man exposed to! (4) The woman, presented with the chance to take over the inheritance by the handicap to her stepson and the old age of her husband, saw that all that was lacking to her opportunity for crime was to have the blind man blackened as a parricide in advance. Seeing, therefore, that the young man did not think of himself as a stepson,[24] she hid in the poor man's pocket poison which she was going to find on him,[25] and told the father of it, making it seem that parricide was being planned. (5) And because a lie could easily be uncovered if she gave the name of an accomplice, she organized the whole accusation like this: she was to be believed to have been promised half the estate if she agreed to administer the poison to the old man personally.

urged by Stepmother—until he finds the poison. The theme, however, suggests that Father confronts Son alone and finds the poison himself.

4. Videtis, iudices, qua praeparatione noverca ad testamentum patris accesserit: mulierem, quam credit maritus noluisse partem bonorum accipere pro scelere, necesse

2 est sic remuneret, ut faciat heredem. O quanto aliter probatur parricidium, quod iam potest deprehendi! Mulier, quae se dicebat in conscientiam sceleris admissam, non hoc primum exegit a patre, ut quaereret quis parasset caeco venenum, quis dedisset: unde[14] maximum sciebat posse fieri quaestionis errorem, instituit ut innocentissimus iuvenis interrogaretur repente, subito, infamatura velut deprehensi trepidationem,[15] seu tacuisset caecus,

3 seu negasset. Adductus ad filium senex dixit iuveni quicquid audierat. Numquam, iudices, tam simplicis innocentiae fuit facinus negare; non esset ausus iuvenis coram ea muliere mentiri, quae prodidit et sciit ubi esset vene-

4 num. Ut vero sensit infelix instantem novercam postulantemque ut sinus iuvenis exquireretur, tunc vero attonitus, haerens, et tota malorum suorum cogitatione confusus, intellexit hoc argumentum eius esse, quae parasset, ut posset deprehendi; igitur propere, festinanter omnia membra pertractans, et mersis in sinum manibus, dum cuncta suspicionibus, dum tactu iuvenis explorat, venenum primus invenit. 5. Laudo, iudices, innocentiam silentii, laudo fiduciam, quod interrogatus cui parasset non

---

[14] unde Ⴝ: inde *codd.*   [15] -ne B V

---

[26] I.e., it will be easy to prove parricide, now that the scheme of catching the culprit in the act has been thought up.

[27] Cf. 18.1.1.   [28] To her husband.

[29] The poison.   [30] Because of his confusion.

[31] Cf. n. 25.

4. You see, judges, the way the stepmother made her preparations to arrive at a place in the father's will: if a woman has, her husband believes, refused to take part of his property in exchange for a crime, he will have to reward her by making her his heir. (2) O how differently is parricide proved, when it can now be caught in the act![26] The woman, who (she said) had been made party to the crime, did not begin by requiring the father to investigate who had made up the poison for the blind man, who had given it to him; she arranged instead—knowing that this could throw the investigation completely off track—that the totally innocent young man should be questioned at once, without warning: her plan was to put in a bad light the consternation of one (as it seemed) caught in the act, whether the blind youth kept silent or denied the charge.[27] (3) Brought to his son, the old man told the young man all he had heard. Never, judges, was it in the power of such a straightforward and innocent person to deny a crime; the youth would not have dared to lie in the presence of the woman who told the story,[28] who knew where the poison was. (4) But when the unlucky man realized that his stepmother was pressing him and demanding that his pockets should be turned out, then indeed, thunderstruck and at a loss, and confused at the thought of all his misfortunes, he realized that this incriminating evidence[29] was the work of the woman who had procured it so that it could be found out. So[30] hurriedly, in haste, the young man[31] felt all over his body and plunged his hands in his pockets; exploring everywhere suspiciously, by touch, he was first to find the poison. 5. I applaud, judges, the innocence proved by his silence, I commend his self-confidence:

putavit sibi defendendum venenum. Rem quin immo fecit
eius, qui sciret patrem non crediturum, et, quae maxima
est innocentiae contumacia, persuasionem senis nulla vo-
2 luit excusatione corrumpere. Non fuit illud trepidatio, non
tacita confessio: quisquis habet venenum, habet et quod
respondeat deprehensus.

3   Fecit post haec senex rem hominis, quem non movisset
quicquid invenerat. Non torsit ministeria caeci, et de scelere, in quo solus nocens esse parricida non poterat, non
explicuit ordinem quaestionis, sed, quod plus est quam
4 absolvere, remisit iuveni defensionem. Utrum deinde
intellectis deterrimae mulieris insidiis filium paulisper
voluerit exheredatione protegere, et, diligentius de patrimonio suo deliberaturus, interim captaverit ut videretur
mulieris cupiditati iam non obstare privignus, an facillimum fuerit[16] ut exheredationem quoque impetraret
noverca caeci ab homine cui tam multa persuaserat, cogi-
5 tationibus vestris relinquo; hoc tantum dixisse contentus
sum: testamentum continuo mutavit, et—ne quis miretur
hanc festinationem—statim subsecutum est ut periret. An
interfuerit, iudices, iuvenis huius ut viveret pater, qui iam
alio moriebatur herede, vos aestimabitis; non interfuit ut
occideretur.

---

16 fuerit ς (vd. Kr.-Str.): fuit codd.

---

32 Sc., in his supposed guilt.
33 That he was innocent: for "qui s'excuse s'accuse."
34 So Son's silence shows he is innocent (DAR).
35 I.e., the disposal of it.
36 An alternative reason for the sudden disinheritance.
37 Sarcastic.

when asked for whom he had prepared the poison, he did not think he needed to justify it. Rather, he acted like someone who knew his father would not believe:[32] he refused—something that shows at its height the obstinacy typical of an innocent man—to upset the old man's settled view[33] by offering any excuse. (2) That was not consternation, not a tacit confession: anyone who has poison in his possession also has a reply to offer if he is caught.[34]

(3) After this, the old man acted like a man quite unaffected by what he had found. He did not torture the blind man's servants, and, though this was a crime where the parricide could not have been the only guilty party, he did not go through the normal interrogatory procedure; instead—and this is something that is more than an acquittal—he let the young man off defending himself. (4) Following on that, he perhaps saw through the machinations of this most wicked woman, wanted to protect his son for a short while by disinheriting him, and, intending to think more carefully about his estate,[35] aimed in the meantime at preventing the stepson from being thought any longer to be an obstacle to the woman's cupidity. Alternatively,[36] it was perfectly simple for the blind man's stepmother to win the young man's disinheritance from a man with whom she had been so often influential in the past. I leave *you* to reflect on these possibilities. (5) All I will say is this: he altered his will on the spot, and—in case this haste causes surprise[37]— his death followed close upon it. It is for you to weigh up, judges, whether it was in this young man's interest that his father should go on living, considering that he had a new heir already when he died; for sure, it was *not* in his interest that he should be *killed*.

6. Facinus, iudices, quod illa nocte in cubiculo novercae, quod in lectulo factum est, domus tota sensit, nemo
non sibi visus est iuxta fuisse; excitari sola noverca non
potuit, illo loco unde venerat fragor! Concurrit familia quo
sollicitos atque trepidantis ducebat strepitus quem seque-
bantur: invenerunt senem occisum, novercam iuxta cadaver sic iacentem, ne statim possent interrogare quis occi-
2 disset. Nuntiatum est deinde facinus et caeco: inventus
est—quod innocentiae sufficit—non a scelere rediens,
stans[17] in limine cubiculi sui, animo quo discurrebant vi-
dentes. Ut deinde ferrum iuvenis inquireretur, exegit ea-
3 dem utique quae postulaverat de veneno. Quod in lectulo
gladius cruentatus inventus est, non deprecor, iudices,
quin contra caecitatem non minus argumentum putetis
quam quod inveniri potuit venenum.[18] In parricidii suspicione gladius cruentatus novissima probatio debet esse,
non sola.
4 Ignoscite, magnorum[19] periculorum metus, ignoscite,
humana discrimina:[20] defensionem iuvenis lacrimis primum gemituque prosequimur. Perdidit infelix patrem,
perdidit [et][21] caecitas illum senem, cuius oscula, cuius
amplexum imponebat vulneribus oculorum, cui praesta-

[17] ‹sed› stans *Håk.*[2] *28–29, at vd. Kr.-Str.*
[18] *dist. Håk.*[2] *29*   [19] magno- *Sch.*: malo- *codd.* (*def. Leh.*[1]
420–21 utpote substant.)
[20] ignoscite—discrimina *dist. et interpr. Str.*[12] *32–33, cf. Kr.-
Str.*   [21] *del. Håk.*

[38] She was deliberately acting like this, to avoid being questioned and let all suspicion fall on the stepson at the discovery of
the sword.

6. Judges, the whole house was aware of the crime that took place that night in the stepmother's bedroom, in her *bed*: everyone had the impression they were close at hand. Only the stepmother could not be roused—and in the very place the noise had come from. The whole household ran to where the fracas they were tracking down led them, anxious and confused. They found the old man murdered, the stepmother lying by the corpse in a condition that made it impossible for them to ask her straight away who the killer had been.[38] (2) Next, the crime was reported to the blind man too. He was found (proof enough of his innocence) not on his way back from the crime, but standing at the threshold[39] of his bedroom, no less perturbed than the sighted people scurrying around. After this, a search for the sword was demanded, of course, by the same woman who had insisted on the search for the poison. (3) As to the discovery of the young man's sword in his bed, covered in blood, I do beg you, judges, to think this no more telling a proof that the blind man was responsible than the finding of the poison. When parricide is suspected, a bloodied sword ought to be the final proof, not the only one.

(4) Forgive me, fears of great dangers, forgive me, hazards of human life, if I begin the young man's defense with tears and groans.[40] An unlucky boy has lost his father, a blind son has lost the old man whose kisses, whose embrace he kept pressing to his wounded eyes, for whose

[39] A possible reminiscence of Verg. *Aen.* 2.485, *armatos . . . vident stantis in limine primo.*

[40] = Forgive me if I use pathos before argument, despite the dangers the young man is facing. Conversely, cf. 2.23.1.

5 bat caecus ut viveret. Misera ignorantia,[22] misera debilitas,
quod te noverca non sic potius decipere maluit, ut biberes
venenum!

7. Facinus est, iudices, comparationem fieri, utri credibilius[23] sit parricidium. Idem vos putatis efficere noctium merita et affectus osculis blanditiisque quaesitos
2 quod natalium pignorumque reverentiam?[24] Nullas ego
facilius perire crediderim quam corporum caritates, et,
licet matrimoniis paulatim reverentia gravitatis accedat,
possunt tamen distrahi facilitate qua coeunt. Uxor est
quam iungit, quam diducit utilitas, cuius haec sola reve-
3 rentia est, quod videtur inventa causa liberorum. Aspici-
mus matrimoniorum singula momenta rixantia: mutant
cotidie domos et per amplexus lectulosque discurrunt.
Placet etiam post liberos alius maritus, et, unde deprehen-
das omnium scelerum facilitatem, possunt non amare ‹per
4 se›[25] viventes. Quid, si huic uxoriae vilitati novercale nomen adiungas? Mulieri, quae post liberos inducitur, matri-
monii non contingit[26] tota reverentia.

8. Quanto alios praestat affectus diligere vitae, lucis
auctorem! Liberi ac parentis non alius mihi videtur affec-

---

[22] innocentia M² A, *sed vd. Kr.-Str.*   [23] utri *Dess.¹ 95,*
credibilius *Håk.* (-le *Dess.¹ 95; cf. 2.16.4*): ut incredibile *codd.*
[24] -am *Håk.*: -as *codd.*   [25] *add. Str.⁷ 300–301*
[26] -igit B V AC P

---

[41] Of the plots against you.   [42] For you would have
avoided being accused of killing Father.
[43] On this commonplace cf., e.g., Ov. *Ars am.* 2.153; Juv.
6.268–69.

sake the blind man went on living. (5) Pitiful your ignorance,[41] pitiful your disability: if only your stepmother had
chosen to trick *you* into drinking poison instead![42]

7. It is outrageous, judges, for a comparison to be conducted as to who is the more likely murderer. Do you think
that the same weight attaches to nocturnal favors and affection sought by kisses and endearments as to the reverence owed to blood relatives? (2) I am inclined to think
that no fondness perishes more easily than the physical:
though respect for their important status gradually ac-
crues to married women, they are capable of getting separated as easily as they unite in matrimony. A wife is someone whom *expediency* weds to a man and divorces from
him, and she commands respect only in so far as matrimony seems to have been instituted for the sake of children. (3) We see married women quarreling all the time;[43]
they change houses from one day to another, skipping
around from embrace to embrace and bed to bed.[44] Even
after children have arrived, another husband takes their
fancy, and—something that enables you to detect women's
liability to commit any crime—they are capable of not
loving those who owe their life ⟨to them⟩.[45] (4) Wives are
thus low enough on the scale anyway: what if you add in
the name of stepmother? A woman brought on the scene
after children have been born does *not* command the absolute respect accorded to marriage.

8. How much greater than other emotions is love for
the author of one's life, of one's seeing the light! Love
between child and parent is in my view identical with that

44 Cf. Juv. 6.224–30.
45 Cf. Juv. 6.638–42.

tus quam quo rerum natura, quo mundus ipse constrictus
est. Quisquamne mortalium confodiet illud sacrum
venerandumque corpus, quod potest ex ignibus rapi, pro
2 quo bene consumuntur oculi? Non invenio, iudices,
quemadmodum possit esse citra[27] liberos salva reverentia:
non est difficile ut maritum uxor occidat, si non est difficilius ut filius patrem.
3   Non est, iudices, quod putetis inter mulierem et virum
de scelere quaeri, neque est quod se noverca sexus occa-
4 sione tueatur; maior est caecitatis infirmitas. Sunt et feminis ad scelera vires, cum habent causas virorum.[28] Quin
immo, si interroges, facilius haec pectora metus, odium,
ira corrumpunt, et, quoniam non habent roboris tantum,
unde vitia mentium vincant, plerumque facinus infirmi-
5 tate fecerunt. Sane tamen illis sceleribus sufficere non
possint, quae discursum, quae exigunt laborem; quod vero
tam muliebre possis invenire facinus quam occidere hominem iuxta te iacentem, aggredi senem, qui se tuis crediderit amplexibus, cuius somnos ipsa disponas, ipsa custo-
6 dias? Omnis alius percussor deprehendi potest antequam
feriat; uxor non sentitur, nisi dum occidit. Non est, iudices,
incredibile ut occiderit mulier hominem, quem dicitur
potuisse caecus occidere.
    9. Facinus est, iudices, si caecos habere non credimus
nisi necessitatis innocentiam. Prima est infirmitas caecita-

---

27 citra *Sh. B.*[2] *190*: contra *codd.*
28 -sas, vi- *dist. Håk., sed vd. Kr.-Str.*

---

46 = Killing your father is far more unnatural than killing your
husband.   47 I.e., than the weakness of a woman.
48 *Robur* is here moral strength: women are not strong enough

which binds together the world, the universe itself. Will any mortal stab that sacred and revered body, which can be rescued from fire, for the sake of which eyes are gloriously sacrificed? (2) I do not find, judges, how there can be true respect except from children: it is not difficult for wife to kill husband—but only if it is not more difficult for son to kill father.[46]

(3) You should not think, judges, that in identifying the criminal the choice lies between woman and man, nor should the stepmother look for defense to the accident of her sex; the handicap of blindness is greater.[47] (4) Women too have the strength to commit crimes, when they have the motives men have. Indeed, if you put the question, fear, hate, anger corrupt these breasts more easily, and since women do not have the strength to overcome their vices, they often do wrong out of weakness.[48] (5) Of course, though, they cannot measure up to crimes that require great activity, that demand hardship; but what crime could be found more womanly than to kill a man lying by your side, to assault an old man who has surrendered himself to your embraces, whose hours of sleep you yourself regulate, you yourself keep watch over? (6) Every other killer can be detected before he strikes a blow; a wife is only felt while she is killing. It is not incredible, judges, that a woman should have killed a man whom a blind man is said to have been capable of killing.

9. It is wicked, judges, to believe that the blind are innocent only out of necessity. The foremost disability of a

morally/mentally to resist emotions, so they may do wrong things because of this aspect of their general infirmity (DAR). We pass to physical capabilities in the next sentence.

tis ut nolit. Fallitur, quisquis hanc calamitatem non animorum putat esse, sed corporum: totius hominis debilitas est
oculos perdidisse, et, si diligenter actus intuearis huma-
2 nos, ministeria luminum sumus. Caecus non irascitur, non
odit, non concupiscit, et, cum corpora nostra vigorem de
luminibus accipiant, pereunt cum suis vitia causis. En ad
quod erumpant manus, quae proxima quaeque tamdiu
quaerunt, manus, quae sua quoque ministeria non ex-
3 plicant! Audebit quicquam corpus illud, quod ad singulos
sibi videtur decidere motus, cui quicquid ante se est,
donec exploretur, abruptum est? Facinus admittet in quo
nihil ipse facturus est, facinus quod totum credat alio?[29]
4 Quid, si caecitas sit quam fecerint ignes? Nemo in incendio solos ex homine perdit oculos: tunc facies sentit
incendium, cum ambusti defecere gressus, cum opponi
non possunt pro oculis manus, et ad lumina nostra flam-
5 mas omnium membrorum vulneribus[30] admittimus. Caecum vel hoc faciet innocentem, quod licet viribus, licet
sufficiat audacia, non habet persuasionem hominis qui
possit imponere.

10. Nefas est, iudices, hunc iuvenem reliquarum debi-
litatium ratione defendi; quam incredibile est ut occiderit
2 patrem, qui pati non potuit ut perderet! Rogo, quid opus
gladio, quid veneno parricidae? Quantulum fuit potius
servare matrem! "Rapiatur ex parentibus illa infirmior, illa

---

29 alio V (*cf. Leu. 480*): alio (*eraso tamen puncto, ut vid.*) B:
alii Φ   30 <confecti> vul- *Wint. ap. Kr.-Str.*

---

49 According to the other side.
50 Cf. 2.1.1: this would not do justice to the filial affection he
has so heroically shown.

blind man is that he lacks will. It is wrong to think this misfortune affects the body only and not the mind: it is a handicap to the whole person to have lost one's eyes, for if you look carefully at human actions you will see that we are the slaves of our sight. (2) A blind man does not grow angry, does not hate, does not feel lust, and just as our bodies receive their strength from their eyes, so their vices perish along with what causes them. Behold what a bold exploit[49] hands may strive for that have to explore everything around them for such a time, hands that cannot even carry out all their own natural functions! (3) Will a man allow his body to venture on anything when he thinks he may fall down at every move he makes, when everything in front of him is a precipice until his touch explores it? Will he commit a crime in which he will not be able to do anything on his own, a crime which he must leave entirely to another? (4) What if the blindness was caused by fire? In a conflagration no one loses only his eyes out of his whole person: his face feels the flames only when his feet have been roasted and refuse to carry him forward, when he cannot put his hands up to shield his eyes—so that we take the flames in our eyes after *all* our limbs have been injured. (5) Even this will make a blind man innocent: he may possess strength enough, boldness enough, but he does not have the self-confidence that marks a man capable of deceiving.

10. It is quite wrong, judges, for this youth to be defended in the same way as other blind people.[50] How incredible it is that someone who could not bear to lose his father should have killed him! (2) Why, I ask, did the murderer need a sword, need poison? How simple a matter to save his mother instead! "Out of the parents let the woman,

77

peritura." Parricidium sic facere potuisti, ut optimus filius
videreris.

3   Quantum deinde putatis impatientissimis affectibus
accessisse? Post caecitatem carior est pater, cum in locum
successit oculorum, et tunc est infinita pietas, cum in illa

4   debeas amare quod feceris. Quid dicitis, iudices? Trans-
feret in facinus hunc caecitatis suae iuvenis favorem, ad
quem cotidie laudatura civitas coit, cui assident omnes
liberi, omnes parentes? Faciet se pariter pietatis et sceleris exemplum? Facilius est ut occidas patrem a quo sis ipse
servatus.

5   Nullius umquam, iudices, parricidii magis debuistis
excutere causas. "Cupiditas" inquit "iuvenem egit in facinus." Hoc si credibile, si verum est, debet videri, mulier
heres maritum an patrem caecus exheredatus occiderit.

6   Habeant sane, iudices, hanc nefariae cupiditatis festinationem, quos vitiorum ardor, quos cotidie luxuria praecipitat;

7   quo caeco hereditatem vel innocenti?[31] Oculi sunt, oculi,
per quos paupertatem ferre non possumus, oculi tota nostra luxuria. Hi nos in omnia cotidie vitia praecipitant:

---

31 -ti ς: -tem *codd.*

---

51 An imaginary comment by the youth.

52 Had he saved only his *mother* from the fire, the youth would
have been praised for his heroism, and at the same time would
have achieved his alleged purpose of getting the father out of the
way.

53 Once he had saved Father at the cost of his own eyes, Son
could not help but love him yet more than before.

54 Sc., than one you have yourself saved (DAR).

55 A blind man has no reason to wish for an—albeit legiti-

the weaker partner, the one more likely to die, be res-cued!"[51] You *could* have committed parricide in such a way as to be thought to be the best of sons.[52]

(3) How much do you think his fondness increased after that—passionate though it already was? Since his blinding, his father is yet dearer to him, now that he has come to fill the place of his eyes: filial affection becomes boundless precisely when you are to love what you have performed out of it.[53] (4) What do you say, judges? Will the young man turn the favor accorded to his blindness into blame for a crime, this man to whom each day the city comes in force to sing his praises, at whose side sit all children, all parents in attendance? Will he make himself into a paradigm equally of devotion and of crime? It is easier to kill a father by whom you have yourself been saved.[54]

(5) You were never obliged, judges, to inquire into the motives for a parricide more carefully than in this case. "Greed," she says, "led the young man into crime." If this is credible, if it is true, we need to ask whether a woman killed her husband when she was in line to inherit the estate, or a blind man killed his father after being disin-herited. (6) Yes, judges, let those hurry into a wicked greed who are driven over the brink by the fire of their vices, by their daily indulgence in luxury. But a blind man, what will an inheritance mean to him, even if he is innocent?[55] (7) It is the eyes, yes the eyes that make us unable to bear poverty, eyes are the whole of our thirst for luxury. It is they who plunge us each day into every vice: it is they

---

mate—inheritance, as he cannot even see it (cf. 1.17.4): why should he go as far as to commit a crime to obtain it?

8 mirantur, adamant, concupiscunt. Facilius impleas animi
satietatem. Quo, per fidem, divitias iuveni, apud quem
omnium rerum diversitas perît?[32] Circumdes licet hanc
debilitatem fulgore, divitiis, caeco tamen tunc magis
cuncta desunt, cum contigerunt, nec invenias debilitatem,
9 cui magis cum paupertate conveniat. Homo in honorem
parentum excaecatus patrimonio sub patre melius utetur.

11. Et quod, per fidem, parricidii genus iuvenis elegit?
"Venenum" inquit "paravit." Cur, per fidem, si sufficit
ferro,[33] facinus adgreditur cui adhibere conscium, cui
praestare debeat ministrum, cum maius[34] habere possit in
2 gladio parricida secretum? An postea iuveni succurrit quid
possent facere manus, et se circa venenum deprehensa
debilitas collegit in vires? Nemo, iudices, nemo nescit
quemadmodum possit occidere.

3 Intellexit, iudices, noverca quam incredibile esset ut
videretur caecus parasse venenum; igitur adiecit temptatam se ut illud ipsa porrigeret. Date, per fidem, iudices,
invenite[35] verba. Secreto privignus et noverca de parrici-
4 dio loquuntur: ita se non putet[36] uterque temptari? Quid
dicitis, iudices? Nullumne tota domo, quod corrumperet,
aliud parricida pectus invenit? Difficilius hoc credas no-

[32] -iit *Helm*² 91, *sed vd. Kr.-Str.*
[33] *dist. B. Asc.*²: *ante* ferro *vulg.*
[34] magis V J   [35] -ite B V γ δ (*damn. Hâk., sed vd. Sh. B.*⁴
190 et Kr.-Str.): -it β
[36] -tet M: -tetur B: -tat V Φ

---

[56] Cf. 1.6.7.
[57] Those that passed between them.

which feel amazement, they which fall in love, they which feel lust.[56] (8) You would find it easier to satisfy your *mind*. What, I ask you, do riches mean to a young man to whom everything now looks the same? Surround though you may with gleaming riches someone so handicapped, a blind man lacks everything the more when he has got everything: you could not find a bodily impairment that is on better terms with poverty. (9) A man who has lost his sight for the sake of his parents will use his patrimony better while he is under the tutelage of his father.

11. And what type of murder did the young man choose, I ask you? "He got poison ready," she says. Why for goodness sake, if he is up to using a sword, does he enter on a crime where he has to bring in an accomplice, provide a helper, given that a parricide can find greater secrecy in a sword? (2) Or did it occur to the young man only later what his hands could do: did this weak and handicapped man summon up his physical strength only after he was caught in possession of poison? No one, judges, no one is ignorant of the way he can commit murder.

(3) The stepmother, judges, realized what an implausible idea it was that a blind man employed poison; so she added that she had been sounded out to see if she would administer it herself. I ask you, judges, produce us, find for us the words.[57] Stepson and stepmother are talking about parricide in private: in such circumstances should not *both* parties be conscious that they are being tested? (4) What do you say, judges? In all the household did the murderer find no one else to corrupt?[58] If you reckon you

---

[58] I.e., to persuade to support his evil plan.

5 vercae, si te a nullo alio putes impetraturum. Non ergo
iuvenis credit hanc[37] omnia[38] loqui cum patre, omnium
blanditiarum primum esse sermonem? Novercam timeas
<nec>[39] negantem. Non habet fidem ei credere parrici-
dium, quem scias proditurum, nisi impetraveris.

12. Per fidem, iudices, diligenter attendite criminis
diversitatem: temptatam se in parricidii conscientiam[40]
mulier affirmat. Quis vero dubitet numquam hoc privig-
num fuisse facturum, si habere conscium potuisset alium?

2 "Atqui venenum iam paravit, emit." Et cum haec ipse facere non potuerit caecus, quis est iste, cui parricidii tantum instrumenta creduntur? Cur non idem porrigit seni?
Vel, si non potest decipi maritus nisi manibus uxoris, cur
ante parricidium struitur quam sciat an noverca promittat?

3 Nam, quod vult videri promissam sibi partem bonorum,
non est argumentum, nisi et ipsum probatur. Mulier, quae
sollicitatur ad facinus, quemadmodum sibi consulit ne illam parricida decipiat![41] Et probationes prospicere debuit

4 seu factura quod rogabatur, seu proditura. Adde quod neque odit novercam caecus, cui parricidium credit, neque
hereditate corrumpitur, cuius contentus est parte dimidia.
Nemo, iudices, parricidium faciet quo alius utatur.

---

[37] hanc *Sh. B.*[2] *190:* hoc *codd.*
[38] -nia *Håk.:* -nes *codd.*
[39] *add. Håk.*[2] *30:* <vel non> *B. Asc.*[2]
[40] -am *Bur.:* -a *codd.*
[41] quemadmodum—decipiat *dist. et interpr. Kr.-Str.*

---

[59] I.e., did not refuse to help.
[60] Literally, "hands."

will fail to win assent from anybody else, you'd think it harder still to entrust this to your stepmother. (5) Does the young man then not believe that she talks everything over with his father, that all intimacies start with conversation? You'd fear a stepmother ⟨even⟩ if she did not say no.[59] It is not a credible course of action to entrust a murder to someone you know will betray you if you do not win their assent.

12. I beg you, judges, listen carefully to the contradiction involved in the charge. The woman alleges that she was sounded out to take part in the parricide. But who would doubt that the stepson would never have done this if he could have found a different accomplice? (2) "Yet he had already procured, already bought poison." And since a blind man could not have done this himself, who is this person to whom only the *means* for the murder is being entrusted? Why does not this same person give it to the old man himself? Or, if the husband can only be deceived by his wife's agency,[60] why is the murder being organized before the boy knows if his stepmother will promise her help? (3) And as to the fact that she wants it to be believed that she was promised half the estate, that is no proof unless it is proved in its turn. When a woman is approached to take part in a crime, how careful she is to make sure the murderer is not double-crossing her! And she should have thought up ways of testing him in advance, whether she intended to do what he asked or to betray him. (4) Add that the blind man does not hate the stepmother (after all, he is entrusting her with his secret), and he is not influenced by thought of the inheritance, for he is content to take only half of it. No one, judges, will commit parricide for someone else to reap the benefit.

5 Exigo igitur ut istud parricidium caeci tu socia, tu conscia manifestius probes. Quid opus est ut iam venenum iuvenis habeat? Potius sermonibus vestris interpone testes: fac coram servis loquatur, fac intersint amici, fac audiat pater. Facillimum est caeci decipere secretum.

6 Utere, mulier, homine qui se commisit oculis tuis, utere membris quae regis, manibus quas moves: volo venenum ipse proferat, ipse porrigat, volo te rursus in facinus hortetur, volo plura promittat. Parricidium caeci deprehendi potest dum tibi fatetur.

13. "Sed" inquit "inventus est tenens venenum." Exiguum argumentum, noverca, de magna facilitate fecisti:

2 non accusas caecum, sed ostendis. Homo expositus ad omnem occasionem, ad omne ludibrium, quem tactus, quem proxima quaeque decipiunt, quid refert quid in sinu habeat, ille, quem deprehendere possis qualem relinquas, a quo modo noverca digressa est, cuius ordinavit vestes,

3 tetigit sinus, membra composuit? Venenum potest habere sic ut nesciat, potest sic ut aliud putet. Si mehercule volueris, tenebit et[42] palam; si iusseris, accipiet coram servulis, coram amicis; et, si venenum non dixeris,[43] hauriet, bibet.

4 Nullo magis, iudices, argumento potest innocentia cae-

---

[42] et *Håk.*: te *codd.*   [43] dixeris *Sch.* (*firm. Reitz.*[2] *39, Kr.-Str.*): diceres B V δ: dices γ β

---

[61] Before he was sure Stepmother would abet him.

[62] The first time being that "described" in the theme (*sibi promissam* eqs.). Stepmother might well have gathered evidence against the stepson, rather than just accusing him.

[63] I.e., to plant poison on him.

[64] Of tricking him.

(5) I demand then that you, his ally, you, his accomplice, should give a more convincing proof of this murderous plan. What need is there for the young man to have poison already?[61] Rather, make witnesses overhear your conversations with him, make him speak in front of servants, ensure friends are present, ensure the father hears; it is very easy to give a blind man a false sense of privacy. (6) Woman, make use of a man who has entrusted himself to your eyes, make use of limbs you control, hands you move. I want him to proffer the poison himself, administer it himself. I want him to exhort you to crime all over again.[62] I want him to make further promises. Murder planned by a blind man can be detected while he is telling you about it.

13. "But," she says, "he was found with poison on him." Your proof is trivial, stepmother, considering how easy it was![63] You are not accusing the blind man, but showing him to be blind. (2) A man open to every opportunity,[64] to all mockery, who can be deceived by a touch, by anything he encounters—what difference does it make what such a one has in his pocket, a man you may catch in the same condition as you leave him,[65] from whom his stepmother had just gone away, whose clothes she arranged, whose pockets she touched, whom she tucked up in bed?[66] (3) He can possess poison without knowing it, he can possess it—and think it to be something else. If you wish, indeed, he will hold it, and, if you tell him to, he will take it from you quite openly, in the presence of slaves, of friends; and if you do not tell him it is poison, he will drink it up. (4) The blind man's innocence can be recognized by

65 I.e., you can plant anything on him and it will still be there later.   66 All possible occasions to plant the poison.

citatis intellegi, quam quod videtur deprehensus iuvenis:
si parricida est et exquiritur, hanc saltem sibi praestabit
dissimulationem, ne teneat venenum.

5   Neminem, iudices, credo mirari quod iuvenis, interrogatus cui parasset, verba non habuit. Non fuit illud patris
indignatio, non fuit dolor: venenum iuvenis expavit. Auferunt nobis vocem quae fieri posse non credimus, et silen-
6 tium est admiratio subita miserorum. Nescit tacere deprehensorum scelerum trepidatio, et statim respondet illa
cum suo sibi scelere parata defensio: tacere facilius est
7 deceptis quam deprehensis. Quid, per fidem, facere vultis
iuvenem, quem de parricidio consulit pater ille servatus?
Miror hercule non dixisse: "Volui: sum veneficus, sum
8 parricida." Et invidiam putarem, si confessus esset. Bene
quod nescit iuvenis quemadmodum parricidium neget,
neque habet illa deprehensorum multa verba. Venenum
quod tenet caecus ipsius est, si illud excuset.

14. "Sed" inquit "exheredatus a patre est." Poteram,
iudices, secretum hoc senis profundumque vocare consilium; contra iuvenem tamen esse non debet, etiam ut de
2 parricidio crediderit novercae. Notum hoc, iudices, ac
vulgare facinus est, quod plerumque contra liberos aman-
tur uxores, et sequentium matrimoniorum non aliunde

---

[67] I.e., of the innocent.   [68] Rather than "questions": the
choice of words suggests that Father does not believe Son to be
guilty and discusses with him the charge brought by Stepmother.

[69] His being disinherited.

[70] The speaker has suggested that Father did not really believe the accusation of parricide (2.5.3–5). Now he argues that,
even supposing he believed it, he might have been influenced by
love for his wife rather than by hate for his son.

no better proof than this, that the young man was to all appearances caught out; if he is a murderer and is being searched, he will at least give himself a chance to dissimulate by not having poison on him.

(5) I imagine, judges, that no one is surprised that the young man was lost for words when he was asked whom he had got it ready for. It was not his father's anger, not his own resentment that silenced him: the blind man took fright at the poison. We lose our powers of speech when we hear of things we do not believe to be possible: silence signals the sudden amazement of the distressed.[67] (6) Someone who is scared when detected in crime is incapable of silence: a reply is forthcoming at once, in the form of an exculpation prepared at the same time as the crime was planned. It is easier for the deceived than for the detected to keep silent. (7) What, for heaven's sake, do you want the young man to do, when the father, the father he saved, consults[68] him about parricide? Heavens, I am astonished he did not say: "I wished it, I am a poisoner, I am a parricide"; and if he *had* confessed it would, I think, have been because he had taken offense. (8) It is a good sign that the young man doesn't know how to deny killing his father, and lacks the flow of words typical of those caught in the act. The poison a blind man has on him belongs to him—if he explains it away.

14. "But," she says, "he was disinherited by his father." I might, judges, call this a deep-laid plan, kept secret by the old man: but it[69] is not necessarily aimed against the young man, even admitting that the father believed the stepmother as to the "parricide."[70] (2) It is a well known and commonplace crime, judges, that wives are mostly loved to the detriment of children: the love marking sec-

quam de damno pietatis affectus est. Genus infirmissimae
servitutis est senex maritus, et uxoriae caritatis ardorem
3 flagrantius frigidis concipimus adfectibus. Quid, quod
necesse est impatientius amet maritus uxorem, qui sibi
videtur filium iam perdidisse? Facillimum est de caeco
parricidium credere, cum hucusque erraveris, ut inqui-
4 reres. Volo scire, iudices, quid fecerit homo senex, qui
parricidam filium sciat. Non culleum parat, non illud
porrigit venenum, non saltem abdicatione dimittit; testamentum tantummodo mutat, et parricida sola paupertate
5 punitur. Rogo, quis praecipitat, urget? Adeone non potest
fieri idem postero die? Gravius hoc faciet pater, si non
6 praestiterit uxori. Quid, quod hoc ipsum tam placide, tam
quiete facit, quasi captet imponere? Quid dicitis, miserorum parentum affectus? Exheredaturus filium pater non
advocat propinquos, non contrahit amicos, nullis lacrimis
7 tabulae, nulla vociferatione complentur? Nescis, senex,
quanta tibi opus sit ratione tabularum:[44] exheredas mise-
rabilem parricidam. 15. Non est, iudices, quod putetis

---

[44] *interrog. distinxerit Wint.*[9]

---

[71] Cf. the *senex amator* of the comedy.

[72] Because of his blindness: cf. 2.3.2.

[73] As is alleged.   [74] Sc., to have planned to kill him.

[75] The traditional punishment for parricide was the *poena
cullei*: the convicted man was sewed in a sack with various animals
(a snake, a cock, a dog, a monkey) and thrown into the Tiber or
the sea.   [76] As another father will do, e.g., in *DM* 17.

[77] Father immediately changes his will, but his calmness suggests that he is actually devising a trick to save Son from Stepmother.

ond marriages arises from loss of paternal affection. An old husband is a paradigm of helpless slavery:[71] we feel ardor for a wife more passionately when our feelings have otherwise grown cold. (3) What of the fact that a husband necessarily loves a wife more ardently when he thinks he has already lost his son?[72] It is all too easy to credit parricide in the case of a blind man, when you have gone so far in error as to conduct an inquiry. (4) Tell me, judges, what an old man did who knows[73] his son to be a parricide.[74] He does not get a sack ready,[75] he does not offer him that same poison to drink,[76] he does not even forbid him the house; all he does is change his will, and the parricide is punished only with poverty. (5) I ask, who is hurrying him on, who is pressing him? Can't the same thing be done next day, then? The father will give the matter more serious thought—unless he has meant it to be a present to his wife. (6) And what of the fact that he acts as he does so coolly, so calmly, as if his aim is to hoodwink?[77] What do you say, you emotions of unhappy parents? Does not a father with a mind to disinherit summon relatives, assemble friends? Are the tablets completed without tears, without cries of distress? (7) You do not know, old man, how careful you have to be when you make a will: you are cutting out a parricide who deserves *pity*.[78] 15. Do not think, judges, that no codicil[79] was added for the dis-

---

[78] Because of his blindness.

[79] The *elogium* was a codicil appended to a will, especially to explain the reasons for a disinheritance. In this case, Father is said to have made a new will, disinheriting Son without any explanation: such an absence shows—according to the speaker—that the man did not believe in the parricide plot.

ideo nullum adiectum ad exheredationem iuvenis elogium, quia de scelere constaret: nemo umquam ideo non
obiecit filio parricidium, quia crederetur.[45]

2   Per fidem, iudices, duorum, inter quos de scelere
quaeritur, aestimemus mutato testamento proximam noctem. Iuvenis, seu innocens, seu parricida est, adhuc in suo
silentio stupet, nec facile dixerim unde maior trepidatio,
3 si alienum tenuit an suum venenum. Noverca rem inter
manus habet anxiam, trepidam. Nihil est difficilius quam
differre gaudium quod scias te non mereri, et filio se esse
praelatam non est longa persuasio: expectat[46] nunc ut
iuvenis agat causam postero die, ut credulum senem pro-
pinqui, ut civitas universa castiget, et se noverca sensit
4 unius tantum noctis heredem. Non creditur testamento
hominis qui, eadem nocte qua filium exheredavit, occiditur.

16. Tractemus nunc, iudices, ipsius sceleris comparationem. Caecus ignorat ubi iaceat senex, an iam quiescat; et
quam difficile est ut credat illum, qui modo de parricidio
suspicatus est, dormire patrem! Tu sentis quando senem
2 vicerit lassitudo curarum. Caeco quis renuntiat quid diei
noctisve, secretine[47] an[48] sitis pariter, an una quiescentium

⁴⁵ -ret *Franc.*, *sed vd. Kr.-Str.*   ⁴⁶ -tet B E
⁴⁷ quid d. n., *Wint.*⁷ *137,* secretine *Russ.*² *ibid.* (quod d. n.
‹tempus, an› secreti *Håk.*): quod d. n. secretum *codd.*
⁴⁸ an M²: aut B V δ (*def. Wint.*⁷ *137, sed cf. 2.20.1* utrum . . .
an . . . an): *om. γ β*

⁸⁰ = "because it was apparent without it" (Warr [1686, 44]).
⁸¹ If he is innocent, he will be shocked that someone has

inheritance of the young man just because there was no doubt about his crime;[80] no one ever failed to accuse a son of parricide just because people believed in it.

(2) Believe me, judges, we should take a look at the night following the change of will: how was it spent by the pair between whom we have to choose in investigating this crime? The young man, whether an innocent or a murderer, is still sunk in his customary silence, and it would be hard to say what was more worrying for him, the poison found on him being another's or his own.[81] (3) The stepmother is preoccupied with something that perturbs and frightens her. Nothing is harder than to postpone a joy you are conscious you do not deserve, and that she has been preferred to the son is not a long-lasting conviction: even now she is anxious that the young man will bring a case the following day, that his relations, that the whole city will upbraid the old man for his credulity—and lo and behold! the stepmother has come to realize that she is heir only for a single night. (4) No credence is given to the will of a man who gets killed the very night he disinherited his son.

16. Let us now, judges, conduct a comparison of the actual crime. The blind man does not know where the old man lies, whether he has already gone to sleep; indeed how hard it is for him to credit that a father who recently entertained suspicions of parricide should be asleep! *You* are aware when the old man has been overcome by tiredness brought on by his troubles. (2) Who would report to the blind man what time it is, day or night, whether you are apart or together, whether attentive slaves have barred

planted poison on him; if he was actually planning the parricide, he will be anxious because his plan has been revealed.

91

fores vallaverit cura servorum? Tu facere potes occa-
3 sionem, uxor et domina. Caeco fortassis ad aliud limen
errandum est; tibi hoc solum restat, ut ferias. Caecus necesse est quietem patris ipsa corporum electione confun-
dat; tu iugulum, tu potes pertractare pectus, dum amplec-
teris. Nobis iterum casus, rursus reditus incerta temptanda
sunt; tibi restat ut statim membra componas, ut quiescas.
4 Non sufficiunt facinus facturo solae cogitationes, et vix
tam multa pariter sciretis, oculi. Per fidem, iudices, ab
utro credibilius est occisum senem: a noverca, quae pro-
spexit ut et alius possit esse suspectus, an a iuvene, cuius
invidia periturus est, etiam ut illum alius occidat?

5   Intuemini, per fidem, iudices, procedentem parricidam. Quos non ista vestigia frangant rumpantque somnos! Vestigia dura[49] semper errantium, quae non valent
suspensis praetemptatisque gressibus librare corpus et,
quia diu sunt incerta, nutantia, necesse est gravius pre-
mant solum cui crediderunt. Quanto ex hoc plus accipiat
6 necesse est illa nocturni silentii quies! <Quid,>[50] quod
ambulantis caeci nec manus cessant? Praemittuntur, ex-
plorant, et adesse se nuntiant illa quae per[51] complexus
7 veniunt. Non sit in potestate caeci quin tanto[52] se fateatur

    [49] dura *Bur.*: plura *codd.*   [50] *suppl.* (*et dist. post* quies)
Håk.   [51] quae per *Str.*[7] *301* (*firm. Kr.-Str.*): per quae (quam
A *β*) *codd.* (*frustra def. Hamm.*[1] *55, Beck.*[2] *45.2*)
    [52] quin N (*cf. Hamm.*[1] *56*), tanto *Håk.*: qua toto B V Φ*: quin
isto *Russ. ap. Kr.-Str.*

    [82] Cf. 19.11.4.   [83] The husband's.   [84] See 1.1.3 n. 6.
    [85] = even the sighted would find it hard to . . .
    [86] Like *exploratores*.

the doors[82] as you sleep in each others' arms? *You*, as wife and mistress of the house, can make your own opportunity. (3) The blind man may perhaps stray perforce to another threshold; all *you* have to do is strike. The blind man must disturb his father's sleep by having to choose between the bodies; *you* can feel for his[83] throat, his breast, even as you embrace him. We[84] have to experience all over again the uncertainties of chance on the return trip; *you* need do no more than settle down straight away and go off to sleep. (4) It is not enough for one about to commit a crime merely to have planned it: indeed you, eyes, would scarcely take in so much at the same time.[85] I ask you, judges, which of the pair is it easier to believe killed the old man: the stepmother, who took precautions that another should be suspected too, or the young man, who will be blamed for the old man's death even though he is killed by someone else?

(5) I ask you, judges, to look carefully at the parricide as he makes his way along. What sleep would not be broken and interrupted by that tread!? Those who are unsure where they are going never put their feet down lightly; their steps can not keep the body in balance as they proceed tentatively on tiptoe, and because they are for a long time unsure and wavering, they are necessarily placed more heavily on ground they have found they can trust. How much more impression must this make on the absolute quiet of night! (6) ⟨What is more,⟩ not even a blind man's hands are motionless as he walks. They are sent out in advance,[86] they spy out the land: things only announce their presence as they come within grasp. (7) A blind man could not help making himself known by all that noise.

strepitu: quicquid occurrit, nequaquam potest evitare caecitas nisi offensa. Ut ambulare, ut ingredi nocte possimus,
dies facit.

17. Quam multa deinde supersunt, postquam ad patrem perventum est! Exploretur necesse est pariter iacen-
tium prima diversitas, vultus, ora tractentur, detrahantur
velamenta corporibus, quaeratur vulneri locus: ita ex duobus neutrum excitat? Gravior semper dexterae tractatus
2 errantis. Paulatim deinde admovendus est pectori mucro,
et, ne qua confundatur ignorantia nimium liber ictus,
praecedat oportet gladium manus. Unde tantum virium
caeco, ut in uno statim ictu mors tota peragatur? Incertum
vulnus sit necesse est, cuius impetum non regitis, oculi,
nec possis[53] custodire destinatum ferro locum, dum ad
colligendum vulneris pondus dexterae redire permittitur.
3 Utrum deinde iuvenis post vulnus unum continuo fugit (et
quemadmodum scit an facinus expleverit?), an potius expectat ut de parricidio cadaveri credat? Ecce iterum per
eadem incerta redeundum est, omnia rursus periculose
4 temptanda ‹temptata›[54] venienti. Fidem vestram, iudices,
ut nobis prosit argumentum criminis nostri: caecus si nec
venire nec reverti sine strepitu potest, neque sic occidere
potuit, ut deciperet novercam.

---

[53] -itis *Russ. ap. Kr.-Str., sed vd. ibid.*   [54] *add. Wint. ap.*
Kr.-Str.: ‹quae› *Watt[1]*: ‹quae temptata› *Sh. B.[4] 190*

---

[87] A blind man cannot get accustomed to a route in daylight,
as the sighted ("us") can.   [88] Cf. the parallel scene in 1.9.3.

[89] Sc., of the right spot.

[90] Without the aid of the eyes, the killer cannot be sure to hit
the spot he had chosen for his blow.

One who is without sight has no chance of avoiding an obstacle—unless he has bumped into it. It is daylight that makes walking, that makes progress at night possible for *us*.[87]

17. How much more remains to be done after he gets to his father! First of all he has to explore the differences between them as they lie there together, feel their faces and mouths, take the bedclothes off them, find the right place to strike.[88] Can it be true that he does not wake either of them in the process? An uncertain hand always operates more heavily. (2) Then the blade has to be brought by degrees up to the chest, and to prevent too wild a blow being confounded by ignorance,[89] hand has to precede sword. How does a blind man summon the strength to make sure that death is achieved instantly with a single blow? A wound must be unsure when you, eyes, cannot control the force of the blow, and no one could keep to the place destined for the steel while the right hand is being allowed to draw back to gather force for the blow.[90] (3) Does the young man make his escape then, after a single blow (and how can he know if he has completed the deed?), or does he instead wait to take it on trust from the dead body that the parricide has been carried through? Look now, he has to go back again along that same uncertain route, all the things have to be perilously tested all over again <that had been tested> on the outward journey. (4) Frankly, judges, so that we can benefit from this reconstruction of our "crime," let me say this: if the blind man could not go or return without making a noise, neither could he have killed in such a way that his stepmother did not notice.

18. Te, te hoc loco, mulier, interrogo: quae tam gravis quies, ut te mors tam vicina non excitet? Parvulis noctium turbamur offensis, excitant nos exigui plerumque motus, vox incerta, longinqua, et aliquando ipsum silentium. Illorum sane iuxta te suprema non sentias, quos senectus languoresque dissolvunt; hominis, qui ferro occiditur, tumul-

2 tuatur exitus et similis est repugnanti. Quid, quod necesse est nulla mors inquietior sit, quam quae statim tota est? Nam quod dormiens occisus est, non est quod sic aestimetis, tamquam per illam quietem transierit in mortem; sit aliquid necesse est inter soporem mortemque medium, nec potest iungi tanta diversitas, cum sit somnus ipse pars

3 vitae. Non multum interest, quietem nostram ratio vitae rumpat an mortis: hominem, qui dormiens occiditur, ipsa mors excitat. Sane non habuerit supremam vocem; habet utique palpitationes, habet motus et quicquid totus lectu-

4 lus sciat. Ecquando,[55] mulier, seni tuo blandius implicita iacuisti? Sicine dormis, quae modo turbasti totam domum,

5 cuius privignus parricida, miser est maritus? En[56] ecce vitalibus ruptis in amplexus tuos effunditur cruor, et fugiens per vulnus anima agit ante se anhelitus, agit crebra suspiria; en iterum[57] largus ille sanguis circa tuos duratur artus, stringeris deficientium rigore membrorum: non

---

[55] ecqu- *Marsh. 182*: et qu- *codd.*
[56] *om.* Φ   [57] interim *Håk., sed vd. Kr.-Str.*

---

[91] Cf. Verg. *Aen.* 2.755, *ipsa silentia terrent.*
[92] Sarcastic.   [93] By having poison found on Stepson, so that (see below) he now appears to have intended parricide and Father is miserable about that.

18. At this point I must ask you, yes you, woman: what sleep is so sound that a death so close by doesn't rouse you? We are disturbed even by little things breaking into the still of the night; small movements often wake us up, an indistinct voice far away, and sometimes silence itself.[91] True, you may not feel the death of those next to you if they succumb to old age or illness; but when a man is stabbed, his end is anything but peaceful: he is like one fighting back. (2) Further, it is inevitable that no death is less tranquil than one that is all over at once. Yes, he was killed while he slept, but you should not suppose that he passed straight through that quiet repose into death; there has to be some midpoint on the way between sleep and death: such opposites cannot be joined directly, for even sleep is part of life. (3) It makes little difference whether life or death interrupts our slumbers: a man who is killed in his sleep is woken by death itself. He may have uttered no last words, but he twitches, he moves, he does things that the whole bed can feel. (4) Did you ever, woman, lie more cozily entwined with your old husband?[92] Can you really be sleeping like this, you who have just brought the whole house into confusion,[93] whose stepson is a parricide, whose husband is in distress? (5) Look, the vitals have been broken open and blood is spurting out on to your encircling body, the soul is escaping out of the wound, driving before it gasps, and sighs thick and fast. Look, now[94] that gush of blood is congealing on your limbs, you are gripped by his stiffening limbs as he dies: are you not

[94] Here, *iterum = porro*, literally, "next," "further." After describing the spurting out of blood, the speaker moves on to what happens next, when blood solidifies.

moveris, non expavescis, sed dormis per tot diversitates?
6 Non relinquitur quid[58] aliud simulare possit mulier, cui
necesse est iuxta eum inveniri, quem occidit.

19. Non est, iudices, quod incredibile putetis ut quis
perferat dormientis simulationem: nihil est quod facilius
humana calliditas possit imitari. Sic quidam cadaverum
expressere pallorem, et contra verbera,[59] experimenta
2 telorum, mortium pertulere patientiam. Quanto facilius
simulare rem, cuius imitationi sufficit clusisse lumina,
laxasse membra, dedisse suspiriis modum et anhelitus
neglegenter egisse! Inter dormientem simulantemque
3 non est nisi conscientia. Nam quod ad tot vestigia, tot
manus, tot proclamationes in eodem tenore duravit, nolite
mirari: facilius excites dormientem, et haec est omnium
natura rerum, ne quid diutius perferas quam quod imita-
ris. Simulare somnum habet et hanc facilitatem, quod vi-
4 detur similis excitato qui deprehensus est. Quid hoc esse
vis, mulier, quod te non excitat res, qua domus tota turba-
tur? Illam servilis neglegentiae quietem, illos sine curis,
sine adfectibus somnos, illos, qui non statim primo timore
5 prosiliunt, fragor noctis agitavit. Quantus deinde fremitus
discurrentium tota domo! Prima sunt evigilantium prae-
sidia clamores, nec potest quieta res esse noctis auxilium.
6 Minore strepitu commota es, cum excitareris. Ecce cubi-

---

58 quod *Russ. et Wint. ap. Kr.-Str.*   59 -ra et M γ β

---

95 I.e., apparent death.
96 A possible reference to the poking of corpses on the battlefield, to expose soldiers who pretend to be dead.   97 If you are
caught out you can pretend you have just woken up.

worried, not scared, but sleep on through all these various disturbances? (6) *That* is the only pretense a woman can make when she needs to be found alongside her victim.

19. Do not think it beyond belief, judges, that someone should take pretense of sleep to the bitter end: there is nothing that human cunning can imitate more readily. People have reproduced the pallor of corpses just like this, and have maintained the passivity of death[95] despite being whipped or prodded with spears.[96] (2) How much easier it is to pretend to be doing something which can be sufficiently imitated by just closing the eyes, relaxing, breathing regularly and easily! Only consciousness makes the difference between sleep and feigned sleep. (3) No, do not be surprised that she did not react to all those footsteps, all those hands, all those shouts: you would more easily arouse someone properly asleep, and it is a general rule that there is nothing which one goes on doing longer than what one is pretending to do. Pretending sleep has this advantage too, that someone caught in the act resembles someone who has been woken up.[97] (4) How do you explain this, woman, that you are not wakened by something that sets the whole house in uproar? The noise during the night woke the slaves from their carefree repose, those slumbers without worries or feeling—and they are people who do not jump out of bed at the first alarm. (5) How great, following on that, was the hubbub as people rushed all over the house! When people are woken up, they turn for aid first to cries, so help in the night cannot be a quiet affair. Less noise was used to wake you up![98] (6) Look, your

[98] The noise that eventually "woke" her from her feigned sleep was less than the general hubbub that did not disturb her.

culi vestri fores trepidae festinationis effringuntur impulsu, en lumen super lectulum ingerunt multae manus et, ad prostratorum corporum spectaculum,[60] cubiculum gemitu, vociferatione completur: tu iaces et in cadaveris similitudinem usque resoluta es. Hoc tu quietem putas esse? Patientia est.

20. Vestrae, iudices, aestimandum relinquo prudentiae strepitum, quem in cubiculo senis fuisse confessi sunt qui illo potissimum concurrerunt, utrum putetis factum conluctatione morientis, an a[61] peracta caede referentis gladium mulieris fuisse discursum, an hoc quoque inter artes novercae, ut omnibus sceleris sui partibus sensim quieteque dispositis ipsa ad excitandam familiam fecerit strepi-
2 tum, cui hoc solum supererat, ut sic inveniretur. Fragor, quo familia excitata est, si redeuntis caeci fuit, deprehensus iuvenis esset antequam gladium referret.

3 Ut sciatis, iudices, neminem fuisse in domo, quem non fragor ille confuderit: caecus quoque inventus in limine est.[62] Si autem[63] solet ultro citroque commeare iuvenis, si inter suum patrisque cubiculum facile discurrit, quid ad-
4 huc in limine facit? Evasit, effugit, gladium iam reposuit: et quanto facilius est caeco simulare somnos, vultum quietis imitari! 21. Quod, per fidem, maius subitae con-

---

[60] spectaculum *Str.*[8] *234.123*: similitudinem *codd. (sc. e seq. sententia)*: aspectum *Wint.*[3]

[61] *om.* V DE   [62] *dist. Sh. B.*[2] *191*

[63] si *Wint. ap. Kr.-Str.*, autem *[Kr.-]Str.*: sicut *codd.*

---

[99] Persistence in simulation. Cf. 2.19.3.   [100] To his room.   [101] Of his own room.   [102] Sc., after that.
    [103] I.e., supposing the blind man had killed his father, after

bedroom door is broken open by the press of frightened people in a hurry, look, many hands bring lights to shine over your bed, and at the sight of prostrate bodies the room is filled with groans, with cries: *you* lie there, reduced to a corpse-like state. Do you think this is sleep? It is stamina.[99]

20. I leave it to your sagacity, judges, to pass judgment on the uproar which took place in the old man's bedroom—as is proved by the fact that the household rushed en masse precisely *there*. Was it caused by the death agonies of the husband? Or was it the result of the woman hurrying to replace the sword after committing the murder? Or was it another part of the cunning stepmother's plot that, after she had step by step and at her leisure seen to every detail of her crime, she herself made the noise to rouse the household, and all that was left for her to do was to be found in the state in which she was found? (2) As for the racket that roused the household, if it had been caused by the blind man returning, the young man would have been detected before he took the sword back.[100]

(3) To convince you, judges, that there was no one in the house who was not disconcerted by the fracas: the blind man too was found on the threshold.[101] Now, if the young man is used to going to and fro, if he finds it easy to move quickly between his room and his father's, what is he doing, still there on the threshold? (4) He has got away, he has made his escape, he has already put the sword back in its place; how much easier it is[102] for a blind man to feign sleep, to look as if he is in repose![103] 21. What better proof

the murder he should have gone to bed and pretended to be asleep, rather than staying on the threshold.

fusionis argumentum est, quam quod caecus exiluit et
stetit? Gravius necesse est expavescant quibus de sollici-
tudine sua non renuntiant oculi, et, cum clusus[64] animus

2 non exit in visus, non habet unde timori suo par sit. Deprehensus est iuvenis ubi illum destituerat impetus timoris. Potest neglegere caecitas in cubiculo suo ducem, in
quo dies omnes cunctasque noctes agit iter quod iam multis offensis, multis edidicit erroribus; extra limen caecitas

3 est, inde error ac tenebrae. Nihil est innocentius caeco qui
nec in scelere deprehensus est, nec in dissimulatione.

4 Proclamat hoc loco iuvenis: "Ut primum" inquit "me,
pater, fragor domus et velut tui confudere gemitus, iterum
tamquam te rapturus exilui. Tunc primum miser sensi
facinus caecitatis: steti, donec mihi nuntiareris occisus, et
in illa discurrentium trepidatione tenui miser otium timo-

5 ris. O, si numen aliquod paulisper accommodasset oculos!
Primus[65] in cubiculum intrassem patris, invenissem fortassis adhuc aliqua verba morientis, loqui, interrogare potuissem. Tarda et trepida[66] sunt officia servorum: ego te de-
prehendissem, noverca, vigilantem."

22. "Sed" inquit "gladius caeci cruentatus inventus

---

[64] cum clu- AC *β*: conclu- *cett.*: ⟨cum⟩ conclu- *Sch.*: cui clu-
Sh. B.⁴ 190   [65] -us *ς* (*def. Watt² 20*): -um *codd.*
[66] tep- S, *sed cf. 2.6.1, 2.19.6, 2.21.4*

---

[104] Of his room.

[105] On the threshold.

[106] Not in a crime (cf. 2.21.3), but at the place where he was
when his first impulse on hearing the noise was replaced by fear
of the unknown.

[107] The first being when he rescued Father from the fire.

of the blind man's sudden state of confusion, I ask you, could there be than that he sprang out[104] and took his stand?[105] Graver must be the panic of those who are not given reports by their eyes on what alarms them, for when the mind is closed in and cannot come forth to see something, it has no means of mastering its fear. (2) The young man was caught[106]—where he had been left helpless by his attack of panic. A blind man can manage without a guide while he is in his own bedroom, where every day and every night he takes a route that he has memorized at the cost of many a collision, many false moves; but beyond the threshold is blindness, from there on perplexity and utter darkness. (3) Nothing is more innocent than a blind man who has been detected neither in crime nor in pretense.

(4) At this point the young man cries: "Father, when the uproar in the house and what sounded like your groans first threw me into confusion, I sprang forth as if to come to your rescue a second time.[107] Only then (ah me!) did I feel the real curse of being blind: I stood there till they told me you were dead, and in all that panic and bustle I, poor wretch, was too frightened to do anything. (5) O, if only some divinity had lent me eyes for a while! I should have been the first to go into my father's bedroom, I should perhaps have found him still able to utter some dying words, I could have talked to him, questioned him. Slaves do their duties slowly and timidly: *I* would have caught you, stepmother, while you were still awake."[108]

22. "But," she says, "the blind man's sword was found

---

[108] After committing the murder and before you could pretend to be asleep.

est." Non est, iudices, caecitatis audacia de parricidio referre gladium, et homo, cuius paulo ante exquisiti sunt
sinus, non referret in cubiculum suum ferrum, quod non
tegere[67] posset, non abscondere, et tamen cruentatum
2 sciat. Quis hanc, iudices, impudentiam ferat? Negat caeco
surripi potuisse gladium mulier,[68] quae se quiete defendit;
et[69] quanto facilius est somnos decipere miserorum! Gravior est quies quibus ex lassitudine calamitatium venit.
3 Caeco vero facile est etiam vigilanti subripere gladium.
4 Quemadmodum paratur argumentum?[70] Quaedam facere
non potest neglegentia, et[71] facilius est ut caecitatem imitentur oculi. Gladium cruentatum reponendi[72] hic[73] tantum causas habet, qui occidit alieno.[74]

23. Sentio, iudices, iamdudum indignari miserrimum
iuvenem quod argumentis, quod probatione defenditur.
Reddenda sunt maximo virorum patrocinia tam piae cae-
2 citatis, et agenda reliqua pars causae admiratione. Intueri
mihi, iudices, videor expeditionis illius incredibilem no-
vamque faciem: vadit rapto patre iuvenis per ardentes
crescentesque flammas—dicturum me putatis ut evadat,

---

[67] terg- *Bur.[1]*   [68] m. ⟨quiescenti⟩ *Russ. ap. Kr.-Str., fort.
recte* [69] at *Sch.*

[70] quemadmodum paratur (-itur J) arg- *codd.* (*def. Str.[9]*): *del.
Dess.[2]*: quam commodum paratur arg-! *Håk.*

[71] at *Russ.[3]*   [72] -ntes M[2] γ β: -ntis δ

[73] hic *Eng. 84*: has *codd.*: is *Vass. 114*

[74] gladium—alieno *sententiam efficere dispexit Vass. 114*

---

[109] Cf. 2.16.1.   [110] Sc., out of the fact that the young
man's sword was found bloodstained under his pillow.

[111] It is easier for a sighted person to give the impression of a

covered in blood." A blind man, judges, would not be bold enough to bring back his sword after killing his father, and a man whose pockets have been gone through a little while before would not take his blade back to his bedroom, where he could not hide it, could not conceal it—yet he knows it is bloodied. (2) Who would put up with such impudence, judges? The woman, who bases her defense on being asleep herself, says the sword could not have been stolen from the blind man; yet how much easier it is to deceive the unhappy when they are asleep! Sleep comes heavier upon those worn out by misfortune.[109] (3) But it is easy to steal a sword from a blind man even when he is awake. How can a proof be made out of this?[110] (4) There are some things that cannot be the result of carelessness, and it is easier for the sighted to feign blindness.[111] The only person who has reason to put a bloodied sword back in its place is one who has used someone else's to commit murder.

23. I am well aware, judges, that this most unhappy youth has for a long time been feeling angry that he is being defended by argumentation, by proof. He is the greatest of men, and he deserves a plea appropriate to such dutiful blindness.[112] Accordingly, the rest of his case must rest on admiration for him. (2) In my imagination, judges, I am watching that rescue, an incredible and unprecedented spectacle: the young man has snatched up his father, and is marching through ever-increasing flames— you think I am going to say, in order to get out, to escape?

crime having been committed by a blind man (than for a blind man to be so careless: cf. 1.2.2).

[112] Incurred in trying to rescue his parents.

3   ut fugiat? Properat miser ut revertatur! En membra
     contactu stringuntur ignium, pater tamen toto cooperitur
     amplexu, et ardentibus tunc quoque paene luminibus
     texerunt manus alterius oculos. Hoc nunc me putatis stu-
     pere, mirari, quod huic iuvenis oneri per medios ignium
     globos et ruentia tecta sufficit?[75] Illud est, cui vix habere
     possit mortalitas fidem: visus est sibi fecisse rem facilem.

4   Quantae, dii deaeque, pietatis audacia est ire rursus in
     flammas, illo ubi patrem paene perdideris! Iam non erat
     illud penates, iam non erat domus, ubique tamen iuveni
     videbatur ardere mater. Iam miser undique flagrantibus
     membris, cum discurrentem clusisset ignis, quod solum
     supererat virium genus, matrem quaerebat oculis. 24. Non
     fuit illud praemium[76] ignium, perire[77] lumina candentia:[78]
     non protexerunt flagrantem sua membra faciem, et oculi

2   quaerentibus matrem[79] manibus arserunt. Rursus infelix
     totum tactu perlustrat incendium, et, unde maximus est
     conlabentium culminum fragor, illo debilitas tamquam
     inventura revocatur. Solus omnium servatus est beneficio
     caecitatis.

---

[75] -fec- ⟨, haud male   [76] praemium Wint. ap. Kr.-Str.:
primum B V Φ*: crimen Bur.: pretium Wint.[7] 138

[77] (primum) igni, operire Plas. 40

[78] cad- S, sed vd. Reitz.[2] 39.5 et Kr.-Str.

[79] matrem ⟨iam⟩ Helm[1] 366

---

[113] At *that* time, contrasting with his later attempt to save his
mother, when he *did* lose his sight (DAR).

[114] I.e., he could not any more search with his body.

[115] I.e., the fire did not have to "defeat" the youth, for he made
no attempt to defend himself (see below).

No, the poor man is in a hurry to *return*! (3) Look, his
limbs are now in close contact with the fire, but his embrace completely protects his father; and though his own
eyes are—then too[113]—all but ablaze, his hands have
shielded the eyes of the other. Do you think I am now
astonished, amazed that the young man is capable of bearing his burden amid the balls of fire and the falling ma-
sonry? In fact, what is barely credible to mortal man is that
he thought he had done something simple. (4) How great,
gods and goddesses, must be the filial affection that in-
spires you with the courage to go back into the flames,
back to where you almost lost your father! That was now
no longer his home, no longer a *house*, but the young man
thought he saw his mother burning in every part of it. Now
the poor man's whole body was ablaze, fire had cut him off
as he hurried this way and that. He searched for his mother
with his eyes: they were all the strength he had left.[114] 24.
It was not a prize won by the fire[115] that his eyes perished
in the white-hot heat: his limbs did not protect their[116]
blazing face, for his eyes went up in flames while his hands
were searching for his mother. (2) Going back on his
tracks, the unfortunate boy traverses the whole fire by
touch alone, and, now sightless, is recalled to where there
is the greatest din of collapsing roofs, thinking to find her.
Alone of all men, he was saved thanks to his blindness.[117]

---

[116] Explained by the following words: the youth did not protect his eyes from the fire, even though hands and eyes were part
of the same body. Cf. 4.8.7.

[117] He is led back (*rursus*) out of the house by the sound, for
he can no longer see where he is going. Presumably, the noise
comes from the collapse of the outer walls. Cf. 2.2.5.

3   Protrahatur, iudices, si videtur, in medium reus: plurimum probationibus adicere debent truces vultus, terribilis minaxque facies. Hic est, iudices, qui dicitur tota nocte
discurrisse, hic ille circumspectus, hic ille felix parricida.
4 Recesserunt cuncta debilitatis officia, et hominis, qui circa
genua vestra ducendus est, non est qui dirigat gressus: non
servuli supersunt, non penates. Respondete, per fidem,
respondete, mortales: utrum hic patrem occidit an perdi-
5 dit? Quid agis, infelicissime iuvenis? Rogandum est, neque habes totas[80] preces; perît ille vester ambitus, vestra
6 miseratio. Sed nefas est ut reatus iste sentiat debilitatis
adversa. Nos agedum, iuvenis, ducamus:[81] nostris[82] humeris, nostris manibus innitere, nos tibi pedes,[83] nos accom-
7 modamus oculos. Quid aversaris,[84] infelix, quid repugnas?
Scimus te non rogare pro vita. Sed dura, miser, dura; saltem vive dum vincas. Decet te hic quoque virtutium tuarum cumulus: decet ut digneris moriturus absolvi.

[80] tuas *Håk., sed vd. B. Asc.[1] xv r. et Russ. ap. Kr.-Str*
[81] ducamus *Wint.[7] 138:* ducimus B: dicimus V: duc immo Φ:
ducemus *Sch. (firm. Russ.[2] 138.2)*
[82] *ante* nostris *dist. Sch.*
[83] pedes *Håk.:* preces *codd.*
[84] av- V: adv- B Φ

(3) If you please, judges, let the defendant be brought forward: his fierce expression, his terrifying and menacing[118] appearance should be a crucial addition to the proofs. This is the man, judges, who is alleged to have scurried around all night, this is the careful, this the successful parricide. (4) All those who should have attended on a handicapped man have disappeared, and there is no one left to guide the steps of one who has to be led around to beg before your knees: there are no slaves any more, no household.[119] Reply, I beg you, reply, mortal men: did this man kill his father or lose him?[120] (5) What are you doing, most unfortunate youth? You need to beg, but your prayers are incomplete. Your own means of arousing favor, of winning sympathy have disappeared.[121] (6) It is wicked, though, that this defendant should feel the adversities of physical impairment. Come now, let *us*[122] lead you: lean on our shoulders, our hands, we are lending you our feet, our eyes. (7) Why are you reluctant, unhappy man, why do you resist? We know you are not asking for life.[123] But endure, unfortunate man, endure: at least live until you win. It is fitting that you should crown your great deeds in this way; it is fitting that you deign to be acquitted before you die.

[118] Ironic.

[119] Because he has been disinherited.

[120] His father too is not available to help him.

[121] *Vester* = of you blind people. Being blind, he is incapable of tears (cf. 1.17.6), the best aids to arousing pity (DAR).

[122] Implying a supporting team, or used emphatically for the advocate alone.

[123] Because he will commit suicide after his victory.

DECLAMATION 3

INTRODUCTION

Marius' Soldier is unusual in what remains of Roman declamation, and unique in our collection, in that it is set in
the real world, and indeed based on an event recorded in
history.[1] Marius, who had triumphed over Jugurtha, king
of Numidia (104 BC), next confronted a Germanic tribe,
the Cimbri, when it invaded northern Italy. During this
war, which culminated in victory at Vercellae (101), a tribune related to Marius was killed by a soldier whom he
had attempted to seduce. In *DM* 3, Marius presides over
a military court (3.2) trying the soldier, whose advocate—
apparently a soldier himself (17.5, *commilito*)—speaks.

Roman verisimilitude is achieved in various ways. The
contrast between the sordid attempted rape and the im-
peratives of war is repeatedly stressed (1.1, 6.6–7, 13.5).
The fearsome Cimbri are described in lurid detail (4.2,
13.1–2—though see 16.5–6). Parallels from Roman myth
and history are exploited at some length (11.1–3, 17.2–5).
Above all, the declaimer draws a Sallustian moral from the
whole affair: the tribune's action is not just an individual's

---

[1] Plut. *Mar.* 14.3–9 (cf. also *Apophth. reg. et imp.* 202b–c),
identifying the tribune as Marius' nephew Lusius and the soldier
as Trebonius. The episode is further referred or alluded to by Cic.
Inv. rhet. 2.124, *Mil.* 9 (cf. Quint. 5.11.15); Val. Max. 6.1.12;
Quint. 3.11.14. See now Traina (2021, 440–43).

act of madness (1.1, 2.1, 12.3); it is portrayed as typical of an age of decadence (1.2, 4.4, 11.5) brought on by aristocratic excess (4.3, 14.3). Against this corrupt society is set the figure of Marius, who, coming from humble stock himself (10.4), measures virtue not by wealth but by deeds (5.3; cf. 19.2). He is frequently addressed by the advocate, with praise and flattery. He embodies Roman and even divine *virtus* (2.5, 3.2, 10.4). If he overlooks his kinship to the tribune, and acquits the soldier, that will be an enhancement of his fame (10.2, 18.1). The defendant is called "your soldier" (1.3, 2.1); that is designed to sound more emotive, and more egalitarian, than "your kinsman."[2]

The soldier is Marius' counterpart:[3] born and bred to the military life in the rigors of the countryside (3.5–4.1), he is a hero both on the field and when he is assaulted by a superior officer (for the relationship between officer and man see 15.2–16.5), whose previous blandishments he had been too naive to understand (6.3). We are not to picture him as a shrinking violet: he is armed to the teeth, and to the helm (12.3). He does not repent of his deed (2.2), and is ready to die for it (2.3): he has always been aware that death is round the corner (1.4). What matters is his honor (2.3, 2.5, 6.7).

The attitude displayed toward homosexual acts is of interest. Commerce with boys is comparatively venial (6.1–2, 11.5). It is when a male consorts with an adult male, and of course especially when he uses force to press his suit (1.1), that disapproval is called for (cf. 10.3). The

2 This relationship is problematized in 18.1–7.
3 See especially 19.1.

tribune is repeatedly stated or implied to be "prostituting" the soldier (1.1, 3.1, 6.6, 9.2, 12.3, 16.5). His taste, though, is not for pretty boys but for scarred heroes (6.1–2)— which might imply a "shameful" desire for passive sex. There is much talk, too, of chastity (dismissed at one point as a virtue for women: 3.3; cf. 11.4) and its opposite (2.2). For the soldier, chastity implies refusal to take part in homosexual amours. Even to mention details of the attempted rape may offend Marius' chaste ears (1.1, 8.3; cf. 6.2), and the speaker himself is reluctant to go into details (6.4–5).[4]

The structure is:

> PROEM 1.1–3.3
> NARRATION 3.4–8.5
> ARGUMENTATION
> *Confirmatio* 9.1–15.1
> *Refutatio* 15.2–18.7
> EPILOGUE 19.1–6

Schneider's more detailed schema[5] marks *excessus* (digressions) at 6.4–5, 8.4–5, 14.2–15.1, 16.1–17.1. Historical *exempla* (probably from some anthology akin to Valerius Maximus' work)[6] are adduced at 11.2–4, 12.2, and 17.2–5.

DM 3 is arguably the most ancient speech in our collection: it may be dated to the very beginning of the second century AD.[7] The same case is briefly argued, on both sides, in Calpurnius Flaccus, *Decl.* 3 (late 2nd century

---

4 Cf. Langlands (2006, 265–75).

5 (2004, 17–19); cf. Brescia (2004, 63ff.).

6 But not from Valerius Maximus himself: cf. Reitzenstein (1909, 75–76), and in detail Schneider (2001, 228–37).

7 See General Introduction, §4.

AD?). In the fourth century, a passage of *DM* 3 is echoed both in Jerome and in the *Panegyrici Latini*;[8] another one might be alluded to in the *Historia Augusta*.[9] Later on, perhaps around 600, the pseudo-Quintilianic defense speech provoked a reply: the anonymous *Tribunus Marianus*.[10] In the twelfth century Osbern of Gloucester, in his *Derivationes*, interestingly cites a phrase from *DM* 3 in its correct form, against all manuscripts of the *Maiores*.[11] More recently, an antilogy to the *Miles Marianus* is due to Patarol.[12]

[8] 16.2–3, *non aestivi solis ardorem nec sub pellibus actam hiemem (sc. recusamus). Ferienda sit fatigato fossa, pro vallo portisque vigilandum. Fortiter ancipites inibimus pugnas* ~ Jer. *Ep.* 14.2.1, *Quid facis in paterna domo, delicate miles? Ubi vallum, ubi fossa, ubi hiemps acta sub pellibus?* and Pan. Lat. 2.8.3 Lassandro, *actas sub pellibus hiemes, aestates inter bella sudatas, dies noctesque proeliando aut vigilando consumptas, gravissimas pugnas terra marique pugnatas.* Cf. Stramaglia (2006, 557n13).

[9] 3.2, *C. Marium, quod exemplum divinitus nobis datum videtur, quid in homine virtus possit* ~ SHA *Tyr. Trig.* 5.5–6, *in Gallia primum Postumus, deinde Lollianus, Victorinus deinceps, postremo Tetricus—nam de Mario nihil dicimus—adsertores Romani nominis extiterunt. Quos omnes datos divinitus credo, ne ... possidendi Romanum solum Germanis daretur facultas.* Cf. Schneider (2004, 104–5n52).

[10] *DM* 3b in Lehnert's Teubner, but omitted in Håkanson's. The piece has recently been edited, translated, and annotated by Winterbottom, building on a draft by Håkanson: see Håkanson-Winterbottom (2015); also Winterbottom (2017). Some valuable insights by Burman (±1700), hitherto overlooked, can now be read in Capizzi (2020–21).

[11] See apparatus to 3.4.

[12] (1743, 137–53). Schneider (2016) has reprinted the Latin text and provided a French translation.

Miles Marianus

Bello Cimbrico miles Mari tribunum stuprum sibi inferre conantem, propinquum Mari, occidit. Reus est caedis apud imperatorem.

1. Satis dedecoris atque flagitii castra ceperunt, cum haec furenti tribuno mens subiecta est, ut in medio belli Cimbrici strepitu ante signa (tuis honos sit habitus sanctissimis auribus) iuberet prostare gladio cinctum et vim turpissimam ac nefariam temptaret inferre—ne quid aliud dicam—fortiori. Haeret[1] aeterna labes, et in exemplum, in quod facillime vitia proficiunt, nova culpa pernotuit. Et licet impunita sit reo virtus sua, tamen in hoc ruentis in deteriora saeculi cursu, adfirmo, plures erunt qui tribunum imitentur quam qui militem. Etsi nil minus convenire videtur partibus advocati, summe imperator, quam reo

2

3

---

[1] haeret *Kroll*: haberet B V δ: habetur M: habet M² γ β

---

[1] If the soldier were found guilty, the camp would suffer an even greater disgrace. Cf. 3.8.4.

3

Marius' soldier

In the war against the Cimbri one of Marius' soldiers killed a tribune, a kinsman of Marius, when he tried to rape him. He is charged with murder before the general.

(Speech of the soldier's advocate)

1. Our camp suffered enough[1] scandal and disgrace when it came into the head of a tribune, in a fit of madness, amid all the tumult of the Cimbrian war, and in the presence of the standards, to order (here I speak with all due respect to your chaste ears, general) a soldier with a sword at his belt to prostitute himself, and to attempt to bring force, such shameful and abominable force, to bear on someone (to use no other word) braver[2] than himself. (2) The blot thus caused is lasting: a new crime has become notorious, creating a precedent—as vices so readily succeed in doing. And even if the defendant's courage goes unpunished, yet, in this age of ours that is rushing headlong into decadence, there will—I maintain—be more people to imitate the tribune than the soldier. (3) Nothing, supreme general, could be less fitting for one acting as advocate than that a

2 = braver, but also better in every way.

capite periclitanti subsidium miserationis auferri,[2] memor
tamen pro quo et apud quem loquar, audacter atque—ut
spero—tuto profiteor militem tuum, quicquid adferat casus hodie, sub ipso fortunae minantis ictu stare securum:
aut enim absolves tamquam innocentem, aut punies tam-
4 quam virum. Fas est vita periclitari, qui natum se meminit
lege pereundi, neque in militiam gravissimo asperrimoque
bello ita venit, ut nesciret sibi mortem in procinctu ha-
bendam, neque est tam imbellis, ut non forti pectore adversa, dum non inhonesta, toleret. 2. Adfirmo tibi, C.
Mari: non sic nuper repugnasset, si illum tribunus voluisset occidere. Neque ignoravit quae manerent eum peri-
cula, cum obscenos furiosi corruptoris amplexus gladio
divelleret, nec habeo sane quid in milite, praesertim tuo,
2 laudem, si pudicus est tantum quia expedit. Nec si sit vitae
cupidissimus, paenitere eum facti sui potest. De inter-
fectore corruptoris fortasse dubites; illud utique scio, de
3 impudico milite non deliberasses. Hunc vero, C. Mari
(defendatur[3] enim tam fortiter miles tuus quam vindicatus
est), nec si damnaveris paenitebit: si fors ita tulerit, ibit ad
poenam pleno gradu, tam paratus mori pro pudicitia quam
occidere, laudemque perpetuam fortissimi pudoris secum

---

2 -re 𝖢 (*prob. Reitz.*[2] *28.10*), *sed vd. Eng. 63*
3 -detur B^ac (*prob. Reitz.*[2] *51*)

---

3 The soldier.

4 Literally, "that he must always have death to hand."

5 The ideal of *pudicitia* for a Roman freeborn man was to
preserve intact his own sexual integrity (opposing—as in this
case—any sexual assault, which would constitute a disgrace).

6 I.e., because he was influenced by the perils just mentioned.

defendant on a capital charge should be deprived of the
help afforded by pity; but, conscious as I am for whom and
before whom I am speaking, I declare boldly, and—I
hope—without running any risk, that your soldier, whatever may befall him today, stands here without a qualm,
beneath the impending stroke of fortune: you will either
acquit him as innocent, or punish him as one who acted as
a man should. (4) It is right and proper for someone to put
his life at risk, when he knows full well that he was born
under sentence of death. This man[3] did not come to serve
in a crucial and bitterly fought war without knowing that
death is always round the corner;[4] nor is he so unwarlike
as to be unprepared to put up bravely with adversity, so
long as it does not bring dishonor. 2. I assure you, Gaius
Marius: he would not have fought back like that the other
day if the tribune had wanted to *kill* him. He knew the
perils that awaited him when he used his sword to break
away from his mad seducer's obscene embrace, and I certainly find nothing to praise in a soldier, and especially a
soldier of yours, if he is chaste[5] only because it is to his
advantage.[6] (2) However much he may long for life, he
cannot repent of what he did. You may perhaps have your
doubts in judging the killer of an abuser: but this I do know,
that you would not have paused to think in the case of an
unchaste soldier. (3) As for this man, Gaius Marius (let
your soldier be defended as bravely as he avenged himself), he will not repent even if you find him guilty. If it so
chances,[7] he will go to his death at the double, no less
ready to die than to kill in order to keep his name clear;
and he will take with him a lasting reputation for so brave

[7] Cf. Verg. *Aen.* 2.94.

4 feret. Omnis licet delatorum vis ingruat, numquam tamen
effici poterit ut miles tuus magis doleat quod accusatus
quam quod appellatus est.

5 Sed neque hoc Mars[4] parens nec signa militaria aqui-
laeque victrices nec tua, summe imperator, divina virtus
sinat, ut tua quoque sententia quisquam vir et Romanus
et miles nimium pudicus sit. [Apud quos ante principia
gerendum est.][5] 3. Ecce cum maxime hoc agitur, ut inter
Romanarum[6] legionum manipulos scorta deligere et ad
stuprum trahere sacramento rogatos post haec liceat ex

2 decreto tuo. Nec pudet accusatorem apud C. Marium,
quod exemplum divinitus nobis datum videtur, quid in
homine virtus possit, adsidentibus legatis praefectisque et
istis illi prodigio dissimillimis tribunis, toto armatorum
iudicio, obicere militi quod vir sit, tantumque non durum
ac rusticum et parum meretriciis artibus queritur educa-

3 tum.[7] At ego, si qua est fides, pudicitiam in milite etiam
laudare erubesco: feminarum est ista virtus; aliter mihi
laudandus est vir fortis: idoneus bello, promptus ad peri-
cula, praestantis[8] animi—libere dicam: dignior qui tribunus esset. Hoc enim propinquo, Mari, non erubesceres.

---

4 Mars ⸤ (*def. Helm[1] 355*): Mari B V δ: Roma M γ β
5 *del. Håk.*[2] *32 utpote glossema* (*in codd. varie corruptum*) *ad*
Mars—victrices   6 -nar- π CD O β: -nor- *cett.*
7 -cat- V γ β: -ct- *cett.* (*longe rariore clausula*)
8 -ns *Bur.* (*corrob. Beck.*[2] *16*)

---

8 Marius would be coming to such a verdict if he found the
soldier guilty. "Too" alludes to the tribune's coming to that "verdict" when faced with the soldier's reaction to his advances.

a defense of his honor. (4) Let denouncers assail him in full force: it can never come about that a soldier of yours finds it more distressing to be accused than to be propositioned.

(5) But let not Father Mars, the military standards and our victorious eagles, let not your own godlike virtue, supreme general, allow you too to come to the verdict that any man, any Roman, any soldier, is over-careful of his honor.[8] 3. What is in question here and now (mark it well!) is that, in accordance with *your* decision, it may in future be permissible to recruit prostitutes from the ranks of Roman legionaries, by luring into debauchery men who have been asked to swear the military oath.[9] (2) In the presence of Gaius Marius, who has apparently been granted by heaven[10] to show us what virtue is capable of in a man, and before a panel of legates, prefects, and you tribunes so different from that monster, a jury consisting only of men under arms, an accuser has the effrontery to reproach a soldier with being a man, and all but complains of his being a rough peasant,[11] ill-educated in a harlot's arts. (3) But, believe me, I blush even to praise chastity in a soldier: that is a female virtue. I have to praise a hero in other terms: as fit for war, ready to face danger, outstandingly brave, a man—to be frank—more worthy[12] to be a tribune. You would have no reason to blush, Marius, if it was *he* who was your kinsman.

[9] Rather than being asked for sexual favors.

[10] This passage is perhaps echoed in SHA *Tyr. Trig.* 5.5–6: see Introduction to the present declamation.

[11] I.e., of being a genuine Roman of other times (cf., e.g., Mart. 7.58.7–9; Juv. 3.67).

[12] I.e., than his seducer.

4   Pater huic emeritis bello stipendiis tum, cum tota subnixum Numidia fregimus Iugurtham, exauctoratas armis
manus agresti labori[9] subegit. Praedura priscis moribus
mater, frigoribus ac solibus perusta et in plerisque ruris
operibus marito particeps, adfirmo, quam nemo appellas-
5   set impune. His ortus ipse procul ab omni contactu reces-
serat puerilis quoque annos aliquo semper opere durando:
sequi pecora primo, arcere gregibus feras, aliquid semper
audere maius annis. 4. Ludus fuit rotare saxa, vibrare iam
tum[10] sudes, saltus agitare venatu; mox vigentibus[11] lacer-
tis humum scindere, segnem futuris novalibus eruere sil-
vam. Sic effectum est ut, quemadmodum aliqui putant,
posset cito militare.

2   Interim ex ultimo litore Oceani et dirempta frigoribus
plaga gens a rerum natura bene[12] relegata, stolida viribus,
indomita feritate, insolens successu, nec minus animorum
immanitate quam corporum beluis suis proxima, Italiam
3   inundavit. Nec tamen tantum vi sua quantum luxuria
socordiaque nostrorum ducum elata, dum nos in bello[13]

---

[9] -ri *Osbern*. Deriv. *e.56* (*I.228 Bertini et al.*), *et cf. Helm*[2] *93:*
-re *codd.*   [10] lamtum B: iactu M E O: amento *Reitz.*[2] *90*
[11] vig- ς: ing- *codd., sed vd. Håk.*
[12] paene *B. Asc.*[1] *xvi v., sed vd. et ibid. et Bur.*
[13] bella *Sch.*

---

[13] Compare the portrait of the primitive Roman woman in
Hor. *Epod.* 2.37–46; Juv. 6.5–10.   [14] Later—it is implied—
he would use them as weapons.   [15] Some object that the
soldier on trial joined the army when he was too young (cf. 3.5.4),
but he *deserved* this thanks to his early training. For *cito = citius*
("too soon") see *ThlL* III.1210.67–69 (AS).

(4) The defendant's father, having completed his military service at the point when we crushed Jugurtha, with all Numidia behind him, applied his hands, now discharged from armed service, to work in the fields. His mother was the hardiest of women, old-fashioned in her ways, pinched by frost and burned by the sun, her husband's partner in many a country task:[13] I can tell you, no one would have got away with propositioning *her*! (5) He himself, with parents like this, had kept well away from any contagion. Even in his boyhood years, he never stopped toughening himself up with some task or other, herding cattle to start with, keeping wild animals away from the flocks, always taking on something beyond his years. 4. Sport for him consisted in hurling rocks, flinging stakes (even then!),[14] scouring the wild countryside for game; then, as his limbs grew strong, he would break up the ground, and tear out unproductive forests to make new fields for the plow. The result was that, as some think, he was all too soon[15] able to serve as a soldier.

(2) Meantime, there flooded over Italy, from the furthest shores of Ocean and a region isolated by the cold, a people providentially exiled from the world:[16] strong brutes, of unconquerable fierceness, overbearing in success, resembling the wild beasts of their country in their savagery of mind and body alike.[17] (3) But even more than by their own violent nature, they were swept on by the luxury and sloth of our generals: the vices of peace clung

[16] The Cimbri and the Teutones, who left their original lands on the shores of the Baltic Sea and invaded the Roman territories on the Danube in 113 BC.

[17] Cf. 13.11.4.

123

quoque vitia pacis secuntur et delicati sumus etiam miseri,
vastitatem agris, solitudinem iuventuti,[14] periculum imperio ac prope exitium adtulit, apparuitque numquam
populo Romano ad propulsandam perniciem magis viris
4 opus fuisse. Itaque cum appareret solutam militiae disciplinam[15] et non minorem[16] nobis pugnam[17] cum moribus esse[18] quam cum hostibus, ad unicum, C. Mari, cum
virtutis tuae, tum sanctitatis severitatisque praesidium
confugimus. 5. Et, mehercules, festinarunt parentes ad
nomen liberos mittere quamvis asperrimo bello velut
occasionem complexi, ut sub te ponere rudimenta militiae
contingeret, cernere cotidie divinae virtutis exemplum,
2 te hortatorem operum habere, te testem. Et cum haec
communis totius exercitus esset felicitas, dux Marius,
tamen—o facinus indignum!—plus reliquis[19] consecuti
videbantur, quibus tribunus contigerat propinquus tuus.
3 Quanta cura robora militum legeris, imperator, ut hostibus
prope humanas vires excedentibus opponeres parem dilectum, vel ex eo manifestum est, quod, cum scires non
ex censu esse virtutem, praeterita facultatium contempla-
4 tione vires animosque tantum spectasti.[20] Quid prodest?

14 sol- iuv- *probum, cf. Str. ap. Schn.*[1]

15 -tam . . . -nam *Eng. 62:* -ta . . . -na *codd.*

16 -or Φ*   17 -na Φ   18 -e V: -et B Φ: -uta m. -ina
[et] non -rem n. -nam . . . esse *Reitz.*[2] 27

19 -is C²E O²: -i *cett.*   20 sp- ς: exp- *codd.*

18 Because the massacres caused a depopulation that was to
affect the next generation(s) too (AS).

19 *ad nomen,* sc. *militiae dandum* (Badius Ascensius [1528,
xvii *r.*]).

to us in war too, and we were dissolute even in ill fortune. So it was that this people brought devastation to our fields, loneliness to our young people,[18] danger and near dissolution to our rule. It was obvious that the Roman people had never had greater need of *men* to ward off destruction. (4) And so, as it was quite clear that military discipline had been fatally weakened, and that we had on our hands a war against our morals as serious as that against our enemies, it was in you, Gaius Marius, that we found refuge, looking to the help that only your valor, your probity and severity could afford. 5. And indeed parents hastened to send their sons to join up,[19] as though taking the opportunity, however bitter the fighting, to give them the chance to start their military careers under you, to see every day the example set by your godlike courage, to have you to spur them on in their exertions, you to witness them.[20] (2) And though it was a felicity shared by the whole army to have Marius as leader, those to whom it fell to serve under a tribune related to you were thought (the shame of it!) to have been favored above the rest. (3) What care you took, general, to choose élite troops, so as to deploy against an enemy of almost superhuman strength a force to match them, is clear from this one fact: knowing that valor does not depend on a man's property rating, you took no account of financial means but had regard to strength and spirit alone.[21] (4) To what avail? Look at the

[20] Cf. 8.7.2.

[21] The Marian reforms of 107 BC permitted the landless citizens, formerly excluded from active service, to enlist in the army. Cf. Sall. *Iug.* 86.

En quanta dilectui tuo fit invidia! Diceris adversum Cimbros puerum probasse!

5   Sed neque te militaris aetas fefellit, cuius certissima mensura est posse fortiter facere, 6. neque illa libido fuit saltem vitiis usitata, quae ad obscenos veneris impetus formae cupidine incenditur, sed quidam perditus contumeliae amor ac summa flagitiorum voluptas, inquinare honesta:²¹ hoc ipsum, quod primus ante signa procurrit, quod veteranos tiro praecedit, quod redit pulvere et

2 cruore concretus, istud, istud quod tam²² vir est. Vulgaria inritamenta sunt cupiditatis forma, aetas; singularis res est fortis concubinus: illas cicatrices, illa vulnera, illa tot eximiae decora militiae—quid exequar ultra, imperator?

3 Pudet me quod intellegis. Transeo oblatam nolenti munerum vacationem et blandius quam militiae disciplina postulat adulatum militi tribunum; imperatas asperrimas expeditiones, ut remitterentur; saepe ordinis, saepe adfinitatis tuae iactatam gratiam. Confitemur, C. Mari: diutius vixit obscenus corruptor, dum ista miles non intellegit.

---

²¹ voluptas—honesta *dist. Gron.* (*vd. Str. ap. Wint.*⁷ *139*)
²² iam *Russ.*³

---

²² Cf. 3.4.1: those favoring the tribune slur the soldier as being young enough to be a boy-partner; the speaker, however, implies that the defendant is no child but a brave *man*.

²³ The argument (justifying the link *neque . . . neque*) is: He was very young, but chosen for his valor nevertheless; equally, the tribune was not attracted by the soldier's boyish looks but by his prowess. Construe (AS): *neque illa* (= indefinite *illud*, subject, agreeing by attraction with its first predicate *libido*) *fuit libido . . . , sed . . . amor*, etc. Cf. Krapinger-Stramaglia (2015, 145–46n95).

disfavor that attends your levy! You are said to have recruited a *boy* to fight the Cimbri![22]

(5) But you were not mistaken as to the age for starting military service, which is measured most surely by the ability to fight bravely. 6. Nor[23] was the tribune's the—for the vicious, at least—usual kind of lust, fired up to obscene sexual impulses by a passion for physical beauty. Rather, it was a sort of perverse passion to insult, an extreme pleasure in outraging—namely, the defiling of what is honorable: of the very fact that he is the first to run out in front of the standards, that though a tyro he goes ahead of the veterans, that he comes back caked in dust and blood, and of this, this, that he is so very much a man. (2) Beauty and youth are but ordinary incitements to desire; what is unique is a *heroic* bedfellow. Those scars, those wounds, all those badges of outstanding service[24]—why should I go on, general? I am ashamed that you understand me.[25] (3) I pass over in silence relief from duties offered to a soldier loath to accept it; a tribune praising a soldier more flatteringly than military discipline requires; orders to undertake the most difficult missions, assigned only to be countermanded; constant boasts of the influence he commanded thanks to his rank, thanks to his connection with yourself. We confess, Gaius Marius: this obscene abuser went on living only so long as the soldier did not understand what all this meant.

[24] The badges Marius was known to pride himself on (cf. Sall. *Iug.* 85.29; Plut. *Mar.* 9.2).

[25] There seems to be a heavy sexual innuendo: the tribune was excited by the very manliness of the soldier, so—it is implied—he even wanted passive sex with him. Cf. 3.11.5 (AS).

4   Non audeo dicere, imperator: "Concipe animo temporis illius habitum, reforma cogitatione tua."[23] In aliis forsitan causis permittatur indignitatem rei in[24] oratione exaggerare; de iniuria nostra Latine queri non possumus.

5   Parcendum verbis est, inhibenda magna ex parte veritas.

6   Praevaricandum mihi est, si pudorem habeo. Conlatis cum hoste gravissimo comminus castris, cum totum bellum quodam genere ad pedem venisset et omnium mentes imminentis pugnae cogitatio implesset, circumfremente undique barbaro ululatu, Romano militi pro vallo excubanti meretriciam obscenae libidinis patientiam aliquis

7   imperat? Suum quisque habeat fortasse iudicium; mea sententia non satis pudicus est miles, qui armatus tantum negat.

7. Hoc expositionis loco, imperator, malo accusatoribus credas. Illi narrarunt rem viro et Romano et milite tuo

2   dignam: ad primum statim obscenae libidinis sermonem, non aliter quam si in hostem classicum cecinisset, gladium illum, quem a te pro pudicitia nostrarum coniugum acceperat, per pectus infandi corruptoris exegit; et inlatum

---

23 -ne -a *Sch.*: -nes -as *codd.*
24 *del. Wint.*[7] 139

---

26 A metarhetorical allusion to *deinosis/exaggeratio* (cf. Quint. 8.3.88).   27 "Sociative" plural: cf. 1.1.3 with n. 6.

28 Literally, "speak Latin."

29 By underplaying the truth.

30 Sc., was about to be decided in a close combat.

31 A recurring motif; cf., e.g., Plin. *HN* 26.19.

32 Cf. Quint. 4.2.75–76: "Suppose the accuser has delivered a Narrative, not only showing what was done, but throwing in prej-

(4) General, I dare not say: "Imagine what it was like at that moment, reconstruct it in your thoughts." In other cases, perhaps, it may be permissible for a speaker to exaggerate the outrageousness of an action;[26] of the injury inflicted upon *us*[27] we cannot speak in plain language.[28] (5) One must be sparing of words, the truth has to a large extent to be suppressed. If I have any shame, I am forced to collude with my opponent.[29] (6) Camp had been pitched close to a most formidable enemy. The whole war had in a way come to a head.[30] No one was thinking of anything except the impending battle. From all sides resounded the shrieks of the barbarians.[31] Amid all this, does someone order a Roman soldier, on sentry duty at the ramparts, to submit to obscene lust like some prostitute? (7) Everyone can perhaps judge for himself; in *my* view a soldier is not sufficiently aware of his honor, if he bears arms—and merely says no.

7. At this point in my narrative, general, I prefer you to believe the accusers.[32] They told of an action worthy of a man, of a Roman, of your soldier. (2) At the very first mention (they said) of obscene lust, just as if the trumpet had sounded for battle, he drove through the unspeakable seducer's breast the sword he had received from you to defend the chastity of our wives.[33] Their words made us *see*[34]

---

udice . . . The judge is naturally waiting to hear our Narrative. If we give none, he is bound to believe the facts to be what our opponent said and to be such as he described" (trans. Russell).

[33] Sc., against the barbarians.   [34] A hint at the rhetorical technique of *enargeia*, i.e., the use of particularly vivid language or descriptions intended to prompt a listener to picture in his mind the scenes narrated, almost as if he could see them.

129

ultro[25] pedem tantumque non ardorem luminum, horro-
rem capillorum, fremitum indignationis ante oculos di-
cendo posuerunt. Si omnes milites tales habemus, Mari,
3 vicimus. Verebar equidem ne fugandi corruptoris causa
ferrum strinxisset, et, quod accidere interim solet, dum
alter recessurum putat, alter percussurum non putat, tam
4 honestum opus casus fecisset. Neque enim, ut opinor, hoc
quoque exigendum fuit, ut, cum caecus amentia corruptor
per vulnera ipsa rueret ad praebendos amplexus, miles
etiam gladium reduceret. Ego vero[26] parum viriliter istum
indignatum puto, si in tanto dolore tribunum potuit agnos-
cere. Ipse nihil excusat: 8. "Percussi" inquit, "—gratia[27]
Marti signisque!—, occidi, hausi noxium ultrice dextera
sanguinem, sive licuit, sive non licuit." Atque utinam
plures mortes cepisset, ut impurum spiritum renascens
2 poena torqueret! Parum severe militarem clementibus[28]
suppliciis disciplinam continemus, si[29] tribuno post hoc
factum bene cessit, quod occisus est. Reum ergo caedis
non infitiatione defendam: viro, forti praesertim et in-
3 nocenti, nihil facere convenit quod negandum sit. Non
abnuo crimen, immo, si accusatores tacerent, ipse narras-
sem. Obicite igitur, sed, ut delatores decet, totum. Vere-

---

25 -ro *Reitz.*[2] 27 (*et vd. Håk.*[2] 33): -ra *codd.*
26 -re *Håk.* (*mendo typoth., ut vid.*)
27 -a π E (*def. Leh.*[1] 422): -am *cett.*
28 clemen- *Håk.*[5] 242: redeun- *codd.*
29 nisi *Håk.*[5] 242 (si . . . <non> bene *Dess.*[2]), *invito sensu*

---

35 The incident, therefore, is to be placed before the decisive
Roman victories of Aquae Sextiae (102 BC) and Vercellae (101
BC).

his spontaneous attack, and, almost, his burning gaze, his hair standing on end, his cry of rage. If all our soldiers are like this, Marius, we have won![35] (3) I was for my part afraid[36] that he unsheathed his sword only to put his seducer to flight, and that—as sometimes happens—, while one party thinks the other will retreat, one that the other will not strike, chance was what brought about so noble a deed. (4) For (I presume) *this* was not to be expected of him either: that when the abuser, blinded by madness, rushed to embrace his victim despite the wounds he might receive, the soldier should actually put up his sword. No, for my part I think his indignation would have been less than manly if he had, in the grip of such resentment, been capable of recognizing the tribune. He himself makes no excuses. 8. He says: "I struck him down (thanks be to Mars and the standards!), I killed him, I drew guilty blood with my avenging right hand, whether it was permissible or not." And would he had had more deaths to die, so that his foul spirit could be tortured by a penalty ever born anew! (2) We maintain military discipline with too little rigor, by exacting punishments that are too clement, if after a deed like this a tribune was fortunate enough to be *killed*.[37] My client is on trial for murder, but I shall not defend him by saying he did not do it: it does not befit a man, especially when he is brave and innocent, to do anything that has to be denied. (3) I do not reject the allegation. Indeed, if the accusers were silent, I should have told the story myself. Bring your charge, but in full, as de-

---

[36] Apparently when he heard the description in the accuser's speech (DAR).   [37] I.e., military discipline should exact a punishment more severe than immediate death for such an action.

[QUINTILIAN]

cundissimum enim militem apud sanctissimas imperatoris
aures minus pudet confiteri quam queri.

4   Parumne dedecoris subimus quod non de honoribus
fortissimi viri quaeritur, et, ut longissime vota procedant,
rem honestissimam militi fecisse impune erit? Damnetur
5   etiam, et pudicitiam supplicio pendat![30] Convenite, legiones, intendite animos, contracta undique auxilia: lex
dicitur castris, nec pauci sunt qui hoc nolint licere, illud
velint.

9. Non mehercules possum teneri[31] quominus in accusatorem dolor meus erumpat. Quid dicis? Tu si tribunus
2   esses, hoc fecisses, si miles esses, hoc tulisses? Date prae-
cepta, componite disciplinam: miles hac contumelia percussus est. Indignis vero vocibus contaminatus nihil
amplius aliud[32] quam renuet? Et quis[33] non illum inter
prostitutos habeat, si commiserit ut possit iterum appel-
3   lari? "Neget tamen, et ultionem iniuriae suae differat." Ita,
4   puto, cum inluxerit,[34] tribuno queretur![35] Inicitur manus,
et ab adsignata statione miles abducitur, ut stuprum patia-

---

[30] *sic fere dist. vulg.: interrog. Håk.*   [31] -ri *Bur.* (*cf. Sen.
Ben. 3.20.1, Suet.* Tib. *35.2*): -re *codd.*: <me> -re *Wint.*[9]

[32] aliud *om.* ς, *sed cf. e.g. Plaut.* Asin. *724, Sall.* Iug. *2.4, Plin.*
HN *37.185*

[33] ecq- *Marsh. 182* (*et iam B. Asc.*[1] *xviii r. in paraphr.*)

[34] inluxe- (ill- B[2]) B V (*def. Helm*[2] *94*): illuse- Φ

[35] -ret- ς (*def. Eng. 27.4, Helm*[2] *94*): -rit- B V Φ*

---

[38] Of the tribune's behavior.   [39] Which he did later obtain:
Marius rewarded the soldier with the crown for brave exploits,
"declaring that at a time which called for noble examples he had
displayed most noble conduct" (Plut. *Mar.* 14.8; trans. Perrin).

nouncers should. Before the pure ears of the general, so modest a soldier is less ashamed to confess than to complain.[38]

(4) Have we not been disgraced enough already, because the investigation does not concern the honors deserved by a hero?[39] Will impunity be the most that we can ask for a soldier who has done something so honorable? No, let him be sentenced too, let him pay with his life for being chaste! (5) Gather round, legions; pay heed, you auxiliaries recruited from every part of the world: a law is being laid down for the army, and there are not a few who wish the one thing to be permitted, and not the other.[40]

9. Heavens, I cannot restrain myself from venting my resentment on the accuser. What do you say? If *you* were a tribune, would you have done this? If *you* were a soldier, would you have tolerated this? (2) Give orders and lay down rules as much as you like: still a *soldier* has been outraged in this manner.[41] Stained by indecent language, shall he do no more than shake his head? Who would not count him a prostitute, if he acts in such a way that he can be propositioned a second time? (3) "Let him say no, rather, and put off the time for avenging himself." Yes, indeed: when day breaks, I suppose, he will complain—to the tribune. (4) Hands are laid upon him; a soldier is haled off from his assigned post to be violated. I ask you, accus-

---

[40] Homosexual rape and murder, respectively: ironic.

[41] The speaker is now addressing the senior officers attending the trial (cf. 3.3.2): they may issue the most strict rules of discipline; but who will follow their regulations, if they let a soldier be treated as a prostitute?

tur: vos interrogo, accusatores, quid faciet? Feret libidino-
sas manus vulnera sua tractantes? Deponet arma, an op-
5 ponet?[36] Vir est enim. "⟨At⟩[37] auctorem habet. Hoc primi
ordines iubent:[38] aequum est tribuno militem parere. Inde[39] sperare etiam processus potest: pro hoc merito accipiet fortasse vitem, ordines ducet, et sub illo alii milita-
6 bunt." Si haec condicio causae est, si defensio sui non
permittitur, indicate, praedicite. Si corruptorem non licet
feriri,[40] feret;[41] non enim potest nuda manu repelli: me-
7 mentote, corruptor armatus est. Implicitus tamen infando
nexui, cogitate quid sibi fecisset; utrum[42] sic,[43] si plura,[44]
despiciat,[45] immo (si videtur), quo iustius queri possit,
patiatur[46]—istud vero flagitium in conatu pereat: nam si
libido ad votum obsceni corruptoris processerit, duo occi-
dendi erunt.

10. Libere itaque dixerim, C. Mari: quam de fortissimo
milite sententiam feras, magis tua interest. Huius quidem

---

[36] an oppo- *Håk.*[2] 33–34: an nepo- B: an ne po- V: an repo- M[2]
γ β (*quod pro glossa hab. Sh. B.*[2] *192*): anne po- δ
[37] *suppl. Håk.*   [38] hoc (*om.* V) -mi -nes (-nis A) -ent B V
Φ* (*def. Russ.*[1] *44*): homo -mi -nis -et *Håk.*
[39] inde *Reitz.*[2] *28*: in diem *codd.*
[40] -re *Franc., sed vd. Eng. 62–63*
[41] feret N C: ferit B: feriret A: fieret D: feriet B[2] C[2] *cett.*
[42] *solitarium* (*H.-Sz. 466*), *propter inseq. aposiopesin*
[43] sic β: sit *cett.*   [44] sic—plura *distinxi* (*vd. ad Angl.
vers.*)   [45] des- V E β: dis- *cett.*
[46] *aposiopesin signif. Str. ap. Schn.*[1]

---

[42] Sc., the centurions, properly the highest noncommissioned
officers.

ers, what is he to do? Put up with lustful hands caressing his wounds? Lay down his arms, or use them to defend himself? He is after all a *man*. (5) "<But> he has someone over him. This is what the officers[42] command: it is right and proper for a soldier to obey a tribune. He can even hope to win promotion from this: as reward for this service he will perhaps get a centurion's staff. He will lead the ranks, and others will serve under him." (6) If these are the terms of the case, if self-defense is banned, well, tell us that, give due notice. If it is illegal for an abuser to be struck, then his victim will put up with it: he cannot repel him with his bare hands—remember, his seducer is armed. (7) In the grip of such a foul assailant, ask yourself, what was he to do for himself? In his present situation is he either, if there is more,[43] to make light of it, even (if you like)[44] submit to it, to gain better grounds for complaint . . . ?[45]—no, let this crime perish in midattempt, for if lust goes as far as the disgusting seducer wishes, two will have to be killed.[46]

10. So, Gaius Marius, I may speak freely: what judgment you pronounce on a heroic soldier matters more to

---

[43] I.e., if there are more explicit advances from the tribune: *si plura*, sc. *evenerint, fuerint*, or the like. For a similar "euphemistic" *plura*, cf. 14.5.5 (AS).

[44] Sarcastic.

[45] I.e., in court (cf. 3.9.3). An *an*-clause (responding to *utrum*) would be expected, with an alternative option for the soldier: but the advocate cuts himself off (aposiopesis), to make it clear that no other principled action was possible but killing the assailant.

[46] I.e., both the tribune (by the soldier) and the soldier (by legal process): sexual relationships between fellow soldiers were forbidden and harshly punished.

gloriae nihil plus adici potest, quam si pro re tam honesta
2 moritur. Hunc mirabitur sola virtutium incorrupta testis
vetustas, hoc factum patres liberis vel post poenam prae-
3 cipient. Tu cogita quid te sensisse homines sciant. Hoc
exemplum in neutram partem potest taceri; [cogitare][47]
certum est id quemque, cum iudicat, probare, quod[48] in
re simili ipse fecisset. Omnibus enim ad virile robur per
pueritiam iter est, et iam contra libidinem maturuisse non
4 prodest. Recognosce incrementa tua et honestam tantae
magnitudini memoriam pristinae tenuitatis: sine dubio te
ad tot consulatus et actos aut destinatos triumphos divina
virtus tua sustulit; memento tamen, et tu sub tribuno mili-
tasti, nec ad hoc fastigium dignitatis tam brevi tibi venire
contigisset, si sero coepisses.

11. Dicam nunc ego praecipuam semper curam Roma-
2 nis moribus pudicitiae fuisse? Referam Lucretiam, quae
condito in viscera sua ferro poenam a se necessitatis exegit, et, ut quam primum pudicus animus a polluto corpore
separaretur, se ipsa percussit, quia corruptorem non po-

---

[47] del. Wint.[7] 139 (sc. e cogita male repet.): -ta: Sh. B.[2] 192:
-tari ("sc. vulgo") Håk.   [48] quod V (def. Sh. B.[2] 192): quid B Φ

---

[47] Sc., than to him.   [48] I.e., as an example for good or bad.
[49] Cf. 5.6.5–7.   [50] The soldier not having been a pretty
boy (cf. 3.5.4–6.1), but a grown man.

[51] Cf., e.g., Sen. Controv. 1.6.4; Juv. 8.245–53.

[52] Marius could not have reached such a great glory if he had
not (like this soldier) started so early in his life; but when he was
a young soldier, he himself might have come across a lustful tribune: therefore (it is implied), he should be able to empathize
with the defendant.

you.[47] To *his* glory nothing can be added, except death in
so honorable a cause. (2) He will be wondered at by posterity, the only incorruptible witness to virtue; this deed
will be cited by fathers advising their sons, even supposing
he is punished. It is for *you* to bear in mind what men are
to know your feelings to have been. (3) This example cannot but be spoken of, whichever way it is taken[48]—there
is no doubt that in passing judgment everyone gives his
approval to what he himself would have done in a similar
position.[49] For all men have to journey through boyhood
to manhood; and indeed nowadays being a grown man is
no help against lust.[50] (4) Bear in mind the stages of your
own advancement, the memory of your original poverty—
the memory that reflects such credit on your present
greatness;[51] without doubt it was your godlike virtue that
raised you to so many consulships and triumphs past or to
come, but remember: you too served in the army beneath
a tribune, and you would not have reached these heights
in so short a time if you had started late.[52]

11. Need I say at this point that Roman morality has
always been especially concerned with chastity? (2) Need
I tell[53] of Lucretia, who plunged a sword into her belly in
order to exact punishment from herself for what she did
out of necessity, and who, that her modest soul might
be parted as soon as possible from her tainted body,
slew herself because she was unable to kill her seducer?

[53] The stories of Lucretia (Livy 1.57–59) and Virginia (Livy
3.44–48) are traditional examples of *pudicitia*, often quoted together in rhetorical texts: cf. Val. Max. 6.1.1–2; Sen. *Controv.*
1.5.3; Calp. Fl. 3 (p. 3.15–17 H.); Juv. 10.293–95.

3   tuit occidere? Si nunc placet tibi miles, quin[49] ego Virgi-
nium narrem, qui filiae virginitatem, qua sola poterat,
morte defendit raptumque de proximo ferrum non re-
cusanti puellae immersit? Dimisit[50] illaesum[51] Appium,
quem tamen populus Romanus secessione a patribus et
prope civili bello persecutus in vincula duci coegit, neque
ulla res tum magis indignationem plebis commovit, quam

4   quod pudicitiam auferre temptaverat filiae militis. Haec
sunt honesta, haec narranda feminarum exempla—nam

5   virorum quae pudicitia est, nisi non corrumpere? Non sit
mihi forsitan querendum adversis auribus saeculi in tantum vitia regnare, ut obscenis cupiditatibus natura cesse-
rit, ut pollutis in femineam usque patientiam maribus in-
currat iam libido in sexum suum. Finem tamen aliquem
sibi vitia ipsa exceperunt, ultimumque adhoc huius flagitii

6   crimen fuit corrupisse futurum virum. Hoc vero cuius
dementiae est? In concubinatum iuniores leguntur, et in

7   muliebrem patientiam vocatur fortasse iam maritus. Ego
vero gratulor militari disciplinae, gratulor opinioni castrorum, si huius mentis tribunus in hunc primum incidit.

    12. Itane tandem (iuvat enim velut praesentis insequi
furorem) scorta tua stipendium merentur, et sub signis

---

[49] quin *Str. ap. Wint.[7] 140*: quid *codd.* (*unde* quid? *Russ.[2]
ibid.*): quidni *Wint.[7] ibid.*
[50] dimi- *Anon. teste Bur.*: divi- *codd.*
[51] illaesum *Helm[2] 94–95*: illi solum *codd.*

---

[54] From a butcher's shop nearby (Livy 3.48.5).
[55] I.e., "natural" sex.

(3) If you would like an example of a soldier next, why should I not tell of Virginius, who defended his daughter's virginity in the only way he could, by her death, snatching a sword that was at hand[54] to plunge into the girl, who made no demur? He left Appius unscathed, but the Roman people, by seceding from the senate and almost starting civil war, hunted down the criminal and had him fettered: and nothing on that occasion angered the ordinary people more than the fact that he had made an attempt on the virtue of the daughter of a *soldier*. (4) These are truly noble examples to narrate—concerning women, of course: for what counts as chastity in men except not to be corrupters? (5) Perhaps I should not complain, in an age so loath to listen, that vice reigns so widely that nature[55] has given place to obscene desires, that males have been corrupted even to the extent of submitting like women, and men's lust now assails their own sex. Vices have found themselves some limit, though: up to now the worst crime has been the corruption of someone yet to grow to manhood. (6) But as for *this* deed, what can be said of its madness? Young men are recruited as bedfellows, and perhaps even some husband is nowadays being summoned to submit as women do. (7) I, for my part, congratulate the army on its discipline, the camp on its good repute, if this was the first man on whom a tribune with such inclinations has lit.[56]

12. So then (I enjoy directing my invective at the madman as though he were here in person),[57] do your tarts earn army wages, do you drag your studs to serve under

---

[56] Because this means that no one in the camp has ever submitted to his lust.　　[57] Cf. Quint. 4.2.93.

exoletos trahis? Ideo meretrices ab exercitu summoven-
tur, intrare castra feminis non licet? Ita, puto: non opus
2 est. Militem, hoc est plus quam virum, iamiamque in acie
staturum, cui pro virili portione salutem suam patria commisit, appellas. Fortasse classico sonante ideo stationes
circuis, ideo vigilias ambis. En quem tribunum faceres,
3 cum praetextati militabant! Non hic profusus[52] est furor,
non manifesta dementia est? Vides munitum gladio latus,
loricam ferro asperam, clausam galea faciem et ad ter-
rorem belli cristas minantis, inscriptum in scuto C. Mari
nomen, totum denique virum Martio habitu horrentem:
4 hic tibi cultus prostituti videtur? Appellabis de stupro?
Vim adferes? Quid deinde?[53] Expectas ut ille te tribunum
5 putet, cum tu illum non putes militem? Vacat enim vitiis
nostris et ad omne votum fluente fortuna lascivit otium?
Aut in eo saltem statu res publica est, ut ad restituendam
eam satis[54] sit milites impudicos non esse?[55]

13. Non de prolatando tibi imperio res est, nec trans-
marinas, ut nuper, provincias petimus; de Italiae posses-
sione certatur, pro aris focisque constitimus: an haec omnia igni ferroque vastentur, an nobis caput barbarus hostis

[52] -fessus *Obr.*
[53] *dist. Wint.*[9]
[54] satius *Håk., sed vd. Sh. B.*[4] 191
[55] *interrog. dist. Håk.*

---

[58] As in past emergencies (cf., e.g., Val. Max 7.6.1 on *praetextati pueri* enlisted after the battle of Cannae in 216 BC). The
minimum age for military service was seventeen years (Gell.
10.28.1), roughly the age of the entry into adulthood; before that,
a boy would wear the *toga praetexta.*

the standards? Is that why harlots are being banished from the army, why women are not allowed to enter the camp? Yes, I suppose so: there is no need for them. (2) You proposition more than a man: a *soldier*, ready before long to stand in the battle line, one to whose best efforts the fatherland has committed its safety. Perhaps that is why, when the trumpet sounds, you go round the posts, why you inspect the watches. What a tribune you would have made, in the days when teenage boys went to war![58] (3) Is this not unbridled madness, obvious insanity? Here are hips girt with a sword, a breastplate bristling with iron, a face shut up in a helmet and plumes threatening the terrors of war, Gaius Marius' name inscribed on the shield, the whole man in the hideous garb of Mars: do you think *this* the getup of a prostitute? (4) Will you propose sex? Will you use force? Well then? Do you expect him to regard you as a tribune, when you do not regard him a soldier? (5) Is there time to indulge our vices, is there a surfeit of leisure, with the tide of fortune answering all our prayers? Or at least is the republic in such a state that, if it is to be put back on its feet, it is enough for soldiers not to be unchaste?[59]

13. It is not now for you a matter of extending the empire, and we are not, as we were quite recently, seeking provinces overseas; the struggle is for the possession of Italy, we have taken a stand in defense of our altars and hearths: what is at stake is whether all this is to be devastated by fire and sword, whether a barbarian foe is to cut

[59] = Is all we need of our soldiers that they should be free of sexual wrongdoing? No: we need them to be real men (DAR).

2 excidat, an Cimbrice loquendum sit. Vita omnium nostrorum[56] et salus (namque aliud ne sub hoste quidem viri
timemus) in ultimum discrimen adducitur. Influxit Italiae
inaudita multitudo, quam ne ea quidem potuit sustinere
terra, quae genuit; inusitata[57] corporum magnitudo; mores
3 etiam Germanis feri. Strage nostrorum campi latent, iam
fugatorum Carbonis atque Silani sub comparatione felix
militia est: iacet post amissum Scaurus exercitum, Servili
Manliique bina cum tot legionibus castra perdidimus.
Gens maiorem terrarum partem victoriis pervagata tan-
4 tum in Mario stetit. Libere[58] te, imperator, interrogo: in
hoc rerum statu tales milites habere malis, an tales tribu-
nos? In tanto belli discursu ne concessae quidem veneri
darem veniam: nam quo ad altiorem quisque honorum
gradum escendit,[59] magis in exemplum spectantibus pa-
5 tet. Cum alii excubent armati, alii claustra portarum
tueantur, alii vallum fossasque scutis innixi cingant, cibum
ipsum stantes capiant, tribunus inter scorta volutabitur, et
has solas vigilias aget? Ac ne ideo quidem brevem saltem

---

56 nostrum 5, *sed hic* nostri *spectantur* (*velut 3.13.3*)

57 invis- *Lips* (*corrob. Marsh. 182*)

58 -ere *Hâk.*: -enter *codd.*   59 esce- *Grut. § II.14,* asce-
"docti viri" teste Bur. (*utrumque firm. Beck.*[2] *74*): exte- B V γ H
β, *unde* <se> (5) ... exte- *Bur.*: extenditur πM O (*def. Gron.*[2] *335*)

---

60 For this traditional representation of German "barbarians,"
cf., e.g., Caes. *B. Gall.* 1.39.1; Juv. 8.251–52.

61 The consul Cn. Papirius Carbo was put to flight with his
army in 113 BC by the Cimbri, who had invaded northern Italy;
M. Iunius Silanus, consul in 109, attacked them and was defeated
in Gallia Transalpina.

off our heads, whether we are to be forced to talk Cimbric. (2) The life and safety of all our dependents (for *we* are *men*, and fear nothing else apart from that—even if we fall into enemy hands) is in extreme danger. A horde without parallel has flooded into Italy, such as could not be supported even by the land that bore them. Their bodies are gigantic; their behavior ferocious even for Germans.[60] (3) The plains lie hidden under the bodies of our men, and to serve with the routed Carbo and Silanus was fortunate by comparison.[61] Scaurus lies dead after the loss of his army, we have lost the two camps of Servilius and Manlius with so many legions.[62] The tribe that roamed victoriously over the greater part of the world has come to a halt only when faced by Marius. (4) I ask you frankly, general: in such circumstances, would you prefer soldiers like this, or tribunes like this? At so chaotic a moment of the war I should not condone even legitimate sexual activity: for the higher a man's rank, the more conspicuous an example he gives to those who keep their eyes fixed on him.[63] (5) While some keep armed guard, others watch the barricaded gates, yet others ring the vallum and ditches, leaning on their shields and eating where they stand, will a tribune roll in the hay among his lovers, and will these be the only watches he keeps? Will he not make a pretense of decent

[62] In 105 BC the consul Cn. Manlius Maximus and Q. Servilius Caepio, proconsul of Gaul, sent their legate M. Aurelius Scaurus to halt the advance of the Germanic coalition, but he was defeated, captured, and executed; Servilius and Manlius were in turn defeated shortly thereafter. [63] Cf. 3.15.2; Plin. *Pan.* 45.6, *vita principis censura est eaque perpetua: . . . ad hanc convertimur, nec tam imperio nobis opus est quam exemplo.*

frugalitatis perferet simulationem, ne haec illum facere
milites sciant?

14. Age porro, si viveret tribunus, et hoc ad te factum,
imperator, deferremus, ⟨si⟩[60] circumstaret universus exercitus, nec hanc militis contumeliam sed militiae puta-
ret, quid ageres, quid constitueres? Beneficium accepisti,
Mari, beneficium: non habes necesse propinquum tuum
2 occidere. Nam si vere aestimemus, imperium populi Romani ad hanc diem militari disciplina stetit. Non enim
nobis aut multitudo maior est quam ceteris gentibus aut
vehementiora corpora quam vel his ecce Cimbris aut
maiores opes quam locupletissimis regnis aut mortis con-
temptus facilior quam plerisque barbaris causam vitae non
habentibus; principes nos facit severitas institutorum,
ordo militiae, amor quidam laboris et cotidiana exercitati-
3 one assidua belli meditatio. Itaque plura paene moribus
quam viribus vicimus, cum captivae quoque sancte habe-
bantur, et contumelia etiam hosti aberat. Quae omnia
longa superbae nobilitatis intermissa luxuria tui nobis
mores retulerunt. 15. Di profecto magnitudinem tuam
curant, imperator, ac dirigunt,[61] qui tibi super ceteras
laudes obtulerunt tam honestae sententiae occasionem:
quod miles fortiter fecit, si absolvis,[62] tuum exemplum est.

[60] *add. Wint.[7] 140*: ⟨cum⟩ *Russ.[2] ibid.*
[61] dili- M
[62] -vis B[pc] V Φ*: -vas B[ac]

---

[64] Cf. Livy 8.7.16.

[65] Romans have a greater fear of dying than barbarians, as
they live a more worthwhile life (due to their virtue, their greater
cultural advancement, etc.).

conduct at least for a short time, if only to prevent the men knowing he is behaving like this?

14. Well now, if the tribune were still alive, and we were bringing this matter before you, general, <if> the entire army were standing around us, regarding it an outrage not to a soldier but to soldiering, what would you do, what would you decide? You have received a boon, Marius, a boon: you do not have to kill your kinsman. (2) For if we judge aright, the empire of the Roman people has to this day stood on the foundation of military discipline.[64] We do not have a larger population than the rest of mankind, or more active bodies than even these Cimbri you see in front of you, or greater resources than the richest kingdoms; nor do we despise death more readily than so many barbarians, who have no reason to live.[65] We are superior thanks to the rigor of our institutions, our military organization, our love of hard work, and our constant practice of war by daily exercises. (3) And so we won almost more victories by character than by strength, in the days when women prisoners too used to be treated decently, and even the enemy suffered no outrage. All these things lapsed during a long period of aristocratic arrogance and luxury; but your[66] moral standards have brought them back to us. 15. Surely the gods must be taking care of your greatness, general, and guiding it: besides all your other claims to fame, they have offered you an opportunity to pass so righteous a verdict. This soldier's heroic act, if you acquit him, is an example which *you* will have established.

[66] Addressed to Marius.

2   Nisi forte hoc me perturbari putatis, quod tribunus
fuit. Ideo hercule turpior, ideo morte omni dignior. Haec
enim condicio superiorum est, ut, quicquid faciunt,
praecipere videantur, et perniciosissimus est malae rei
3 maximus quisque auctor. Quis continebit militiam, quis
castrensis disciplinae praecipiet severitatem? Quis te,
imperator, maioribus curis districto delicta militum coer-
4 cebit? ‹Tribunus? Et quis›[63] tribuni [corpus et][64] peccata
corriget?[65] Ad quem confugiam, cui querar? Sic fit ut
necesse habeamus ipsi nos vindicare. "Tribunus fuit"; et
5 hic miles fuit. "Tribunus": hoc[66] dicis, cui parere caligatum
lex iubet, qui non solum militibus, sed centurionibus prae-
positus partem quandam imperatoriae potestatis optinet.
6 Ita, opinor, contra iura castrorum fecerat miles, etiam si
tantum negasset. Nescit quod istius honoris fastigium,
7 quae potestas ordinis: tiro est.[67] Age si ad te, C. Mari,
aliquis impudicum militem detulisset, ferres dicentem:
"Tribunus me iussit"? Quodsi par in utraque parte de-
lictum est, hoc tamen crimen militem saltem decet.

---

[63] *lac. stat. Reitz.*[2] *29, suppl. Håk.* (‹tribunus. quis est qui›
Helm[1] *357)*   [64] *secl. Wint.*[7] *140 utpote (Russ.*[2] *ibid.) corrup-
tam anticip. v.* corriget (tribuni corpus *del. Sh. B.*[2] *192):* corruptoris *Obr.:* correctoris *Str. ap. Sch.*[1]   [65] -gat B V

[66] miles—hoc *dist. Reitz.*[2] *29–30 (firm. Pas.*[3] *536)*

[67] nescit—est *del. Reitz.*[2] *30 et Håk., sed totum argumentum*
(ita, opinor—saltem decet) *elucid. Helm*[1] *357–58*

---

[67] Cf. 3.9.5.   [68] Cf. Juv. 6.O31–32, *Sed quis custodiet
ipsos / custodes . . . ?*   [69] Cf. 3.9.3. The advocate here speaks
in the first person instead of his client; then he returns to the
"sociative" plural (*habeamus ipsi nos*): compare 3.6.4.

(2) Perhaps, though, you all think I feel upset that he was a tribune. Heavens, that makes him the more disgraceful, the more worthy of any kind of death. The position of superior officers is such that whatever they do is thought to be an order, and it is the highest in rank who are the most dangerous initiators[67] of evil deeds. (3) Who will keep the troops under control, who will enjoin strict discipline in the camp? At times when you have more important matters clamoring for your attention, general, who will restrain the misdemeanors of the soldiers? ⟨The tribune? (4) And who⟩ will correct the tribune's faults?[68] With whom shall I seek refuge, to whom shall I complain?[69] In these circumstances, we have to look to avenging ourselves. "He was a tribune": and this man was a soldier.[70] (5) "A tribune." You mean by that a man whom the law orders the private soldier[71] to obey, a man who is placed above the troops, and over centurions too, and wields some part of the general's power. (6) On[72] that basis, I presume, the soldier would have infringed military law even if he had just said no. Well, he does not know how high a rank it is, what power it carries: after all, he is only a recruit. (7) Seriously, Gaius Marius: if some one had denounced a licentious soldier to you, would you tolerate him saying: "A tribune ordered me to"? The offense may well be equal on both sides,[73] but at least *this* crime befits

---

[70] Who, as such, could not leave himself unavenged. Cf. 3.15.7.   [71] The private soldiers wore leather boots (*caligae*), the officers shoes (*calcei*). This contrast in footwear became the symbol of the different ranks in the army.

[72] The whole of §6 is ironic.   [73] I.e., the attempted rape by the tribune, the murder by the soldier.

16. "Tribunus fuit." Videor mehercules, imperator, oblitus mediocritatis meae, cum vix unius defensioni sufficiam, quaedam pro universo dicturus exercitu; omnes has, quae circumstetere legiones, florem Italiae, civium sociorumque robora una voce proclamare apud tribunal existima:

2 "Non ignominia tribunis parere possumus. Nemo nostrum recusat itinerum laborem nec iniustum super arma fascem, non aestivi solis ardorem nec sub pellibus actam hiemem. Ferienda[68] sit[69] fatigato fossa, pro vallo portisque

3 vigilandum. Fortiter ancipites inibimus pugnas, vulnera laude pensabimus. Mors erit ignominia potior. Quicquid

4 in pugna patimur, virorum est. Imperet asperas tribunus expeditiones, si quo vertice montis hostis pellendus est, si inter infestos armatis saltus speculandum; saeviat denique in terga verberibus, exigat servilem plagarum patientiam.

5 Leno etiam servis excipitur; fortasse hac lege captivos vendes. Si meretricia imperatur necessitas, si adversus obscenam vim corruptoris arma tantum contumeliae causa habemus, potius castra capiantur, et vim tribuni

---

68 fodi- *Pass., sed cf. Beck.*[2] 75 et ThlL VI.1.516.77–81
69 -da est sic β, *sed cf. Str.*[15] 55.96

---

74 To kill to protect his own *pudicitia* befits a soldier (3.15.4); to proposition a subordinate does *not* befit a tribune.

75 Cf. 3.19.1.

76 This passage (3.16.2–3) is echoed by Jerome and a Latin panegyrist: see Introduction to the present declamation.

77 You = Marius. In a contract of sale for a slave, a special provision (*exceptio*) could be added disallowing the prostitution of the person concerned (cf. Papin. *Dig.* 18.7.6.pr.); and even prisoners of war might be sold on the same condition. It follows

a soldier.[74] 16. "It was a tribune." By heaven, general, I feel I will now forget my own modest abilities[75]—scarcely capable as I am of defending a *single* man—and speak out on behalf of the whole army; imagine that these legions gathered around us, the cream of Italy, the élite force of citizens and allies, declare with one voice before your tribunal: (2) "We cannot obey tribunes at the cost of disgrace. No one of us rebels at the toil of route marches or the excessive packs that we carry in addition to our weapons, at the blazing summer heat or winters spent in tents of hide. Let us have ditches dug when we are dog-tired, watch kept at rampart and gates. (3) We shall go bravely into the hazards of battle,[76] and regard praise as recompense for our wounds. Death will be preferable to disgrace. Whatever we suffer in battle is *men's* work. (4) Let a tribune order dangerous enterprises, if the foe has to be driven from a mountain crest, if reconnaissances have to be undertaken across wild country infested with armed men. Let him beat our backs savagely, expect us to bear our stripes like slaves. (5) But even in the case of slaves, sale to a pimp may be excluded; and perhaps you will sell captives on the same terms.[77] If *we*[78] are ordered to prostitute ourselves, if in the face of the obscene force of a corrupter the weapons we bear do no more than taunt us, better the camp were captured, better a Cimbrian

that soldiers serving under this tribune underwent a fate worse than slaves and prisoners, as they incurred harassment that the latter are normally spared (see now Santorelli [2020a]).

[78] Soldiers, far superior—in principle—to slaves and captives.

6   interpellet Cimber. Nihil tale novere Germani, et sanctius vivitur ad Oceanum." 17. Quid futurum est, imperator, si ad pudicitiam militum pertinet vinci?

2   An ignoramus, imperator, quanta quondam populi Romani exarserit seditio, cum ex domo feneratoris addictus lacero verberibus tergo prorupisset in publicum, et illas suppliciorum notas tulisse se quereretur, quod vim 3 corruptoris pati noluisset? Et ille tamen, quamquam hoc flagitium conatus in addicto ac paene vix libero, videbatur aliquatenus memor fuisse Romanae sanctitatis, qui vim obscenissimam non temptaverat nisi adversus alligatas 4 manus. Eo tamen usque populi Romani vindicta processit, ut ardentibus bello finibus ad dilectum nemo responderet, nisi et poena corruptoris et abrogatione legis satisfactum esset. Nolebant militare, quamvis hanc iniuriam non miles 5 acceperat. Quid de Fabio Eburno loquar, qui filium impudicum[70] cognita domi causa necavit? Iam iam, commilito,

---

[70] impudicum E δ: in iudicium B V: in -cio *cett.*

---

[79] This anecdote is mentioned in Cic. *Rep.* 2.59, Dion. Hal. *Ant. Rom.* 16.5.9, Livy 8.28, and Val. Max. 6.1.9, with significant variations as to the dating (at some point in the late fourth century BC) and the characters involved. An uprising of the Roman people is mentioned in Dionysius and Livy. See Santorelli (2018a, 31–34).   [80] In *that* condition the man was made equivalent to a slave, expected to submit to his master's requests. Cf. Sen. *Controv.* 4.pr.10 (Haterius), *Impudicitia in ingenuo crimen est, in servo necessitas, in liberto officium.*

[81] In reality, early Roman law on insolvent debtors was (however greatly) *mitigated* only, after this episode, thanks to the new *lex Poetelia Papiria de nexis.*

obstructed the tribune's violence! (6) The Germans know nothing of such things: life is conducted more decently on the shores of the Ocean." 17. Where will it end, general, if the chastity of soldiers is guaranteed by their defeat?

(2) Do we not know, general, what a great sedition of the Roman people blazed forth once in the past, when an indentured servant burst into the street from the house of a moneylender, his back torn by whips, and complained that these were the marks left by his punishment for refusing to submit to the violence of a seducer?[79] (3) The usurer perpetrated this outrage on someone indentured for debt and scarcely to be counted as free, but he did seem to some extent to have been aware of what Roman standards require, for he had aimed his utterly obscene force only at a man in chains.[80] (4) Still, the Roman people went so far in its revenge that, though the frontiers were ablaze with war, no one went to answer the call for recruits before they were placated by the punishment of the corrupter and the annulling[81] of the law. They refused to serve as soldiers even though it was not a soldier who had been thus outraged.[82] (5) And what should I say about Fabius Eburnus, who tried his immoral son in his own house, and put him to death?[83] Now, fellow soldier, whatever is in

[82] Cf. n. 79. The declaimer draws this ending from another anecdote in Livy 2.23–24, where the plebeians refuse to enlist for the imminent war against the Volsci at the sight of an old former centurion enslaved for debts and tortured by his master (but without references to sexual harassment).

[83] Q. Fabius Maximus Eburnus was censor in 108 BC. Val. Max. 6.1.5 mistakenly ascribes this action to his father, Q. Fabius Maximus Servilianus. Cf. also Oros. 5.16.8.

quicumque casus[71] manet, etiam si te imperator damnatu-
rus est, habes solacium: satius est quam a patre occidi.

18. "At propinquus[72] C. Mari fuit." Corrumpitis iudi-
cem, et damno alioquin levi[73] gratiae pondus imponitis.
"Propinquus tuus fuit." O rem omnibus narrandam, cum
2 absolveris! Nam si quid tibi iudicandi fides tua causa facere permittit, cogitas profecto quantum tibi hoc ipsum
apud aemulos, quos virtutibus offendis, adlaturum sit invi-
diae, cum videberis aut corruptorem militis iudicasse[74]
innocentem aut propinquum tuum etiam nocentem[75] vin-
3 dicasse.[76] Olim iam, imperator, inter fulgentes virtutes
tuas livor locum quaerit, et natura quidem omnibus novi-
tatis incrementis adversa nobilitas, tuis tamen laudibus
pressa et obruta, rimatur occasionem criminum. Quodsi
bene invidiam novi, hoc quoque tibi obicietur, quod sal-
4 tem propinquus tuus peccaverit. Quare abdicandus, eiu-
randus[77] est non tuus sanguis. Certe nihil minus commit-
tendum, quam ut ⟨non⟩[78] ulciscaris hoc flagitium, in eo
praesertim, qui apud malignos poterit videri te permit-
5 tente fecisse. An ille, si umquam cogitasset se propinquum
tuum, non has virtutes, inter quas fortuna tua minima est,

---

71 ⟨te⟩ casus *Beck.*[2] *19, sed vd. ThlL VIII.290.71ss.*
72 -ncus B   73 damno... levi *Håk.*[4] *152:* animo (ammo
B[ac]) . . . levi *codd.:* animo . . . leni *B. Asc.*[1] *xxi r., sed vd. Str. ap.*
Schn.[1]   74 -are ς
    75 noc- *h.l. habet* V (*def. Golz 77, Wint.*[7] *140): post* vind- B Φ
    76 -asse *Wint.*[7] *140:* -are *codd.*
    77 eiur- *Håk.*[2] *34* (et eiur- ς): et iur- *codd.:* et abiur- *Leh.*[1] *423*
(*cf. Håk.-Wint. 80*)   78 *add. Helm*[2] *95*

---

84 = You want Marius' judgment to be influenced by the loss

store, even if the general is going to find you guilty, you have something to console you: it is preferable to being killed by your father.

18. "But he was related to Gaius Marius." You are trying to corrupt the judge, adding the burden of bias to a loss in itself slight.[84] "He was your kinsman." What a tale for all to tell when you pronounce acquittal! (2) For if your integrity as a judge allows you to do anything in your own interests, you surely have in mind how much hostility this very fact will bring down upon you among the rivals you offend by your virtues, if you seem either to have adjudged innocent the abuser of a soldier or to have avenged a kinsman even though he was guilty. (3) For a long time now, general, envy has been looking for a weak point amid your shining virtues.[85] The nobility is of course inherently opposed to every advancement of new men, but it feels oppressed and overwhelmed by your glorious career, and is ferreting out an opportunity to accuse you. Indeed, if I know how envy operates, even so much as a relative of yours doing wrong will be brought against you. (4) Accordingly this man must be disowned and disavowed, as not being of your blood. Certainly no course of action is less to be recommended than to ⟨fail to⟩ punish this outrage, especially as it concerns someone who may be thought by the malevolent to have acted with your approval. (5) If he had ever thought of himself as your kinsman, should he not have drunk deep of your virtues (among which your

he sustained by the tribune's death; however, such a loss is light, both in itself (cf. 3.18.5–7) and when compared with the harm Marius would suffer, should he not keep his oath of impartiality as a judge (cf. 3.18.2–4).   [85] Cf. Sall. *Iug.* 85.5.

cum ei velut propius contemplare[79] licuisset, toto pectore
haurire debuerat, non huic affinitatis suae felicitati referre
6 gratiam? Milites te melius imitantur. Quodsi post hanc
mentem[80] viveret tribunus, necessarium forsitan erat hac
quoque eum premi invidia, quod ista fecisset Mari propinquus, quod ex ipsa stirpe virtutum sustulisset se flagi-
7 tii[81] suboles. Iam[82] cum bene sit liberata probro familia,
quid attinet illud subinde Mario obicere? Optimum fuerat
non habuisse talem, proximum est[83] libenter perdidisse.

19. Perorata, imperator, ut mediocritas ingenii mei
tulit, causa scio commendationis partis esse reliquas, sed
has supervacuas facit sanctitas tua: quid enim verear ne
noceat reo humilitas apud te, cui vel gratior potest esse
nuda virtus, apud quem maximum est ex se coepisse?
2 Commendem tibi ordinem caligati militis, quem velut
incrementorum tuorum natalem libenter ab alto respicis?
Adhuc fortasse patricium valuerit genus, sed nunc tu[84]
tuae[85] longa serie dignitatis ordinem[86] ipse[87] virtutum

---

79 -ri Φ, *sed cf. ThlL IV.650.15ss.*

80 amentiam *Watt*[2] *20, sed vd. Hâk.*

81 -ii V AE δ (*def. Eng. 90–91, Helm*[2] *95*): -iis *cett.*

82 iam *Franc.*: nam *codd.* (*frustra def. Hâk.*): nunc *Gron.*

83 est *Leh.*: et *codd.*: aut ς: talem ⟨propinquum⟩, proximum
[aut] *Dess.*[1] *86* (-mum est *Hâk.*)   84 nunc tu *Helm*[1] *358*: duc
tu V: ductu B Φ*: ducta *Pas.*[2] *239–40*

85 tuae *Str. ap. Schn.*[1]: eius E: tuis *cett.*

86 origine (ipsa) *Pi. ap. Pas.*[2] *240*

87 -se *Helm*[2] *95–96* (*firm. Wint.*[7] *140–41*): -sam M: -sa *cett.*

---

86 Cf. Soph. *OC* 1224–27: "Not to be born comes first by every
reckoning; and once one has appeared, to go back to where one

good fortune is the least), considering that he had been in a position to observe them from so close at hand? Should he not have made some requital for the good luck of being related to you? The common soldiers imitate you better. (6) But if, after this display of his cast of mind, the tribune had gone on living, he would perhaps have had to feel heavy upon him the burden of disfavor for this too, that it was a kinsman of Marius who had acted thus, that from the very stock of virtues had sprung a scion of disgrace. (7) Anyway, now that the family has been well and truly rid of the stain on it, there is no point in continually throwing the outrage in Marius' teeth. It would have been best not to have had someone like that: next best[86] is to be glad to have lost him.

19. General, I have now completed the defense so far as my modest abilities allowed.[87] I know that it remains to commend the defendant;[88] but this is rendered superfluous by your integrity. Why should I be afraid that his low birth might harm him in the eyes of you, for whom virtue can be even more welcome when it is unadorned, and whose greatest claim to glory is that you started from yourself? (2) Am I to commend to you the "order" of private soldiers,[89] on which you look back from your lofty station as the origin of your advancement? Hitherto, perhaps, patrician descent may have had weight; but now, thanks to your long history of high office, you have yourself estab-

---

came from as soon as possible is the next best thing" (trans. Lloyd-Jones).　　[87] Cf. 3.16.1. The speaker is supposed to be a soldier, not a professional advocate.

[88] As usually required in an epilogue (a metarhetorical hint).

[89] Cf. n. 71.

3 condicione[88] meliore[89] fecisti. Nondum potuit altius pro-
cedere vir adhuc huius aetatis; tamen, cum virum fortem,
cum dignum tuis castris, tuis auspiciis probarim, com-
4 mendo tibi quicquid melius miles fieri potest. Hoc quidem
profecto non expectas, ut in extrema actione miserabili
fletu et humili obtestatione vitam genu nixus petat: nec tu
rogari ab innocente exigis, nec viro forti opus est preca-
ria[90] absolutione.[91] Unum rogat, ut, si quid de causa illius
dubitas, des dilationem usque ad proximum proelium.
5 Pone in prima acie, pone ante signa—fortiter dixerim: non
inter tirones; ubi plus[92] periculi, quo maximus hostium
globus ingruet,[93] specta pugnantem. Adfirmo: tunc minus
6 ignosces tribuno. Liceat ire in aciem, congredi cum hostibus. Si perire debet, rogat te, imperator, miles tuus,
opera[94] mortis suae utaris.

88 -ne Φ (*def. Wint.*[7] *140–41*): -nem B V
89 -re *Wint.*[7] *140–41*: -rem *codd.*
90 -ria E: -ri *cett.*
91 -ne B V E: -nem *cett.*
92 plus πM[2] E (*def. Helm*[1] *358–59*): su`s´ B: usus *cett.* (*def. Leh.*[1] *423*)
93 signa—ingruet *sic distinxi*
94 -ra M[2] E: -re B[2]: -ris *cett.*

lished, on a better basis, an "order" of virtues.[90] (3) A man still so young could not yet have gone higher; but[91] in demonstrating that he is worthy of serving in your camp and under your auspices, I am commending to you everything that this soldier can rise to in the future. (4) You do not expect, I am sure, that at the end of the hearing he should go down on his knees and ask for his life with pitiable weeping and humble appeals: you do not ask prayers from someone who is innocent, and a brave man needs no acquittal that depends on entreaty. He asks only this: if you have any doubts about his case, grant an adjournment till the next battle. (5) Place him in the front rank, place him before the standards, and not (to say it boldly) among the raw recruits; watch him fighting where there is more danger, where the enemy will attack in the largest numbers. *Then*, I promise, you will be less inclined to forgive the tribune. (6) Let him go into action, engage with the enemy. If he must die, general, your soldier asks you to make good use of his death.

[90] A wordplay on the meanings of *ordo*: Marius's example has shown that the "rank" a soldier can achieve by proving his virtue (*ordinem . . . virtutum*) is more important than the grade he is assigned in the army (*ordinem . . . militis*) or the authority that comes from an aristocratic descent (*patricium . . . genus*).

[91] This soldier is too young to have reached the heights of Marius already; but he could yet fly high.

DECLAMATION 4

INTRODUCTION

A man, about to become a father, consults an astrologer on the destiny of his unborn child: the astrologer predicts that a son will be born, who will first become a hero, then will commit parricide. Years later, the son fights heroically in war: to prevent the second part of the prophecy from happening, he wishes to end his own life, but his father objects.

Two of the most popular rules of "Sophistopolis," the city of declamations, interact in this *controversia*: the law granting a war hero a reward of his choice,[1] and the provision requiring that any suicide who has failed to account for the reasons for his act before the senate be left unburied.[2] The background to this case is provided by astrology,

[1] Cf., e.g., Sen. *Controv.* 10.2; Quint. 7.5.4; [Quint.] *Decl. min.* 258 and 371. The main legal issue raised by this law was whether a hero could choose *any* reward, especially when his choice created a conflict with another legal provision. Cf. Lentano (1998); Stramaglia (2013b, 83–84n1) for further references.

[2] The speech of self-denunciation given by the aspiring suicide to disclose the reasons for his death, known as προσαγγελία, was a very popular exercise in both Greek and Roman declamation: cf., e.g., Quint. 7.4.39; [Quint.] *Decl. min.* 335 and 337; Calp. Fl. 20, 38, 53. See Stramaglia (2013b, 85n3), with previous bibliography; add Manzione (2014, 190–95) and Hatzilambrou (2015).

which is in turn a topic addressed in ancient rhetorical theory, in real forensic speeches, and especially in declamation.[3] The mythical paradigm of Oedipus—as developed especially in Seneca's tragedy—is also clearly discernible.[4]

In our case, Father has already spoken against Son's resolution to commit suicide. He has argued that the astrologer's prediction rested on no solid grounds, for there is no art of astrology (13.2). Son's reply to this assertion (13.4–14.5) deploys traditional arguments,[5] rising to heights of philosophical eloquence: our awesome universe cannot be the product of chance, and when man stirred himself to examine it he saw that signs can be found in the stars (16.1–3 and 16.5); man's destiny, like everything else, is predetermined and predictable.

This formal defense of astrology is tied to the case in hand by the use of an *ad hominem* argument: Father himself must have been a believer, for otherwise he would not have felt frightened enough to consult an astrologer in the first place (cf. the start of the narration in 3.1–2). Son puts especial emphasis on the coherence of the prediction: eventual parricide is proved by past heroism in war (4.1–2;

In reality, the only postmortem sanction a suicide could incur in Rome was the confiscation of his property: but this applied only to those who took their life while facing a trial and arguably committed suicide to prevent an unfavorable judgment that could result in their death or in the confiscation of their assets; see now Petrucci (2017, 110–16).

[3] For a detailed survey, see Stramaglia (2013b, 13–19); on *DM* 4 specifically see now [Krapinger-]Zinsmaier (2021, 151–55).

[4] See Brescia (2021).

[5] Those in favor of suicide draw largely on the younger Seneca: see Pasetti (2009b).

indeed, the two have much in common psychologically: 17.4–6). The point was hinted at very early on (1.1) and will be developed in a brilliant passage (17.3) where prediction and outcome are set side by side.

From his faith in the prediction, Son draws a clear message: he must die, for otherwise he will kill (2.3). Indeed, he had hoped to die in battle (4.6–5.1); but fate decreed otherwise (5.2). He craves for the certainty of suicide (12.5). There is always the risk he may kill, by mistake if not intentionally (5.4, 19.3–6), a motif that reaches a climax in the last words of the piece (23.4). Not only, though, *must* he die: he *wishes* to die (8.1). There may have been reasons to stay alive in the past, but they do not apply now, when he loathes life (8.4–8). Every man has good reason to wish to die (9.4–6), but none more than a past hero with nothing left to live for (11.1–6).

Father is painted sympathetically. He does not fear Son now (1.3) any more than he had in the past (4.4). He sees in him only a hero, not a potential parricide (2.4). If Son commits suicide, Father will think of that as a murder for which he will himself be responsible (2.5). Son advises him not to love but to distrust and fear him (20.1–3). He should let his son die and see to his burial (22.3).

The structure can be analyzed thus:[6]

> PROEM 1.1–2.6
> NARRATION 3.1–5.9
> ARGUMENTATION
> *Confirmatio/Refutatio* 6.1–20.3
> EPILOGUE 20.4–23.4

[6] Stramaglia (2013b, 21–22).

In the development of this speech of self-denunciation,[7] the declaimer adheres to the theoretical positions of Quintilian. The prevailing practice in both Greek and Roman declamations was to treat such cases as *controversiae figuratae*, in which the speaker asks permission to die only to put in a bad light the person who pushes him to such a decision, thus ensuring his life being saved.[8] Quintilian, on the contrary, considers such a strategy deeply flawed and mocks the declaimers who make their characters ask for their own death while hoping to achieve the opposite end.[9] Our speaker makes clear that his *only* concern is to die, taking Quintilian's side against the usual practice (21.3–5).

DM 4 comes strikingly close to *DM* 17 in language and content and is clearly known to the author of *DM* 8; this suggests the dating of the *Mathematicus* to the early third century AD.[10] The arguments in favor of astrology exploited in our declamation were later taken over (word for word, at times) and adapted by Firmicus Maternus in his treaty *De errore profanarum religionum* (written in 346–50);[11] and a late antique (fourth–fifth century) commen-

[7] Cf. above, n. 2.

[8] See Stramaglia (2013b, 23, 120–21n103). In general, on the concept of figured speech, see Breij (2015, 70–77).

[9] Cf. Quint. 9.2.85–86: "Another common error . . . is to think that some people say one thing but mean another, especially when the theme involves a character asking permission to die . . . I merely laugh, because these declaimers are as frightened as if they were going to die themselves" (trans. Russell).

[10] See General Introduction, §4.

[11] See Stramaglia (2013b, 37), with earlier modern bibliography; the first to notice this was—as it now turns out—Burman (±1700).

tary on Lucan quotes a passage from the *Mathematicus* (10.6), ascribing it to "Quintilian."[12]

We have a dramatization of the story in elegiac couplets, the work of Bernard Silvestris or his circle in Tours in the twelfth century.[13] Much later, there is Patarol's antilogy.[14]

---

[12] Cf. *Comm. Bern. ad* Lucan. 4.478 (p. 138.1–3 Usener) *Unde Quintilianus: "Faciamus de fine remedium, de necessitate virtutem. Solus vixit quoad voluit, qui mori maluit."*

[13] *Mathematicus*, now edited with English translation by Wetherbee (2015, 183–245; notes: 264–65, 268–69, 301–2); for further bibliography, see Stramaglia (2013b, 38n145); Kauntze (2014, 28–31).

[14] (1743, 154–76).

4

Mathematicus

VIR FORTIS OPTET PRAEMIUM QUOD VOLET. QUI CAUSAS MORTIS[1] **IN SENATU NON REDDIDERIT, INSEPULTUS ABICIATUR.** Quidam de partu uxoris mathematicum consuluit. Is respondit virum fortem futurum qui nasceretur, deinde parricidam. Cum adolevisset qui erat natus, bello patriae fortiter fecit. Reddit causas voluntariae mortis. Pater contradicit.

1. Positus, P. C., in ea condicione tristissimae sortis, ut nec morte dignus sim, nisi me parricidam putetis, nec praemio, nisi innocentem, adeoque ludibriis miserrimae[2] di-

---

[1] ‹VOLUNTARIAE› M. E, *sed vd. Str.*[7] *301–2*
[2] -rrimae *Dess.*[1] *95 (firm. Håk.*[2] *35–36):* -rae sim *codd.*

---

[1] A *mathematicus* was properly an astrologer who claimed to predict persons' futures from the position of stars at the moment of their birth; since this baby has not yet been born, the astrologer must have based his prediction on the moment of conception (a

4

The astrologer

A HERO MAY CHOOSE THE REWARD HE WISHES. SOME-
ONE WHO HAS COMMITTED SUICIDE WITHOUT GIVING
HIS REASONS TO THE SENATE IS TO BE CAST OUT UN-
BURIED. A man consulted an astrologer[1] about his wife's
unborn baby. He replied that the child would be first a
hero, then a parricide. When the boy had grown up, he
fought heroically for his country. He now gives reasons for
committing suicide. His father objects.

(Speech of the son)

1. Senators, my most unhappy lot has placed me in a dilemma: if you do not think me a parricide, I do not deserve
death; if you do not think me innocent, I do not deserve
my reward.[2] I am so cruelly sported with by this contradic-

---

practice theoretically discussed in antiquity, but obviously difficult to implement).

[2] Son will try to prove that he may kill his father, and so deserves to die; at the same time, he wishes to show that his intentions are innocent, and that he therefore deserves the reward he
requests for his heroism—burial after suicide.

versitatis [necessitatis][3] implicitus, ut impetrandum a vobis habeam odii mei favorem, quaeso, praeter omnia quae
ante hoc tempus circa nos ordo praedictae veritatis explicuit, attulisse me credatis urgentium malorum probationem: de parricidio venit quod occidere me possum, de
2 fato quod mihi non licet mori. Non solus[4] mathematicus
saeculo temporibusque praedixit has manus: et ego me
parricidium credo facturum. Plus quam responsum, quam
sacrae artis triste praesagium est quod mihi sic minatur
3 animus meus. Non habeo infelix in cogitationibus unde
non timeam, et facinus, quod sibi pro me pietas patris,
quod singularis[5] innocentia abrogat,[6] sentio, patior,
agnosco. Ne quis me tamen laborare putet miserae persuasionis errore, accipite cur non possim dubitare de fato:
parricidium credit qui facturus est, non timet qui periturus est.

2. Ante omnia igitur a gravitate publica peto ne pro tota
innocentia mea contenti sitis hoc, quod volo mori; nec,[7]
quia videor contendere cum mathematico, vincere necessitates, expugnare fatum, ideo mihi bene credi putetis
et vitam. Aliud est facinus non esse facturum, aliud mori

---

[3] *del. Dess.*[1] 95 (*firm. Håk.*[2] 35–37), *et om.* V: [div-] nec-
Reitz.[2] 37   [4] -um M AD J[ac] β
  [5] -laris *Håk.*[2] 37: -lorum *codd., sed vd. Str.*[10]
  [6] abro- *Sh. B.*[2] 192–93: ro- *codd.*   [7] mori, ne *Wint.*[9]

---

[3] Sc., so as to think me better dead, and thus agree to my request.   [4] I.e., to court, to form part of this speech (cf. 7.12.4;
Quint. 5.10.44).
  [5] This "proof" are the two sentences that follow ("it is . . .
dying").

tion that I cannot but ask a favor of you: that you hate me.[3]
I must ask you to believe that besides everything else that
has hitherto, step by step, been unfolded by the fulfillment
of the prediction concerning me, I have brought with me[4]
proof[5] of the evils that press upon me: it is the prospect of
killing my father that makes me ready to kill myself; it is
fate that prevents me from dying.[6] (2) It is not only the
astrologer who forecast, for this generation, for this time,
what these my hands will do: *I* too believe that I will commit parricide. Over and above the response, over and
above the dire prediction given by the sacred art, is this
menace from within *me*. (3) Ah me, every thought I have
adds to my fear. I feel, I suffer, I recognize the terrible act
in which my father, out of love for me, refuses to believe—
such is his affection, such his unparalleled innocence. But
let no one imagine that I am laboring under an unfortunate misconception. Listen to why I cannot have doubts
about fate: the man who is going to commit parricide believes he will do it; the man who is going to die[7] is not
afraid.[8]

2. First of all, then, I ask this of the weighty authority
of the state: do not think that the fact that I wish to die is
enough to make me wholly guiltless; and, just because I
seem to be in contention with an astrologer, just because I
seem to be trying to overcome necessity and to vanquish
fate, do not think that I can safely be trusted with life
as well. It is one thing not to be going to commit a
crime, quite another to wish to die to avoid committing

[6] He sees Father's objection as the hand of fate (cf. 4.4.3),
which prevents him from dying before he commits parricide.

[7] Father.

[8] = does *not* believe that he will be the victim.

2 velle ne facias. Quin immo, si qua est fides, hoc, quod vos
constantiam putatis, infirmitas est. Quod ad suprema
confugio, animum meum novi. Novissima victae[8] mentis
integritas est in mea potestate; brevi non habebo[9] nec
3 mortem. Fidem vestram, P. C., ne quid amplius de misera
pietate speretis. Qui mori volo ne parricidium admittam,
non invenio quemadmodum illud possim non facere vic-
4 turus. Nam quod ad patrem pertinet, qui me retinet vivere
nolentem, non miror quod adhuc recenti gloriae nostrae
gaudio stupet, et, in opera mea totus oculis animoque con-
5 versus, parricidam non videt per virum fortem. Hic est
animus, quo me quamvis denuntiatum praedictumque
servavit, et, cum incertis adhuc dubiisque virtutibus praestiterit ut viverem, praestat meritis actisque ne moriar.
6 Nunc ille, quod pietate, quod videor istius perire reverentia, vocat parricidium suum, et in orbitate, quam facere
sibi videtur, non remedium meum, sed suum spectat adfectum. Filium,[10] qui vult mori ne parricida sit, aliter sibi
videtur remunerare[11] non posse, quam ut ipse moriatur.

[8] vite M^2 A δ β (*ut sit* vitae, me-), *sed vd. Ellis 330*
[9] -eo B AD: -eam E
[10] -um *Reitz.*^{2} 59 (*corrob. Str.*^{10}): -us *codd.*
[11] -ri B^2 AD P, *sed vd. Wint.*^{7} *141*

---

[9] Someone who is not going to commit a crime can be safely
entrusted with life, as he is not harmful; someone who wishes to
die to avoid committing a crime can still commit it in the end: so
he should be given leave to die.

[10] Son fears he will soon lose his mind and so no longer be
able to commit suicide—his only way to avoid killing Father.

[11] Sc., than my death. The judges could ask Son, e.g., to go on
living and make every effort to avoid parricide, so as to spare his

one.[9] (2) In fact (believe me!), what you regard as determination on my part is really weakness. If I take refuge in death, that is because I know myself so well. I have in my power the last means by which my mind, now quite overcome, can keep control over its innocence; in a short while I shall have no control even over my death.[10] (3) I appeal to you, senators, do not look for anything more[11] from my ill-fated filial affection: I wish to die to avoid killing my father, I see no way not to kill him if I go on living. (4) So far as concerns my father, who is trying to keep me alive even though I do not wish to live, I am not surprised that he is spellbound by the still fresh joy he feels at my glorious feats. Eye and mind, he concentrates totally on my deeds, so he does not see the parricide behind the hero. (5) This is the frame of mind in which he let me go on living[12] despite what was pronounced and predicted about me. When my bravery was still uncertain and in doubt, he responded to it by granting me life; now that it has been translated into actual deeds, he responds to them by refusing me death. (6) I may appear to be dying out of affection and reverence for him; but he calls that "his" parricide.[13] Faced with the prospect of a bereavement for which he holds himself responsible, he is concerned not with the resulting remedy for me, but with his own affection. He thinks that only by dying himself can he reward a son who wants to die to avoid killing his father.[14]

father a life of bereavement; but this would be too heavy a burden for the young man (cf. 4.19.1–5).   [12] Rather than killing him at birth.   [13] I.e., a death (of his son) that *he* will bring about.

[14] Father wants to reward Son for his generous intentions by arguing for his life; yet (as Son sees, but Father does not) he is thereby bringing his own death upon himself.

3. Merito prorsus, merito miserum senem tristes sollicitudines et praescii metus ad mathematicum et responsa
miserunt. Debui vir fortis nuntiari, parricida praedici.

2 Sive enim miserae coniugis prodigiosa fecunditas tumul-
tuosis pulsibus maritales inquietavit amplexus, seu per
anxias noctes dirosque somnos feralibus senex imaginibus
agitatus ‹est›,[12] dicitur ad notissimum sacrae artis antisti-
tem non spes, non avida vota, sed suspiria, metus et prae-

3 sagum magni nesciocuius incerti detulisse pallorem. Quid
aliud hoc esse vultis, P. C., quam primam fatalis instinctus
necessitatem? De partu uxoris non potuit non interrogare,
deinde non credidit.

4 Referam nunc, P. C., cuius artis, cuius fuisse dicatur
auctoritatis, quem putavit adeundum qui sic timebat?[13]
Homo qui, quod certum habeo, plurimis meruerat ex-
perimentis ut ad illum velut ad oracula deorum plenumque
sacro spiritu pectus hominum sollicitudines metusque
confugerent, dicitur inspecta totius ratione caeli, digestis
sideribus in numeros, ad publici privatique fati stupuisse
conspectum, et tanta prosperorum tristiumque congerie
magis ipso consultore perterritus diu non commississe
verbis quod videbat. 4. Sed o virum gravitatis antiquae,
dignumque cui se fatorum arcana nudarent! Cum partus,

[15] His public destiny is to become a hero, his private one is to
kill his father (cf. 4.4.1).

3. There was reason, good reason, why the wretched old man should have been prompted by his gloomy anxieties and foreboding fears to consult the astrologer and hear his responses: I *had* to be announced to be a future hero, foretold to be a future parricide. (2) Perhaps the monstrous fetus in his unhappy wife's womb disturbed their marital embraces with its energetic kicking; perhaps the old man <was> disturbed by funereal apparitions during anguished nights full of terrifying dreams. Whatever the case, he took (it is said) to the celebrated minister of the sacred art not hopes, not greedy wishes, but sighs, fears, a pallor that presaged some great but undefined event. (3) What was this, do you think, senators, if not the first necessity imposed by the instigation of fate?—he could not but ask about his wife's child, but then did not believe the reply.

(4) Am I now to describe, senators, the reputed art and authority of the man whom one who was a prey to such fears thought he must approach? He was someone who had—I know this for sure—, by giving frequent proofs of his skill, earned such a reputation that he was turned to by anxious and fearful men, who had recourse to him as though to an oracle, as though to a breast filled with a holy spirit. After examining the whole state of the heavens and making calculations based on the position of the stars, he was horrified (it is said) when he saw the child's public and private destiny.[15] More frightened even than his client by such an accumulation of good and bad fortune, he for a long time hesitated to put what he was seeing into words. 4. Here truly is a man of antique integrity, who well deserved to have the secrets of fate lay themselves bare to him! Though the unborn child, the subject of the inquiry,

de quo quaerebatur, multa praestaret,[14] propiora pros-
pera, laetos incipientes annos, non fuit contentus meliora
praedicere, et, quae certissima est vera proferentium fides, quicquid deprehenderat protulit in medium et pro-
2 clamavit futurum virum fortem, deinde parricidam. Quis
umquam, P. C., fiducia maiore respondit? Cum summum
facinus denuntiaret, ante se dixit probaturum.

3   Fecerat profecto, P. C., interrogando mathematicum
pater rem non educaturi, si quid tristius comperisset, nisi
hoc primum de fato fuisset, ut viverem. Sed nec mathe-
matici fides circa momentum aliquod neque[15] cessavit
ordine:[16] non numerus fefellit, non sexus in partu, non
4 iuventa, non robur. Illa quoque, quae velut extrinsecus
consentiebant, adfuere responso: bellum, hostis, acies ad
illam ipsam, qua fortiter facere poteramus, aetatem. Pater
vero, periculi sui denuntiatione non territus, arma mihi
(pro tristis necessitas!), arma ipse circumdedit et suis ad
pugnam manibus aptavit, tamquam mathematico iam cre-
5 didisset. Quis miretur quod responsum non[17] contempse-
rit, dum sperabat ut fortiter facerem? Mori me non vult,
et iam non superest nisi parricidium.

---

[14] *dist. Reitz.*[2] *50*   [15] -quod neque *Helm*[2] *96–97*: -quodque
B[pc] (-idq- B[ac]) V: -quemve AD β: -quem cumque E: -quemque δ
[16] -e *Helm*[2] *96–97*: -em *codd.*
[17] *del. Sh. B.*[1] *74, sed vd. Di St. 604 et Wint.*[7] *141*

---

[16] I.e., when the boy (as he predicted) became a hero.
[17] Cf. 4.17.3.
[18] Father *believed* the warning of the danger to himself but
was not *frightened* by it; and no wonder he believed in the as-

had much to offer, good fortune in the nearer period, happy first years, the astrologer was not content to predict merely the better part; *everything* he had discovered he revealed (and that is the surest test of those who are telling the truth): he proclaimed the child would be a hero, then a parricide. (2) No one has ever given a response more worthy of belief, senators: in announcing the ultimate crime, he said that he would prove his prophecy in advance.[16]

(3) No doubt, senators, by consulting the astrologer my father had acted like someone unprepared to rear his son, if he had learned anything dire: but it was the first requirement of fate that I must live. Indeed, the astrologer showed himself trustworthy in every detail, and in the order of events too: he was right about the number of births, and my sex, about my growing up and becoming strong.[17] (4) Circumstances too that—as it were—gave their assent from outside were at hand to confirm the prediction: the war, the enemy, a battle at the precise time at which I was of an age to act heroically. But my father, in no way frightened by the danger to himself, personally armed me, yes, armed me (how sinister the workings of fate!): he prepared me for the fight with his own hands, as though he had already believed the astrologer. (5) Who would be surprised that he did not shrug off the prediction, at a time when he was looking forward to me being a hero?[18] He does not wish me to die:[19] yet all that now remains to be accomplished is his killing.

trologer's prediction at the point when he was looking forward to it being fulfilled by his son's heroism.

[19] Now, just as at the time of my birth.

6   O mors laudanda fortibus, expetenda miseris, non re-
cusanda felicibus, quantum te quaesivimus in bello! Tuli
enim—deos testor—in aciem, tuli non virium iactationem,
non gloriae cupiditatem, sed ut patriae praestaret aliquid
vilitas mei, ut hunc mihi deploratum spiritum, hoc destinatum damnatumque corpus publicarum utilitatium usus
absumeret. 5. Ibi primum miser didici quam multa nesci-
entes, quam multa faceremus inviti! In medios hostium
globos perditus pugnator exilui: cessit acies; densissima
quaeque certamina solus invasi: resistere nemo sustinuit;
obviis[18] ictibus membra nudavi et ad incurrens ubique
ferrum vitalia parata circumtuli: vacua circa me tela ceci-
2   derunt. Miserum me deceptae cogitationis eventu! Fortiter feci, dum mereor occidi.

3   Recedite, gratulationes, abite, laudantes; non circumeo
templa, non reddo vota numinibus: ad parricidium veni.
4   Quem ego paulo ante passus sum miserae conscientiae
pudorem! Ad patrem arma non rettuli; timui quin immo
ne mihi, dum revertor, occurreret, ne in oscula mea ple-
nasque adhuc victricibus telis manus incauto rueret am-
5   plexu. Quam tunc inter ceteras exclamationes deducen-
tis exercitus vocem, quod circumstantis populi murmur
excepi: "Magnum felicemque iuvenem!" Si subito moreretur!

18 -vus B^ac: -vius E

---

20 To be executed as a parricide.   21 On the imperfect
subjunctive (*faceremus*) for an expected present, cf. Ter. *Haut.* 7;
Hofmann-Szantyr (1972², 547).   22 With the implication
that he may yet kill his father unawares: see, e.g., 4.5.4.
23 Cf. 4.8.4.   24 To thank the gods, as expected of a victorious hero: cf. 11.9.5.   25 From war.   26 Cf. 4.4.4.

(6) O death, which the brave must praise, which the wretched must seek, which the fortunate must not refuse, how I looked for you in the war! Into the fray I brought (the gods be my witness!), I brought not a desire to show off my strength, not a thirst for glory: only the wish that my valueless person might have something to contribute to my country, that serving the public interest might finish off this spirit which I had given up for lost, this body that was doomed and condemned.[20] 5. It was there (poor wretch!) that I learned for the first time how much I do[21] in ignorance, how much against my will.[22] I darted into the midst of the foe, a combatant with nothing to lose: the battle line yielded before me. I plunged alone into the thickest of the fray: no one could withstand me. I bared my limbs to the blows I faced, I bore around with me vital parts ready to receive every weapon that came my way: the missiles fell vainly around me. (2) Ah me, how false my plans turned out to be! I acted like a hero—while deserving to be killed.

(3) Withdraw, congratulations! Depart, encomiasts![23] I am not doing the rounds of temples,[24] I am not fulfilling vows to the gods: I have come home[25]—for parricide. (4) What pangs of conscience I was unfortunate enough to suffer only a short while ago! I did not bring my weapons back to my father:[26] indeed I was afraid that on my return he might cross my path, might rush into an incautious embrace while seeking to kiss me, and be clasped in hands still bearing the missiles with which I had won victory. (5) What words did I hear spoken amid the other cries of the army as it escorted me home, what words murmured by the crowd around me! "A young man great and fortunate!" Yes, if only he were to die—at once!

6   Adiuvate, dii pariter atque homines, dum perire concupisco, dum volo; miseremini, ne hunc ardorem fugientis animae dilatione laxetis. Proclamo, testor: in novissimo fati stamus abrupto; prope est ut occidat patrem parricida
7   praedictus, cum est mori paratus. Quid me, pater, adhuc detines, quid moraris abeuntem? Melius quidem fuerat hunc spiritum aut in ipsa maternorum viscerum sede comprimere aut, ut primum contactu suo caelum terrasque
8   polluerit, festinata morte dimittere. Sane tamen caritas[19] patriae privatos vicerit metus, et in honorem virtutum scelera nutrita sint; quicquid est, propter quod educari me tanti fuit, explicitum peractumque est. Restat una pars
9   fati: ultimum solumque facinus. Frustra me consolaris aequanimitate patientiae tuae;[20] non idem utriusque nostrum discrimen agitur: tu mori periclitaris, ego patrem invitus occidere.

    6. Hoc primum itaque excuso vobis, P. C., quod praemium peto. Satis sit hactenus viri fortis nomen agnoscere, hucusque auctoritatem sacrae legis attingere, ut illam
2   advocationem [sacrae][21] mortis adducam. Relaturum me putatis illa optionum verba sollemnia: non capere magnorum pretia meritorum solas aequitates; tanta remuneran-

---

[19] tamen cum ca- B, *unde* tamen, cum—metus, [et] in *Reitz.*[2]
43   [20] -tia (*nec plura*) V: -tia tua A: -tiaque tua δ β
    [21] *del. Sh. B.*[2] *193, sc. e* sacrae legis *male repet.*

---

[27] Parricide pollutes the world: see the "archetypal" Cic. *Rosc. Am.* 71–72.   [28] I.e., (DAR) to recognize my position as a *vir fortis* as far as this grants me the privilege of choosing my reward, in accordance with the relevant "sacred" law.

(6) Help me, gods, and men no less, while I long to die, while I wish to die; pity me! My soul wants to escape: do not slacken its ardor by holding it back. I declare, I bear witness: I am on the very brink of the cliff of fate. When a son predicted to be a parricide is prepared to die, he is very near to killing his father. (7) Why are you still holding me back, father, why are you delaying me just when I am departing? It would have been better to suppress this breath while I was still in my mother's womb, or to hurry it away to death the very moment it came to pollute heaven and earth with its contagion.[27] (8) It may be that my father's patriotism overcame his personal fears, and that a criminal was bred up out of consideration for his virtues: whatever the case, the reason for which it was so important for me to be reared is over and done with. There remains only a single step in the fated series: the ultimate, the unique crime. (9) It is in vain that you try to console me by being so patient and unperturbed. The two of us are not equally at risk: *you* are in danger of dying, *I* of killing my father against my will.

6. Now, this is the first thing for which I have to excuse myself to you, senators: that I am asking for a reward. Let it be enough for me to acknowledge my title of hero[28] just so far, to touch on the authority of the sacrosanct law[29] just to the extent, that I may adduce that law to support my claim to die. (2) You think, perhaps, that I am going to say what is so often said in option cases:[30] that great services are not necessarily to be rewarded with strict equality, that

[27] Cf. Introduction to the present declamation, n. 1.
[30] Cf., e.g., *Decl. min.* 266.7, 293.1.

dum benignitate quod fortiter fecit aliquis, quanta[22] sol-
licitaretis ut faceret? Nemini umquam minus solvendo
civitas fuit: praestiti post quod mori continuo deberem.

3   Sed securi estote de aviditate summae potestatis. Illud
infinitum, illud immodicum, quod nobis voluerunt licere
leges, intra se consumit ille qui meruit.[23] Titulos, ima-
gines, honores servate victuris; mihi praestate salutem

4 patris, innocentiam meam, temporum pudorem. Quaeso,
ne mihi ideo praemium negetis, quia fortassis et hoc debeatis odisse, quod fortiter feci. Extra invidiam est optio,
cum id exigam, quod impetrare potuissem etiam ante-

5 quam fortiter facerem. Nam quod obiter optionis[24] reddo
rationem, quaeso, ne quis ideo me parum aut praemio fi-
dere credat aut causis, quia utriusque iuris miscui preces;
ignoscite ardori perire cupientis, quod pariter imploro
quae singula sufficere potuissent. Fidem quin immo vestram, si qua adhuc lex est, quae adiuvare possit mori vo-

6 lentem, commodate, conferte. [Est quod in][25] Utriusque

    [22] -ta ⟨sedulitate⟩ *Russ.*[3]
    [23] moritur *Håk.*[2] 39 (*unde* mori vult *Sh. B.*[1] 74), *sed vd. Str.*[7]
302–3   [24] ⟨et⟩ op- *Wint.*[7] 141–42
    [25] *secl. Håk.*[2] 39–40: in *om.* γ β (*et del.* M), *unde* est q. u. i.
[et] -tati [est quod] in mea *Sh. B.*[2] 193

[31] = I am not arguing, as heroes so often do, that the reward
should be disproportionately *large* in comparison to the service.
I am asking for something disproportionately *small*, so the city is
unprecedentedly in my debt.   [32] The absolute discretion to
choose anything I like.   [33] A hero is allowed to choose *any*
reward, but the city need not fear any abuse on this man's part:
he wishes only to ensure burial after his suicide, so that his choice
will not affect anyone but himself.

a man is to be recompensed for heroism with the same generosity with which you would encourage him to act heroically. Well, the city was never less able to pay its debt to anyone: I have done for it something that had to be followed immediately by my death.[31]

(3) But you need have no concerns about the greed that might accompany my position of supreme power.[32] The infinite and boundless privilege which the laws wished to grant me is being used up within himself by the man who has deserved it.[33] Titles, statues, honors you may keep for those who will go on living; grant *me* the safety of my father, my own innocence, and the good repute of our times. (4) I beg you, do not refuse me the prize on the grounds that you perhaps have reason to dislike even the fact that I acted heroically.[34] My option is beyond the reach of envy, for I am asking something I could have been granted even before I became a hero.[35] (5) As to the fact that I am justifying my choice of reward at the same time,[36] no one—I ask—should imagine that I have no confidence in the prize or in my reasons just because I have combined both laws in my pleas. Forgive the strong feeling, natural to one who longs to die, that causes me to make two conjoined requests when either would have been enough on its own. Rather, indeed, I beg you, if there is yet some law that could help me in my wish to die, put it at my disposal, let me benefit from it. (6) You can in the case of my death

[34] The senators ought to hate his heroic act because it is only the fulfillment of his unhappy destiny.

[35] Through the "regular" request of permission to commit suicide.

[36] I.e., he is putting forward his choice of reward at the same time as stating his reasons for committing suicide.

iuris [et] auctoritati[26] est quod in mea morte tribuatis: praestate causis ut moriar, praemio ut sepeliar.

7   Sentio, P. C., hoc primum ab adfectibus publicis petendum, ne quis ideo mori me velle non credat, quia potius ad causas ac verba confugi, quia a vobis malui petere quicquid ab his potui manibus accipere. 7. Merui, fateor, malignas interpretationes: vir fortis ut morerer a bello reversus,[27] arma posui, populi favorem, gaudia civitatis intravi.

2   Sed sive hoc est sepulturae suae magna reverentia, pessimeque additae pectoribus humanis infirmitatis,[28] ut esset quod timeret qui non timet mortem, seu[29] decuit innocentiae amore pereuntem tranquillitas magna pereundi, ignoscite—quaeso—cunctationi, patientiae, morae: si me continuo occidissem, tamquam parricida moriebar.

3   Neque est, P. C., quod excludi praemium putetis contradictione patris. Eximus per magnorum operum reverentiam de necessitate parendi, et aut interim nobis magna venit contra nominis huius potentiam de virtutum favore

---

[26] [et] -tati *Håk.*[2] *39–40:* et -tas (-tatis E) *codd.*
[27] vir—reversus *distinxi*
[28] -tis π[pc] (*def. Str.*[10]): -tes π[ac] *cett.*
[29] seu *Dess.*[1] *93:* sed *codd.*: sive ς

---

[37] The speaker is clarifying that this is *not a controversia figurata* (see Introduction to the present declamation).

[38] I.e., of committing suicide at once: but then he delayed, because he decided to give reasons to the senate and thereby avoid being cast out unburied. See 4.7.2.

[39] Cf. Sen. *Controv.* 8.4 (p. 231.14–15 H.), *Contra hos inventum est ut aliquid post mortem timerent, <qui> non timent mortem.*

concede something to the authority of both laws: to my reasons, grant that I may die; to my prize, that I be buried.

(7) I am aware, senators, that I have first to ask something from the feelings of the public: let no one refuse to believe that I wish to die just because I have had recourse to reasons and words, just because I have preferred to seek from you something that these hands of mine could have given me.[37] 7. I have deserved, I confess, that my actions should be judged unfavorably: I came back from the war with the intention of dying as a hero;[38] instead, after laying down my arms, I plunged into the cheering crowds, into a rejoicing city. (2) Perhaps this was because one has a feeling of deep reverence for one's own burial, the result of a weakness that has deplorably been put into human hearts so that a man unafraid of death might still have something to fear;[39] or perhaps it was a completely tranquil mind[40] at the point of dying that befitted someone dying for love of innocence.[41] Whatever the case, I ask you to forgive this hesitation, this moment of weakness, this delay: if I had killed myself immediately, I should have been dying as a murderer.

(3) Nor should you think, senators, that my receiving the reward is ruled out because of the opposition of my father. By evoking the reverence due to great feats of arms, we pass beyond the need to obey. Sometimes to counter the power of this name[42] comes a wide freedom given by the popularity of virtue; or else we shall renew

[40] Not attainable if the suicide is hurried, and especially at a moment of triumph in war.

[41] Cf. 17.4.4, 18.17.5.

[42] I.e., "father."

libertas, aut obsequia, peracta demum optione, repete-
4 mus. Non est quod vos resistentis moveat auctoritas; neminem invenias mori volentem, qui non habeat aliquem
vetantem. Ille, cui praesto non sunt pignera caritatis, lacrimis tamen audientium et consolationibus et promptissima
5 semper exhortatione retinetur. Parentibus vero circa liberos unus adfectus est: favere vitae, timere mortem. Non
habent patientiam nec iustae orbitatis,[30] et inter supplicia
[nemo][31] poenasque omnes tamen illis innocentes, omnes
6 miseri sumus. Ego, P. C., communem hanc impatientiam
senis accendo pietate, reverentia. Fieri non potest ut se
mori debere persuadeat patri filius, propter quem se videtur occidere.
7   Hactenus leges, hactenus merita virtutum; veniamus
ad necessitates. 8. Mori volo: ita [ut][32] non[33] reddidi causas? Ita non ex hac destinatione sentitis quicquid dici po-
2 test, quicquid dici non potest? Viderit,[34] quid[35] nos hucusque protulerit; hinc incipit ratio, quod volo.[36] Fingite
unum ex populo turbaque petere ius supremorum:[37] non
debet hoc vetari, quotiens habet causas; non potest, quo-

   30 -tes V   31 del. Reitz.[2] 80, et om. E δ (vd. Str.[10])
   32 del. Reitz.[2] 80, et om. π[ac]   33 om. Φ
   34 -ritis ς, sed cf. Sh. B.[1] 74–75 et Str.[10]   35 qui Dess.[1] 83–84
   36 protulerit—volo sic dist. Obr.   37 ius supremo- Reitz.[2]
80: ius supraemio- B[ac]: iussu praemio- B[pc] V: ius praemio- Φ

   43 According to Sen. Controv. 1.8.7, Roman ears would not
tolerate a speech in which the merits of a war-hero son straight-
forwardly outweighed paternal authority. See Lentano (2014,
esp. 173–75).   44 Cf. 16.5.6.   45 Cf. Decl. min. 335.3,
Mori volo. . . . Et iam satis rationem videor reddidisse.

our obedience *after* the choice is made.[43] (4) You should not be swayed by the authority of the opposer; you would find nobody wishing to die who is without someone to forbid it. A man without any loved ones is nevertheless held back by the tears of those who hear him, their consolations, their exhortations always readily available. (5) On the other hand, parents have one emotion in regard to their children, and one only: they want them to live, they dread them dying. They cannot bear losing a son even when he dies justly, and if we are being tortured and punished, still in *their* eyes we are all innocent, we all deserve pity.[44] (6) This natural inability to endure bereavement *I*, senators, exacerbate in my father by my affection and my respect for him. It is not possible for a son to convince his father that he must die when he appears to be killing himself for his father's sake.

(7) So much for the laws, so much for the deserts of valor. Let us now come to what is unavoidable. 8. I wish to die. Have I not given my reasons, merely by saying that?[45] Do you not, from this expression of my fixed purpose, gather all that can be said, all that cannot be said? (2) As to what brought me to this point, let it go;[46] my motivation begins from here: I wish.[47] Imagine that some ordinary person is asking for the right to die. His wish ought not be turned down, if he has good reasons; it can-

---

[46] *Viderit* = *nihil refert*, "it does not matter" (cf. 19.11.2); the subject is the clause *quid . . . protulerit.* The hero's wish to take his own life is the only consideration that should weigh with the judging senators.

[47] Cf. 9.4.2; Juv. 6.223, *hoc volo, sic iubeo, sit pro ratione voluntas.*

3 tiens non habet. Scilicet enim verendum est ne ad hoc inconsulte, ne temere levitas humana prosiliat, et credibile est ut quicquid apud hominem pro vita dici potest, ipsa sibi vita non dixerit?

4   Abite, gratulationes, silete, blanditiae; quotiens iam putatis noluisse me mori? Primum hoc maximumque[38] pro incolumitate hominis natura commenta est, ut periremus inviti, ut[39] contra tot adversos casus patientiae nobis aequanimitate succurreret. Inde est quod inter luctus et 5 desperationes foeda vivacitate duramus. An vos me movere non creditis quod iuvenis sum,[40] quod modo vitae voluptates, modo gaudia lucis ingressus sum? Quantopere mihi blanditur, quod publicis ex acie reportatus umeris 6 laetitiam civitatis implevi! Quotiens mehercule haec vulnera et rorantia hostili cruore arma conspexi, animum 7 supra necessitates erigo, supra fatum[41] pono. Sed omnia mihi iam discussa, consumpta sunt, et honeste[42] pereundi ratione victa cesserunt. Quid mihi amplius cum corpore, quod oderunt oculi sui, cum quo cotidie properans anima rixatur? Non sunt mea membra, quae possim velut hostis

---

38 -umque *Reitz.*[2] 80: -um quod *codd.*
39 ut *Reitz.*[2] 80: et *codd.*: et ⟨ut⟩ *Håk.*
40 sum E (*cf. mox* ingressus sum): sim *cett.*
41 fat- ⟨: fret- B V Φ*   42 -ta V Φ

---

48 As he will take action, without anyone being able to prevent it. Cf. 4.23.2.
49 People might congratulate and flatter Son for his apparent equanimity at the prospect of death.

not be turned down, if he does not.[48] (3) Indeed, is there any fear that human levity might take such a step lightly or rashly? Is it credible that anything can be said to a man in favor of life which life has not already said to him?

(4) Away then with congratulations! Flattery, fall silent![49] How often do you imagine I have *not* in the past wanted to die? This is the first and greatest device of nature to ensure that man does not come to harm: that we should be reluctant to die, that she should give us the equanimity to help us endure so many adverse circumstances. Hence our ability to stick it out, clinging shamefully to life, despite moments of grief and despair. (5) Do you suppose that I am not influenced by my being a young man, entered only now on the pleasures of life, the joys of this world? How flattered I am by the thought that I was carried home from the battle line on the shoulders of my fellow citizens, and filled their cup of joy to the full! (6) By heaven, as often as I have looked at these wounds of mine,[50] at my arms dripping with the blood of the enemy, I raise my mind high above necessity, place it above fate. (7) But everything is now scattered to the winds and exhausted, defeated and surrendering to my reason for dying an honorable death. What further use is my body now to me? Its own eyes[51] loathe it; my soul, in its anxiety to depart, quarrels with it every day. These are not *my* limbs: I could tear and stab them as though they belonged to some

[50] The display of a hero's wounds is a traditional commonplace (cf., e.g., 3.6.2). Here (and in 4.11.5) it leads the speaker to contradict what he has stated at 4.5.1.

[51] Rather than "my eyes," to emphasize the distance between the speaker and the limbs of his own body. Cf. 2.24.1.

8   alicuius[43] lacerare, confodere. Homini, qui semel renun-
tiavit rebus humanis, non redditur vita, sed tempus, et ipsa
cupiditas ratioque pereundi hoc ipso quo[44] vetamur ad-
9   crescit. Felicior mehercules qui moritur antequam debeat, antequam velit; paene sero renuntiat vitae quisquis
sic[45] ad exitum pervenit, ut hoc illum facere nemo miretur.
10   Ei tantum debet mors negari, de quo non sufficit hoc
poenae genus, ut ipse se potius occidat.

    9. Nam quod lex iussit ut moriturus redderet causas,
quod insepultum voluit abici, si sic properasset erumpere
ut non nuntiaret hoc prius, non fateretur, fallitur quisquis
2   ideo factum putat, ut teneremur in vita. Illa vero non timet
pereundi temeritatem, nec secretum doloris alieni libenter inquirit. Sciebat illos non aliter[46] ausuros proferre causas, quos sceleris conscientia, quos maioris cruciatus me-
3   tus in suprema compelleret. Igitur, ne supplicia properato
lucrarentur obitu, rursus in poenam nocentis insepulti
corporis revocavit iniuria. Lex placida, mitis, causas mortis
reddi voluit, non aestimari.

4   Possum igitur, P. C., publica quadam voce generis humani respondere quaerentibus causas mortis interrogatus;

[43] aliquis *Franc.*   [44] quod *Helm*[2] *97, sed vd. Håk.*[2] *42*
[45] -quis sic E (*def. Håk.*[2] *42*): -quis δ: -que sic B V γ* β
[46] *del. Reitz.*[2] *73, sed vd. Wint.*[1] *314:* ante *Håk.*[2] *42–43:* alteri
Watt[2] *20*

[52] Cf. *Decl. min.* 337.3, *Nullam tam inhumanam quisquam
crediderit esse legem, ut hominem innocentem et invitum detineat
in luce.*
[53] = it was not laid down out of fear that . . .

enemy. (8) Once a man has renounced human affairs, you can give him time, but not life. The very longing and motivation to die grows the more death is forbidden. (9) Happier, by heaven, he who dies before he must, before he wishes to! It is almost too late to renounce life if you come to your end in such a way that no one is surprised that you do it. (10) Death should only be denied to one for whom it is not punishment enough to die at his own hand rather than another's.

9. Now, the law required that one intending to die should give his reasons; it wished him to be cast out unburied if he was in such a hurry to escape life that he did not announce it, did not confess it in advance. But it is quite wrong to think that the intention of the law was that we should be held back from dying.[52] (2) In fact, the law is not afraid of death being sought rashly,[53] nor does it wish to pry into the secret grief of another. Rather, it knew that those driven into extreme courses by remorse for a crime, or their fear of a worse torture, would not dare to publicize their reasons[54] on different terms.[55] (3) So, to prevent them evading their penalty by hastening on their end, it called the guilty back to punishment by inflicting the injury of a body unburied. Restrained and gentle as it is, the law wanted motives for death to be stated, not assessed.[56]

(4) If therefore I am asked, senators, I *can* give an answer, as it were on behalf of the human race as a whole, to those who seek to be given reasons for dying; indeed

54 For wishing to die.

55 I.e., in the absence of any sanction.

56 For they would *ipso facto* be unexceptionable if the applicant was ready to state them (AS).

at ego difficilius redderem vitae. Quid iuvat, o misera mor-
talitas, animam per tot annos, etiam, si natura patiatur, per
infinita temporum spatia tristissimo corporis retinere
5 complexu? Si cuncta gaudia nostra, si voluptates et quaecumque ex hac universitate mundi vel sollicitant aspectu,
vel blandiuntur usu, diligenter excutias, tota vita hominis
unus est dies. Humiles prorsus abiectaeque mentes, quas
non implent haec eadem ⟨semper⟩[47] semperque redeun-
6 tia. At qui[48] honestis operatus artibus sciat quis finis bonorum, quae vera felicitas, numquam sibi videbitur prae-
matura morte periturus, et lucis causas ad animum
mentemque referentium neminem cotidie vita non satiat.
10. Relaturum nunc me putatis quanto plura sint in hac
aevi brevitate fugienda, comparaturum gaudiis, prosperis
2 metus, calamitates?[49] Illa,[50] illa aestimemus, propter quae
fatigamus votis deos, propter quae brevem querimur aetatem. Nempe sunt vanitas, cupido, luxuria, libido. Non pudet propter haec ferre debilitates, luctus, spatia morbo-
3 rum, et, cum liceat evadere, malle pati? Finge tibi velut
ipsam proclamare naturam: "Receptus es in hoc pulcher-
rimum mundi rerumque consortium, et per succedentium
vices in ordinem mortalitatis natus bona nostra vidisti;
4 admitte posteros, cede venientibus." Nescis te, quanto
diutius vixeris, tanto magis impatientem perire?[51] Quan-

---

[47] *add. Cast. 105 (firm. Str.[10])*   [48] *at Sh. B.[2] 193,* qui ς: ut
quis *codd.*   [49] g. metus, prosperis c. *Russ.[3]*   [50] *om.* M γ β
[51] -tem *Franc.,* perire *Watt[2] 21:* -tiam parere *codd.*

---

[57] Looking back to 4.9.3, *reddi . . . non aestimari.* We should
assess the reasons for our complaints about the shortness of life,
not for our seeking death (cf. also 4.9.4).

what I should find harder would be to offer reasons for *living*. Wretched mortal men, what is the good of keeping the soul in the grievous embrace of the body for so many years, or even—if nature allowed it—for infinite periods of time? (5) If you take the trouble to examine all our joys, our pleasures and everything in this wide world that entices us by its appearance or pleases us to use, the whole life of man is but a single day. Minds are altogether humble and low if they do not come to feel cloyed by these things, ⟨always⟩ the same, always returning. (6) But a man who has applied himself to the liberal arts and knows what the highest good is, what true happiness is, will never think he can die before his time: everyone every day feels sated by life, if he cares to analyze his reasons for staying alive. 10. Do you suppose that I am now going to describe how many more are the things that are to be shunned in the short life that is all we have, or to compare fears and disasters with joys and successes? (2) What we *should* assess[57] are the reasons, yes the reasons for which we weary the gods with prayers, for which we complain that life is short. They are vanity, lust, luxury, appetite. Are we not ashamed for their sake to put up with disabilities, grief, long periods of illness, and to prefer to endure them even though it is possible to escape them? (3) Imagine that—so to say—nature herself is declaring to you: "Received as you are into this most beautiful community, the universe, and born to take your place in the succession of mortal men as the generations follow upon each other, you have seen the good things I have to offer. Now let posterity in, make room for those who are to come!" (4) Do you not realize that the longer you live, the more unaccepting you are when you die? However

tumlibet prorogentur tempora, iungantur aetates, quandoque tamen non potest non exitu perire miseri, qui mori-
5 tur invitus. Miraris quod suprema mea ipse praecipitem?
Numquid enim non hoc agunt singuli dies? Omnis nos
hora per tacitos fallentesque cursus adplicat fato, et in hac
turpissima perpetuitatis cogitatione districti[52] per exigua
6 festinantis aevi momenta praemorimur. Faciamus potius
de fine remedium, de necessitate solacium: exeamus
sponte, consilio, pleni securitatis, gratias agentes. Solus
vixit quoad voluit, qui mori mavult.

11. Indulgete, quaeso, saevae tristesque causae, indulgete, virtutes, ut mori tamquam magno animo velim. Ita
2 non sufficit ad maturandos exitus quod fortiter feci? Infir-
mae prorsus terrenaeque mentis est, ut numeretis[53] annos;
ego, quae felicissima vel lassitudo vel satietas est, virtute
consenui. Quid adhuc inter accidentia fragilesque casus
3 ago? Homo receptus in publicas gratulationes praesentiae
humilitate decresco: minores fiant necesse est diuturni-
tate, quorum initia confirmavere successus.[54] Cum iam
nec operibus nec felicitati possit accedere,[55] cum fortuna
4 ruere dementia est et aetatem trahere pereuntem. Nullos
ego senes degere turpius puto, quam qui fortissimi fuerunt. Vultis expectem ut putres artus foedet pudenda canities, ut sanguine membra vacuata vix nitantur ad gressus,

---

[52] dis- π: des- *cett.*   [53] -retis *codd.* (*def. Håk.*): -ret
Reitz.[2] 63: -ret aetatis *Plas. 63.10*   [54] *gravius dist. Håk.*
[55] -ced- M (*def. Str.*[10]): -cid- *cett.*

---

[58] See Introduction to the present declamation, on *controversia figurata.*

[59] As an ordinary private citizen, no longer a public hero.

long his time is extended, generations merging into each
other, one day or other the man who dies unwillingly must
inevitably die the death of a wretch. (5) Are you surprised
that I wish to hasten my end? Does not each single day
do that? Every hour, by its silent and unnoticed passage,
brings us closer to fate, and, taken up with our so shameful notion of living for ever, we die in advance, at every
brief moment of time as it hurries on. (6) Let us rather
make a remedy out of our end, a consolation out of what
must happen. Let us make our exit voluntarily, deliberately, free of care and giving thanks. The only man who
has lived as long as he wished is the one who chooses to
die.[58]

11. Grant, I beg you, my savage and melancholy motives, grant, my courageous acts, that I may die voluntarily,
as though with a high spirit. Is it not in fact reason enough
to hasten my departure that I have been a hero in the past?
(2) It is the mark of a weak and earth-bound soul to count
up your years: I have grown old in valor, the happiest kind
of weariness or, if you will, of satiety. What am I doing here
still, in a world of accidents and uncertain chances? (3)
Once I was welcomed back with public congratulations;
now I am diminished by my present low condition.[59] If
one's early days were given strength by success, one can
only be lessened by the passage of time. When nothing can
be added to one's feats or one's felicity, it is sheer madness
to collapse in ruin along with one's fortune, to drag on a
life that is passing away. (4) I think no old men live more
degradingly than those who have in the past been most
heroic. Do you want me to wait till my crumbling limbs
are disfigured by shameful gray hairs; till my legs can
scarcely struggle along for lack of blood; till these hands,

ut hae laudatae manus nec ad cotidianae vitae ministeria
5 sufficiant? Quam miserum, quam deforme est meminisse
quod fueris, referre cicatricum tuarum redundationes et
frigidam praeteritorum memoriam, cum iam fidem mem-
6 bra non habeant supra tua[56] facta rideri! Festinato exire
de saeculo debeo, dum alacre corpus, dum spiritus viget,
dum teneor, dum desideror, et hoc volo deberi manibus
meis, animo meo. Favete, dii pariter atque homines: mortem viri[57] fortis inveni.

7   Est haec communis mihi cum multis fortasse causa, sed
veniamus ad meam. 12. Si mihi mathematicus denuntias-
set damna membrorum, gravem corporis perpetuumque
2 languorem, ignosceres tanta mala vel incerta fugienti. Plus
est quod expavesco, quod timeo: minatus est mihi manus
meas meus animus, nullumque voluit esse momentum
quo securus intrepidusque requiescerem. Iussus sum vi-
3 tam per anhelitus metusque consumere. Quis inter haec
spei, quis consolationis est locus? Mori debeo tamquam
nocens, si mathematicus verum dixit, tamquam miser, si
mentitus est.

4   Quid, quod me futurum dixit parricidam? En quem[58]
5 mittamus in experimentum, cui credamus! Placet potius[59]
futurorum incerta <certa>[60] tractare ratione[61] quam[62] ad

[56] tua *Str.*[10]: sua *codd.*
[57] viri *Håk.* (*corrob. Str.*[10]): vir *codd.*
[58] en q- B V γ β: ecq- δ
[59] potius *Sch.*: post *codd.*
[60] *add. Sh. B.*[1] 75
[61] incertă . . . ratione *Håk.*[2] 44: -tam . . . -nem *codd.*
[62] quam *Håk.*: qui *codd.*

once the theme for praise, are unable to serve me even in the everyday routines of life? (5) How wretched it is, how ugly to remember what you once were, to rehearse the story of your innumerable scars with its cold remembrance of the past,[60] to be laughed at for your deeds because your limbs no longer make them credible! (6) I must hurry away from this world, while my body is active, while my spirit is high, while I am held on to, while I am still wanted; and I wish this to be the work of my hands, of my conscious intent. May gods and men alike favor me: I have found a death worthy of a hero.

(7) This is, perhaps, a motivation that I have in common with many men. Let us now come on to what is peculiar to myself. 12. If the astrologer had warned me of loss of limbs, a serious and continuing bodily illness, you would forgive me if I fled from such misfortunes, even if they were not certain. (2) What I now dread, what I am afraid of, is yet more than that. My mind has threatened me with what my hands may do; it wanted there to be no quiet moment in which I could relax, free of worry and trepidation. I was bidden to use my life up in gasps and fears. (3) Amid all this, what place is there for hope, what for consolation? I must die as a guilty man, if the astrologer told the truth; as a wretched one, if he lied.

(4) What of his prediction that I should kill my father? Look who we're supposed to use to test it, who we're supposed to rely on![61] (5) I am determined to face an uncertain future on a basis ⟨of certainty⟩, rather than to vary

[60] Cf. n. 50, with, e.g., Sen. *Controv.* 1.8.3.

[61] Himself (sarcastic). Son refuses to be experimented on: he wants the certainty of suicide.

diversas persuasiones et ad loquacissima humanorum pec-
torum ingenia variari.[63] Parricidium dictus sum facturus;
si possum post hoc vivere, non sum innocens, etiamsi non
fecero.

6   Interrogare mehercules hoc ⟨loco⟩[64] libet vos, omnes
liberi, omnes parentes: quem mihi post hanc denuntia-
7   tionem adsignetis animum? Homo sum, cuius corpus ira-
tum fortasse saeculo numen velut aptissimam facinori videtur elegisse materiam, cui in primis continuo natalibus
adsignata est virtus pariter et facinus, omnium incredibilium diversorumque pariter capax, omnibus difficultati-
bus novitatibusque sufficiens, sceleribus miser et, sine
morte sua, nocens, in quo debeatis ipsas quoque odisse
virtutes.

13. Nescioquae me prodigiosa feritas in patrem velut
telum aliquod casurumque pondus librat, impingit. Facinus me manet, quod contra fidem est, quod profuturum
mihi negatur ut nolim, cuius non tempus, non locus, non
causa praedicitur. An mori debeam, vos aestimabitis; non
debui nasci.

2   Sentit pater quanta sit praedicti sceleris immanitas, et
ideo temptat efficere ut mathematicam artem[65] non putetis: ac modo contendit non esse fatum, et cuncta casu
fortuitoque decurrere, modo, etiam ut providentia regan-
3   tur, non posse tamen humana scientia deprehendi. Dum
utrumque colligo, interim apud gravitatem vestram de-

---

[63] -ri *Håk.*: -ris *codd.*   [64] hoc ⟨loco⟩ *Dess.[1]* 87 (*vd. Håk.*,
Pas. 151–52.215): hoc *codd.* (*quod prolept. capiunt Leh.[1]* 425, *Di
St.* 604): hic ϛ   [65] artem ⟨esse⟩ *Watt[3]* 47 *coll.* 4.14.6

---

[62] Cf. Sen. *Suas.* 3.3 (Cestius): "gods do not make their wishes

according to the different convictions and the whims of human hearts, expressed in all too many words. It has been foretold that I shall kill my father. If I can go on living after this, I am guilty, even if I do not do the deed.

(6) All you who are children, all you who are parents, I should—by heaven!—<now> like to ask you: how do you expect me to react to such a warning? (7) I am a man who seems to have been selected as the subject most fit to commit a crime by a divine power angry, it may be, with this generation of men; a man marked out at his very birth by both virtue and crime, equally capable of everything incredible and inconsistent, well able to cope with every difficult and unprecedented situation, both pitiable for his crimes and guilty—unless he dies; a man in whom you ought to hate even his very valor.

13. Some monstrous, savage force is projecting me at my father like some missile, or a weight about to drop on him. A terrible deed awaits me, one that is beyond belief, one that (it is said) it will profit me nothing to be unwilling to commit. The time, the place, the cause are not specified. It is for you to judge if I ought to die: certainly I ought never to have been born.

(2) My father is aware of all the enormity of the crime that is predicted, and that is why he is trying to make you believe that astrology is not an art. At one moment he contends that fate does not exist, that all things proceed at random, subject only to chance; at another that, even if they are steered by providence, their rules are beyond the reach of human knowledge.[62] (3) I shall weigh up the two

felt in human affairs; even if they do, men cannot know their will; even if men do know it, the fates are irrevocable."

pono sensisse aliquid etiam patrem, cum metuit. Ego mathematicum probavi dixisse verum, ille credidit[66] esse dicturum.

4   Casune tibi, pater, haec diversitas videtur in corpus unum dissentientibus solidata primordiis, ut summo vertice locatus igneus vigor cuncta gravia[67] calidi spiritus ardore suspenderet, profundus umor ad ima demersus, unde cotidie superpositi caloris alimenta traherentur, terrenum pondus in medio quanto superne spiritu, tanta penitus inanitate subnixum librata mole consideret, ut saeculorum infinita series per adsiduas temporum vices sua

5   lege festinet?[68] Quid haec fulgentium siderum veneranda facies? Quod quaedam velut infixa ac cohaerentia perpetua semelque capta sede conlucent, alia toto sparsa caelo vagos cursus certis emetiuntur erroribus,[69] ista credis passim fortuitoque disposita? Rogo, quid melius ratio fecisset? 14. Deus haec, deus, fabricator operis immensi, ex illa rudi primaque caligine protracta[70] posuit in vultum, digessit in partes. Postquam dederat universitati parem dignamque faciem, spiritum desuper, quo pariter ⟨omnia⟩[71]

2   animarentur, immisit. Inde est quod quidquid nascitur

---

[66] credidit ⟨ (def. Helm[2] 97): credit codd.

[67] levia ⟨, sed vd. Leh.[1] 425 et Str.[10]   [68] expectes -naret, sed vd. Str.[10]   [69] levius dist. Håk.: interrog. vulg.

[70] -ta Obr.: -tum codd. (auctorisne error e super. operis immensi ortus? Håk.)

[71] h.l. add. Håk.[2] 45: ante pariter Hamm.[1] 57

---

[63] Cf. 4.3.1–3.   [64] On the good record of the astrologer, cf. 4.3.4; see also 4.14.6.   [65] What follows is a summary of Stoic cosmology: see Diog. Laert. 7.137–40.

positions, but for the moment here is something for you to consider in your wisdom: even my father had some glimmer of knowledge, when he felt afraid.[63] I have shown that the astrologer told the truth, my father believed he would tell it.[64]

(4) Father, do you really suppose that[65] it was by chance that this variegated sum of things was made from discordant elements into one solid body; that the vigor of fire[66] took its place at the top and kept all the heavy elements suspended in space by its burning breath; that wetness plunged down to take its place at the bottom, in order to provide daily sustenance for the heat above; that the weight of the earth settled in equilibrium in the middle, between the air above and the void below; that an infinite series of ages hurries on, in obedience to its own laws, through an unending cycle of seasons? (5) What then of this awesome spectacle of the brilliant stars? Some shine as though they are fixed to the sky and of a piece with it, in unchanging positions that they have taken up once for all, while others, scattered all over the heavens, trace out wandering courses, erratic yet predetermined. Do you imagine all these things were set in order at random or by chance? I ask you, how could reason have done any better? 14. God, yes, god, the maker of the whole immeasurable structure, drew these things forth from that primordial shapeless darkness and gave them an appearance, dividing them up into parts. After he had conferred on the universe the uniform appearance that befitted it, he introduced spirit into it from above, to animate ‹the whole›. (2) Hence it is that everything that is born is marked by an

66 Cf. Verg. *Aen.* 6.730–31; also 10.17.3.

consociata numinis proprietate signatur, et in totam aevi
sui brevitatem compositum firmatumque[72] sic accipit fu-
3 tura quasi vitam. Haec credo, pater, terrori primis[73] fuisse
mortalibus, mox admirationem consumpta novitate me-
ruisse. Paulatim deinde hoc, quod stupemus, animus ausus diligenter adtendere in arcana naturae sacrum misit
ingenium,[74] et ex adsiduis observationibus notisque re-
deuntibus latentium ratione collecta pervenit ad causas.
4 Miraris fatum hominis posse praedici? Defectiones siderum laboresque narrantur, nuntiantur origo tempestatum,
lassitudo ventorum, quod sidus immodicos solis ardores,
quod severas[75] minetur hiemes, quid significent sparsi
longius crines, quid ardentius solito iubar, quid excussa
5 flamma sideribus. Non invenio quid esse possit certius
verae artis ingenium[76] quam dicere quid futurum sit, fieri
deinde quod dixerit.
6   Quodsi esse artem mathematicam probant natura, ratio, experimenta, pater quoque, qui credidit consulendum,
superest ut ostendamus verum dixisse de futuris, quem de
praeteritis non possumus probare mentitum. 15. Accipite
primam certissimae scientiae probationem: homo, qui de
partu consulebatur, non confudit turbavitque responsum,
nec per varias ambages indeprehensibilem sparsit errorem; nihil ita locutus est, ut illud[77] audientium interpreta-

---

[72] form- *Sch.* (*corrob. Beck.*[2] *75–76*), *sed vd. Håk.*

[73] -mum *Beck.*[1] *477 ex Firm.* Err. 17.4

[74] sacrum… ingenium π γ β (*def. Reitz.*[2] *36*): -ro … -io B V
δ: -ro ⟨se⟩ … -io *Hamm.*[1] *57*

[75] severas ς: serenas *codd.*

[76] -ium *Sch.* (*firm. Str.*[10]): -io *codd.*

[77] -ud ς: -um *codd.*

attendant divinity unique to it; shaped and given solidity for the whole of its short existence, it receives its future just as it receives its life. (3) Father, I think all this struck terror into the first mortals, but later, when the novelty had worn off, it won their admiration. Little by little, the mind found the courage to pay close attention to what bewilders us, and dispatched its sacred intelligence to probe the hidden secrets of nature. By drawing inferences about what lay hidden, on the basis of constant observation and recurring signs, it arrived at causes. (4) Does it surprise you that the destiny of man can be predicted? We can tell the tale of the travails suffered by heavenly bodies in eclipse, receive news of coming storms and periods of calm, of which constellation threatens immoderate heat from the sun and which one severe winters, of what is signified by comets especially long or unusually bright, or by flames struck off the stars. (5) I can imagine nothing more characteristic of an art based on truth than this: it says what is going to happen, then what it said happens.

(6) That there is an art of astrology is proved by nature, reason, experience—and by my father too, who thought fit to have a consultation. It remains for me to show that the astrologer spoke the truth about the future: for we cannot prove that he lied about the past.[67] 15. Let me tell you the first proof of how completely sure he was of his knowledge. When consulted about the coming birth, he did not offer a confused and disorderly response, he did not use ambiguous verbiage to spread about error that no one could detect; he did not speak in such a way that hearers

[67] When the first part of the prophecy came true.

2 tio traheret dirigeretque quo mallet. Atquin in eo tota
ratio fallendi est, non dare consulentibus quod deposcant,
sed caligine magnaque promissorum vanitate suspensos
sic dimittere ut, quicquid casus attulerit, putent esse praedictum. An scilicet haec fuerit ratio fingendi, quod dicebat
usitata, communia, quae futurus pater facile crederet,

3 libenter audiret? "Fortiter" inquit "faciet filius tuus."
Rogo, ubi magis desinit qui mentitur? Sed quibus ille—dii
deaeque—signis, quibus impletus est notis, qui de parri-

4 cida dissimulare non potuit, cum quaereret pater! Artem
tantum mirari me, pater, putas? Ego miror animum, stu-

5 peo constantiam. "Erit" inquit "vir fortis—et parricida."
Rogo, quae ratio fallendi est ea adicere,[78] propter quae
nec prioribus debeat credi? In parricidio quod prospicie-
bat mathematicus, haec sola ratio fuit mendacii, ne prae-
diceretur.

6   Fero tamen ut quis in aliis consultationibus decipi possit; at[79] errare de futuro parricida non magis mathematicus
potest quam pater interrogare. 16. Omnes ⟨homines⟩,[80]
sicuti apud sacrae artis antistites satis constat, animae pro-
prietates et futuras mentium corporumque formas ex illo-

---

[78] adi- *Reitz.*[2] 65: di- *codd.*
[79] at (*et ante dist.*) *Håk.*[2] 45: aut *codd.*
[80] *suppl.* ⟨*vd. Str.*[10]⟩: homines *pro* omnes *coni. Hüb.-Hei.*

---

[68] Answer: no. Besides ambiguous verbiage (4.15.1), astrolo-
gers can deceive through vague statements.
[69] I.e., when it would have been natural to soften the blow by
keeping quiet about the parricide.

could interpret and turn his words in any way they chose. (2) Yet the whole art of deception is this: not to give your clients what they are asking for, but to send them away in a suspense induced by obscurity and a great show of vain promises, so that, whatever chance comes up with, they may think it to have been predicted. Or was *this* really his method of deceiving, to predict ordinary and common things that the future father could readily believe and be glad to hear?[268] (3) "Your son will act heroically," he said. Where better to stop, I ask you, if one is lying? Well—ye gods and goddesses!—, how many signs and indications he must have had available to him, if he was unable to pretend he knew nothing about a parricide when it was a father who was putting the question![69] (4) Do you imagine, father, that all I am doing is marveling at the man's art? No, I am marveling at his courage, I am staggered by his strength of mind. (5) "He will be a hero—and a parricide," he said. Tell me, what kind of deception is that, to add words that make it hard to believe what went before as well? When the astrologer foresaw parricide, the only way to lie was not to predict it.

(6) In any case, I am prepared to admit that one may be deceived in other consultations; but concerning a future parricide an astrologer can no more err than a father can inquire.[70] 16. All <men>, as is well known to ministers of this sacred art, receive the characteristics of their souls, the future forms of their bodies and minds, from the state

---

[70] As to parricide, the astrologer cannot err, because the signs are so clear; the father cannot inquire, because the crime is so incredible that he has not contemplated it (cf., e.g., 4.18.4).

rum siderum qualitate, quibus in ortu suo coniunguntur,[81]
2 accipiunt. Aliquis vagi numinis errore perstrictus est: vitam transiget[82] ille discursibus. Placida conceptum stella
signavit: erit modesta lenitate conspicuus. Ardens nascen-
tis horam sidus accendit: viribus pariter moribusque fla-
3 grabit. <***>[83] languidi et[84] iam vergentis in proclive
mundi: hebescentibus tardior membris similis senectae
iuventa pigrescet.[85] Iam si cui principalium deorum fulgor
4 inluxerit, in populi consurget imperium. Credo mehercules in illum natalem monstri mei diem iratorum numi-
num conspirasse violentiam sedemque prodigiosi spiritus
conlato pariter igne pressisse. Si verum est post vetusta
saecula et innumerabiles annos reddi rursus aliis corporibus animas, fortassis in me renatus sit aliquis ex illis, quorum scelere violatus dies mundum subito mutavit, quos
<per>[86] maria terrasque fugientes furiales faces et ultri-
cum dearum terror agitavit.
5   Necesse est et maiores notas ventura praemittant,[87]

---

[81] coniunguntur *Hüb.-Hei.*: cuncta gignuntur *codd.*: iuncti
signantur *Håk.*   [82] -get *ς*: -git *codd.*
    [83] *lac. stat. Dess.[1] 91*   [84] -di et M E (*def. Str.[10]*): -do *cett.*
    [85] -cet *Obr.* (*et iam B. Asc.[1] xxvi v. in paraphr.*): -cit *codd.*
    [86] *add. ς*   [87] praemittant *Gr.-Mer.* (*firm. Str.[10]*): promit-
tant (-ent E) V *γ* H P: permittant O S: promittunt *cett.*

---

[71] What follows is a summary of the alleged ways in which
human destinies are affected by the seven planets of the Ptole-
maic system: Mercury (the errant deity), Jupiter (the peaceful
star), Mars (the blazing star), Saturn (the languid star), Sun and
Moon (the major gods). Absent from this list is a reference to the
planet Venus, which has doubtless been lost in the lacuna at
4.16.3. See Stramaglia (2013b, 171–72n259).

of the stars with which they are joined at their birth.[71]
(2) One man is brushed by an errant deity in its wander-
ings: he will lead a roving life. A peaceful star has marked
another's conception: he will be remarkable for a modest
gentleness. A blazing star has lit up the hour of another's
birth: he will be afire in physical strength and character
alike. (3) ⟨. . . Another is born under the mark⟩ of a languid star, already on its way downhill in the sky: his youth,
all too slow because of its sluggish limbs, will be prone to
idleness, just like old age. Finally, if someone has been
shone upon by the brilliance of the major gods, he will rise
to rule over a people. (4) By heaven, I believe that against
the notorious day when the monster that I am was born
the violence of angry powers directed their combined influence, bringing their fires down together on the body
housing so portentous a spirit. If it is true that after long
ages and years past number souls are brought back to
animate different bodies, perhaps there has been reborn
in me one of those sinners whose crime polluted the day,
causing sudden change in the whole world,[72] or who were
driven in flight ⟨over⟩ land and sea by the Furies' torches
and the terror inspired by those avenging goddesses.[73]

(5) It must be that when things come about that are not

[72] A reference to Atreus, who killed the sons of his brother
Thyestes, cooked their bodies, and served them to their father.
Horrified at the sight of this crime, the sun inverted his course
(cf. Sen. *Thy.* 789–883; the myth is alluded to also in 12.26.6).

[73] An allusion to Orestes, hunted by the Furies for killing his
mother, Clytemnestra, and her lover, Aegisthus, in a scene all too
often referred to in declamation (see, e.g., the parody in Petron.
1.1).

quae non temere nascuntur. Sic futuras tempestates pelagi fragor et conscium nemorum murmur enuntiat, sic periturorum fata populorum ardentes caelo faces et crinita siderum flamma praecurrit. 17. Praedicebar bello, monstrabar armis: agebat ante se ventura feritas publicas calamitates, et omnium malorum consummatione parricida ponebar. At si nunc ista putet aliquis fortuito, non arte sentiri, possit fortasse casu evenire quod futurum sit; non potest casu fieri quod praedictum est. Ecquando[88] umquam, pater, explicuit manifestius ullius[89] fati necessitatem totus ordo responsi? "Vir" inquit "nascetur"; evenit. "Educabitur, quamvis praedictus[90] sit"; accidit. "Perveniet ad iuventae robur"; adolevi. "Viribus erit conspicuus"; eminui.[91] "Aderunt bella"; venerunt. "Ibit in aciem te volente"; misisti. "Fortiter faciet"; feci. "Erit parricida"; si vixero.

Si, pater, tam[92] secretae profundaeque artis ratio reddenda est, nonne habere tibi grande consortium praedicti videtur ipsa diversitas? Virum fortem dixit et parricidam: vicina sunt haec, etiam ut dissimilia, paria viribus, etiam ut mente dissentiant. Quid enim me aliud notabilem fecit in bello, quam quod non parco caedibus, cruore non satior, exultans super stratorum corporum strages palpitan-

2

3

4

5

---

88 ecq- δ: et q- *cett.*
89 ull- M: ill- *cett.* 90 -us *Håk.*: -um *codd.*
91 eminui *Bur.¹*: et minis AE: et nimis (-io O) *cett.*
92 tam M² (*def. Wint.⁷ 142*): tamen *cett.*

---

74 The war in which he fought so bravely is a forewarning of the parricide (and also a foretaste of it: cf. 4.17.4–5).

just random, they send in advance even greater signs. Coming tempests, accordingly, are announced by the crashing of the sea and the complicit moaning of woods, and in advance of the fates of peoples doomed to perish there appear torches burning in the sky and the flowing hair of flaming stars. 17. *I* was predicted by war, pointed out by arms: the savage act to come brought before it public disasters,[74] so I was put down for the role of parricide by the accumulation of every kind of evil. Now if anyone at this point should think such forewarnings to be due to chance, not art—well, perhaps something in the future may happen by chance; but something that has been predicted cannot be the result of chance. (2) Has the whole sequence of an oracular response, father, ever made clearer the necessity of any fated event? (3) "A male child will be born," he said: so it turned out. "He will be reared, despite what had been predicted of him": so it proved. "He will live to be a strong youth": I grew up. "He will be remarkable for his strength": I stood out. "Wars will come": they came. "He will go to battle with your consent": you sent me. "He will act heroically": I did. "He will be a parricide": yes—if I live.

(4) If, father, I have to give an account of the workings of an art so secret and profound, don't you think that even the contradictory elements of the prediction show striking coherence? The astrologer talked of a hero and a parricide: these things are neighbors, even though they are not alike. They have the use of force in common, even though the intentions are different. (5) Indeed what was it that made me so prominent on the battlefield if not that I am unsparing in slaughter, that I can never have enough of gore, that I am eager to tread on still quivering corpses as

tibus adhuc cadaveribus alacer insisto? Virtutis sunt ista,
cum hostis contigit; pax est quae nos deprehendit, et, cum
iusta grassandi materia consumpta est, in facinus necesse
6 est otiosus ardor erumpat. Ecce iam rei publicae praebita
est quies; mihi tamen plurimum est cum gladio meo: totis
diebus tracto ferrum, ad arma respicio, tela mea laudo,
admiror, adloquor. Crede, pater: et parricidium tam facile
est quam fortiter facere, cum utrumque de fato est.

18. Sed quousque ratione colligam quod exitu iam pro-
batum est? Quod nullis mathematicus dixit ambagibus,
2 nullis dissimulari artibus potest.[93] Partem responsi futu-
ram in alio opere iam vidisti, et, quod praecipue torquet
animum, fides sceleris virtus fuit. Explicata est auctoritas
responsi, cum de duobus praedictis unum factum est, nec
possis de veritate dubitare, quotiens cum incertis experi-
3 menta consentiunt. In responso cui cuncta cesserunt, fieri
non potest ut hoc solum falsum sit, quod novissimum est.
4   "Non potest" inquit "fieri parricidium." Vis mirer, pater, si non creditur futurum quod, etiam cum factum est,
5 vix creditur? Falleris, si adversus praedictas necessitates
sufficere credis quod ego bonus filius sum, quod tu optimus pater. Tu non mereris [scire]. Credo. Ego utique nolle
me[94] scio.[95] Quid est ergo fatum, nisi quod fit et non habet

---

[93] est—potest *sic dist. Gr.-Mer.*

[94] tu non—me *sic constituit Plas. 68.1, interpunctionem expo-
livit Wint. ap. Str.*[7] *303–4 (et cf. OLD*[2] *credo §8.b)*

[95] -io *Obr.*: -ire *codd.*

---

[75] Sc., as wrongdoers.   [76] Cf. the same morbid attach-
ment to weapons in 1.14.2.   [77] Cf. 4.17.3.   [78] I.e., experience of a past event and forecast of a future event.

I exult over heaps of bodies laid low? Such things count as valor, when an enemy has come your way; it is *peace* that catches us out:[75] when there remains no legitimate scope for running amok, our frenzy lacks employment, and has to burst out into some outrageous action. (6) Now, as you see, our state has been granted peace and quiet. But most of my business is with my sword. All day and every day I handle cold iron, gaze upon weapons; I praise my spears, admire them, address them.[76] Believe me, father: even killing one's father is as easy as heroism in the field—when both are fated.

18. But how long shall I go on arguing logically for something that has already been proved by the outcome? What the astrologer said without ambiguity cannot be shrugged off by any device. (2) The part of the prediction that is to come, you have already seen in the other act, and (what especially anguishes me) it is my heroism that makes my crime credible.[77] The response had its authority made manifest at the moment when one of the two things foretold took place: you cannot doubt of truth when experience and uncertainty are in agreement.[78] (3) In a prediction where everything else has come true, it is impossible that the only false stage is the one that comes last.

(4) "Parricide is impossible," my father says. Do you want me to express surprise, father, that belief is denied to something before it happens when it is scarcely believed even when it has happened? (5) You are mistaken, if you suppose that my being a good son and you an excellent father is protection enough against events that have been predicted as inescapable. You don't deserve such a fate. Sure. For my part, in any case, I am quite certain that I do not wish it. But what then is fate, if not what happens

6 causas? "Quemadmodum ergo" inquit "istud vitari potest, si fieri necesse est?" Scilicet hac sola ratione, ut mors inter facinus hominemque ponatur. Vincitur, pater, fatum, si
7 resistas, vincit, si contempseris. Ago quin immo gratias hoc solo nomine crudelissimis fatis, quod maximum facinus non in prima aevi mei parte posuerunt, quod praemissae sunt ante virtutes, magnorumque operum prior ordo defluxit. Potest, puto, caveri parricidium quod et praedicitur et novissimum est.

19. Fingamus, pater, mathematicum de hac sola vitae meae parte mentitum; quid tanti est, ut credam ista et vivam? "Occidi non potest pater"; sed quid refert, si diffi-
2 cultas ista non est salva animo meo? Excedit omnem calamitatem innocentiae suae non credere, diebus ac noctibus timere, suspectum habere animum suum, calumniari manus, incausare visus et parricidalem agere cogitationem. Maior mihi ratio moriendi est, si parricidium fieri
3 non potest, et ego me credo facturum. Quem tu mihi, pater, imperas laborem, quam asperam exigis patientiam! Horreo oscula tua, ne seniles artus nimium gravis amplexus elidat. Non sustineo eosdem expetere convictus, ne, quos porrexerim cibos, venena fiant. Timeo eiusdem peregrinationis adire comitatum, omne fugio secretum,
4 ne quid fortuna, ne quid afferat casus. Quousque timebitur animus? Mors mihi praestare potest, ne parricidium
5 faciam, mors, ut videar nec fuisse facturus. Sed me infeli-

---

79 Sc., no causes *we* can perceive.
80 Sc., for I would spend my entire life in fear.

and yet has no causes?[79] (6) "How then," he says, "can this be avoided if it cannot but happen?" Only, surely, by death being set between the crime and the man. Fate is conquered, father, if you stand up to it; it conquers if you shrug it off. (7) In fact I am grateful to the ruthless fates on this count alone, that they did not place the ultimate crime in the first part of my life: they allowed heroic deeds to precede, and it was early on that my series of great feats unrolled. One can, I think, take precautions against parricide if it is predicted—and comes last.

19. Let us imagine, father, that the astrologer lied about this part of my life, and this only. How can it be worthwhile for me to believe the prediction, and go on living?[80] "One cannot kill one's father." But what if that objection does not hold in my state of mind? (2) It is the worst possible misfortune to be distrustful of one's innocence, to be afraid night and day, to suspect one's own character, to speak ill of one's hands, to accuse one's eyes and have thoughts of parricide. I have the greater reason for killing myself if parricide is impossible, yet I believe I am going to commit it. (3) What a task you are laying upon me, father, what burdensome self-control you ask of me! I shrink from your kisses, for fear too hearty an embrace crush your aged limbs. I cannot bring myself to wish to have you dine with me, in case the food I offer turns out to be poisonous. I am afraid to accompany you on a journey, I avoid every occasion to be alone in your company, for fear of some stroke of fortune, of chance. (4) How much longer shall I have to go on being afraid of my own frame of mind? Death it is that can prevent me committing parricide, that can make it seem that I would not even have committed it. (5) But unhappy me, how much I have

211

cem, quam multa sunt quae timere debeam etiam citra[96] animum meum! Unde scio, an expulsum me repente sensibus meis aliqua magni discriminis imago raptura sit? Prosilibo fortasse, tamquam sequar classici vocantis instinctum, tamquam me ruentis patriae fragor et vociferatio captae civitatis exciverit. Me sane custodire possum, sed unde scio quid adferat nox, casus, error? Mathematicus hoc non futurum dixit, ut vellem, sed ut occiderem.

20. Tu quoque, pater, quanto graviores passurus es ex ipsa dissimulatione cruciatus! Felicius[97] illud[98] prorsus est, palam odisse[99] quem timeas. Cum bene in osculis meis amplexibusque requiescas, subeat necesse est tacitas cogitationes praedicti periculi metus, et, licet componatur ad fortem superbamque constantiam, naturalis tamen hominis infirmitas potest tam percussorem timere quam mortem. Explica nos, pater, tam misero tristique complexu, et longissimas sollicitudines brevi recide patientia; minus indignum est ut moriar, si innocens futurus sum, quam ut vivam, si parricida.

Denuntio tibi, pater, et de suprema necessitate confiteor: iam non sunt meae potestatis hae manus; non regere dexteram, non retinere sufficio. Venit ille nescioquis ardor: non sentio, non intuentur oculi; tunc omnia incipio

[96] citra *Håk.*: contra *codd.*
[97] -ius *5*: -ior *codd.*
[98] -lud *Leh.¹ 440*: -le *codd.*
[99] odisse *Sh. B.² 194*: occidisse *codd.*

[81] This picks up 4.19.4, *Quousque timebitur animus?*: Son is now passing from fear of things he might do consciously, to fear of actions in a state of hallucination.

to fear quite apart from my state of mind![81] How can I tell if I may not suddenly be deprived of my senses and carried away by the impression of some imaginary crisis? Perhaps I shall leap forward, as though responding to a peremptory trumpet call, as though roused by the crash of my country falling, by the screams of my city taken captive. (6) I can of course control *myself*; but how do I know what night, chance, mistake may bring? The astrologer did not say I would wish to kill, but that I would kill.

20. As for you, father, how much worse tortures will you suffer from the very pretense that you feel nothing! Better by far to show open hatred of the man you fear. (2) Although you relax as I kiss you, as I embrace you, you cannot in your unspoken thoughts help dread of the predicted danger coming over you: even though he makes a show of strong and proud firmness, a man in his natural weakness may well fear the killer no less than death itself. (3) Father, free both of us from our pitiable and unhappy embrace, cutting short so long a period of worry by a brief time of endurance. It is less of an outrage for me to die if I am going to turn out innocent[82] than to live if I am going to turn out to be a parricide.

(4) I solemnly warn you, father, and make confession from the depth of ultimate necessity: these hands are no longer in my power; I am not capable of controlling my right hand, or holding it back. That old mysterious impulse[83] has come over me: I have no feeling, my eyes have no sight. I only begin to be conscious of what I do when

---

[82] Sc., even though, if I lived, I were not going to kill my father.

[83] Last seen on the battlefield (cf. 4.17.5).

5   scire, cum gesta sunt. Quid?[100] Tu me lacertorum vi-
riumque beneficio stravisse nuper hostes putas? Quantum
dicuntur narrasse captivi,[101] nescioquem in me monstruosi
6   vultus horruere conspectum. Non tela iaciebam, non iacu-
labar ignes:[102] furialibus miser facibus ardebam, et pectus
istud non lorica, non ferrum, sed diri serpentium clause-
rant nexus. Non fuit illud pugna, non acies: in bello parricida vincebam; excesserunt opera mea humanarum virium
mediocritatem: quicquid factum est, rabies, insania fuit.
21. Praedico, testor: non ego parricidium faciam, non ego
fortiter feci.

2   Quodsi ulla ratione casuve effici potest ut praedicta
non fiant, fidem vestram, P. C., ut mihi potius innocentia
quam fato debeatur: ego dicar expugnasse constitutionem,
fregisse vincula necessitatis, mea pietas, mea laudetur
integritas! Dii non sinant ut inter me responsumque de-
cernat exitus; mathematicum vincere malo quam reprehendere.[103]

3   Quid nunc agam, P. C., quemadmodum me vir fortis
ad preces, quemadmodum parricida componam? Dicam
"Miseremini," dicam "Succurrite"? Sic rogari contra mor-
4   tem solet. Novo mihi inauditoque opus est ambitu:[104] malo
mortem.[105] Nisi morior, periclitor: ideo videbor[106] causas

100 *dist. Sh. B.*[2] *194*   101 *levius dist. Scheff. 442: interrog.*
vulg.   102 ignes *Sch. (firm. Watt*[3] *47–48, Str.*[7] *304)*: ictus *codd.*
103 dep- *Sh. B.*[4] *193, sed vd. Str.*[10]   104 *sic dist. Reitz.*[2] *72.1*
105 malo mortem *Wint.*[7] *142*: malorum *codd., damn. Håk.*
106 -ebor *Plas. 72.1*: -eor *codd.*: -eri *Str.*[7] *304–5 (sed vd. Wint.*[7]
142)

84 "Son would sooner defeat Astrologer by voluntarily dying

all is done. (5) What? Do you really think that I laid low the enemy not long ago by virtue of brawn and strength? According to what the prisoners are said to have related, they shuddered at the sight of something monstrous in my face. (6) *I* was not casting spears, or hurling fiery darts: I was—alas!—myself ablaze with the torches of the Furies, and this breast had not been encased in plate of iron but in terrifying coils of snakes. That was no fight, no battle line: in war I conquered—as a parricide. My feats went beyond mere human strength: whatever was done was the work of madness and insanity. 21. I proclaim, I declare with all solemnity: it is not I who will kill my father; it was not I who played the hero.

(2) But if by some means, by some chance, it can be brought about that the predictions are not fulfilled, I ask you to believe me, senators: my innocence should be marked up to me, not to fate. Let *me* be said to have conquered what was written in the stars, to have broken the bonds of necessity! Let *my* filial affection, *my* integrity, be the subject of men's praise! Heaven forbid that the outcome of events should decide between me and the prophecy! I wish to defeat the astrologer, rather than prove him wrong.[84]

(3) What now, senators? What stance should I, a hero, a parricide, take up to entreat you? Am I to say "Pity me," am I to say "Help me"? Those are requests men make when they are trying to *avoid* death. (4) I need a new and unheard method of winning favor: I *opt* for death! Unless I die, I am in danger: I will be thought to have put forward

---

before the prophecy was fulfilled than prove him a liar by living on and not fulfilling it" (Shackleton Bailey [1984–97, 193]).

reddidisse, ut contradiceret pater, et, si bene novi malignas interpretationes, non exitum captasse dicar sed ex-
5 cusationem. Explicate, per fidem, miseri pudoris aestum:
numquam videbitur mori voluisse parricida, si vixerit.

22. Ad tua nunc genua porrigo, optime pater, has, si vis,
tantum fortes manus. Per ego, si fas est, quicquid feci, per
hanc ipsam mei caritatem, qua me nondum timere coe-
pisti, miserere, filium pietate pereuntem ne velis exitum
2 facere parricidae. Praesta mihi patientiam, qua me modo
bello credidisti. Finge nos in ipso prosperi Martis ceci-
disse complexu confectumque magnis vulneribus cadaver
adferri. Relinquo tibi pro me omnes ⟨liberos, omnes⟩[107]
3 parentes. Hunc, quo nos retinere voluisses, in suprema
mea transfer adfectum, tuis manibus compone corpus,
exstrue rogos, funeri iusta persolve. Deinde,[108] cum iam
novissimis osculis supremoque discedens satiatus fueris
amplexu, tunc te fas est sublatis ad caelum manibus proclamare: "Mathematice, mentitus es!"

23. Reddidimus causas, peregimus preces. Reliqua[109]
2 vos, manus, vos adiuvate, cives. Non ut liceat mihi mori:
licet istud, etiam ut negetis. Vir fortis commendo vobis
3 exitum meum. Si non continuo letale vulnus impressero,
si non cum sanguine totam animam properans ictus eges-

---

107 *suppl. Reitz.*[2] 71–72
108 deinde B: dehinc S: dein *cett.*
109 -a M: -as B V Φ*

---

85 And not those of a parricide.   86 Mention of his heroism
might be thought inappropriate, as presaging the predicted parricide (cf. 4.17.1).   87 Sc., to comfort you.
88 Or "to my remains" (Breij [2015, 368n657]).

reasons to die just to ensure my father spoke on the other side, and—if I am right in knowing how actions are misconstrued—it will be said that my aim was not death but an excuse to avoid it. (5) I beg you, resolve the perplexity caused by my unhappy sense of honor: no one will ever think a parricide wished to die, if he goes on living.

22. Now, best of fathers, I stretch out to your knees these hands, which, if you are willing, will only be those of a hero.[85] In the name—if this is appropriate[86]—of all my exploits, in the name of the very love you feel for me, which has not allowed you to start to fear me even now, take pity: do not wish your son, who longs to die out of affection for you, to die as your killer. (2) Show me the forbearance with which just now you so trustingly let me go to war. Imagine that I have died at the very heart of a victorious battle, and that my body, dispatched by gaping wounds, is being brought to you. I leave you, to fill my place, all ‹sons, all› parents.[87] (3) Bring to my last rites[88] the affection with which you would have wished to keep me with you: use your own hands to lay out my body, raise the pyre, perform the due funeral offices. Then, when you go away after having your fill of the last kisses and the final embrace, then and only then can you properly lift up your hands to heaven and cry: "Astrologer, you lied!"

23. I have stated my reasons, my prayers are over. As for the rest, it is for you my hands, for you my fellow citizens, to help me. (2) I do not ask that I may be permitted to die: that is permitted even if you forbid it. Rather, speaking as a war hero, I commend to you my last moments. (3) If I do not at once give myself a mortal wound, if in my hurry the blow does not drive out my whole soul along with my blood, do you assist my right arm, press

serit, adiuvate dexteram, deprimite telum, et ante omnia detinete patrem. Nescio quam longe manum sparsurus sit fugientis animae dolor, quo cadat extractus mucro visceribus, in quem se collabentis corporis ruina praecipitet. 4 Vultis scire quantum debeam timere victurus? Metuo ne patrem, dum morior, occidam.

down the steel, and above all else keep my father out of the way. I do not know how far the agony of my departing soul may make my hand wander, where my sword may light when I pull it from my guts, on whom my falling body may dash itself as it collapses. (4) You may judge how great is my fear, were I to go on living: I am afraid that I may kill my father at the moment I die.

DECLAMATION 5

INTRODUCTION

The case hinges on two issues: (1) What is a father supposed to do, if both his thrifty and his (now ill) prodigal son have been seized by pirates,[1] and he has money
enough to ransom only one of them—at *his* choice? (2)
Once the man has chosen Prodigal Son and this son has
died soon after, leaving Father in beggary, is the abandoned Thrifty Son—who has meanwhile escaped from the
pirates and returned home—bound to feed Father, as a
specific law prescribes?[2] The former issue has a remote
ancestor in a puzzle about ransoming raised in Aristotle
(*Eth. Nic.* 9.1164b.34–1165a.2): a reminder that at the
heart of our piece is an acute moral problem. Thrifty Son
and Prodigal Son are paired elsewhere in declamation (as
in comedy); most notably, they are involved with pirates—
though rather differently—in Sen. *Controv.* 3.3.

DM 5 gives Father's speech against his surviving son.
The unfortunate parent, eloquent though he is on the

[1] On this recurring motif, see Introduction to *DM* 6, n. 1.
[2] Cf. the theme of our piece ("CHILDREN ARE TO SUPPORT
THEIR PARENTS IF THEY ARE IN NEED, OR BE IMPRISONED"),
and, e.g., Sen. *Controv.* 1.1, 1.7, 7.4; Quint. 5.10.97. By the second century AD, Roman law enjoined on sons the duty of supporting their parents but did not provide for detention of trans-
gressors: see in detail Stramaglia (2018b, 50n1).

topic of love as extending to all a man's sons (12.1–3), represents himself as having a pronounced preference for Thrifty Son (3.3, 13.6). He chose to ransom his brother, not as a result of a comparison of their characters (1.5, 13.6) but only because he was ill (5.1–2, 14.1 and 3, 15.3–8, where the claims of the sick and dying are enlarged upon): it was a matter of necessity (as stated already in the proem, 1.5; cf. later 6.1, 18.8: "the sick son *had* to be ransomed, but I *wanted* to ransom you").

Near the end, Prodigal Son is made to raise the objection that he is *unable* to feed his father (22.1): an odd plea, easily answered, and perhaps included only so that, as the epilogue approaches, Father can draw a pathetic contrast between Son's youthful strength and his own failing powers (equally in 11.1 Son twits his father with squandering *his* riches, just so that Father can retort: "On you!"). But Son's main plea has been that he is under no obligation to support his father. Father's reply is that that is the law, though it is outrageous that there needs to be a law for that at all (7.4–8). If there is, it is only because some sons do not show the proper respect (and it is the fault of sons if fathers prove less than kind: 8.6). It is a law of nature to support a parent, just as it is to help others in distress (6.5–7.3). Father may not have ransomed Son: but he gave him life (9.6–10.3).

While not concealing his love for Thrifty Son, whom he has no wish to see punished (23.1–2), Father makes sharp points against him. Son is looking to revenge himself for being passed over (1.3, 9.5–6, 21.4). He complains he was left behind, but he did not need freeing as he was capable of escaping by himself (1.3; cf. 5.6). As the better son, he should have agreed willingly to the ransoming of his sick brother (2.1–2; cf. 6.3). On his return, he should have been supportive of his father (6.4). As it is, he has lost the right to be thought better at all (2.1). Still, the epilogue dwells on the piquant picture of the two in harmony, the upright father begging, the thrifty son looking after their finances (23.6).

The declaimer is conscious, however, that Father's self-representation is crucial to the speech. He milks the pathos of his own poverty (1.1–2, 9.1–5, 22.4), the result of his generous response to the kidnappers' demands (4.1). He had to think long and hard which son to choose (4.7, 18.5–8). By the time Prodigal Son returns, Father is busy scraping together money to ransom him (6.2). He had the interests of both his sons at heart (10.5–8), but his dilemma was inescapable (15.1–3). His decision, though "mad" (17.3–4), was understandable.

In the end, however—as the chorus of a Greek tragedy might have concluded—the blame lay on Fortune. It was luck that things went the way they did (14.4; cf. also 3.5, 5.6, 14.10, 18.3, 21.1); Father had no real choice.

The (rather complex) structure of the speech can be outlined as follows:[3]

> PROEM 1.1–2.4
> NARRATION (I) 2.5–6.4
> ARGUMENTATION (I)
> > *Propositio causae* 6.5
> > *Confirmatio/Refutatio* 6.5–18.4
> NARRATION (II)[4] 18.5–20.8

[3] Cf. Stramaglia (2018b, 26).

[4] According to Quint. 4.2.128, such "additional narrations" (*epidiegeseis*) are typical of declamations rather than forensic

ARGUMENTATION (II)
 Refutatio/Confirmatio 20.9–22.7
EPILOGUE 22.8–23.7

There are reasons that suggest the piece should be dated to the early third century AD.[5] It was known to the author of *DM* 8.[6] Later, in the sixth century, Ennodius of Pavia wrote a declamation on the same theme, where the speaker is the son (*dictio* 21). Ennodius says that he is replying to "Quintilian," but there is remarkably little in common between the two pieces, and three *exempla* that Ennodius claims to have found in his source are in fact absent from *DM* 5—at least in its present form. Different explanations for this anomaly have been proposed.[7] Much later we have, as ever, Patarol's antilogy.[8]

---

speeches, and their main aim is the arousal of either aversion or pity. They can be placed either within the argumentation (thus here, as well as in *DM* 10) or at the end of it, before the epilogue (thus in *DM* 8 and 19, and possibly 12). See Vottero (2004, 248n105); Schneider (2013, 18–19); Stramaglia (2018b, 26).

[5] See Stramaglia (2018b, 26); General Introduction, §4.

[6] Cf. Reitzenstein (1909, 67–68); Deratani (1927, 297–303); L. Greco in Stramaglia (1999b, 17–21).

[7] See Reitzenstein (1909, 3–4); Håkanson (1986, 2285–90); Winterbottom (2003–19; with English translation of, and notes to, the Ennodius speech); Bureau (2007); and the surveys by Stramaglia (2018b, 26) and van Mal-Maeder (2018, 45–47).

[8] (1743, 177–202). See van Mal-Maeder (2018, 47–50).

5

Aeger redemptus

LIBERI PARENTES IN EGESTATE AUT ALANT AUT VIN-
CIANTUR. Quidam duos filios habebat, frugi et luxuriosum. Peregre profecti sunt capti a piratis. Luxuriosus languere coepit. Ambo de redemptione scripserunt. Pater
universis bonis in unum[1] redactis profectus est. Dixerunt
illi praedones non attulisse illum nisi unius pretium, et
eligeret utrum vellet. Aegrum redemit. Qui, dum rever-
titur, mortuus est. Alter ruptis vinculis fugit. Alimenta
poscitur. Contradicit.

1. Quamvis, iudices, in tanta malorum continuatione iam
poteram[2] nihil ex accidentium meorum novitate mirari,
nullumque mihi reliquerint impatientiae genus adversa,
quae de solaciis remediisque creverunt, confiteor tamen
hoc solum me prospicere nullo metu, nulla tristium recor-

---

[1] in nummum *Kuy., sed cf. Str.*[7] *305–6*
[2] potuerim *B. Asc.*[1] *xxix r.* (*cf. mox* reliquerint), *sed vd. H.-Sz.*
604 et Str.[15] *50.8*

5

Sick son ransomed

CHILDREN ARE TO SUPPORT THEIR PARENTS IF THEY ARE IN NEED, OR BE IMPRISONED.[1] A man had two sons, one thrifty, the other prodigal. The pair set off abroad and were captured by pirates. The prodigal son fell ill. Both wrote asking to be ransomed. Their father put together all he had[2] and set out after them. The pirates said he had brought only enough money to pay for one: he must choose the one he wanted. He ransomed the sick one, who died on the return journey. The other broke free and escaped. His father demands support from him. He refuses.

(Speech of the father)

1. Although, judges, amid such a long sequence of misfortunes, I could no longer find cause for wonder in any of the strange things befalling me, and although my adversities, that have only increased from my attempts to relieve and cure them, have kept in store for me no type of suffering I cannot bear, I must nevertheless confess that this is the only thing I could not have foreseen, out of fear for

---

[1] See Introduction to the present declamation.
[2] I.e., to be sold.

datione potuisse, ut post piratas, orbitatem, famem hinc
quoque calamitatibus nostris pondus accederet, quod re-
2 versus est filius meus. Vivebam miser ut hunc viderem,
solaque superstitis expectatione suspensus avidissimam
moriendi cupiditatem contentiosa mendicitate fallebam.
3 Pudet persuasionis! Redisse se iuvenis adfirmat ut vin-
dicaretur morte fratris, ut patris orbitate gauderet, nec
intellegit maiorem se factis meis auctoritatem hac indignatione conferre; nunc magis sentio quantum facinus fuerit aegrum non redimere: queritur se relictum
4 qui potuit evadere. Utcumque igitur, iudices, poteram
redemptionis illius reddere de praesenti iuvenis impietate
rationem, et mihi crudelitas ista praestabat ut filium vide-
rer elegisse meliorem; non utor tamen occasionis huius
invidia nec, quicquid miserae pietatis impatientia feci,
5 querela malo defendere. Ego vero tunc non mores liberorum mentesque tractavi, nec mihi in illa tristissima condicione succurrit de comparatione consilium. Sola, quid
facerem, necessitas, sola iuvenum meorum adversa sua-
serunt. Ex duobus liberis neutrum magis amat, qui redi-
mit aegrum.

2. Illud plane, iudices, ultra omnem malorum meorum
fateor esse tristitiam, quod hac asperitate iuvenis, hoc inopiae squalorisque despectu, famam optimi fratris inces-

---

3 Cf. 5.21.4.

4 Whereas the sick brother could not do so and needed to be
ransomed. Cf. 5.13.1.

the future or by remembering past sorrows: that after
pirates, loss of a child, hunger, an extra burden should
be added to my calamities even by the return of my son.
(2) Unhappy though I was, I was going on living just to see
him. It was only because I was buoyed up by the prospect
of seeing my surviving son that I went on foiling my ardent
eagerness to die by begging so aggressively. I am ashamed
of that resolve! (3) The young man asserts that he has
come back to use his brother's death as a way of avenging
himself,[3] to take pleasure in his father's loss; he fails to see
that by this show of anger he is making what I did the more
defensible. Now I feel still more how wrong it would have
been not to ransom the sick son: he complains that he was
left behind, this man who proved capable of escaping![4] (4)
So I might, judges, in any case have justified the choice I
made by pointing to the youth's present lack of filial affection: this cruelty of his could have afforded me the chance
to be seen to have chosen the better son. But I am not
trying to use the present circumstances to rouse hatred
against him, and whatever I did under the intolerable burden of my unhappy affection, I do not choose to defend it
by making complaints. (5) In fact, I did not on that occasion review the behavior and the character of my sons, and
under those tragic circumstances I was not guided by a
comparison between them. Only necessity, only the troubles of my young men moved me to act as I did. A father
who of two children ransoms the sick one does not love
one more than the other.

2. What, to my mind, judges, exceeds all the sadness
brought about by my troubles is that the young man has
been so harsh, has so disdained my poverty and squalid
appearance, as to do violence to his reputation for being

sit. Hominem qui piraticum carcerem, qui praedonum
2   vincla discusserat, decuerat nec voluisse[3] aliter reverti. Ex
quo se nobis tanto virium labore restituit, poterat eius
quoque admirationem mereri, qui pretio paulo ante ces-
sisset. Dii immortales, quam laudem, quem gloriae favorem impleverat, si pasceret patrem:[4] redemerat fratrem!

3   Relaturus vobis, iudices, ordinem[5] [nam][6] hic malorum
meorum ⟨et⟩[7] eventum, quem nemo tam crudelis, nemo
tam saevus audiet, ut me non pascat, hunc ante omnia, qui
se queritur in fratris comparatione damnatum, secreti
4   doloris indignatione convenio. Quid agis, impotens, su-
perbe? Tu nescis utrum fuerim redempturus ex duobus
sanis, ex duobus aegris?

5   Habui enim, iudices, filios diversissima mentium corporumque qualitate compositos, et, sicut mox probavit
saeva captivitas, in totam dissimilitudinem vitae quoque
genere diductos. 3. Hic namque robustus ac patiens, non
molliri prosperis facilis,[8] non accidentibus frangi, et quem
de voluptatum gaudiorumque contemptu scires parem

---

[3] nec voluisse *Reitz.[1]* 106: ne voluisset *codd., sed cf. Str.[15]*
51.24   [4] *dist. Wint. ap. Str.[15]*: patrem, ⟨qui⟩ *Steff.*
[5] -nem B V H (*cf. 18.3.1, Str.[12] 36–38*): -ne *cett.*
[6] *del. Reitz.[2] 46.5 (cf. antec.* -nem): nam hic *om. Φ*
[7] *add. Håk.*: -rum meorum, ev- *υM.-M.*
[8] -lis W (*def. Bur. et Longo[1] 176.39*): -le *codd.*

---

[5] By disdaining his father's sufferings, the surviving son is
ruining his own reputation—which was once better than his
prodigal brother's.   [6] Cf. 5.6.4.
[7] Wished, that is, to be ransomed rather than to have escaped.

the best brother.[5] It would have been fitting[6] for a man who had forcibly broken free of the pirates' prison, the plunderers' chains, not even to have wished to return in any other manner.[7] (2) After restoring himself to me by such an exploit, he could have also[8] won deserved admiration for having, not long since, given up the chance of being ransomed.[9] Immortal gods, what praise, what favor and glory he would have won if he were now feeding his father—after ransoming[10] his brother!

(3) As I begin to recount at this point, judges, the course <and> outcome of my misfortunes—and no one who listens will be so cruel, so savage as to refuse me sustenance—I accuse first and foremost, with the indignation resulting from pent-up pain,[11] this man who complains that he was condemned as inferior in comparison with his brother. (4) What are you about, insolent and overweening youth? Do *you* not know which of the two I should have chosen if you had both been in good health, or if you had both been sick?

(5) Indeed, judges, I had sons of very different mental and bodily makeup, ones who, as their harsh captivity soon demonstrated, had become complete opposites as a result of their manner of life too. 3. One was strong and hardy, not easily softened by prosperity or broken by circumstance: from his disdain of pleasure and enjoyment you

[8] I.e., as well as winning admiration for his spirited escape.
[9] Literally, "for being the one who . . . had given up his claim to the ransom money," i.e., agreed that his sick brother, not he, should be ransomed.   [10] I.e., by acquiescing in him being ransomed; see previous note.   [11] Father had listened to Son's complaints without showing his pain—which now bursts out.

quandoque fortuitis; traxerat ex firmitate mentis magnam
protinus et in membra constantiam. Ille vero pariter in
laetitiam metusque resolutus, alienus a curis, sollicitudi-
2 nibus impar, delicatus, impatiens, et iam similis aegro. Sed
apud patris affectus haec ipsa liberos dissimilitudo iunge-
bat, et erat quaedam in inaequalitate caritatis aequalitas,
quod hunc serio[9] laudatumque semper, illum iam quadam
3 miseratione diligerem. Quid profuit individua pietas? Erat
etiam me nolente manifestum, utrius magis colloquiis,
magis laetarer aspectu. Velit nolit, iudices, ipsa quoque
querela iuvenis, quid de patris fateatur animo, probat:
irasci quod non sit fratri praelatus aegro, impatientia est
4 hominis qui magis ametur. Accipite, iudices, maiorem pietatis aequae probationem: filium nec peregre dimissurus
elegi; iunxi fratrum artavique comitatum, et utroque patris latere nudato visus sum mihi magis habiturus utrum-
5 que mecum, si pariter essent.[10] Hanc apud me iuvenum
aequalitatem etiam in calamitatibus fortuna servavit: uterque captus est, ambo de redemptione scripserunt. Dissimules licet, iterum tamen et inter adversa persuasionem
carioris invenio: in captivitate communi, puto, minus spe-
ravit ille de patre, qui languere coepit.

[9] serio ς: -ie B V Φ*: severe *Sh. B.*[1] 75: -rum *Håk.*
[10] abes- *Wint.*[3] (<ambo> abes- *Reitz.*[1] 106), sed vd. *Str.*[15] 52.45

---

[12] I.e., conscious of being the favorite son, he complains when
his father favors his brother for a change.   [13] Being simul-
taneously deprived of the company of both sons. Cf. conversely
8.3.1–2.   [14] Cf. 5.3.3.   [15] Thrifty Son had more hope
of his father's help than his brother did (cf. 5.5.1, 5.19.7–20.4);
this shows that he was aware of being the better loved, despite
what he claims now.

might have been sure he was equal to anything that might
come his way; and from his firmness of mind he had derived at the same time great physical endurance as well.
The other was liable to give himself up alike to uncon-
trolled exultation and to fear, averse from cares, unable to
face up to worry, soft, no match for suffering, already like
a sick man. (2) But in a father's affections this very difference put the boys on a level, and, unlike as they were, they
were in a way equally dear to me, for I loved the one with
sober, constant praises, the other—already then—with a
sort of pity. (3) What good did this impartial affection do?
Even against my will, it was obvious which of the two I
enjoyed talking to more, looking at more. Whether he
likes it or not, judges, the young man's very complaint
proves what he acknowledges about his father's state of
mind:[12] to be angry at not being preferred to a sick brother
is the petulant reaction of a man who is loved more. (4)
Let me give you, judges, an even better proof that my affection was equal: I did not make a choice between my
sons even when I was about to let them go away abroad. I
joined the brothers and made them close companions; and
though, as their father, I was now left bare on both sides,[13]
I reckoned I should have them both with me more closely
as long as they remained together. (5) This equality in my
regard for the young men was preserved by Fortune in
their sufferings. Both were captured, both wrote for a
ransom. You may not admit it, but even amid their adversities I can detect again[14] which of the two was convinced
he was the more dear: in their shared captivity, it was,
I think, the one who fell ill who placed less hope in his
father's help.[15]

[QUINTILIAN]

4. Tu mihi nunc, impotentissime[11] iuvenis, tu, quaeso,
responde quid aliud facere debuerit pater duos redempturus. Cunctas facultates in pretia collegi:[12] rus, servulos,
penates et omnia viliora properantius,[13] festinatione per-
dentis addixi, et, ultra quam non potest excogitare sum-
mus adfectus, nihil senectuti meae, nihil dubiis casibus
(pro inconsulta pietas!), nihil neque illis[14] reservavi, quos[15]
2 redemissem. Quantum, iudices, ad piratas tulerim, scire
potestis ex hac fame: fuerit pretium licet exiguum par-
vumque, dum totum. Fingite quamlibet divitem, quamlibet pauperem patrem: nemo umquam plus pro liberis
dedit, quam qui sibi nihil reliquit.
3 Utrumne igitur, iudices, nemo mortalium habet pretium plurium[16] liberorum, an piraticae feritatis ingenium
est in captivorum taxatione solos aestimare redimentes?
Dii immortales, quam arrogans me pirata, quam superbus
4 excepit! "Parum" inquit "attulisti, senex; languet alter."
Quid ego a diis hominibusque merui, quod mihi non red-
5 diturus utrumque non ipse potius elegit? Saevus et humani doloris artifex negavit a me duos posse redimi,
deinde, ut hoc tristius, ut difficilius esset, redditurum se
dixit utrum maluissem. Vides, iuvenis, quantum pietati

---

11 -puden- *Meurs.*[3] *II.168, sed vd. Håk. et vM.-M.*
12 coegi *Meurs.*[3] *II.168, sed vd. Bur.*   13 -ius *Guil. Malm.*
(*vd. Wint.*[6] *258); cf. 5.18.2, Dess.*[1] *98:* -ibus *codd.*
14 illi Φ   15 quem V Φ
16 -ium ς: -imum *codd.* (*vd. ad 16.6.5, Sant. 284–85.167*)

---

16 I.e., to pay the *two* ransom demands. Cf. 5.10.8.
17 The pirate makes use of Son's illness to ask Father a higher
price (exploiting his foreseeable anxiety to rescue a son in need

234

4. It is for you now, young man, beyond control as you are, for you, please, to answer me: what else should a father have done when he had two sons to ransom? I hurriedly realized all my property for the ransoms:[16] the country estate, the slaves, the house, and all the lesser items I knocked down with the haste of one who was throwing them away; going beyond anything the greatest affection can conceive, I laid aside nothing for my old age, nothing for emergencies (such was my heedless love!), nothing even for the sons I hoped to ransom. (2) You may reckon, judges, how much I took to give to the pirates from the hunger I now endure: the sum may have been small and slight, but it was all there was. Imagine a father as rich as you like, as poor as you like: no one ever gave more for his children that one who left himself nothing.

(3) Does then, judges, no mortal man have the means to pay for more than one child, or is it the cruel cunning of pirates to have regard only to the means of the ransomers when they put a price on their prisoners? Immortal gods, the arrogance, the effrontery of the pirate's greeting! (4) "You have brought too little, old man," he said. "One of them is sick."[17] What had I deserved from gods and men that, resolved as I was not to hand both over, he did not himself make the choice?[18] (5) This savage, adept at causing pain to men, said I could not ransom two; then, to make it more painful, more difficult, he said he would give back the one I preferred. You see, young man, what a

of help). Contrast 5.15.2–3, where the sick prisoner seems to be less valuable to the pirates.

18 Rather than leaving it to me.

meae testimonium reddiderit ipsa crudelitas: condicio
non ponitur nisi duos redempturo.

6   Expectatis, certum habeo, iudices, ut in tristissimae
necessitatis positus abrupto ad aegrum continuo propera-
verim. Quis non putet audita condicione vincula me statim
7 detraxisse languenti? Oderitis licet confessionem meam,
deliberavi. Tenuit inter illos inexplicabiles doloris aestus,
quam longum tenuit[17] pietas misera consilium, et, quod
numquam satis manibus filii, numquam satis excusabo
conscientiae meae, non statim mihi ille deficiens unicus
fuit. 5. Dissimules licet, orbitas, ego mihi plurimum mor-
bis,[18] plurimum videor adiecisse languori cunctationis
mora, et sensit infelix quid in electionis huius necessitate
2 fuerim neutro languente facturus. Tandem, quod solum
habebat ambitus genus, desperatione praevaluit: accepi,
fateor, illum, qui solutus quoque non sequebatur, quem
non gaudium redemptionis, non laetitia praelati, non hor-
tantis erexit patris amplexus. Si esset in rebus humanis ulla
clementia, merueram etiam de piratis ut mihi duo red-
derentur.

3   Utinam, iudices, iuvenis illius vita praestaret ut videretur non periculi miseratione sed caritate praelatus! Me

---

[17] om. Φ, sed vd. Str.[11] 105–6
[18] -bis C β (def. Håk.[2] 47–48): om. DE: -bi cett.

---

[19] The pirates offered him the choice of one son because they
knew he would come back with more money to rescue the other
too (as he was in fact trying to do: cf. 5.6.2–3).

[20] Sc., me to say.   [21] My own.

[22] = the one who really mattered (cf. 5.12.1).

[23] Now that I have lost him, I try to tell myself that I was ready

testimony cruelty itself paid to my affection: a bargain is only offered when someone is prepared to pay for two.[19]

(6) I am sure, judges, you expect[20] that on this knife edge of tragic necessity I hurried straight to the sick man. Who would not imagine that, when I heard the terms proposed, I at once took the chains off the man who was ill? (7) In fact, deplore this admission though you may, I paused to consider what to do. Amid those inescapable surges of suffering[21] my unhappy affection deliberated— and deliberated for what a time! I shall never be able to justify it sufficiently to the shades of my son, never to my own conscience: I did not immediately think of the dying man as being my only son.[22] 5. You may pretend otherwise, bereavement, but I think I added a great deal to his diseases, to his illness by my delay[23]—and the unhappy youth understood what I would have done in this forced choice if neither had been ill. (2) In the end, he prevailed thanks to his desperate condition, the only means he had to sway me: I confess it, I took the one who even after being freed was not in a position to follow me, who was not put back on his feet by the joy of being ransomed, the happiness of being the one preferred, the embrace and encouragement of his father. If there were any mercy in human affairs, I would have deserved even of pirates that *two* should be handed over to me.[24]

(3) I only wish, judges, that the young man's manner of life permitted it to be thought that he was put first out of affection rather than out of pity for his dangerous position.

---

to rescue the sick son immediately; however, I am aware that I *did* delay, and this may have contributed to his death.

[24] Because even the pirates would have seen how torn I was.

4 infelicem, quod bonam habeo causam! Explicuit iustitiam comparationis qui decessit etiam redemptus, et in peri-
5 turo filio nihil aliud electum est. In quo fui miser famae periculo! Filius meus languore defunctus est; tamen pater occiderat aegrum, si reliquisset.

6 Videram continuo, iudices, in carcere illo, quantum promitteret constantia hominis quem non captivitas, non expectatio patris, non fratris fregisset infirmitas, nec immerito cuncta de fortissimo iuvene speravi, si fuisset ad omnes conatus explicato languente liberior. Tandem miseros fortuna respexit et, puto, contra praedonum commenta[19] feritatem, ipsa consensit ut nobis quem negaverant non abstulissent. 6. Non quidem mihi, iudices, arrogo temporis illius providentiam; nihil me fateor fecisse consilio. Potest tamen utriusque iuvenis exitus necessitatibus meis adsignare rationem: periit quem redemi, reversus est quem reliqui.

2 Invenisse te putas, iuvenis, patrem cibos et alimenta
3 poscentem? Quaerebam pretium tuum. Testor clementiam mitissimae civitatis, hae preces, hic rogantis ambitus fuit: "Miseremini, date stipes, indulgete, conferte! Repe-
4 tendus est ille, qui redimi maluit fratrem." Sed et hac te decebat reversum proclamare voce: "Erige vultus, pater,

---

19 -mota *Obr., sed vd. Str.[11] 106 et vM.-M.*

---

25 He no longer had to worry about the pirates taking it out on his brother.

26 I.e., retrospectively.

27 Sc., on your return (cf. 5.6.4).

O the wretchedness of my having such a compelling motive! (4) By dying even though he had been ransomed, he showed the justice of the choice I made between them: a son was doomed to die, and nothing but that determined my decision. (5) Alas, what danger my good name was running! My son died of his illness, but it would have been his father who killed him if he had left him there on his sick bed.

(6) I had seen straight away in that prison, judges, how much promise there was in the firmness of mind of the one who had not been broken by imprisonment, by the wait for his father, by the sickness of his brother, and it was right to have the highest hopes of so brave a youth, once he was made freer for all attempts by the release of the invalid.[25] Fortune at long last looked favorably upon the unfortunate, and, I think, scheming to counter the barbarity of the pirates, itself conspired to ensure that they did not deprive me of the son they had denied me. 6. To be sure, I take no credit for any foresight on that occasion; I own, I did nothing by design. But the eventual fate of both youths can supply a reason[26] for what I did out of necessity: the one I ransomed perished, the one I left behind came back home.

(2) Do you think, young man, that you found[27] your father begging for food and maintenance? No, I was trying to raise the money to pay the price for your ransom. (3) I call as witness the clemency of so soft-hearted a city—these were my prayers, this is how I went around begging: "Show pity, give a mite, be indulgent, make a contribution! I have to go back to look for a son who preferred his brother to be ransomed." (4) But on your return *you* should have cried: "Look up, father, raise your sad face:

239

attolle[20] tristitiam: vindicati de saevissimis praedonibus sumus; duos redemisti."

5   Alimenta posco—poteram non adicere filium pater, sed mendicus hominem, sed iuvenem senex. Quis[21] enim magis ex ipsis rerum naturae sacris venerandisque primordiis descendit affectus? Quid etiam citra[22] liberos ac parentes tam commune, tam publicum, quam ut alicuius

6 famem proximus quisque depellat? Voluit nos ille mortalitatis artifex deus in commune succurrere et per mutuas auxiliorum vices in altero quemque, quod pro se timeret, asserere. Nondum hoc caritas est, nec personis impensa reverentia, sed similium accidentium providi metus et

7 communium fortuitorum religiosus horror. In aliena fame sui quisque miseretur. Sic cibos obsidio partitur, sic inopiam pariter navigantium frequenter unius alimenta pa-

8 verunt. Hinc et ille venit affectus, quod ignotis cadaveribus humum gerimus,[23] et insepultum quodlibet corpus nulla festinatio tam rapida transcurrit, ut non quantulocumque veneretur aggestu.

   7. Parentibus vero liberi non praestatis alimenta, sed redditis. Quanto, dii deaeque, breviora, quanto minora pro tot infantiae, tot pueritiae sumptibus, tam variis vel

2 abstinentissimae iuventutis impendiis! Si mehercules hoc

---

[20] ac tolle *Beck.¹ 478, Beck.² 76* ([at]tolle *Sch.*), *sed cf. Håk.² 49 et vM.-M.*

[21] qui B V, *sed cf. 5.16.6, 5.18.5 et saep., H.-Sz. 540–41*

[22] citra *Str.¹¹ 106–7*: inter *codd.* (*unde* <non> i. *Sch.*): extra *Wint. ap. Str.¹¹*

[23] ge- (conge- E) *codd.*: inge- ⛬, *sed vd. Str.¹¹ 107*

we have been avenged on those ruthless pirates; you ransomed two."[28]

(5) I am asking for support—I could have added not "as father from son," but as a beggar from a human being, as an old man from a youth. Indeed, what feeling is more directly derived from the very foundations of nature, sacred and venerable as they are? Again, what is so ordinary, so generally observed, even where children and parents are not involved, as that everyone should drive away his neighbor's hunger? (6) The god who designed mortal men wished us to give help to each other, and by mutual aid to assist another to avoid what one would fear for oneself. This is not yet affection, or respect granted to particular persons, but a matter of farsighted fear of similar circumstances and a superstitious dread of the chances to which we are all subject. (7) When another is hungry, each man feels pity for himself.[29] Thus a city under siege shares out food, thus one individual's provisions have often fed starving fellow passengers at sea. (8) This is the source, too, of the feeling that leads us to bring earth to the corpses of people unknown to us: no one passes by an unburied body so hastily that he does not show his respect by sprinkling at least a little soil upon it.

7. On the other hand, children, you do not provide food for your parents: you give it them as their due—and (gods and goddesses!) for how short a time, in how small a quantity compared with all they spent on your infancy and on your childhood, on the so varied expenses of even the most frugal youth! (2) Indeed, if nature allowed this kind of

[28] Cf. 5.2.1.   [29] Thinking of the hunger he might suffer himself in the future (AS).

quoque officii genus natura permitteret, bene pro defi-
cientibus aliquid et vita vestra dependeret, iterumque ex
illa, quam traxistis, anima portio brevis in suum rediret
3   auctorem. Vultis scire quantus nomini nostro debeatur
affectus, quanta veneratio? Non est beneficium quod
pascitis, sed est facinus quod negatis.

4   LIBERI PARENTES ALANT. Pudet sacrorum nominum,
pudet religionis humanae: hoc ergo lex erit? Quid impre-
cer homini, qui primus fecit ut pietatem iuberemus?[24]
5   LIBERI PARENTES ALANT. O crudele factum, o numquam
6   tristior fames! Ita pascit ille qui cogitur? "Non meruisti"
inquit "accipere." Discede, pietas, quiesce paulisper, infir-
7   mitas;[25] remunerandum sit primum.[26] Lex severissima est,
ut fortius alimenta poscantur. Perdiderunt pulchritudi-
nem sanctitatemque naturae, qui putant illis parentibus
iura succurrere, quibus apud liberos salva est de mutua
caritate reverentia; collisis prospexere pignoribus, et inter
tam venerabiles affectus hoc quoque dignum providentia
fuit, ut aliquid et odia praestarent. Quereris, irasceris, et
8   ideo iuberis. Expectandum est videlicet ut liberorum pa-
rentumque concordiam perferant totius merita vitae,
[et][27] ut pietas, natura, sanguis accipiant cotidie tamquam

---

[24] -tem iuberemus *Gron.*: -te iuvaremur *codd.*: -tem iubere-
mur *Reitz.[1] 109 (sed vd. Str.[15] 55.93)*   [25] dist. *Håk.[2] 50 cum*
ς: *post* paulisper *vulg.*   [26] -ndum est primum. lex *Sh. B.[1]*
75–76, sit pr- *repos. Str.[15]:* -nda sit (sic S) primum lex *codd.*
[27] *del. Wint. ap. Str.[15]:* et ut B V γ δ: ut et (ut *s.l.* S) β

---

[30] "Father" and "son": cf. 1.6.3.   [31] I.e., as those (properly
obtaining) between father and son.   [32] To give sustenance.
[33] Ironic. The speaker dismisses the idea that hatred between

service too, it would be no bad thing if you made, even, some sacrifice of life to them when they are failing, so that a small portion of the breath you drew from them returned back to those who gave it. (3) Do you want to know how much affection is owed to the name of father, how much respect? If you give us food, that is not a favor; but it is an outrage if you deny it.

(4) CHILDREN ARE TO SUPPORT PARENTS. I am ashamed for these holy names,[30] ashamed for men's moral standards: shall this then be a *law*? What curse am I to lay on the man who first caused us to *order* sons to be dutiful? (5) CHILDREN ARE TO SUPPORT PARENTS. O cruel act, o hunger never more bitter! Is one who is forced to feed really feeding at all? (6) "You did not deserve anything," he says. Stand aside, filial duty, be silent for a while, weakness: the first thing must be for recompense to be given. (7) The law is extremely rigorous precisely to make it possible for sustenance to be demanded the more forcefully. You destroy the beauty and sanctity of nature, if you think that these legal provisions are in place to bring aid to parents whose children maintain the respect that arises from mutual love. No, the law was framed to cover cases where father and son are in conflict: where such revered relationships are concerned,[31] it was thought worthwhile to provide that those who hate should make a contribution too. You complain, you are angry, and so you are subjected to an order.[32] (8) Must we wait, forsooth, for concord between children and parents to be preserved only at the cost of a whole lifetime of services?[33] Must we wait for

father and sons should be avoided by a lifetime spent by the father in cajoling and flattering the sons.

amicitiae nexum, et, nisi vos promeruerimus obsequiis, adulatione, patientia, natales ortus et pignora prima perierunt? 8. Si vultis, iudices, ut huic nomini salva sit in omni personarum diversitate veneratio, bonum patrem filius alat, lex malum.

2   Non faciam hanc rerum naturae, non faciam contumeliam legi, ut excusem vel pessimum patrem, ut sacro nomini temptem gratiam petere de venia. Sim licet crudelis 3 ac saevus, filium tamen diutius amavi. Clauserim paternos penates, de testamento, de spe successionis expulerim, oneraverim vinculis manus, foedaverim membra verberi-4 bus: persolvi gratia non potest nec malo patri. Arrogans, impotens sum? Nolo cotidie mereri quicquid mihi deberi 5 coepit primo die. "Facilis, mitis, indulgens": vocabula sunt ista minoris affectus; propter haec aleretur amicus, pasce-6 retur extraneus. Vestrum quin immo crimen est, quod interdum aliud sumus, et, unde manifestum est diversitatem nostram venire de moribus liberorum, non invenias 7 asperum patrem nisi iam peccantis aetatis. Quid ais? Rigidus, immitis sum? Ideo pasce tantum,[28] pasce, non ultra. 8 Malo pro reverentia nominis nostri quicquid praestatis inviti, et, cum alitur pater quem quereris indignum, acci-

---

[28] *dist. B. Asc.*[2] (*et vd. Watt*[2] 22)

---

[34] "Father."

[35] He was for a long time a loving father, which should earn him Son's gratitude; but even if he had been the worst of fathers, he would still have been entitled to Son's support, out of respect for his authority (cf. 5.8.7–8).

[36] Cf. 5.7.8.   [37] I.e., we become harsh.

filial affection, nature, blood to form, as it were, a bond of friendship every day?—So that, unless we win your favor by our attentions, by our flattery, by our forbearance, the debt you incurred when you first came into the world has gone for nothing? 8. If, judges, you want that name[34] to retain its proper respect despite all variations of person, let a son feed a good father, the law a bad one.

(2) I shall not insult nature, I shall not insult the law, by submitting excuses for having been—say—the worst of fathers, by seeking pardon in order to try and win favor for my sacred name. I may be cruel and harsh now, but for a long time I did *love* my son.[35] (3) Suppose, though, I closed the doors of his father's house to him, cut him out of my will and any hope of coming into my property, loaded his hands with chains, disfigured his limbs with lashes: it is still impossible to repay even a bad father for his services to you. (4) Am I arrogant, overbearing? I am not prepared to try every day to deserve[36] what my son began to owe to me on the first day of his life. (5) "Easygoing, gentle, indulgent": these are words for a lesser affection; for these qualities a friend would be fed, a stranger would receive nourishment. (6) Rather, it is the fault of you sons that sometimes we change:[37] in fact, you would not find a harsh father unless his son is of an age to misbehave—which clearly shows that variations in us[38] result from the nature of our children. (7) What do you say? Am I inflexible, brutal? In that case just feed me, feed me, no more than that.[39] (8) I prefer whatever you sons give us unwillingly out of respect for our name; and if a father is

38 I.e., differences in the behavior of us fathers.
39 = without feeling affection.

9 pere mihi videntur omnes parentes. Si vis, affectum[29] debes; sin minus, necessitatem,[30] servitutem, patientiam. Non tamquam pater alitur, qui tamquam bonus amatur.

9. Sepone, iuvenis, differ querelas; tunc irasceris, tunc obicies mihi, cum prosperitatium, cum secundorum officia deposcam. Non talis ad tua genua provolvor, ut aestimandus sim: nulli malus est pater, cum esse coepit
2 infelix. Aspicis collapsum et ex omni calamitatium genere miserum et, ultra quod accidentium mensura non exit, in orbitate mendicum. Riget squalidi capitis concreta canities, vigor pristini vultus vacuis luminibus intabuit et per obstantium crinium inluviem tenuis[31] arentium iactus oculorum. Haeret adstricta nudatis ossibus cutis et, in fame sua homine consumpto, iam membra sine corpore.[32]
3 Iterum bonus sum, in pristinam religionem de calamitatium honore restituor. Adeone non habent haec ipsa supplicia poenas, quod posco, quod rogo, quod mendicus
4 sum filii mei? Et quanta,[33] dii deaeque, non possunt pro nobis impetrare leges! Quanto plura sunt quae negantur,

---

[29] -tu (d., s. m., -tate) *Best 255–56*

[30] -tem πM ψ (*vind. Russ. ap. Str.*[15] *56.116*): -te *cett.*

[31] *sc.* est. *alii aliud verbum in* et—oculorum (*moxque in* et—corpore) *desideraverunt, sed vd. Str.*[11] *107–8*

[32] *sc.* sunt (*vd. super. adn.*)

[33] quanta B (*def. Str.*[15] *57.129*): quam multa V Φ

---

[40] A person who is loved may be fed out of affection; a father must be fed out of respect for his position as father.

[41] Now, he is asking only what he needs to survive.

[42] Sc., so that you may decide whether I am a good father,

fed even when you complain that he does not deserve it,
all fathers—it seems to me—benefit. (9) If you are willing
to give it, you owe me affection; if not, you owe me com-
pulsion, servitude, compliance. Anyone who is loved for
being good is not fed as a father.[40]

9. Put your complaints on one side, young man, postpone them; you will have cause for anger, cause to accuse
me, when I ask for services appropriate to a prosperous
man, for whom things are going well.[41] I am not, in the
state I am in, throwing myself at your feet in order to be
judged:[42] no one's father is bad when he falls on evil times.
(2) You see me laid low, made wretched by all manner of
calamities, and—the extreme point affliction can reach—
begging after losing a son. The white hair on my filthy
scalp is matted and stiff, my eyes are empty, the old liveli-
ness of my glance has wasted away, and through the bar-
rier of a filthy thatch of hair my dried up eyes can cast only
a feeble glance. My bones are bare, and the skin hangs
tight on them;[43] the man has been consumed by his own
hunger, and I am now limbs with no body. (3) I am good
again,[44] I am being given my old sanctity back out of respect for my calamities. After all, do these very torments
not constitute sufficient punishment—that I make demands, that I ask, that I beg from my own son? (4) Besides,
how many are the things, gods and goddesses, that the
laws cannot obtain for us! How much more is denied,[45]

---

deserving of gratitude, or a bad one, not deserving to be fed. I am
in such a desperate condition that you cannot doubt what to do.

[43] Cf. 6.3.4.   [44] Now that my misfortunes have reduced
me to such a state (cf. 5.9.1–2).

[45] Than given.

5 cum praestant[34] inviti! Non exigo ut tuis manibus porrigas
cibos, ut consoleris, ut foveas. Proice quod rapiam, abice
quod colligam. Genus ultionis est pascere nec misereri.

6   Si tamen, iudices, fas est impietatis huius ullas accipere
causas et filium qui non alit putatis reddere posse rationem, aestimate, per fidem, quod sit facinus illud, cuius

7 ultionem debeat exigere aliquis[35] de fame patris. "Captum
me" inquit "non redemisti." Quis non putet queri de filio

8 patrem? Quemquamne dicentem feram: "Nihil tibi debeo,
quia mihi vitae lucisque beneficium semel praestitisti,
quia hunc spiritum, hoc corpus non ex indulgentia tua
rursus accepi"? 10. Iniquissima magnorum condicio meritorum est, si quicquid non fuerit adiectum de prioribus
perit, et pessimo exemplo gratiam praeteritis auferunt re-

2 liqua cessantia. Non redemi. Non tamen ideo minus est
quod in hunc te divinorum humanorumque conspectum

3 de nostra protulimus anima. Maria terrasque, infatigabiles
siderum cursus et cuncta sacro fulgore lucentia nos, ut
fruereris, ostendimus. Has quas subtrahis manus, haec
verba quae negant, de meo spiritu, de meis visceribus

4 hausisti. Gaude potius, exulta quod tibi patris asperitas
praestat boni filii iactationem; solus habet quod imputet
patri qui queritur et pascit.

5   Quam multa, iudices, huic querelae respondere pote-

---

[34] -atis *Reitz.[1] 111*   [35] -is M ψ: -id *cett.*

---

[46] By escaping from the pirates.
[47] A further variation on the point already made at 5.7.8, 5.8.4.
[48] Cf. 5.11.5.
[49] I.e., a son who fulfills his duty even toward a bad father.

when those who offer are unwilling! (5) I do not insist that you proffer food with your own hands, that you console me, that you cherish me; just toss me something to grab at, throw something away for me to pick up. It is a kind of vengeance to feed without feeling any pity.

(6) But if, judges, it is possible to be given any reasons for such lack of affection, and if you think that a son who withholds food can justify his behavior, take the measure, I beg you, of a crime for which someone has to claim requital by starving his father. (7) He says: "You did not ransom me when I was a prisoner." Who would not think this the complaint of a father about a son? (8) Am I to tolerate someone who says: "I owe you nothing, because you gave me the boon of life and light only once, because it was not thanks to your generosity that I received this breath, this body a second time"?[46] 10. Great services are set impossibly unfair terms if failure to do more is regarded as diminishing what went before: it sets an evil precedent if later delays remove favor from past actions.[47] (2) I did not ransom you, true. But that does not detract from the fact that I brought you forth from my soul to gaze on things human and divine. (3) I showed you for your enjoyment the seas and lands, the unwearied courses of the constellations, and a world lit up with a holy glow. These hands which you withdraw from me, these words that say no to me, you derived from my breath, from my vital organs.[48] (4) Rejoice rather, exult, that your father's harshness gives you the chance to boast of being a good son. The only son who can claim credit from his father is one who complains and yet supports him.[49]

(5) How much, judges, I might say in reply to the

ram, propter quae[36] filium salva pietate non redemissem!

6 Quis non acciperet excusationem, si dicerem: "Impediit quamvis properantem senectus, inopia, languor. Pretium non tam festinanter inveni. Explicare non potui navigationem iuvenibus quoque fratribusque difficilem: solus ac senex non illa, qua speraveram, prosperitate direxi; per quos metus, per quae peregrinationis incerta properavi!"?

7 Remove, iuvenis, indignationem; nihil plus pro filio factum est quem recepi. Non fortunam tibi debeo sed affec-

8 tum, non exitum sed voluntatem. Pro duobus pretia contraxi, pro duobus maria conscendi, pro duobus genua tenui. Rogo, uter magis amaretur, si mihi piratae duos reddidissent?

11. Age tu nunc, iuvenis, ad faciendam inopiae patris invidiam, si videtur, exclama: "Famem obtendis, ad quam luxuria prodigarumque voluptatium continuatione venisti.

2 Exhausisti senex census in pretia meretricum." Quamquam et huic iubetur necessitati pietas vestra succurrere, et lex quae inopem, quae patrem nominare contenta est,

3 filium non remisit ad causas. Quid vero si in educationem, in discursus, in pretia vacuatus sum? Excedit omnem scelerum comparationem patrem mendicum facere nec pascere.

4 Temptat, iudices, hoc quod non est redemptus ampliare alia iuvenis invidia: "Fratrem" inquit "mihi praetu-

---

36 quae D (*def. Reitz.[1] 112*): quod E: quam *cett.*

---

50 Son should consider the efforts Father made to save him (as well as his brother), not the outcome.

51 For a father's poverty.

charge being brought against me to show that I did not neglect my duties as a father, even though I failed to ransom my son. Who would not accept the excuse, if I were to say: (6) "I tried to make haste, but I was held up by old age, want, sickness. The ransom money I could not find as quickly as that. Nor could I manage a sea journey that was difficult even for young men—and brothers: alone and aged, I did not carry it through as prosperously as I had hoped; amid what fears, amid what uncertainties of travel did I hasten!"? (7) Young man, stop being angry: I did no more for the son who was restored to me than I did for you. I owe you not good luck but affection, not the outcome but the intention.[50] (8) I raised money for two, I embarked on the seas for two, I supplicated for two. I ask, which of the two would now be the more loved if the pirates had given me two back?

11. Well now, young man, if you see fit to arouse feeling against your impoverished father, cry aloud: "You are making a pretext of a hunger to which you have been reduced by your own debauchery, by an unbroken career of expensive pleasures. You have spent—at your age!—all your substance on paying for whores." (2) Yet a son's sense of duty is bidden to come to the rescue even of this state of need: the law is content to speak of a "poor man," of a "father"; it did not require a son to investigate the reasons.[51] (3) But what if I lost my all on bringing you up, on your jaunts, on your ransom money? It is wickedness beyond compare to beggar your father and refuse to support him.

(4) The youth is attempting, judges, to build on the plea that he was not ransomed by introducing another slur: "You preferred my brother," he says, "to me." Let us grant

listi." Fateamur paulisper hoc crimen, agnoscamus hoc
nefas: impudentissime generis humani, tu non feres ut
5 frater tuus vel magis ametur? Vides enim, praelatus est tibi
nescioquis affectus, possident caritatis tuae locum pignora
de minoribus sumpta nominibus: ille[37] nempe, cuius ae-
que spiritus de visceribus his trahebat ortum, qui patrem
vel solus impleret. Pessimus est mortalium, qui amari fra-
6 trem suum sine sui caritate putat. Tu custodies utrum
frequentius osculer, utrum stringam magis artiore[38] complexu? Non est hoc impatientia, nec circa patris adfectus
sacra de pietatis contentione rixa; eum tantum fratrem
putes amari magis, quem non ames.
7   Falleris, iuvenis, longeque te ab intellectu rerum naturae seposuit prava persuasio, qui putas ex paternis affectibus filio perire quicquid in altero de necessitate praepon-
derat. 12. Par est in omnes liberos eademque pietas, sed
habet in aliquo plerumque proprias indulgentiae causas,
et salva caritatis aequalitate est quiddam, per quod tacito
mentis instinctu singulos rursus tamquam unicos amemus:
2 hunc primus nascendi locus, illum gratiorem propior[39]
fecit infantia; alium laetior vultus et blandior osculis amplexibusque facies; quosdam magis severitas probitasque
commendat; in quibusdam diliguntur impatientius calamitates et damna corporum debilitatesque membrorum

---

37 -le B. Asc.[1] xxxiii r.: -lum codd.
38 art- π DE: alt- cett.   39 propior Reitz.[1] 113, Ellis 332:
prior B V ACD δ: om. β: prae(fecit) E

---

52 Vides—nominibus is ironic.   53 Cf. 5.10.3.
54 Cf. 5.4.7.

this charge for a moment, let us acknowledge this wicked act: most impudent member of the human race, will you not allow your brother to be loved even more than you? (5) Of course, as you can see,[52] what was preferred to you was some trivial affection, your place in my love has been taken over by a less close relative.—In fact, it was someone whose breath, just as much as yours, originated from these vitals of mine,[53] someone capable even by himself of taking up the whole of his father's heart. Worst of mortals is he who thinks his brother is being loved without any affection left over for himself. (6) Are you going to keep watch to see which of the two I kiss more often, which I hold in a tighter embrace? All this is not passionate love, or dutiful competitiveness in showing affection for a father: you would think a brother is loved more only if you do not love him.

(7) You are mistaken, young man, and your way of thinking is wicked: you are very far from understanding nature, if you think that in a father's heart whatever in an emergency tips the scale to the side of one son is lost to the other. 12. One's affection is equal and identical toward all one's children, but quite often it has especial motives for fondness in a given case: though the feeling for all is unimpaired, there is something that by an unspoken prompting of our hearts makes us love individuals as if they were our only sons turn by turn.[54] (2) This one is made more attractive by having been born first, that by having been an infant more recently, a third by a more cheerful face and an appearance that makes kissing and hugging him more agreeable; some are commended by their seriousness and honesty; in some their distresses arouse more passionate affection: since we feel pity, we

3 notabilius miseratione complectimur. Salva est tamen universitas, cum, quicquid in aliquo[40] cessare creditur, in altero restituit alter affectus. Securus sis: non intercidunt ista, non pereunt, sed invicem vincunt,[41] praevalent, cedunt. Filio non potest praeferri nisi filius.[42]

4　　Blandiar, iudices, paulisper calamitatibus meis et sic agam, tamquam apud piratas invenerim utrumque sanum. Attuli sine dubio pretium duorum, sed utrumque praedo

5 non reddit: offert electionem. Suadete quid faciam. Quid dicitis?[43] Ita pietas est abire, discedere, irasci scilicet, queri et invidiam facere piratis? Vos interrogo, liberi, vos, parentes: non ergo facinus est ideo neutrum redimere,

6 quia utrumque non possis? Egregia pietas aequare liberos iustitia desperationis et ex hoc, quod succurrere non contingit duobus, orbitatem facere totam! Tu vero, senectus, accipe quicquid datur, accipe quicquid offertur, dum hoc saltem feritati libet, antequam impatientia[44] tam saeva

7 recrudescat[45] immanitas. Interim multa possunt afferre casus. Sperare, ‹fili,›[46] licet: repeteris; sperare, pater: fortassis evadat. Quaecumque explicari coacervatione non possunt, per partes vicesque servantur, et facilius est divisa subtrahere, quorum magnitudo laborat in solido.

[40] aliquo *Håk.* (*firm. Str.*[15] 59.170): alio *codd.*

[41] vincunt, ‹vincuntur,› *Reitz.*[2] 4, *sed vd. Helm*[1] 343

[42] ‹miser› fi- *Håk.*[3] 125, *sed vd. vM.-M.*

[43] dicitis M[2] DE: dicis *cett.*　　　[44] -a M O P: -am *cett.*

[45] recrudescat *Reitz.*[1] 114 (*firm. Str.*[11] 108): decrescit (-cat M) *codd.*　　　[46] *suppl. Sh. B.*[2] 194 (spera, fili: rep- *Reitz.*[1] 114.5)

[55] The various reasons for our affection.　　　[56] I.e., understate them, make them sound less bad than they were (AS).

embrace their damaged bodies and feeble limbs more demonstratively. (3) But the total result remains the same, for whatever is thought to be lacking in a child is made up for by reasons to feel affection that differ in each case. Do not worry: these[55] do not disappear, do not perish; they are victorious turn by turn, now prevailing, now yielding. No one can be preferred to a son except a son.

(4) I shall for a short while, judges, soften my calamities[56] and conduct my case on the assumption that I found both sons in the pirates' hands fit and well. I have of course brought money enough to pay for both, but the robber is not giving them both up: he is offering a choice instead. Advise me what to do. (5) What do you say? Is it, I ask you, a sign of paternal affection to go away, retire from the scene, grow cross forsooth, protest, abuse the pirates? I ask you, children, and you, parents: is it then not a crime to ransom neither just because you are unable to ransom both? (6) An excellent manifestation of paternal duty indeed, to put your sons on the same level by the equity of despair, and to make your bereavement complete because you are not in a position to help both! No: *you* are old, and should take all that is being given, accept all that is on offer, while the brute is still prepared to make these terms at least, before he loses patience and all that cruelty breaks out anew. (7) Many strange things can happen in the meanwhile. You can hope, <son:> search will be made for you for a second time; *you* can hope, father: maybe he will escape. Matters that cannot be resolved when they present themselves all together are best approached piecemeal, one thing at a time: where the sum of the whole is daunting it is easier to divide it up and deal with the parts separately.

13. Quantum intellego, iudices, filius, cui profuturum non erat ut eligerem, hoc solum ferre non potest, quod redemptus est frater. Quis hanc, iudices, impudentiam

2 ferat? Obicit mihi quod ullum de liberis meis potuerim facere discrimen, deinde queritur non se potius electum et, cum fratri praeter eiusdem nominis par ac simile consortium reverentia quoque languoris accesserit, indignatur apud affectus patris non eam praevaluisse par-

3 tem, in qua tantum filius erat. Non invenio, iudices, quemadmodum effugere potuerim criminis huius invidiam, si hunc potius recepissem. Patri, cui utrumque pirata reddere nolebat, redimendus fuit aut aeger aut neuter.

4 "Quid, quod" inquit "etiam[47] luxuriosum praetulisti?" Parce, iuvenis, maledictis, parce conviciis; reliquistis haec nomina. Domi erunt ista vitia, domi erunt istae virtutes, sed, dum[48] fueritis reversi, interim nihil aliud estis quam fratres, quam liberi mei, duo captivi, ambo miseri, et diversitas vestra de calamitatium societate consumpta est.

5 Vides quam nefas sit alterum ex vobis mihi esse viliorem: piratarum non interest uter eligatur. Dic nunc:[49] "Luxuriosum redemisti."

6 Comparatione vestra, iuvenis, ‹si›[50] circa patrimonium honoresve contenderes[51]—et ego proclamabo—, vicisses.

---

47 quid—etiam *dist. Reitz.[1] 116*
48 dum (*et comma post* reversi) *Håk.[2]* 50–51: cum *codd.*
49 dic nunc V: dignum nunc B Φ (*sc. per diplogr.*)
50 *add. Klotz[1]*
51 -tenderes C[2]: -cederet B: -tenderet *cett.*: -tenderetur *Dess.[2]*

---

57 He did not need ransoming, for he was, as he proved, capable of escaping. Cf. 5.1.3.   58 I.e., not ill too.

13. As I understand it, judges, a son whom it would not have helped for me to choose him[57] cannot tolerate this one thing—that his brother was ransomed. Who could bear such impudence? (2) He charges me with being able to make any distinction between my children, then complains that he was not chosen for preference: in a case where concern for illness was put in the scales alongside the precisely equal claims of brotherhood, he professes indignation that in his father's affections the part in which he was a son and no more[58] did not prevail. (3) If I had taken him instead, I don't see, judges, how I could have avoided this same damaging charge.[59] A father to whom the pirate refused to hand over both had to ransom the sick son, or neither.

(4) "What," he says, "of the fact that you gave preference to the son who was actually a prodigal?" Let us have none of this reviling, young man, none of this abuse: you have both left such appellations behind you.[60] Home will be the place for these vices, and for these virtues too; but until you come back, you are meanwhile just brothers, just my children, two prisoners, both in distress: the difference between you is swallowed up in your shared misfortune. (5) You can see how wrong it is for one of you to be cheaper in my eyes: it makes no odds to the pirates which is chosen.[61] *Now* say: "You ransomed the prodigal."

(6) In a choice between the two of you, young man, ⟨if⟩ you had been competing for inheritance or for honors, *you*

---

[59] Which would have been lodged by the other son, in that case.   [60] We are still in, or rather revert to, the pirate camp (cf. 5.12.4).

[61] But contrast (again) 5.15.2–3.

Sed ventum est illuc ubi non probitas, non mores aesti-
7 mantur, et de corporibus sola taxatio est. Unde tristes tole-
raret casus, ferret sordes vinculorum, piraticam famem
iuvenis, quem torquere solebat nostra frugalitas? Unde
[et][52] in illa solitudine carceris duraret[53] animus convic-
8 tibus semper comitatibusque laetatus? Expecta tu, quem
decet honesta patientia, laudabilis labor, qui tibi difficul-
tatium reddis ipse rationem. Tu differris, luxuriosus relinquitur.
9   Quid ais? Praetuli illum de quo soli tibi querebar, quem
cum vellem castigare, reprehendere, te solebam laudare,
mirari? 14. Exaggera quantum voles vitia fratris, luxuriosum, perditum voca, dum scias te sic magis probare non
animum fuisse patris, sed de calamitate rationem. Ille eli-
2 git, qui recipit ante meliorem. Sed parce, quaeso, iuvenis,
adversorum interpretationi. Non est electio alterum reci-
pere, cum pretium attuleris duorum; discrimen illud non
3 ego, sed pirata commentus est. Quicquid [inter vos][54] in
alterutro fecero, affectus est quo duos amo, et homo, apud

---

52 *del. Wint. ap. Str.*[15] (*et om.* E S): et B: ut *cett.*

53 -raret *Obr.*: -ret *codd.*

54 *secl. Wint. ap. Str.*[15] (*utpote gloss. ad* in alt-), *et om.* π: *post*
-men illud (*§2*) *transp. Reitz.*[1] *117, Reitz.*[2] *45*

---

62 I.e., just like you would have done.

63 I.e., capacity to endure hardship.

64 Cf., e.g., 6.4.1, 9.4.3, 16.8.6–7.

65 I.e., the son who had proved to be the more deserving.
Father's opting for the less deserving shows that he did not really
make a choice, but acted out of *necessity*.

(I too[62] am ready to shout it aloud) would have won. But we are now in a place where it is not probity, not behavior that is being judged, and the only assessment is of physique.[63] (7) How could a youth who used to find our frugality a torment put up with distressing conditions, bear the filth of captivity and the starvation that pirates always[64] inflict? How could one who always took pleasure in good cheer and good company tolerate life in that solitary confinement? (8) It is for you to be left to wait, to whom honest endurance and praiseworthy toil come naturally, who have only yourself to answer to in confronting difficulties. *You* are merely being put off, the prodigal is being abandoned.

(9) What do you say? That I gave preference to the son whom I used to complain of to you in private?—Indeed, when I wanted to punish and reprove *him* I used to praise *you*, lavish admiration on *you*. 14. Exaggerate the vices of your brother as much as you like, call him debauched, depraved, so long as you are aware that you are thereby proving that what counted was not a father's heart, but a calculation based on calamity. A choice is only made by a father who takes the son who was better hitherto.[65] (2) But I beg you, young man, to refrain from misinterpreting adversities.[66] When you have brought the money to pay for two, it does not count as a choice to take one; that a differentiation[67] was made like that was brought about not by me but by the pirate. (3) Whatever I do in the case of either of you is the result of the emotion that makes me

---

[66] Son is portraying Father's conduct as a deliberate choice; but he was in fact *forced* to rescue the sick son (see n. 65 and below).   [67] Between the two of you.

quem filius sola praevaluit gratia calamitatis, non fratrem
4 tibi praetuli, sed quod in te fratri praetulissem. Consilium
hoc putas fuisse patris? Fortunae[55] est, qua capti pariter
estis, qua decubuit alter, qua non convaluit redemptus.
5 Cum propter duos venerim, quod altero[56] mihi pirata cessit idem est ac si mihi neutrum reddidisset.
6 Sed quousque facti mei dissimulabo rationem? Aeger
7 electus est. Responde[57] nunc, si videtur: "Luxuriosus, perditus fuit." Parcamus, quaeso, memoriae, revereamur su-
8 prema cineris. Paeniteret me fortasse, si viveret. Iterum
ac saepius, iudices,[58] necesse est ipsa criminis mei voce
9 defendar: aegrum redemi. Non habent profecto, non habent discrimen liberi nisi de calamitate, et, inter homines
quos natura pietatis aequavit, differentiam nisi de dolore
non explices. Non cum usu nunc vestro, non cum moribus
loquor: ille anhelat, illius sunt lassa suspiria, ad illum se-
10 rius veni. Excogitasti rursus, fortuna, quod supercresceret
caritati, quod posset sacris nominibus accedere; hic solus
maior affectus est quam filios amare: filii misereri.
15. Me quidem, iudices, si quis interroget, condicio illa
non fuit vera, non simplex, habuitque piraticae feritatis

---

[55] -na W (*et vd. Reitz.[1] 115.2*)   [56] -ro B V (*def. Håk.*): in
-ro Φ   [57] -de *Reitz.[1] 115*: -dete *codd.*
[58] iudices (*h.e.* iuđ, *ut saepius*) *Håk.[3] 125–26*: quod *codd.*

---

[68] I.e., the illness.   [69] Sc., who was ill.

[70] Father's motive has not been hidden so far; but it is only
now that he explains openly that his pity for the sick son was the
reason for his discriminating between the two of them.

[71] Back in the pirate camp: cf. 5.12.6–7, 5.13.4–8, 5.19.1ff.

[72] Literally, "something to develop as an addition to."

love you both, and, as a man who allowed one son to prevail only because of his distressing condition, I did not prefer your *brother* to you, but what[68] would have made me prefer you to your brother if *you* had been the one.[69] (4) Do you think this was a father's considered plan? No, it is Fortune's doing: the chance by which you were both taken prisoner, by which one of you fell ill, by which the son I ransomed did not recover. (5) I came to get both of you back: so, that the pirate gave up one to me is the same as if he had let me have neither.

(6) But how much longer shall I go on disguising the motive for my action?[70] The *sick* one was chosen. (7) Retort now if you like: "He was debauched, depraved." Let us spare, I ask, the memory of the dead man, have respect for the last rites accorded to his ashes—though I should perhaps regret my choice, if he were still alive. (8) Again and again, judges, I have to look for my defense to the very words of the charge against me: I ransomed a sick man. (9) Surely children are not discriminated between, no indeed they are not, except when ill fortune comes into it: between human beings whom the nature of paternal affection has made equal, you can make no distinction except on grounds of suffering. I am not now[71] talking with the habits, the character of the pair of you; *he* is gasping, *his* are the tired sighs, it is to *him* I have come too late. (10) You have, Fortune, thought up something more to swell[72] my affection, something to add to the sacred ties between father and son; this is the only feeling deeper than love for sons: pity for a son.

15. Indeed, if I am posed the question, judges, those terms were not genuine, not straightforward, and they smacked of a pirate's cruelty: I was not really allowed to

ingenium: aegrum mihi non licuit relinquere, licuit eli-
2 gere. An fas fuisse credis ut iuxta moriturum tu reddereris,
et homines eius immanitatis, ut possent liberos cum patre
partiri, paterentur eum sibi relinqui, quem periturum et
3 hoc probabat,[59] quod illum pater non eligebat? Temptata
est misera pietas, et placuit hoc quoque addi calamitatibus
nostris, ut onerarer pudore condicionis partes non ha-
bentis. Cum in comparatione sani aeger offertur, ideo ponitur, ut eligatur.
4 Superest, nisi fallor, iudices, ut, cum sibi praelatum
fratrem queratur, aestimetis utri tunc magis debuerit pi-
5 etas nostra succurrere. Est quidem, iudices, humanae
infirmitatis ista natura, ut ex omnibus accidentibus gravissimum putet quisque quod patitur, et, cum aliena cogitationibus, nostra[60] dolore tractentur, necesse est apud
impatientiam sua[61] vel minora praevaleant. Languor est
tamen, languor, cui merito cesserint cunctae calamitates,
in cuius comparatione consolari se potest genus omne
6 miserorum. Stringat licet manus saeva captivitas, pro-
funda carceris nocte membra claudantur, datur tamen
collidere catenas, artus extrahere nexibus, et habet aliquid
aequanimitatis cum poena sua posse rixari. Saeviunt regna
tormentis, bella vulneribus, sed levius adficit quicquid viribus feras et, cum in plenum adhuc sanguinem adversa

---

[59] et h. -bat *Reitz.*[1] *115, Reitz.*[2] *63.10*: et h. -bant B: ex h. -bant
V Φ (*frustra def. Eng. 58–59*)   [60] -ra V C[2]: -ro *cett.*
[61] suam O, *et* sua *coni. Reitz.*[1] *117.4*: -am *cett.*

---

[73] They wanted to get rid of the sick man, whose death would
leave them with one asset less. But contrast 5.4.4.
[74] Cf. 5.15.1.

leave my sick son behind, all I was allowed to do was to choose him. (2) Do you think it was possible for you to be taken back when your dying brother was by? Would men brutal enough to divide up children with their father have allowed the one to be left with them[73] whose imminent death was proved by the very fact that his father did not choose him? (3) Unhappy paternal affection was put to the test, and it was decided that this too should add to my calamities, that I should be burdened with the shame of a one-sided[74] bargain. When a sick man is offered as against a healthy one, he is put there just to be chosen.

(4) If I am not mistaken, judges, what remains is that, given that he complains of his brother being preferred to him, you are to judge to which son my sense of duty was more bound to give assistance at that moment. (5) Human weakness, judges, certainly has this characteristic, to think what one is undergoing oneself to be the worst of all possible happenings: since the troubles of others are matter for our thoughts, whereas our own are matter for our pain, it is inevitable that a man suffering intolerably should deem his own afflictions overwhelming, even if they are less great. But illness, yes illness is something to which all other misfortunes should rightly yield place. In comparison with illness, every other type of wretchedness can find comfort. (6) Even if cruel captivity pinions the hands, even though the body is confined in the profound darkness of a prison, one can still try to break one's chains, to free one's arms and legs from one's bonds: it eases the mind a little to be able to pick a fight with one's punishment. Tyrants have their cruel tortures, wars their cruel wounds, yet anything you find the strength to bear has less effect: when adversity falls upon someone in rude health, it is

ceciderunt, repugnantis roboris colluctatione vincuntur.
7 Quos cruciatus compares, quem dolorem, cum penitus
visceribus immissa tabes cotidie aliquid ex homine prae-
mittit in mortem, cum cibos, haustus et omnia blandi-
8 menta vitae fames fastidit et poscit? Desiderare assidentium officia, dehinc ferre non posse; gravari quos appetieris
attactus; per totum cubile corpus velut super ardentes
exagitare flammas; lux fatigatis luminibus gravis, vox sola
de gemitu: ⟨hi cruciatus!⟩[62] Cum ex duobus captivis languet alter, una est inaequalitas patris:[63] eligere sanum.

16. Retuli, iudices, usque adhuc in penatibus suis, iuxta
parentes propinquosque languentem. O carcer, o morae,[64]
2 qualem[65] vos non facitis[66] aegrum? Et non ille carcer,
quem severitas legum, quem potestatum iustitia commenta est. Non possunt humani metus, humanarum cogitationum ingenia satis habundeque concipere quae vidi.
3 Iacet sub immensae rupis abrupto tristis et ultra natura-
lem profundae caliginis noctem mersus piraticis artibus
specus, quem tutatur[67] circumfusi[68] vastitas maris et undique minantibus scopulis illisa tempestas terrore ruiturae
4 molis everberat. Horrent cuncta crucibus, squalent cir-
cumiecta naufragiis: nullus nisi in supplicia mortesque

---

[62] *suppl. Str.[11] 108–9 (cf. fere 1.14.2): lac. stat. (post Pagl.)*
Wint. ibid., ⟨haec vera tormenta sunt!⟩ *temptans*
[63] *dist. Str.[15]*   [64] *morae Reitz.[1] 117.4 (cf. 5.18.1):* morbi
codd.   [65] qualem *Str.[15]:* quem *codd.*
[66] non confic- *Håk., sed vd. Str.[15] 63.244–45*
[67] tutatur *Russ. ap. Str.[11] 109:* tota *codd.*
[68] (tota) -fundit *vM.-M.*

---

[75] Cf. 5.5.1, 5.18.1.

conquered by the struggle put up by strength that can fight back. (7) But what torment, what pain is comparable with that felt when decay planted deep in the vitals sends each day some part of a man to death in advance, when hunger rejects and yet demands food, drink and everything that makes life agreeable? (8) To ask for the services of those attending you, then to be unable to tolerate them; to find the touch you longed for a burden; to toss all over your bed as though on burning coals; the light of day troublesome to tired eyes, the voice capable only of groans: ⟨*these* are torments!*⟩* When one of two captives is sick, there is only one way their father can be unfair: by choosing the one who is in good health.

16. So far, judges, I have reported on someone lying ill in his own home, with his parents and relatives in attendance. But you, prison, you, delays,[75] to what a state do you not reduce an ill man?[76] (2) And that was not a prison devised by the rigor of the law, the justice of authority. Human fears, the wit of human imagination, cannot adequately conceive the scene before me. (3) Under the precipitous slope of an immense cliff there lies a gloomy cave, sunk, thanks to the workmanship[77] of the pirates, in the unnatural night of profound darkness—a cave which the expanse of the surrounding sea protects, and which the storms, dashing against the rocks that rise threateningly on every side, lash with terror that the whole mass may plunge down. (4) Everything bristles with crosses, the whole area is littered with shipwrecks, there is nothing to

---

[76] Illness may be unbearable even if the patient enjoys the comforts of home; when he is in prison, it becomes devastating.

[77] They built it: it was not a natural cave. Cf. Heliod. 1.28.2.

prospectus, et ad infelicium captivorum metum prae-
missus de simili exitu dolor. Spiritus solus intus, quem
vinctorum trahunt redduntque gemitus, quem tot contu-
5   lere languentes. Hoc erat ubi iacebat aeger, illud tot anno-
rum, ex quo coepit pirata grassari, idem cubile. Corpus,
quod gravaretur assidentium sedulas manus, iacet inter
vincula quibus instrinxerat adhuc recentem pirata capti-
vum, et, quamvis tenuata de nexibus membra labantur,
rursus in modum stringentium tenent quae nullo suspensa
6   nisu velut victo homine sederunt. Qualis erat ille sub
ferro, cuius exsangues manus vix levia velamenta trans-
ferrent! Quis inter complorationes gemitusque somnus,
7   quem vix silentia sollicita praestarent? Ad quae colloquia
tristitia respiraret? Undique pares similesque miseri, et
veteribus captivis adiectus cotidie novus aliquis impatiens.
8   Compara, si videtur, huic aegro captivitatem tantum
tuam. 17. Tu quereris quod cibos pirata non praestet; ille
remittit oblatos. Te nuda humus, nudum cubile frangit;
ille ad singulos ardentis corporis motus in sua [supra][69]
vincla versatur, et quocumque membra lassata dolore
2   transtulerit, in supplicium redit renovata patientia. Brevi-
ter saevissimi languoris definienda mensura est: non potest ex illo sanari nec quem redemerit pater.

[69] *del. Bur.* (*corrob. Wint. ap. Str.*[15] *64.263*)

---

[78] Cf. 6.18.4–5; Calp. Fl. 4 (p. 4.17–18 H.).
[79] Cf. 5.15.8.
[80] I.e., the bonds have not been tightened up, but he cannot
escape them, so feeble is he.
[81] He feels better for a bit in the new position, then the pain
returns.

look at except executions and deaths: to strike dread into the unfortunate captives, the anguish of a similar fate has been set before them in advance.[78] Inside the only air is that drawn in and breathed out by the groaning prisoners in their chains, air that so many sick men have contributed to. (5) This is where the invalid was lying, on a bed not changed over all the years since the pirates started their depredations. His body, which would have found painful even the attentive hands of people waiting on him,[79] lies in the chains with which the pirates had shackled him when he was first taken prisoner, and though his emaciated limbs tend to slip from their bonds, these keep holding them as though they are tight upon him: he can make no effort that would keep the chains raised,[80] and they have settled on him as on a man defeated. (6) Think of his fate, beneath those irons, when his bloodless hands could scarcely manage to adjust the flimsy blankets! What sleep could he get amid the wails and groans, when even a carefully observed silence could scarcely have offered it? (7) In what conversations could his depressed state find relaxation? All around were others like him, equally wretched, and each day some new, recalcitrant captive was added to the number of the old inmates.

(8) With the plight of this sick man compare, if you will, *your* captivity—for that was all it was. 17. *You* grumble that the pirate is giving you no food, *he* sends it back when it is offered. *You* are worn down by the bare earth, the bare bed; every time *he* moves his fevered body, he rolls over on to his chains: so that, wherever he shifts limbs tired out with pain, his renewed ability to endure ends in new agony.[81] (2) The extent of his dreadful illness can be briefly defined: he cannot recover from it, even if his father chooses to ransom him.

[QUINTILIAN]

3   Insta nunc, si videtur, ac subinde, iuvenis, interroga,
cur aegrum potius elegerim. Reddi a me posse rationem,
cur hoc fecerim, putas? Ego vero non possem, nec si te
4   redemissem. Quid enim, si respondere iubeas orbitatem
cur in exequias totos egerat[70] census, quid sibi velit ille
funebrium longus ordo pomparum, cur super flagrantes
iaceant rogos, cur ardenti non divellantur amplexu? Et ego
dico, proclamo, fateor: error istud,[71] dementiae[72] furor
est—cum feceris.

5   "Hoc est ergo" inquit "quod de te praecipue queror:
moriturum mihi praetulisti." Quaeso, iuvenis, ne nobis
putes tantum inesse feritatis, ut illum potuerimus aestimare moriturum: vis non sperem victurum filium, quem
tunc primum aspicio, complector,[73] aegrum, quem pirata
6   non recusat sibi relinqui? Si persuasionem patris interroges, quicquid est quo[74] miser torquetur, afficitur, non languorem credo, sed impatientiam, desiderium, dolorem.
Hominis, qui apud piratas languet, unum remedium putes
7   ut redimatur. Sed non est, quaeso, iuvenis, quod hoc patrocinium de tam calamitosa pietate concipias,[75] ut dicam:

[70] ege- C[2] δ (def. Håk.[2] 51): exege- B γ β: exagge- V (unde
exaggeret Leh.)
[71] -or istud Reitz.[1] 118.4: -oris ut B V: -or is ut π: -oris aut cett.
[72] -iae M δ β (def. Håk.): -ia B V: clementiae γ
[73] dist. Sh. B.[4] 195   [74] quo B. Asc.[1] xxxv v.: quod codd.
[75] -as Wint. ap. Str.[15]: -am codd.

---

[82] That would have been an equally blind piece of emotional
reaction: see below.
[83] It's only later you see the madness of such behavior.
[84] The emotion of embracing his son for the first time since

268

(3) Press me now, if you like, young man, ask me over and over again why I chose the sick man rather than you. Do you think I can give a reason why I did it? In fact I could not, even if I had ransomed *you*.[82] (4) Suppose you were to tell bereaved men to explain why they are spending all their money on the last rites, what is the point of that long cortège of the funeral procession, why they lie on the blazing pyre, why they cannot be prised away from an embrace already ablaze. Just like them, I say, I declare, I admit it: this is folly, this is raving madness—*after* you have done it.[83]

(5) "This in fact," he says, "is what I especially complain of in your behavior: you preferred to me one who was going to die." I ask you, young man, do not think me so brutal as to have been capable of calculating that he was on the point of death. Do you wish me not to hope that my son will live? After all, I am seeing him, embracing him now for the first time,[84] a sick man, but one whom the pirate is not refusing to have left in their hands.[85] (6) If you ask your father what he really thinks, whatever it is that is torturing and afflicting the poor man is not, to my mind, illness but lack of endurance, longing, pain. You could think of only one cure for a sick man in pirates' hands: for him to be ransomed. (7) But please do not, young man, imagine that, in a case where paternal affection was in such a calamitous dilemma, I propose to defend myself by saying: "I thought he would survive." No,

his departure abroad gives Father the illusion that the young man may survive despite his illness.   [85] I.e., "a sick man, but not hopelessly sick, or the pirates would not be willing to keep him" (Shackleton Bailey [1984–97, 195; cf. 5.15.3 *et al.*]).

"Victurum putavi." Exaggero quin immo invidiam criminis mei: 18. redemi, fateor, illum qui dilationes, qui moras
ferre non poterat, in quo mihi pirata vendebat brevia oscula, paucos dies. Si mehercules uterque fuisset aeger, il-
2 lum redemissem, qui prior languere coepisset. Si duos
pariter naufragia raperent, illi porrigerem manum, quem
iam membrorum contentione lassatum fluctus hauriret.
Si vulneribus confectos remisisset acies, properantius ei
clauderem plagas, per quas animam largior sanguis ege-
3 reret. Ignoscite, dii pariter atque homines: non possum de
liberis, possum eligere de miseris. Gratias quin immo fortunae, gratias ago, quod adhuc aeger sentit, intellegit; alioquin cadaver acceperam et pretia duorum pro funere tan-
4 tum[76] supremisque persolveram. Nescis quantum pudori,
quantum adiciat affectibus meis inter tam impares ae-
quata condicio. Aeger, qui tantundem est piratis, plus[77] est
patri.
5   Velis tamen nolis, infelix senectus, fatendum est quod
merito, quod summa pietate factum est, quam difficile
fecerimus. Quae tunc mihi cogitationes, quis temporis illius animus fuit, cum inter duos liberos incerta miser elec-
6 tione discurrerem! Hunc diutius osculabar: illum putabam
desperatione moriturum; lacrimas ad languentem gemitusque transtuleram:[78] et tu mihi videbaris futurus aeger.
7 Quotiens catenas tuas soluturus invasi! Sed mihi commen-

---

[76] ⟨unius⟩ tantum *Wint. ap. Str.*[15] 65.290
[77] pluris *Wint.*[9]
[78] osculabar—transtuleram *sic dist. Reitz.*[1] 118.4

---

[86] I.e., in selling whom they sold me only . . .

I want to make my crime even more odious: 18. I ransomed, I confess it, the one who could not tolerate delays and deferrals, the one in whom[86] the pirate sold me only snatched kisses, a few days. Indeed if both had been sick, I should have ransomed the one who fell ill first. (2) If the two of them were being swept away together by shipwreck, I should offer my hand to the one being sucked under by the waves, his limbs tired out by his struggles. If they had come home from war with grave injuries, I should now be in more of a hurry to bind up the wounds through which the greater gush of blood is carrying life away. (3) Forgive me, gods and men alike: I cannot choose between sons, I can choose between men who suffer. Rather, I thank Fortune, yes I thank it, that the sick man was still conscious and aware of what was going on. Otherwise I should have taken his dead body, and spent the money meant for two just on his funeral and last rites. (4) You do not know how much it adds to my shame, to my turmoil of emotions, that two sons in such different situations were given equal weight in the balance. The sick son has the same price for the pirates, but for his father he is worth more.

(5) Still, whether you like it or not, my unlucky old age, it has to be confessed how difficult it was to do what was done rightly, done out of the strongest sense of duty. What went through my head then, what was my state of mind at that moment, when I scurried between my two sons, agonized by the difficulty of my choice! (6) I kissed this one the longer: the other I thought would die of despair; I had transferred my tears and groans to the sick one: it seemed to me that you would fall ill too. (7) How often I flung myself on your chains, with the intention of undoing them!

271

8 dabat relictum quod ⟨in⟩[79] te praetulissem. Quam frequenter iam laxata misero vincula rursus imposui, dum mihi tua potius sanitas placet! Dissimulare non possum condicionis illius secretas difficultates: redimi debebat aeger, ego te volebam.

19. Ponere vos, iudices, velut in illa necessitatis meae praesentia volo. Ecce infelix, ad primum aspectum patris conatus assurgere, illas squalentes[80] sordibus manus paululum tamquam amplexus daturus erexit, nec usque in cervices meas spiritu iam deficiente perlatas in suum mi-

2 ser iterum cubile deiecit. Totus ille circa nos carceris populus obticuit et, ne colloquiis nostris terribilis catenarum stridor obstreperet, lassatos artus in sua tenuere patientia. Ego serius, gravis, hinc—si videtur—incipiam: "Luxuri-

3 ose, meruisti!"? Ignorat profecto paterni doloris aestus, quisquis solacium putat ut de languente filio queratur, ut moribus mentique maledicat. Abite, virtutes, ignosce,

4 probitas: ⟨potior⟩[81] est ex liberis ille qui moritur. Mihi vero fateor hinc aliqua languente filio venisse solacia, quod vixit infelix quemadmodum voluit, quod fuit hilaris ac laeta brevis aetas. Crede, iuvenis: et pro te iam maluis-

5 sem ut luxuriosus esses. Cui tu tempori, cui dolori rigorem ultionis, frontem castigantis iniungis! Impatientissima res

[79] *add. Håk.*[3] *125 ex 5.14.3*
[80] squale- *Bur.* (*firm. Håk.*[2] *51–52*): pare- B: palle- B[2] V Φ*
[81] *add. Eng. 94–95:* ⟨cario r⟩ C[2]

---

[87] "what . . . ⟨in⟩ you" = illness: if *you* had been the sick son, I would have preferred you. Cf. 5.14.3.   [88] I.e., was I, at that moment . . .   [89] He might as well have had a merry life too, granted he has ended up in prison—possibly for ever.

But what I would have preferred ‹in› you[87] kept recommending the one I had just left. (8) How often I put back on the poor sick boy the chains I had already loosened, each time your sound health made me prefer you! I cannot hide the difficulties lurking in those terms: the sick son *had* to be ransomed, but I *wanted* to ransom you.

19. I want, judges, to put you there with me—as it were—at the moment when I was forced to make that choice. Look! At the first sight of his father, the unlucky man tried to get up. For a little while he raised his hands, mired with dirt, as though he meant to embrace me. Then he grew faint; he was unable to stretch them as far as my neck, and—poor man—he let them fall back on to his bed. (2) Around us the whole population of the prison fell silent, and, for fear the horrid clank of their chains drown our conversation, they held their weary limbs still, enduring their own pain. Am I,[88] forsooth, to begin, in serious and solemn tones, like this?—"Prodigal son, you deserved it!" (3) A man must be quite uncomprehending of a father's painful emotions, if he thinks it brings comfort to complain about a sick son, to revile his behavior and cast of mind. Begone, virtues, forgive, uprightness: the son ‹to be preferred› is the dying one. (4) But I confess that, though my son was ill, I did find some solace in the fact that the poor boy had lived as he chose to live, that his brief life was happy and full of merriment. Young man, believe me: I should at that point have preferred you too to have been a prodigal, for your sake![89] (5) At such a time, when I am in such pain, do you bid me be severe in vengeance, knit the stern brow of one meting out punishment? It is absolutely intolerable to lose a son you are

273

6   est perdere filium, cui videaris irasci. Corruptum me pre-
    cibus putatis ambituque lacrimarum? Hoc vicit aeger,
7   quod non rogabat. Assidebam misero; demittebat oculos,
    interroganti responsum de lacrimis tantum gemituque
    reddebat. Agebat me deliberante iam victum, cum re-
    pente miseras manus velut recidentis amplexus posuit in
    sinu meo, 20. et cum lassa suspiria per ardentis anhelitus
    egessisset[82] saepe visceribus, cum diu collatis uterque sin-
    gultibus miscuissemus lapsas[83] sine voce lacrimas, tandem
    spiritu vix in paucissima verba collecto, "Tibi quidem"
    inquit "gratias ago, pater, quod redempturus utrumque
    venisti; non adeo tamen sensus meos languor hebetavit, ut
2   exitum condicionis huius ignorem. Ego luxuriosus, ego
    perditus; nunc vero super infamiam nominis huius emo-
    rior. Utinam hoc saltem mihi sero[84] fata praestarent, ut
    residuum laborantis animae in tuo poneremus amplexu!
3   Sed si mora est longior properantibus expectare pere-
    untem, ite superstites, ite felices; has tantum reliquias
    commendate piratis, ne mersus profundo, proiectus in
    fluctus, exitum faciam hominis ad quem non venerit pater.
4   Unde enim sperare possum ut revertaris, ut facias—"
    Tunc super abrupta verba tota defectione conticuit, stric-
    tisque vitalibus circa dolorem suum membra riguerunt.
5   Exclamavi, fateor: "Quid agis, infelix? Cur desperatione

[82] -ssisset *Str.*[11] 109–10: -stis *codd.*: -sta (*sc.* essent) *Håk.*[2] 52
[83] laps- *Sch., Franc.*: lass- *codd.*
[84] mihi sero *codd.* (*def. vM.-M.*[1] 132.47): misero *Bur.*

[90] These things would both suggest choice of the other son.
[91] Sc., to ransom him. Such a person would have been useless
to the pirates, and they would have thrown him into the sea.

thought to be angry with. (6) Do you suppose I was swayed by prayers and the pressure that tears can exert? No, my sick son prevailed just because he did not beg. (7) I was sitting by the unhappy man; he would lower his eyes, and reply to my questions only with tears and groans. While I pondered my choice, he bore himself like one who had already been defeated; but all of a sudden he laid down his poor hands in my lap as though he was failing in the attempt to embrace me, 20. and after he had, amid feverish gasps, drawn many a weary sigh from his vitals, after we had both for some while combined our gulps and mingled tears that flowed without speech, he finally just managed to summon the breath to utter a very few words: "Thank you, father, for coming to ransom us both. But illness has not so dulled my senses that I am unaware of the outcome of the choice before you. (2) I am the prodigal, I am the debauched son; and now, as well as the slur of this designation, I am dying.[90] But would that the fates might grant me at least one late boon: that I may entrust to your embrace what is left of my failing life. (3) However, if you are in too much of a hurry to wait for me to die, go you who will survive me, go in good fortune; only commend these remains to the pirates, that I may not, buried in the deep, cast upon the waves, meet the end of a man to whom his father did not come.[91] (4) For how am I to hope that you will return, that you will perform—"[92] Then, breaking off his words, he fell silent, quite spent. His vital organs tightened where their pain gripped them, and his limbs grew stiff. (5) I cried out—I confess—: "What is this, unhappy son? Why are you collapsing in despair? Raise

[92] My burial.

conlaberis? Attolle paulisper oculos, confirma, dura; te
6 frater elegit." Visa est per[85] hanc vocem meam peracta
condicio: continuo pirata detraxit catenas, vincla laxavit.
7 Vultis elegisse me negem, vultis in lucem diemque pro-
ductus carceri suo reddatur aeger? Ego vero non habui
verba quibus me deliberare, quibus nolle contenderem.
8 Vultis scire quid pater, quid pirata praestiterit? Ego duos
redemi, sed alterum accepi.

9   "Ut scias" inquit "aegrum redimi non debuisse: defunctus est." Crudelissime generis humani, qui nos putas
pretium tuum perdidisse, audi quam multa nobis in mori-
10 turo filio pirata reddiderit: frater tuus ille inter vincula
catenasque deficiens respiravit aliquid in toro tandemque
liberas vinculis manus per totius lectuli spatia iactavit; post
impias carceris sordes illum cum ferali veste squalorem
exuit,[86] paulisper aeger vidit propinquos, allocutus est
amicos, mandavit, exegit, et quamvis suprema sorte conla-
bens, prius tamen luce caeli libera satiatus est. 21. Contu-
lit mihi grande, velit nolit, fortuna in orbitate solacium:
filium, qui relictus mea fuit moriturus invidia, non occidi,
2 sed perdidi. Quid ais, iuvenis? Ita, si moriturum filium
redimere non debui, non sufficit haec tibi de me poena,
3 quod ille decessit? Irasci patri tunc[87] fortasse fas esset, si

---

[85] post V γ β
[86] dist. vulg.: post aeger Håk., sed vd. Str.[11] 110
[87] tunc Reitz.[1] 118.4: tantum codd.

---

93 Sc., to take the sick son thus released.   94 Father had
(duly) brought the money for two; the pirate (unfairly) gave him
only one son back.   95 The implication here is that the sick
son died at home; yet in the theme he died during the return trip.

your eyes for a little while, hold out, endure; your brother has chosen *you*." (6) It seemed that the bargain was sealed by these words of mine: the pirate straightaway removed the fetters, loosed the bonds. (7) Do you want me to say I had not made my choice, do you want me to have the sick man, who had been brought into the light of day, returned to his prison? No, I found no words to protest that I was still deliberating, that that was not my wish.[93] (8) Do you want to know what the father, what the pirate contributed? I ransomed two, but took back one.[94]

(9) "You can tell," he says, "that the sick man should not have been ransomed: he died." Cruelest of the human race, if you think I wasted your ransom money, listen to all that the pirate gave back to me in the shape of my doomed son: (10) your brother, he who was fading away amid bonds and chains, recovered somewhat on his bed, and threw his hands, at last freed of their bonds, all over it. After the unholy filth of the prison, he put off both that squalor and his funereal clothes: for a while, sick though he was, he saw his relatives, spoke to his friends, gave commissions, made requests;[95] and, though he was sinking to his destined end, he was in time to feast full on the free light of day.[96] 21. Fortune, willy nilly, has given me a great comfort in my bereavement. I did not *kill* the son who, had he been left behind, would have been a reproach to me: I *lost* him. (2) What say you, young man? Suppose I was wrong to ransom a son on the point of death: does not his decease punish me enough to satisfy you? (3) It would perhaps be quite proper for you to be angry with your

[96] As opposed to the unnatural night of the pirates' prison (5.16.3).

viveret frater; tunc[88] alimenta quaerenti respondere pos-
4 ses: "Posce praelatum." Quantum intellego, qui de mendicitate patris vindicaris, aegri es redempti, iuvenis, inimi-
cus. Nescis, quid sit invidiam facere patri: melior erat tua
causa, si mei miserereris.[89]

5   At quanto, dii deaeque, alius fuit ille infelicissimi iuvenis affectus! Nuntio enim te audiente[90] et tota civitate
teste proclamo: tibi gratias agebat ille, dum moreretur.
Credo mehercules hoc miserum dolore consumptum,
6 quod sibi videbatur pretium suum[91] mihi perdidisse. Non
aliter igitur quam si te praesente deficeret, "Per illud,"
inquit, "frater optime, natalium nostrorum sacrum venerandumque consortium, per socias peregrinationes, per
adversa communia, per hoc, quod et tu languere potuisti,
si te vel tua quandoque virtus vel satietas secura praedonum piratico carcere emiserit, commendo tibi senem,
quem facimus uterque mendicum. Testor immortalia nu-
mina et infernarum sedum deos: pascerem patrem, si te
redemisset."

7   "Ego tamen" inquit "mihi debeo, quod reversus sum."

---

[88] tunc C^2 *in ras.*: nunc *cett.*

[89] miserereris πM C H P: misereris *cett.*

[90] te au- *Sh. B.*^{2} *195*: et au- *codd.*: et <te> au- *Franc.*: et au-
<te> *Reitz.*^{1} *118.4*   [91] tuum *Reitz.*^{1} *118.4, sed vd. Håk.*

---

[97] Cf. 5.1.3.

[98] Arousing public hostility against your father is going to take
more than you think: he can still count on appreciation for his
efforts and sympathy for his disgrace (cf., e.g., 5.9.1–3, 5.21.1 and
3).

[99] Compare and contrast 5.20.9.

father if your brother were still alive; in that case, when I begged for food you could reply: "Ask the son you put first." (4) So far as I can see, if, young man, you are having your revenge by beggaring your father,[97] it is because of your enmity to the sick son I ransomed. But you do not know how *much* it takes to make your father hated;[98] you would have a better case if you were to pity me.

(5) But, gods and goddesses, how different was the reaction of that most unhappy youth! I announce it in your hearing, indeed, I proclaim it with the whole city bearing witness: as he died he was thanking you. In fact, I believe that the poor boy was overcome by grief because he imagined he had made me waste his ransom money.[99] (6) So just as if you were there as he was passing away, he said: "Excellent brother, in the name of our shared birth, a holy and revered tie, by our joint travels, by the hardships we went through together, by the fact that you too might have fallen ill: if one day either your own courage or the careless satiety of the plunderers[100] releases you from the pirate prison, I commend to you our old father, whom we are both reducing to beggary. I ask the immortal powers and the gods of the realms below to bear witness: I would be supporting our father, if he had ransomed *you*."[101]

(7) "But," he says, "it is to *me* that I owe my return."[102]

---

[100] They were sated because they had been so well paid (cf. 5.21.9).   [101] If our roles were reversed, Father having ransomed *you*, I would still support him. This speech was purportedly given *before* Surviving Son's escape and his dispute with Father; yet it presupposes knowledge of the events to come.

[102] = You didn't ransom me (and so lacked *pietas*), therefore I had to free myself.

Non quidem quicquam velim, iuvenis, de virtutum tuarum admiratione detractum; audias tamen necesse est in
8   hac impietate[92] verum. Evasisse te putas? Ingrate, dimis-
sus es! Mea pietas istud, mea fecit electio. Unde enim
evenit, quicquid ante captivitas tua praestare non potuit?
9   Iacta quantum voles effractum carcerem, ruptas catenas;
vis scire quid neglegentes fecerit securosque piratas? Ac-
ceperant pretium duorum.

22. Intellegit, iudices, et ipse iuvenis non esse se calamitatium nostrarum iustitiae parem, [et] ⟨si⟩[93] sic agit,
tamquam alere non debeat, itaque transfert in hoc defen-
2   sionem, ut posse se neget. Quid dicitis, iudices? Feretis
hoc dicentem iuvenem corpore atque aetate robustum?
3   Non habes opes, sed membra, sed vires. Nam neque ego
laborem nec difficiles posco conatus: contentus sum, iuve-
4   nis, ut velis. Cibos me poscere putas? Humeros, quibus
incumbam, manus, quas eliso pectori apponam, sinus, in
quos egeram exhaustarum reliquias lacrimarum, ut sepe-
lias, ut haec cum miseri illius membris ossa componas.
5   Non alimenta quaero, sed filium. Quid, quod nec[94] grave
longumque supremae pietatis exigimus officium? Non diu
viverem, etiamsi me duo pasceretis. Securus sis: brevi te
gemitus mei liberabunt, assiduis planctibus everberata
6   vitalia. Quid me remittis ad turbam, quid facis rursus

---

[92] impie- *Reitz.[1] 118* (*corrob. Wint. ap. Str.[15] 68.355*): pie-
codd. (*def. vM.-M.*): parte *Obr.*   [93] [et] ⟨si⟩ *Sh. B.[2] 195,
Wint.[3]*: et *codd.*: cum *Obr.*   [94] nec C[2]E: ne *cett.*

---

[103] Picked up by *pietas* below.
[104] Sc., before Father came on the scene.
[105] Cf. 1.6.9, 16.6.2.

I should not wish any detraction, young man, from the admiration felt for your virtues; but you must hear the truth about my "lack of affection."[103] (8) Do you think you got away? Ungrateful boy, you were *sent* away! This was the result of my affection, of my choice. For how did something come about that was impossible earlier[104] in your captivity? (9) Boast all you like of how you broke out of prison, of how you snapped your chains; do you want to know what made the pirates so lax and careless? They had been paid for two.

22. The young man, judges, does not need to be warned that he is not equal to answering the just case afforded me by calamity <if> he pleads that he does not *have to* feed me; and so he transfers his defense to the assertion that he *cannot*. (2) What do you say, judges? Will you tolerate such an excuse from a youth with all the physical strength of his age? (3) You may not have wealth, but you have limbs, you have strength. And I am not demanding hard work or taxing exertions: I am content, young man, that you should be willing. (4) Do you think I am asking for food? No, I am asking for shoulders to lean on,[105] hands to place on my battered breast, a lap into which I may shed the last of the tears I have exhausted, that you should bury me, that you should lay my bones to rest alongside the body of that poor boy. I do not ask for sustenance, but for my son. (5) And what of the fact that I do not even demand burdensome or long duties, in this last act of filial affection? I should not live for long even if there were two of you to feed me. Don't worry: in a short while my groans, my internal organs bruised by continual breast-beating, will set you free. (6) Why do you send me back to the crowds in the street? Why do you make me a burden to all

omnibus gravem? Consumpsi fletus, clementiam civitatis exhausi. Non alit populus hominem, quem pascere filius
7 debet. Quid sibi vult haec aliena calamitatibus nostris, aliena virtutibus tuis, iuvenis, asperitas? Abstulisti mihi malorum quoque meorum verecundiam: quicquid faciebam, mendicitas est, ex quo reversus es.

8 Durat in suscepto rigore iuvenis, et ad misericordiam non memoria fratris, non patris contemplatione deflectitur. 23. Exclamaret alius hoc loco: "Lex, tuam fidem!"[95] Dignus quidem eras, impotentissime[96] generis humani, quem in tormenta mea doloremque redeuntem vincla rursus ac poena carceris exciperet; at[97] insultes huic con-
2 fessioni licet, alligare non possum. Quid mihi miseras ultiones, quid triste monstratis auxilium? Faceret hoc pater, qui redimere noluisset.

3 Age nunc, vivacissima senectus, redeamus ad preces: quod solum ius paternae pietatis agnoscis,[98] hic quoque rogemus. Per ego te, iuvenis, illos meos, de quibus nunc quereris, annos, per expertos tibi notosque humanorum accidentium casus, per infelicis illius manes, cui nec hoc saltem contigit, ut te reverso, te praesente moreretur,

---

95 lex, tuam fidem! *Håk.*[3] *126–27*: ex tuam fidem V: ex -a -de B Φ   96 impuden- *Franc., sed vd. ad 5.4.1*

97 at *Obr.* (*firm. Str.*[15] *69.376*): et *codd.*: set *Reitz.*[1] *119*

98 -is *Russ. ap. Str.*[15]: -it *codd.* (*unde* -na pietas -it *Sch.*)

---

106 Before your return, I begged money in order to ransom you (5.6.2–3); now people think that *you* should be feeding me: therefore, if I ask them for money, they look down on me as a mere beggar.   107 He addresses the jurors, who (he implies) are encouraging him to send Son to prison—thus "showing" him a course of action he rejects.

and sundry once more? I have used up the tears of the city, exhausted its charity. The people does not feed a man whom *his son* should be supporting. (7) What is the meaning of this harshness, youth? It is not appropriate to our calamities, it is not appropriate to your virtues. You have robbed me even of the respect that my plight commanded: all I used to do has become mere begging now that you have come back.[106]

(8) The young man persists in his hardheartedness, and is not inclined toward pity by the memory of his brother, by the sight of his father. 23. At this point another would cry: "Law, I appeal to you!" You certainly deserved, most arrogant of mortals, on your return home to torment and grieve me, to be greeted once more by chains and punishment in prison; but, though you may scoff at this confession, I can't put you in bonds. (2) Why do you point out[107] to me the way to a vengeance that brings sadness, aid that brings no comfort? A father would act like this if he had been unwilling to ransom.

(3) Come now, old man who have lived too long, let us return to prayers; here too,[108] let us beg: the only right of an affectionate father that you[109] now want to be enforced.[110] Young man, I appeal to you by my years, of which you now complain, by the accidents of human life that you have come to know by experience, by the shades of that unhappy boy, who was not even lucky enough to

[108] I.e., in the hearings, after praying Son on his return (see below).   [109] Sc., old man (so addressing himself).

[110] He prefers to act as a good father, appealing to his son in the name of the affection that binds them, rather than enforcing the law that would send him to prison.

pasce nunc quod te redimere volui, pasce quod fratrem
4 tuum redemi. Non ego lassitudinem tuam posco, numquam[99] otium meum, nec, ut ipse securus quietusque
transigam diem, tuas operibus manus, tuum laboribus
assigno sudorem. Iungamus mutuae pietatis officia, par
flebile, par omnibus aetatibus nominibusque reverendum.
5 Est nobis negotium cum civitate mitissima. Quanto liben-
tius dabunt, cum viderint pariter unaque miseros mutua
6 sustentatione conexos! Et ego quidem rogabo, qui soleo;
sed in tuos sinus populus congerat stipes. Quicquid preces, quicquid impetraverint lacrimae meae, accipe, tuere,
7 dispensa. Pro tua fama, pro tua sum pietate sollicitus. Ego
mendicabo, tu pasces.

---

[99] numquam *codd.* (*def. Håk.* = non *coll.* 19.4.2, *sed utrobique*
dubium): non *Franc.*: non, inquam, *Sh. B.*[2] *195*: nequaquam *Str.*[11]
110: nedum *Russ. ibid.*

die after your return, in your presence: feed me now, because I wanted to ransom you, because I ransomed your brother.[111] (4) I do not ask you to tire yourself out while I sit at leisure; or that I should pass the day carefree and at my ease, leaving you to do the manual work, you to sweat over what has to be done. Let us join in doing the duties that belong to mutual affection, a pair to evoke tears, a pair to command the respect of any age and family relationship.[112] (5) We have to do with a very soft-hearted city.[113] How much more gladly will they give, when they see us joined to maintain each other in our distress! (6) Yes, I will do the asking: I am used to it; but let the people throw its pennies into *your* lap. Whatever alms my prayers, my tears may win, you take it, save it up, dole it out. (7) I am concerned for your good name as a dutiful son. *I* will beg, *you* will feed.

[111] Literally, "feed the fact that I . . ."

[112] I.e., of both elderly fathers and young sons. For this use of *nomen* see 5.7.3–4, 5.8.1–2, 5.8.8, 5.14.10.

[113] Cf. 5.6.3.